Revolution and World Politics

Revolution and World Politics

The Rise and Fall of the Sixth Great Power

Fred Halliday

DUKE UNIVERSITY PRESS
DURHAM 1999

First published in the United States in 1999 by
DUKE UNIVERSITY PRESS
Durham, NC 27708-0660
and in the United Kingdom in 1999 by
MACMILLAN PRESS LTD
Houndmills, Basingstoke, Hampshire, RG21 6XS

Library of Congress Cataloging-in-Publication Data
Halliday, Fred.
   Revolution and world politics : the rise and fall of the Sixth
Great Power / Fred Halliday.
      p.   cm.
   Includes bibliographical references and index.
   ISBN 0–8223–2427–X (alk. paper).   —   ISBN 0–8223–2464–4 (pbk. :
alk. paper)
   1. Revolutions—History.   2. World politics.   I. Title.
JC491.H188   1999
321.09'4'09—dc21   99–25824
                                                         CIP

Typeset by Povey-Edmondson
Tavistock and Rochdale, England

Printed in Hong Kong

To Maxine

Contents

**PART II REVOLUTIONS AND THE INTERNATIONAL
          SYSTEM**

La victoire, en chantant, nous ouvre la barrière
La Liberté guide nos pas.
Et du nord au midi, la trompette guerrière
A sonné l'heure des combats.
Tremblez, ennemis de la France.
Rois ivres de sang et d'orgueil,
Le peuple souverain s'avance:
Tyrans descendez au cercueil . . .

Sur ce fer, devant Dieu, nous jurons à nos pères,
A nos épouses, à nos mères,
D'anéantir les oppresseurs.
En tous lieux, dans la nuit profonde
Plongeant l'infame royauté
Les Français donneront au monde
Et la paix et la liberté

(Popular song of the French revolution, in Marcel Merle, *Paci-fisme et Internationalisme XVIIe–XXe siècles*, Paris: Armand Colin, 1966, p. 160)

* * *

A young soldier spoke to us in German. 'The Brotherhood Grave', he explained. 'Tomorrow we shall bury here five hundred proletarians who died for the Revolution.'

He took us down into the pit. In frantic haste swung the picks and shovels, and earth-mountains grew. No one spoke. Overhead the night was thick with stars, and the ancient Imperial Kremlin wall towered up immeasurably.

'Here in this holy place,' said the student, 'holiest of all Russia, we shall bury our most holy. Here where are the tombs of the Tsars, our Tsar – the People – shall sleep . . .' His arm was in a sling, from a bullet wound gained in the fighting. He looked at it. 'You foreigners look down on us Russians because so long we tolerated a medieval monarchy,' he said. 'But we saw that the Tsar was not the only tyrant in the world; capitalism was worse, and in all the countries of the world capitalism was Emperor . . . Russian revolutionary tactics are best. . .'

(John Reed, *Ten Days That Shook the World*, Harmondsworth: Penguin, 1977, p. 227)

In the Name of Almighty God, crusher of tyrants and champion of the oppressed. 'We desired to be gracious to those who have been oppressed on earth, and to make them leaders, and to make them inheritors.' (Koran). This is the voice of right, the voice of the oppressed, this is the voice of the Islamic Republic of Iran. Muslims everywhere, we transmit our programmes to you from Tehran, the bastion of the Islamic revolution, so that they will be a light for all oppressed people everywhere. We pledge to remain loyal to our Islamic mission, the mission of right, justice and freedom. This is Tehran, voice of the Islamic Republic of Iran.

(Opening announcement of Radio Tehran broadcasts in Arabic, *BBC Summary of World Broadcasts*, Part 4, The Middle East and North Africa, ME/7675/A2 21 June 1984)

Preface

Revolutions are important events for individual countries and for the politics of the world. They are events of immense political and moral contradiction, occasions at once for the heroic and the idealistic, and for the cynical, the cruel and the destructive. Revolutions do not achieve what they set out to attain, but in an age where revolutions appear to be events of another time, it has to be remembered how and why millions of people fought, struggled and died for the cause of radical change. In the words of Edward Thompson, we need to rescue revolution 'from the immense condescension of posterity'. What equally cannot be denied is their formative influence on the world in which we live, and in the shaping of the societies and political systems of today. Writing in 1854, when world politics was dominated by the *pentarchy*, the rule of five great powers, and Europe was preoccupied by the Crimean War, Karl Marx argued that it was a sixth great power, revolution, which would prevail over the other five.[1] It was a power which acted as much against states as through them, as much through ideas and social change as through diplomacy and war. The extent of that sixth great power's impact forms the focus of this study.

Every book has a personal element in it, and this one is no exception. One central argument made below is that revolutionaries, for all their exaggeration and tactical accommodations, mean much of what they say. This is as true for the international dimensions, the subject of this book, as for the domestic. The belief that revolutionaries do mean what they say was, of course, long held by those who supported revolutions. It was a belief challenged, quite properly, not only by the course of events, but also by recognition of the constraints, the failures, the limits of what revolutions achieved. The pendulum then swung in another direction – towards seeing revolutionaries as practitioners of *Realpolitik*, or of national interest little different from their non-revolutionary predecessors, or as people only interested in gaining and keeping power. Later sociologists and political scientists theorised this in

terms of the preponderance of structure over agency. These qualifications of the role of agency need to be borne in mind: but they do
not override the fact that, from the French revolutionaries in the
1790s to Iran in the 1980s, revolutionary states have formulated far-
reaching goals for change in both the domestic and international
contexts. What this commitment leads to, and how far those in
other countries follow them, is the central question examined in this
book.

The question of the international dimensions of revolution hung
over the second half of the twentieth century. The world I grew up
in, that of the 1950s and 1960s, was one in which the claims of
revolutionaries, and of those opposed to them, dominated much of
world politics. This was an era of Cold War, of Third World
revolution, and of growing tension, of opportunity and disunity,
within the communist world. The great crisis of the communist
movement, the moment from which in retrospect its internal
dissolution began, was the secret speech by Soviet leader Nikita
Khrushchev in 1956 denouncing the crimes of his predecessor
Joseph Stalin. From this followed not only the split with China,
in the early 1960s, and the breaking away of the Western European
communist parties in the 1970s, but also that inner dissolution, and
loss of faith, which was to end in the disintegration of the USSR in
1991. These were years of continued dispute within the communist
world – the extended polemics between Russia and China of the
early 1960s, the frenzied mobilisations of the Cultural Revolution in
China, the controversy that divided Western communism following
the criminal Soviet invasion of Czechoslovakia in 1968. Yet even as
the Soviet Union came to face the truth about its own horrendous
past, and as its international following began to erode, others, in the
less developed world, remained gripped by the aspiration to make
revolutions and construct states and societies radically different
from those of the West. The 1960s and 1970s were decades in which
the impact of revolution reverberated through the Third World, be
it in the aftermath of the Cuban revolution of 1959 – I remember
the first TV interview with Castro as he spoke on the eve of the
capture of Havana. Later came the charged atmosphere surround-
ing the war in Vietnam in the late 1960s.

Much of my own work was taken up with upheavals in the Third
World. In 1968 I spent a month in Cuba during which I witnessed
two of the contrasted moments of that revolution's relation to the
international: a speech by Fidel Castro in Oriente province inau-

gurating the village of Ñancahuazú, named after the village in Bolivia where Guevara had set up his revolutionary base: and the throttled response of the Cuban state to the political opening in Prague, accompanied by its stifling of debate within. A great admirer of the Cuban revolution, the veteran Italian journalist Saverio Tutino, then correspondent in Havana of *Unità*, told me: 'The atmosphere here is as bad as in Stalin's Russia in 1952.' While studying Middle East politics, I visited the Palestinian guerrillas in Jordan in 1969. In 1970 I embarked on a visit to the newly independent People's Republic of South Yemen and to the neighbouring region of Dhofar, in the Sultanate of Oman; the mountains of Dhofar, source of the frankincense of the ancient world, were at that time controlled by Maoist guerrillas. These South Arabian revolutionary movements, and the broader context of the Arabian Peninsula and the Persian Gulf, were to be the subject of later books – *Arabia without Sultans, Iran: Dictatorship and Development* and of my doctoral research on South Yemen, *Revolution and Foreign Policy*. In 1977–8, together with my partner Maxine Molyneux, I visited Ethiopia, then in the grip of civil war in Eritrea, and of inter-state war with Somalia: this resulted in our *The Ethiopian Revolution*.

If much of the emphasis of the 1960s and 1970s was on radical movements of the secular left – nationalist and communist – the 1980s were dominated by the rise of contestatory movements of Islamist orientation, above all in Iran. In the revolutionary Tehran of summer 1979 all the features of a modern revolution could be seen – mass meetings in the grounds of the university, buildings transformed into centres of radical activity, rhetorical assertions of solidarity with the oppressed of the world, the formation of a new militarised, and coercive, revolutionary regime. Under the chandeliers of the former imperial foreign ministry, I argued with then Foreign Minister Ibrahim Yazdi about the goals of the Islamic revolution. What has never ceased to strike me, and what I have tried to reflect in this book, is that for all the very substantial differences which the Iranian case exhibited in comparison with other revolutions there was much – in cause, development and language – that it had in common with them.[2]

The story of revolution in the twentieth century is haunted by 1917 and its aftermath. I first visited the Soviet Union in July 1982, in the last months of Brezhnevite 'stagnation', and then returned through the increasingly uncharted years of Gorbachev and his successors. The events of 1989–91 were to provide another, dramatic, chapter in the history of revolutions, and of the decisive intervention of peoples into politics. Nothing could more vividly illustrate the import of the collapse of communism in the period 1989–91 than the experience of cities where the old order had crumbled. To walk through streets in Budapest or Moscow that had been only months before ruled by communism, to see the collection of deposed statues – Lenin, Dzerzhinksy, Kalinin – in the garden of the House of Artists in Moscow, to cross at the former Checkpoint Charlie where the Berlin wall once stood and which I had often seen, or visit the gardens of the Lubkovic Palace, the German embassy, in Prague where thousands of East Germans had sought refuge in 1989, was to feel the passage of history before one's eyes. It seemed as if all that the Bolshevik revolution had meant for world history, and indeed all that 'Revolution' had meant, was now reduced to nothing. Demonstrators in Red Square carried the banner, a rebuttal of communist triumphalism about the advances of the Soviet state: '70 Years – On the Road to Nowhere'. In a meeting with the Russian sociologist Tatiana Zaslavskaya I asked her what, in her opinion, would be the significance of the Bolshevik revolution a generation hence: 'Nothing', she replied, and after a pause added, 'except nostalgia for great power status, and for social equality'.

The collapse of communism was, of course, only a European phenomenon: in China the Communist Party still ruled, but here too its authority was being eroded from within. In 1995 I had the occasion to teach at the People's University of Beijing: for 10 yuan, around one British pound, one could climb the stairs to the podium overlooking Tienanmen square and stand on the spot where, in October 1949, Mao Tse-tung announced that China had arisen. I do not know what that history, and clamour, meant to the crowds of young Chinese walking the square in front of me, and where eight years before student protesters had been slain in their hundreds: to my mind, it was part of the challenge that I have tried to address in this book. I asked a Chinese colleague what he now thought of Mao. 'Mao was an ignorant person. He did not brush his teeth. He was a cruel man, who killed millions of people. But I owe him my very existence: without the revolution he made, my father, who was from a poor peasant background, could never have afforded to marry. I would never have been born.'

This concern with political upheavals and with their international consequences was matched by an attempt to understand the broader significance of the revolutions of modern history. As a student at the School of Oriental and African Studies in the period 1967–9 I began research on the comparative political study of revolutions. At that time there were certain books that shaped my interest in this issue: Barrington Moore's *The Social Origins of Dictatorship and Democracy*, Edgar Snow's *Red Star Over China*, and above all Franz Borkenau's *World Communism*, an incisive and comprehensive account of the rise of an international communist movement and its manipulation by the Soviet state. Later books were to develop the themes of this literature – I would mention, above all, on the sociological side Theda Skocpol's *States and Social Revolutions*, and in the charting of international revolution Jorge Castañeda's *Utopia Unarmed*.

In the late 1960s I also worked on the papers of the historian of the Russian revolution Isaac Deutscher, later published as *Russia, China and the West*. Deutscher had been a member of the opposition within the Polish communist party. He had remained loyal to the ideals of his youth, but had become amongst the most powerful critics of Stalin, and of the system, within the USSR and within the communist movement as a whole, that Stalin had created. Deutscher's biography of Stalin, published in 1949, remains as powerful a critique of the USSR, domestically and internationally, as any written in the subsequent half century. Deutscher, like Borkenau, was acutely sensitive to the ways in which revolutions both claim and subordinate an international following. He was a member of a communist party, that of Poland, whose leadership had been murdered by Stalin in the purges. The questions that Deutscher raised – the ideological origins of revolutions, the links between the French and twentieth-century upheavals, the emergence of post-revolutionary bureaucracy and dictatorship, the longer-run evolution of post-revolutionary societies – are ones that framed, and continue to frame, my approach to these questions. Deutscher did not live to see the outcome of the communist period in the Soviet Union and Eastern Europe: his expectations that these societies they could in some way be transformed into something at once democratic and revolutionary, have not been fulfilled. They were to prove unfounded. But the approach which he took – historical, comparative, interpretative, above all critical – and which

I discussed through many conversations with his wife Tamara, is one that has more than stood the test of time.

No topic of this kind is ever thought through on one's own. From the 1960s onwards I had the good fortune to belong to institutions that provided a context for reflection, and much argument, on these issues: first *New Left Review*, and then the Transnational Institute, both sources of immense intellectual stimulation. In 1983 I began teaching at the London School of Economics, and some time later began an MSc course on the international dimensions of revolutions. The debt I owe to the successive years of students on that course and to those who went on to do research related to the subject-matter of that course is unmeasurable. So too is my debt to those who have over the past two decades so developed the academic study of revolutions, in both its sociological and international dimensions: the literature that one has to work on today, itself enhanced by a flood of material following the collapse of communism, adds to the stimulation and the challenge of writing on this subject. I have tried in this book to relate this literature to two other benchmarks: one the Marxist tradition, the most serious engagement with revolution in modern social thought; the other historical events themselves, and the role within history of ideas, beliefs, myths. My writing in this and previous books has been strongly influenced by the Marxist interpretation of the modern world, and by its examination of the role of social movements, and protest, in the shaping of it. Above all it has emphasised that all modern phenomena have to be seen in the context of their over-arching context, that of capitalism and of the contradictions it generates. Theodor Adorno said of fascism, that those who did not wish to speak of capitalism should not speak of it either. I would say the same of revolution, and of international relations: both are formed by capitalist modernity. Marxism has been associated both with great insights and with great illusions: I have tried to write in the spirit of the first, while avoiding the disasters of the second. How far I have been successful, or consistent, is for others to say. As for history, it remains both source and arbiter, a corrective to all theories and an inspiration to analysis.

Among the many individuals to whom I would wish to express gratitude I would mention Masood Akhavan Kazemi, Mariano Aguirre, Domingo Amuchastegui, Matthew Anderson, Perry Anderson, David Armstrong, Anthony Barnett, Robin Blackburn, Wilfred Burchett, Peter Calvert, Carmen Claudín, Mike Davis, Wolfgang

Deckers, Tamara Deutscher, Luis Fernandes, Jon Halliday, Eric Hobsbawm, Monty Johnstone, Nikki Keddie, Saul Landau, Margot Light, Arno Mayer, Francis Mulhern, Justin Rosenberg, Stuart Schram, Teodor Shanin, Hazel Smith, Geoffrey Stern, Göran Therborn, Saverio Tutino, and Pere Vilanova. Jennifer Chapa of the Department of International Relations at LSE was a model of tact and endurance in the preparation of the manuscript for publication. Nick Bisley read the completed manuscript with exemplary editorial and conceptual vigilance. Financial support for teaching replacement was generously provided by the Suntory and Toyota International Centres for Economics and Related Disciplines at LSE.

My greatest debt, in this as in all other respects, is to Maxine Molyneux, who has lived through this history and these debates with me, and who has endured many visits to inhospitable and perilous places. She has been an inexhaustible source of support, ideas, criticism and inspiration. That this book is dedicated to her is a small, but heartfelt, recognition of what her partnership and love have meant to me.

London   FRED HALLIDAY

Notes

1. 'The European War', *New York Daily Tribune*, 2 February 1854.
2. 'The Iranian Revolution in Comparative Perspective' in Fred Halliday, *Islam and the Myth of Confrontation* (London: I.B. Tauris, 1996).

1

Introduction: Revolutions and the International

The Unpeaceful Origins of a Peaceful World

There are few things less becoming to the study of human affairs than the complacency of a triumphal age. At the close of the twentieth century the world was able to contemplate, in a manner never previously possible, the prospect of an age of democratic peace. After two world wars and a forty-year cold war, and the rise and fall of authoritarian regimes of left and right, it appeared to some that the consolidation of democracy in the major states of the world, and its apparent spread to others, would herald an age when inter-state conflict of a military kind would cease. A solution, imperfect but durable, to the twin problems of attaining internal political order, and external, inter-state, peace appeared to have been reached. The agenda for international relations, as for domestic politics, would therefore appear to have been clear: the consolidation of democracy within states, combined with the growth of cooperation between them.

There was much to recommend this argument, both in theory and in fact. Democratic states have had good reason not to go to war with each other. They have never, in any meaningful sense, done so. There were, however, some reasons for questioning the image of world history associated with this vision. It would, in the first place, be misleading to read the present back into the past, to see in the liberal democratic formula an explanation for how the world had reached the condition it had. The past is a corrective to any simple association of peace with democracy: democracy, defined in general terms, is a political system that had taken centuries to achieve, a

1

product even in the more developed countries of the last half of the twentieth century.[1]

There is no such thing, in any country or in international relations, as a peaceful road to modernity: the most apparently tranquil of states – Holland, Sweden, Finland – had periods of convulsion and war. Those hegemonic powers that prided themselves on a peaceful road – Britain, the USA – had their own sanguinary chapters, some within, some visited on others. As for the evidently less peaceful powers – France, Germany, Italy, Russia, China, Japan – their histories are ones in which repression, revolt, aggression and defeat have all combined. Equally, democratisation is not just, as contemporary discussion of a 'Zone of Peace', a region of peaceful, liberal, industrial states, might imply, a condition of inter-state peace but also a result of international factors. It had itself owed much to the external: to the requirement to change and democratise that states felt in competition with others, to the very demonstration effect which democratic change exerted, but also to the inter-state conflicts, the wars, that marked modern history. The apparently peaceful solution achieved at the end of the twentieth century therefore involved decades, indeed centuries, of conflict within and between states.

A recognition of this history, of at what cost and under what conditions the 'Zone of Peace' was produced, is a necessary part of understanding the contemporary international system. This outcome, itself precarious, has eventuated from a very unpeaceful past, one within which revolutions played a constitutive role. It is no more possible to understand how this world was created by ignoring the role of revolutions than it is by ignoring the formative influence of war. Democracy, and a peaceful evolution towards its fulfilment, is therefore only one part of the history of modern society and of the international system. An equally formative process has been that of social and political upheaval in general, and of revolution in particular.

The triumphalist perspective on world politics may be equally misleading as far as the future is concerned. A democratic political order is not something that necessarily lasts: in the course of the twentieth century many countries with constitutional regimes were overtaken by violence. There is no certainty that this could not occur again. Equally, as will be argued in the concluding chapter, the agenda of the revolutions of modern history is still very much with us because the aims they asserted, above all in regard to the rights of individuals and social groups, are far from having been achieved. Within more developed societies with a sustained experience of democracy, revolutions may not erupt to realise those aims, but this is far from meaning that the agenda has been brought to fruition. A picture of the contemporary world, and of the international system in particular, that ignores this unfinished agenda is not only incomplete, but fundamentally distorted.

The Centrality of Revolution

While this book as a whole is a study of one aspect of this revolutionary impact, this introductory chapter summarises the relationship between social revolutions and the international system and the analytic issues it poses. For much of modern history, revolutions have been a major factor, along with war, in the formation of world politics. Throughout this period their fate has been interwoven with that of the international system. Revolutions have aspired to the internal transformation of societies, but equally they have sought to alter relations between states and nations. They have done this not only by provoking conflicts between them and by seeking to promote change in other states, but also by aiming to alter the norms, the very ways, in which states and peoples have interacted. In ideological and programmatic terms, a revolution aims to transform a society within: it has equally to be international, or it is nothing.

The history of revolutionary movements – the French revolutionaries after 1789, the Bolsheviks after 1917, more recently the Islamic revolutionaries of Iran after 1979 – exemplifies an aspiration to change the world both within and beyond frontiers. The French revolution convulsed Europe and the Americas and shaped the politics and political language of the following century. Much of the twentieth century was dominated by the attempts of the communist movement to achieve its internationalised goals. Less socially radical than its successors, the American revolution none the less proclaimed what the Founding Fathers believed to be universal political truths. This process is, however, two-way: for their part, revolutions have been affected in fundamental ways by the international system. International forces have both served to stimulate change within countries and directed or constrained the subsequent development of revolutionary states and aspirations. The French revolution finally succumbed after Waterloo, the Bolshevik revolution to a less dramatic but no less effective challenge in the disintegration of the Soviet system of the late 1980s. A study of how these two factors – the revolutionary and the international – have interacted is therefore part of understanding how the modern world was created. Too easily forgotten in an age of peace and apparently spreading prosperity and democracy, the history of the modern world is one of struggle, suppression and revolt, of protracted conflict within as well as between states, of great myths and aspirations mixed with cruelty and disaster.

A study of how revolutions and the international interact will, in the first place, help us to understand the phenomenon of revolution itself. 'Revolution' as a term in political discourse and social science has a double character: like 'nation', 'society', 'class', 'war' and 'community' it denotes both a reality, something that analysis can identify and study, and an aspiration, a concept with a normative dimension that protagonists advocate and opponents contest. At the same time just as the real character of revolution – the forms it takes, the forces it mobilises, the outcomes it has – have changed, so too has its meaning, for political theorists and political actors, and above all for the social movements that mobilise in support of this idea. Analysis of the history of such ideas is a necessary accompaniment of, while no substitute for, the history of political movements, and will help to chart the word's changing meaning and impact. In common with other political and social terms, 'revolution' has changed meaning and usage over the centuries: this is in part a result of the impact of the tensions of modernity itself, in part in response to changes within particular societies that have then had an international impact. In keeping with the need to study both reality and ideas, we need to examine how the term has evolved: the history of the concept of 'revolution' is in itself an international history, as much in its genesis as in its impact. Equally, the meanings, aspirations, fears and myths associated with the term have been international – in their import and in their diffusion.

A study of revolutions in their international context can, at the same time, help to establish some proportion about their causes and effects. It can do so by correcting the twin excesses of exaggeration and denial. In situations where hostility to revolutions is expressed, there is a tendency to allocate responsibility for them uniquely to international forces – foreign, alien, imported. It is as if there could be no causes, grievance or actor within the society who is responsible for such actions. Karl Marx once poured scorn on those who ascribe revolutionary activity to external conspiracy:

> The police-tinged bourgeois mind naturally figures to itself the International Working Men's Association as acting in the manner of a secret conspiracy, its central body ordering, from time to time, explosions in different countries. Our association is in fact nothing but the international bond between the most advanced working men in the various countries of the civilized world. Wherever, in whatever shape, and under whatever conditions the class struggle obtains any consistency, it is but natural that members of our association should stand in the foreground. The soil out of which it grows is modern society itself.[2]

Marx was, of course, simplifying: once revolutionary states were established they certainly did help their supporters and admirers elsewhere. Moreover, when it suits them, as we shall see, revolutionaries too often make the same mistake: carried away with internationalist intoxication, they exaggerate the 'international' character of their movements, as part of their denial of social and political differences between states. From Anacharsis Cloots in the 1790s, with his 'world map of revolution', through Trotsky in the 1920s, with his 'itinerary of the world revolution', to Mao Tse-tung proclaiming 'The East is Red' and Guevara calling for 'two, three, many Vietnams' in the 1960s and Khomeini and his invocation of the world 'oppressed' in the early 1980s, the delusion of a worldwide revolutionary conflagration has inspired, and deluded, revolutionary leaders. On the other hand, Marx was right to put at the centre of any explanation of revolutions in the social and political context, that 'modern society' which is international as well as national and which is formed by world politics, by the world economy and by the flow of ideas across frontiers. There is much in the Marxist tradition of revolutions which is questionable, not least in the light of history: but the insight, expressed most clearly by Trotsky, into the 'combined and uneven' character of capitalist development, that such development *unifies* the world but in a dramatically unequal and disjointed way, is one of the most important means of understanding the international dimensions of revolution: this development binds the societies of the world more closely together, convening economic, military, political and ideological forces across frontiers even as it creates a world that is more and more uneven and therefore riven by tensions that can explode in revolutionary crisis.

In much of the academic literature, be it that of historians, political scientists, or sociologists, the converse problem, of diminishing the international dimension, arises: when the course of individual revolutions is discussed, this international origin, and the international factors affecting revolution, are too often placed on one side. International factors are too often viewed, by historians and sociologists alike, as marginal or residual factors in the course of what is presented as a discrete national event which then has some international consequences.[3] Equally, a large amount of the literature on the failure of revolutions, most notably that of Soviet communism, pays little attention to external factors: the failure of that system was not absolute, but relative, a failure in the context of the aspiration it had proclaimed to surpass its rival. If revolutions are nothing if they are not international, the same goes for their opposite, counter-revolution, and for their failures.

While in no way denying the role of specific and internal factors in the course of revolutions, the argument advanced here is that revolutions are always in some degree international events and need to be seen in this context. This is not to deny the internal, and in so doing subscribe to the myth of international exaggeration: rather we can establish with some greater comparative perspective and analytic precision the relationship between internal and external. There can be no history of states or of societies that is purely internal: the same applies to those crises of state and society that are revolutions.

If such a study can help to throw light on the phenomenon of revolution, it may also help to look in a new way at the workings of the international system. In the first instance, a focus on revolutions may help to show just how important revolution has been to the history of the international system, from the seventeenth century onwards. The history of that system is not just one of wars, diplomacy, and territorial changes. Hannah Arendt's remark that the twentieth century was one of war and revolution could be extended to the three preceding centuries: it is not that the sole, or always predominant, factor in international relations has been revolution, but that such upheavals have repeatedly affected the international system and underlain conflict between states in a way that most histories of international relations have understated. Beyond historical importance, a study of revolutions in their international context may also help to examine some more general theoretical issues, in regard to the workings of the system and indeed to the role of the international in regard to individual societies.

As will be discussed more fully in Chapter 11, writers on international relations have paid attention to the issue of revolutions, but they have tended to be sceptical of any theoretical implications that might be drawn from this study. Instead, they have taken revolutions, supposedly challenges to the workings and conceptions of the system, as evidence that the system is resistant to such changes and that theoretical conclusions need not follow. The argument advanced here is, by contrast, that a proper understanding of the international dimensions of revolution does entail a revision of our view of the international system as a whole. Beyond that, however, it suggests that our view of an apparently separate, domestic, politics may also have to be revised, since it leads us to see how much more important international factors are in the development and stability of states. The 'international' matters as much when there is no upheaval as when previously stable societies are affected by external factors. The insight which historical sociology has promoted is precisely how the apparently insulated institutions of domestic life – family, education, taxation systems, administrative structures, forms of worship, sport or entertainment – have always been shaped by external factors.[4] The implication of this is that an international study of revolutions can lead to a revision of our view both of international relations itself and of the politics and sociology of individual states.

Structure in Mass Upheavals

There is a further analytic issue that a combined study of the international and revolutions may help to clarify, namely that of the relationship between structure and change. Revolutions have posed, in sharpest form, the question of how to analyse social action. The problem of social action, and the relationship between intentions and outcomes, is by no means peculiar to revolutions. It runs through the whole of modern social and political analysis. However, in the case of revolutions, the debate has taken a particular, acute form, ranging from those, such as revolutionaries, who overstate the potential for conscious human activity, at home and abroad, and those who stress the structural preconditions, and argue that revolutions are not *made*, but happen.[5] It needs, again, to be said that neither of these two positions is adequate. The great voluntarists have seen their schemes confounded by the structures of reality. In 1885, in a letter to the Russian Marxist Vera Zasulich, Engels wrote:

> People who boast that they have *made* a revolution always see the day after that they had no idea what they were doing, that the revolution *made* does not in the least resemble the one they would have liked to make. That is what Hegel calls the irony of history.[6]

That is what Lenin began to learn in abrupt fashion after October 1917. Yet the most assured structuralists have seen their arguments overtaken by mass social action – Gramsci's reaction to 1917 itself was to term it 'the revolt against *Das Kapital*'. Iran and Nicaragua, in 1979, seemed equally to reassert the possibilities of purposive collective action as defiance of the then prevailing structuralism in much of the social sciences. As Eric Hobsbawm has written:

> Irrespective of their general character as phenomena of historic rupture, concretely revolutions are also episodes in which groups of people pursue intended goals, whatever the causes and motives which make them act or the – inevitable – difference between their intentions and the results of their actions. They belong to the realm of politics as well as to that in which political decisions are unimportant. The element of conscious action and decision cannot be left out of the analysis, though both the strategists of revolution and perhaps because they control more power especially those of counter-revolution, tend to overestimate its scope. . . History is made by men's actions, and their choices are conscious and may be significant. Yet the greatest of all revolutionary strategists, Lenin, was lucidly aware that during revolutions planned action takes place in a context of uncontrollable forces.[7]

Structure is unkind to *ancien régime* and revolutionary alike. Nowhere is this limitation more evident than in regard to international factors – those who in a pre-revolutionary period may wish to retain power see their ability to do so eroded, or destroyed by international factors, whilst revolutionaries, intent on transforming the world, find their plans defeated by the realities of the international system.

Here it is important to distinguish, however, between two kinds of structural factors. There are those which militate against change, which represent the immutable, unchanging, features of a political or other situation. This was the central theme of the great single study made of the foreign dimensions of a major revolution – Albert Sorel's *L'Europe et la Révolution française*.[8] The first of Sorel's eight volumes is entitled 'Les moeurs politiques et les traditions' – 'political customs and traditions': like de Tocqueville in his analysis of domestic continuities, Sorel sought to show how the foreign policy and impact of France after 1789 followed from what had gone before. This concern with constraints on human action has, equally, been the main preoccupation of modern social theory: this began with Durkheim's theory of 'social facts', those broader features of society which, as much as the rules and meaning of language, limit what an individual can do. The concern of what are termed, within international relations theory, 'realists', has similarly been on the role of structures in constraining what actors, be they states, social movements, or individuals, can do:[9] whatever the internal composition of states, states assert sovereignty, engage in diplomacy and trade, and are concerned with the power of their rivals.

Critical discussion of structure is therefore usually about what in the face of such inescapable and immutable forces human will, be it that of individuals or social movements, can achieve. Structure may however denote not the limits of the unchangeable, but its opposite, the irresistibility of change: about changes, long-term or abrupt, that human will cannot prevent or resist. 'Structure' is not therefore only a matter of constraint. There are those structural factors which are immune to human control and which make for change and upheavals, whatever human actors may think: ageing is one, climate another, geological movement a third. These may be gradual, or sudden: heart attacks, tornadoes and earthquakes are as structural as anything else, hitting at the foundations of an individual or social entity. The limits on human will in the face of macro-social change apply equally to the counter-revolutionary and the revolutionary; the structural is therefore both a source of change and of resistance to change. The central insight in the eighteenth-century idea of revolution was not that humans made history as they chose, but rather that human actions had to be seen in the context of events and processes that were beyond their control – hence the resort of writers on revolution to such images as a force of nature, an earthquake, a movement in the heavens.[10] At times the individual may have a *greater* role the *less* they understand or control the changes taking place around them: this was most evidently the case with the last Soviet leader Mikhail Gorbachev who unleashed a revolutionary collapse of the Soviet state whilst imagining until the very end that this system could be reformed. It is no diminution of the depth of what Gorbachev achieved to say that he did not anticipate the consequences of his actions. Had Gorbachev realised more presciently what his actions would entail, he might well have done other than he did.

The awareness of structural factors should, therefore, sensitise us to the inhibitions on what revolution can achieve as much as to the endurance of limits on the power of human action, individual or collective, to alter the world in which humans find themselves. For all the volumes written on the subject in modern social theory, it is hard to beat Marx's laconic insight:

> Men make their own history, but not of their own free will; not under circumstances they themselves have chosen but under the given and inherited circumstances with which they are directly confronted.[11]

This is as true for international relations as it is for social and political action within states. Yet while the aspiration to effect a total change of the international system is doomed to failure, revolutions, as much by the structural changes they express as by the intentions of revolutionary leaders and states themselves, are a major component of the development of modern society, and of the modern international system.

Normative Debates: The Challenge to Sovereignty

In addition to being about states and movements, revolutions are also about ideas. A focus on revolutions can thereby provide an alternative perspective on the ethical assumptions underlying international relations. The challenge they pose to established conceptions of the international system involves not just the postulation of a revolutionary internationalism, but also that, through the challenge they pose to established ideas of statehood and sovereignty, they open up alternative conceptions of international relations themselves. The alternative, internationalist, ideology of revolutions will be discussed in Chapter 3. This salience of ideas is evident in three separate but related domains – those of sovereignty, security and non-interference.

The ethical challenge is most acutely shown in regard to the concept that defines modern statehood – sovereignty. Sovereignty in its simplest form is an attribute of states: it denotes a condition in which no higher authority is recognised, and in which the holder of that sovereignty has full authority over the people and territory under its control. It is therefore, like the state itself, two-sided – it faces out, towards all rivals, asserting they have no jurisdiction or power within its territory; it faces inwards, towards any rivals, political and social, and tells them that they must obey the state – hence, amongst other characteristics, the monopoly on the means of violence associated with the modern state. To describe sovereignty as an attribute is, as with any normative concept, to assert something that may not coincide with reality. The assertion of external sovereignty was much easier than that of internal – it was usually easier to prevent an invasion than to maintain full control over your own population. However, with the rise of industrial society, and the new forms of intervention in society that this provided – such as taxing income, or conscripting youth of a particular age – the reality of control came more and more to reflect the ideal.

By the same token, revolutions are, above all, challenges to sovereignty *in both its dimensions*. Internally, they defy the authority of the state, challenging its legitimacy, its monopoly on violence, indeed its very political form and personnel. For revolutionaries, the concept of sovereignty is specific to rulers: it is, in Marxist terms, a class value, a legitimation of the rule of the oppressors over the oppressed. The famous slogan of the treaties of Westphalia, *cujus regio, ejus religio* stated that your religious affiliation depends on where you live and under it toleration of religious diversity could be institutionalised. It could equally be argued to legitimate the division between competing ruling groups, shared but parcelled, of class oppression and exploitation in the early modern epoch: *cujus regio, ejus spoliatio* – that you are exploited by whoever controls the area you live in – would be a fair alternative rendering. Externally, by their internationalist programmes and transnational impact, and by that very ideological universalism which de Tocqueville characterised as religious, revolutionaries challenge the frontiers between political units and the very validity of frontiers themselves. It has been rightly said that in 1789 the French Revolution constituted a rejection of the treaties of Westphalia of 1648.[12] In revolutionary thought frontiers and divisions between peoples are seen as the fabrications of rulers, as myths of division designed to divide the peoples of the world and ensure their continued, fragmented, domination.

Yet in that challenge to sovereignty, revolutions reveal the contradictory character of their programme. For, within states, an initial overthrow of the pre-revolutionary state, and utopian statements about new, spontaneous, forms of political order, are immediately replaced by the formation of recast, authoritarian and coercive institutions. In practice, revolutionary regimes are the more determined defenders of the authority of states within. Post-revolutionary states are more centralised than pre-revolutionary ones. In the international sphere, the same applies. While promoting challenges to statehood and sovereignty without, revolutions deploy their powers to seal their own frontiers, and, in time, come to be among the strongest defenders of state sovereignty. Such a commitment is, in time, also reflected in the sphere of ideology: not only do revolutionary regimes uphold principles of non-interference, sovereignty, inviolability of frontiers and the like, but they also come to espouse nationalism as a legitimating value. Revolutions, therefore, both challenge sovereignty, internally and internationally, and reassert it, often in a more effective form than did the regimes they have overthrown.[13]

Revolutions also prompt a reconceptualisation of the concept of security. Security, in orthodox international relations, pertains to relations between states, above all to military arrangements designed, either individually or conjointly, to limit the possibilities of armed attack by another state. This is what has been referred to as 'vertical security'. It is the kind of security guaranteed in the UN Charter, Article 2, and which is the concern of military alliances, armed forces and so forth. The other concept of security, 'horizontal security', is that of the regimes themselves, against internal challenge. Revolutions highlight not only the uneasy interrelation of these two forms of security, but also, critically, highlight the interests that lie behind particular definitions of security. The security of the 'nation', when defined against a shared external enemy, may slide into being the security not so much of the country as a whole as of particular groups within it.

In terms of the original concept of sovereignty articulated in the seventeenth century, security, seen from without as the defence of a realm, is therefore, internally, a licence to dominate, plunder and exploit. It entails the legitimacy and permanence of established authority. By challenging the power and defying the legitimacy of regimes, revolutions deny the claims of a state or 'national' security. In the same way, in occasioning changes that impact on the international system, they make clear the link between international and domestic security.

The attempts to resolve these problems are as extended as that of revolutions themselves. States confronted with revolutions and their international impact have sought to implement some link between vertical and horizontal security, yet have never been able to sustain a complete fusion of the two. From Vienna in 1815 onwards, and even more so at Versailles in 1919, the illusions of revolutionary internationalism were matched by those of counter-revolutionary interventionism. Guaranteeing a link between the state's definition of security and that of the people it claims to rule is, to some degree, a matter of making that state more representative. The spread of democracy over the past century has turned what were extremely unrepresentative states, whose definition of security was oligarchic at best, into ones commanding broader support within society. Yet this extension of the relevance of security cannot ever be complete: the most democratic societies in the world are pluralistic ones, in which conflicting groups – social, regional, ethnic, gender – will have different conceptions of what their security entails; all modern industrial democracies remain highly unequal societies in which the definition of interest is predominantly in the hands of an administrative and entrepreneurial elite. Once the *a priori* identification of state and nation, and of each with the given definition of 'security', is broken, then security becomes, like other dimensions of any political system, a matter of contested definitions and policies.

Revolutions challenge established notions of states and sovereignty in a third respect, they turn around the debate on non-interference and intervention. In orthodox politics, and international relations, the presumption is in favour of non-intervention: if intervention is contemplated, as it frequently is, then justifications for it have to be found. Such justifications have been formulated, most famously by John Stuart Mill, with his four legitimations: self-defence, secession, assistance to a state faced with invasion, extreme inhumanity.[14] The fact that intervention has been frequently practised does not detract from the fact that, in international relations, arguments have to be provided to justify it, or, as is often the case, responsibility for it has to be denied. In the case of revolution, *the reverse applies.* Revolutions started with a presumption that the boundaries between states are invalid, that sovereignty defined as non-interference is an ideology of the oppressors. Thus in November 1918, in an open letter to the German socialist leader Scheidemann, the Bolshevik Karl Radek declared:

> This principle of non-intervention was the principle which guided legitimist Europe after the Congress of Vienna, while in the struggle for liberation, international Communists all along advocated the energetic intervention in the affairs of the whole world.[15]

The supreme moral value is not, therefore, non-interference, but solidarity, an obligation made possible and at the same time enjoined by the transnational character of the system of oppression. Here, where the presumption is *in favour of intervention*, the arguments on exceptions go in the opposite direction: to justify non-intervention. The long history of orthodox justifications for intervention by status quo powers thus find counterpart in the long history of arguments by revolutionaries as to why they should *not* intervene: the lack of objective conditions, the possible counterattacks of the enemy, the unsuitability, often the 'adventurism', of the revolution that is asking for assistance, the unfavourable nature of the international balance of power or 'correlation of forces'. In the 1790s and again after 1917 left critics of revolutionary states have berated them for not doing more, for not living up to the obligations of solidarity and appropriately taking advantage of a given international revolutionary situation. This was the issue in dispute within the Bolshevik leadership over the signing of a compromise peace with Germany at Brest-Litovsk in early 1918. Those opposed to it have stressed that, while the duty of solidarity endures, it can never be absolute, nor be implemented at the risk of jeopardising the survival of the revolutionary state itself. The Cold War, a conflict in which the dangers associated with inter-state war were compounded by the risks of nuclear war, at once sudden and annihilating, provided many examples of this. Above all, Fidel Castro, in late October 1962, as he ruefully contemplated the withdrawal of Soviet missiles from Cuba, must have had reason to reflect on this recurrence. Little wonder that he was later to question Lenin's decision at Brest-Litovsk to compromise with Germany.

The principles of revolutionary solidarity and of hostility to the state are closely related: hence the appositeness of the term 'revolutionism' which the theorist Martin Wight used to refer to those who sought to displace the state from it place in international relations.[16] Wight's category included thinkers such as Immanuel Kant, who were not in any normal sense concerned with revolution, or any other sort of mass upheavals: rather, they identified a trend in international affairs, one they deemed positive, for the world of states to be replaced by one of cooperation between communities and individuals. Those who regard the states, their sovereignty and legitimacy, as primary, will, as a consequence, support non-intervention: this is as true of post-revolutionary regimes as of *anciens régimes*. Those who oppose the states in question will as a consequence regard intervention as justified, in order to promote other, superior, values. For revolutionaries from Cromwell and Robespierre to Lenin, Castro and Khomeini, this was as clear as it was for counter-revolutionaries of an internationalist bent, from Edmund Burke to Ronald Reagan. This centrality of legitimacy is evidently the case in situations of internationalised conflict: the issue in Central America in the 1980s was not intervention, or who crossed which frontier, but the legitimacy of, respectively, the Nicaraguan and other Central American regimes. The issue in Vietnam in the 1960s was not whether the US was invading South Vietnam, or North Vietnam, but the legitimacy of the southern regime and of the northern claim to be the legitimate government of the whole of Vietnam.

Here it is not merely a question of relating debate on normative issues in international relations to those in domestic politics. The debate on intervention indicates that there can be no normative theory on intervention that is confined purely to international relations. Given the link between vertical and horizontal security, and the instrumentalism of the debate on intervention, two broad schools of thought on revolutions and international security can be identified: for one, the goal is to make the world safe *from* revolutions, by containment and as much counter-revolutionary intervention as is feasible; for the other, the goal is to make the world safe *for* revolutions, again within the constraints of existing states and power relations[17] – Metternich was to term himself 'the doctor of revolutions', i.e. the person who cured society of them. The presumption in favour of security, i.e. of those already in power, entails one conception of world order; the presumption against security entails the other – solidarity with the oppressed, and, where apposite, non-interference by counter-revolution. This entails that, whether arguing for it or against it, the principle of non-intervention is never able to stand on its own: it is, as it were, a dependent value, that presupposes the value placed on the state in question. What appears as a normative debate about international relations, and the pros and cons of intervention, conceals another, *anterior*, debate about the rights and wrongs of states themselves.

Analytic Focuses: Understanding and Explanation

Against this background of both the reality and myths of revolu-tion, there are two broad ways to approach the topic of the international dimensions of revolutions: these correspond to the two characteristic approaches of social science itself, understanding and explaining. The former seeks to get inside the minds of those who made history, the individuals, social movements, and regimes; the latter seeks to look as objectively as possible at what occurred, and assess its causes, course and consequences. The need for the former is widely recognised in social science: we need to know what people think, what their motives are, and what constitutes their ideological appeal to others. It is above all necessary in regard to purposive action, individual or collective. 'Understanding' has, however, its limits: all social actors have their illusions, their half-truths, their preposterous and self-serving claims.

Nationalists are prime examples of this. One cannot write an account of nationalists, let alone assess the historical validity of, say, their territorial claims or conduct in war, by taking what they say alone. The same applies to revolutionaries. On the other hand, a purely explanatory approach too easily misses the point: people acted, individually and collectively, on the basis of certain beliefs, hopes, aspirations. Ideas, true or false, matter. They matter above all in situations of collective action and conflict – in wars, in nationalist movements, in revolutions. This is not just a matter of conceding that in a world of structures and limitations, agency and human intention have effects: it involves exploring what it was that these actors or agents thought they were doing. This is a necessary part of any explanation of their actions. So too is the emphasis on the role of ideas: social science has tended, in reaction against subjective accounts and in sceptical rejection of the motives people give, rather to downplay this side of human action. There can be no study of the causes and outcome of revolutions without giving it due attention.

In the light of these considerations, the study that follows is divided into three parts. Part I aims to understand what revolutionaries said and did. The first step is the reconstruction of the history of the idea of 'revolution' itself, a semantic and political trajectory that reflected an international process, prior to and following the constitutive moment of 1789. This is the reconstruction of an intellectual history that knew no frontiers. The next chapter examines the way in which international aspiration and anxiety was central to all revolutionary thinking, as indeed it was to the whole modern idea of progress. Revolutionaries viewed the international system and the role of the revolutionary state, or movement within it, as part of the unfolding of an inevitable and progressive story. There are striking similarities here, across ideologies, states and periods. Khomeini might have been dismayed to know how much he sounded like Robespierre or Lenin. If this international commitment, or ideology, is important as part of the history of political thought, it is also a factor, if by no means the only one, in the foreign policies of these states themselves: here a critical refutation of ideas, and of utopias in particular, may contain its own limitations. It is too simple to say that such 'internationalist' aspirations were merely the fantasies of dissatisfied intellectuals, the projection on to the international stage of some 'Age of Virtue' originally concocted at home. These ideas, for all their utopian character, had their real world causes, and had their effects on the course of foreign policy, on domestic opinion within states and on those in other countries, either sympathetic or hostile to the particular revolutionary regime in question.[18] To classify something as a myth, without explaining why this myth had such widespread appeal, runs the risk of denying the reasons why millions of people believed in and fought for it.

Central to the analysis of ideas is the aim of exporting revolution, the promotion of change in other states. Revolutionary regimes often, for their own reasons, deny that this is what they are doing, and their friends abroad often seek to downplay it. Such well-intentioned but mistaken analysis was heard frequently with regard to the revolutions of Vietnam, Cuba, Iran and Nicaragua, as it was, earlier, about France and Russia. Equally, disabused revolutionary critics of such regimes are prone to argue that the regime has abandoned its commitments: the Trotskyist critique of the USSR, developed from the mid-1920s, is a good example. What the liberal sympathiser misses is the continued belief by such regimes in the spread of their influence through social upheavals, what the disabused revolutionary underestimates is the way in which the manipulation of foreign support can as easily take an adventurist, military form as that of accommodation. In the aftermath of the Cold War there was much apparent surprise in academic literature about how far the Soviet Union and other states had indeed remained committed to revolution. People should not have been surprised – the archives and interviews only confirmed what was evident at the time, for those who wanted to see it.[19]

One of the central arguments of this book is that revolutionary regimes *do* seek to export revolution, by arms, political support and ideological encouragement: this is a theme I have already analysed with regard to particular regimes.[20] An objective assessment of revolutions may play this down, as such actions would seem forlorn and in conflict with the rational interests of a state. It is only by examining the ideas and record of these states that the endurance of such a commitment can be seen. The commitment to exporting revolution, and more broadly to reshaping the international system, was given effect in the foreign policies of revolutionary states: many generalisations are made about foreign policy in this context, ranging from those who see the foreign policies of states as a complete break with the past, to those who stress the continuities, national or systemic, of pre- and post-revolutionary foreign policies. A comparative study of this question, in terms of goals, capabilities and achievement, may contribute to a broader reassessment not only of individual diplomatic histories, but also of the domestic factors underlying foreign policy.

There is, as already suggested, a distortion latent in any purely internal account, for in charting the history of an idea, and of the thinking of revolutionaries, such an account runs the risk of paying insufficient attention to the course of events and the obstacles such an ideological commitment may have encountered. In Part II of the book I therefore look at broad topics that may help to explain the overall relationship of revolutions and the 'international'. The first of these issues is the question of causation – how, and how far, international factors account for the emergence of revolutionary challenges and their success or failure. There can be no definitive or general answer here: however, a comparative analysis of international causation may tell us a lot about individual revolutions as well as about the more general workings of the international system. This may be a continuous or interactive 'circular' process: an external influence upon a particular society may, in turn, produce changes in that society that lead to further conflict or other change in the international system. The study of cause also draws attention to the broader structures of international relations that to a large degree determine national politics – shifts in world balances of power, transitions in social and economic order.

If revolution has been an important feature of the international system over past centuries, so too has its opposite, 'counter-revolution', understood as the attempt to prevent, contain or reverse revolutions. The outspoken and militant international claims of revolutions were an important factor in shaping not only the policies of revolutionary states, but the response of the international system to such events. Here, as much as in the policies of revolutions, reality and rhetoric often diverge. If it has proved far harder to 'export' revolutions to other states than revolutionaries have imagined, it has also been far more difficult for those opposed to revolutions to impose their will on revolutionary states. Indeed, while revolutions have almost always provoked a response in the international system and calls for the revolution to be overthrown, international 'counter-revolution' in the sense of the successful destruction of a regime in one country by the coercive intervention of another, has been rather rare. Although such absolute reversals have not occurred, with the striking exception of the defeat of Napoleon in 1815 and the subsequent restoration of the Bourbon monarchy, the effects on revolutionary states and their foreign aspirations of such contrary responses have been enormous.

A chapter on the relation of revolution to war is followed by the last of the analytic issues discussed in Part II – the impact on revolutionary states and societies of international factors, or, more broadly, on the fate of revolutions themselves. This goes beyond the study of the international causes and consequences of revolutions into the internal, post-revolutionary, trajectory of such states themselves. This is an essential part of the story, the final, often destructive, link in the circular influence of revolutions and international relations. If revolutions aim, and to some extent succeed, in having an international impact, they are also themselves to a great extent affected by international factors: this is so not only in terms of the spread or international consolidation of their revolutions, but also in terms of the post-revolutionary evolution of their own societies, which remains under the influence of external factors. Much of the literature on revolutions stresses rupture, the separation of these societies from the international system, and the consolidation of new post-revolutionary states able to impose their own policies on the society. Though this may well be the aspiration and, for a while, the reality, over time such 'transformation', under varying degrees of autarchy, can be undermined by external pressures short of actual military intervention. The collapse of the Soviet bloc of communist states in the late 1980s is a striking example of how such a revolutionary autarchy could eventually be eroded, as was, with a different course, the 'Four Modernisations' policy of Chinese communism after 1978. In the latter half of the 1990s the pressures from within Iranian society for greater contact with the West, and not least for more access to its consumer culture and associated individual liberties, have come to the fore.

It was ever thus: whether in the case of the English revolution of the seventeenth century, or the Jesuit experiment in Paraguay in the eighteenth, or with more recent examples, insulation and divergence in the short and medium term seems in the longer scheme of things to yield to collapse and convergence. As with causation, it would be simplistic to ascribe responsibility for this wholly or mainly to external factors: but as the Bolsheviks above all were acutely aware, the success or failure of revolutions depend as much as anything else on the international context in which they are located. In this, as in other respects, revolutions are international, or they are nothing.

This book concludes, in Part III, with chapters analysing the implications of this study for, respectively, the theory of international relations, and the pattern of contemporary history. Both suggest, in distinct lines of argument, why the topic of revolution should be of continued relevance to students of human affairs. Chapter 11 argues for the centrality of revolutions to *international relations theory*, Chapter 12 for its centrality to modern and contemporary history. Both ignore it at a price.

Social Revolutions in Retrospect

This analysis is, as a whole, inseparable from the context of the 1980s and 1990s, from developments in the social science study of revolutions, from world events, and from the impact of these events on social science. As I examine in more detail in Chapter 2, revolutions, unlike war or nationalism, claim to embody something new – indeed it is the factor of novelty, and hence unexpectedness, that helps account for their success. For this reason, in addition to the general reasons as to why there are no 'laws of history', there are limits to any comparative study of revolutions and to the drawing of theoretical conclusions from it. But revolutions, like other political and historical phenomena, are not singular events: they are, as will be argued later, produced by comparable causes, shaped by comparable factors, as well as being influenced in their rhetoric, politics and outcomes by what has occurred, or is believed to have occurred, in the past. It is this possibility for comparison, without inappropriate scientistic or quantitative aspirations, that underlies the following study.

The category of revolution being proposed is straightforward: if, as already indicated, the word 'revolution' has several meanings, over time and within different theoretical approaches, the focus of what follows will be on revolutions in the sense that has emerged from the late eighteenth century – that is, *major political and social transformations in the context of a contradictory modernity involving mass participation and the aspiration to establish a radically different society*. For all the variations involved, a category of this kind has considerable comparative and theoretical relevance and can enable us to examine the major upheavals of modern history, from the American and French revolutions to the contemporary period. Earlier upheavals which bear a partial resemblance to these events and which can in retrospect be vested with the word 'revolution', even when they preceded the tensions of modernity, notably the English revolution of the 1640s, will also be used to provide, where pertinent, illustration and to elicit theoretical challenge.[21]

Nowhere is this issue of challenge more evident than in the outcome of the communist revolutionary experiment in the late

1980s. For if hitherto it had appeared that the communist system provided a further illustration of the impact of revolutions on the international system, the collapse of communism, or its rapid transformation in the Chinese case, would seem to have marked the end of such alternatives in the international system. It is in this context, of course, that there has been much speculation about the end of a historical period, going back to the French Revolution, in which revolution, or the possibility thereof, constituted a central feature of international political and intellectual life. This is, in essence, the thesis of the 'end of history'. Equally, historians such as François Furet and Simon Schama have sought, in revising the orthodox Marxist account of the French revolution, to demystify it as a founding moment in modern history.

Whether or not we are now entering a period when revolution in this sense is no longer a feature of international politics is an open question. As I suggest in chapter 12, the question cannot be answered in advance any more than can the equally debated issue of the end of war between major states. If there is one thing that we could learn from the history of the twentieth century, and of revolutions across several centuries, it is the capacity of history, and not least of social movements, to surprise. The capitalist modernity that provided earlier revolutions is, if less warlike, even more unequal and fast-changing than that of earlier decades. Even if it were the case that 'Revolution' has passed into history, and was specific to the period 1789–1989, we are yet far from reducing the importance of studying the intersection of revolutions and the international. Indeed, the outcome of the communist experiment makes it all the more possible and challenging to look at this issue anew: we now have a historical outcome, a verdict, that makes possible analysis of two hundred years of revolution, as ideology and as historical phenomenon.

The events of 1989 also enable us to pose, more sharply than perhaps was possible previously, the theoretical issues that underlie such a comparative study, with regard to both 'revolution' and the 'international'. These issues are as pertinent as they ever were to the study of both politics and international relations. In this sense, the end of communism and, in whatever qualified way we use the term, the 'end of Revolution' enable a more challenging investigation of the issue to be attempted. The implications for the analysis for individual, bounded societies and for international relations as a whole, are, I shall argue, considerable. Revolutions are part of the foundation, the formative process, of modern states, modern politics, and the modern international system. For this reason, as much as because of the unfulfilled agenda that they asserted, they are part of the present, as well as the past, of world politics. On these bases alone the connection between revolution and world politics merits systematic examination.

Part I
The Internationalist Engagement

2

An Alternative Modernity: The Rise and Fall of 'Revolution'

1989: The Cunning of History Returns

The year 1989 was a challenging one for the student of revolution. In it fell not only the two-hundredth anniversary of the French revolution of 1789, but the fortieth anniversary of the Chinese revolution of 1949 and the tenth anniversary of two of the most resonant upheavals of more recent times, those in Iran and Nicaragua in 1979. In the initial part of the year the battle lines seemed clear enough. For those sympathetic to revolution it was an occasion to proclaim the historical significance of these upheavals, and the legitimacy of at least some of the goals which they had embodied. For those hostile to, or embarrassed by, these events it was the occasion to reassert alternative verities, to warn of the dangers which revolution might bring, as a purported solution to social and political ills.[1]

By the end of 1989 a very different ideological picture had presented itself. While in Western Europe the French revolution, as predicted, was indeed celebrated amidst much political and academic dispute, in the East a contrary and contemporary verdict was being returned, as mass movements and state collapse that were widely regarded as themselves revolutionary precipitated changes against the major revolution of the twentieth century. Within the space of a few months the system of political power, domestic and international built by the Bolshevik revolution of 1917 was swept away, first in Hungary and Poland, then in the remaining East European countries; although the impact on the USSR itself was

27

somewhat delayed, this rejection of the communist model was then replicated in the Soviet Union itself, leading in the latter part of 1991 to the disintegration of the Soviet state and the removal of the Communist Party from power. Therefore, 1989 was a year which confounded both sides of the ideological divide: those who were sympathetic to revolutions seemed to have their expectations refuted by the disintegration of the communist system; those who had begun the year opposed to mass upheavals now found themselves endorsing a form of political action that they had themselves opposed.

While the paradox of bicentenary should not attract too much attention, the events of 1989 challenged all students of revolution. In historical terms, they posed the question of whether the collapse of communism and the discrediting of an alternative social and political system marked the end of the longer period that had indeed begun in 1789. This was one in which revolution, as historical events, and 'Revolution' as historical aspiration and myth, had appeared to be a possibility, desirable or otherwise, in modern society. As will be argued later, the real turning point, or moment of truth, was not 1989 at all, but had come one hundred and fifty years earlier, in 1848. It was then that revolution and 'Revolution' failed to coincide: the emerging state structures of Western Europe held, but, in response to movements of social and national assertion, the states began a process of reform and accommodation. Therefore, 1989 can be said to have confirmed something that, in retrospect at least, had long been the case: revolution had ceased to be a viable option in Western Europe for a century and a half, since the failure of the upheavals of 1848. The last such upheaval in any European society had been 1917, its occurrence a result of the First World War, its later impact sustained not by the revolutionary upsurge across Europe that the Bolsheviks anticipated, but by military victory in the Second World War.

In analytic terms, therefore, 1989 posed the question not only of how and why the communist system had collapsed so quickly, a chapter as fascinating as any in the annals of state collapse in modern times, but also of whether the events of 1989 could be regarded as a revolution at all and, if so, what the implications for theories of revolution were. Not least amongst the issues which any such analysis would have to include would be the role of the international – as a precipitant of change and as an element in any new, revised, theorisation of what constitutes revolution.

The Evolution of a Concept

If the events of 1989 posed a challenge to accepted definitions and theories of revolution they were far from being the first to do so. By looking at the development of this term we may discern something about the assumptions it embodies. Three dangers lurk on the edges of such a history of meaning: one is that of an etymological reductionism, that seeks to read into contemporary meaning residues of a semantic origin – such residues may prevail, but often do not;[2] the second danger is that of a detached semanticism, a study of changing meaning that separates the history of such changes, and the import of words, from their social context; the third danger involves confusing the history of the idea with that of the history of the process itself – of, in this case, confusing 'Revolution' with revolution. None the less, the endeavour of semantic history is possible and significant: revolution, as much as any other word in social science or everyday usage, has evolved over time and moved through several different meanings. If one can trace the changing meaning of other words common in modern political language – nation, class, race, economy, liberalism – then the evolution of the term 'revolution', and the factors determining this development, can also be clarified.[3]

Such chartings of origin and meaning are central to much modern political philosophy, be it in the *Begriffsgeschichte* of Reinhardt Kosseleck or the works of Raymond Williams and Quentin Skinner that focus on context. Such histories have an important clarificatory, not to say secular, role: they show that terms do not have any essential linguistic let alone religiously inherent meaning. It is social change and political history that determine and alter signification. As much as with any of these other political terms, we can therefore show the way in which the term 'revolution', located in one particular language, has shifted meaning over time is itself part of an international process: not only are the events which affect meanings in any one language drawn from a range of countries, but the definition in one idiom is affected by changes in others. Both event and term reflect a process of development within particular states or societies, but also within an international context.

The history of political terms is, it can be argued, international in at least *three* senses: discursive, generative, paradigmatic. First, discursive: words, and symbols, themselves cross frontiers and are picked up, often with different meanings, far from their country of origin. Secondly, generative: this process is itself explained, in large part, by the very shared, internationalised experience of different countries, be this the travails of industrialisation or foreign domination, the tensions of that combined and uneven development which characterises the modern world. Thirdly, paradigmatic: revolutionary movements themselves see themselves, and are seen by others, as models. In this triple internationality – discursive, generative, paradigmatic – is to be found the explanation for the spread and influence of political terms around the world. The fate of core words of modern politics – state, nation, democracy, revolution – is one of such internationalisation. So too is the spread of symbols: the Phrygian cap was the symbol of republican revolt at the end of the eighteenth century, the tricolour became the standard emblem of liberal and nationalist revolt in the nineteenth century, the red flag and the hammer and sickle that in the twentieth, the nuclear disarmament symbol that of youth revolt in the third quarter of the century. Such diffusion did not stop words having very different, and often contrary, meanings: the term 'republican' has meant very different things in, say, Germany, Italy, Ireland and the USA. History has also played cruel tricks with these terms: some of the most oppressive modern states have been termed 'people's democracies', and the most potent symbol of communist collective action, 'solidarity', became the symbol of the very national but spontaneously effective anti-communist workers' movement in Poland.

At the core of the idea of revolution is that of some substantial and potentially violent change in a political system.[4] In that sense an embryonic concept of revolution was present in classical Chinese and Hebrew and in what was most formative for the European political conception, classical Greek thought: Thucydides, the historian, talked of *epanastasis*, revolt, and the dangers of *neoterismos*, or innovation, and Plato argued that this process, to which he also applied the word *neoterismos*, was accompanied by violence. In his schema of degeneration from one political order to another, it denoted a negative process. Aristotle discussed *metabole*, change or transition, and *stasis* or unconstitutional change.[5] Latin political thought contained no systematic discussion of political upheavals comparable to that of the Greeks, but the conception of substantial change was present, with an emphasis above all on the *novelty* of such situations.

Although Aristotle's actual term *stasis* came later to be applied more to sedition than to the process of change itself, another aspect of his thinking was to influence later conceptions, namely the idea of a cyclical flow in history. Hence a radical change was above all something which *returned* to a previous era: it was for this reason that when in the early Italian city states there began to be discussion of such changes, the word *revoluzione*, meaning a turning round in a circle or turning back, began to be used. This Italian term was derived from the verb *revolvere*, meaning to turn around or turn back: it was distinct from the word *revoltare*, meaning to rise up against a ruler. As was also to be the case later, term and event did not correspond. The English events of the 1640s, which much later became known as a 'revolution',[6] were known at the time as 'civil war' or the 'great rebellion' ('rebellion', from the Latin word for re-starting a war, had long been used in a generally negative sense). Similarly, three other upheavals of the pre-1789 era, the German 'Peasant War' of the early sixteenth century, the revolt of the Netherlands, and the American War of Independence, only later and retrospectively acquired the meaning 'revolution'. It was in the sense of a change leading to a return that the word 'revolution' was used of the events in England of 1688, which restored the Stuart monarch to the throne.

In the eighteenth century the modern concept of 'revolution' began to crystallise. Montesquieu wrote of it, in the context of warning that despotic as opposed to properly constituted monarchies were more likely to provoke an overthrow of the system. Voltaire in his *Essai sur les moeurs et l'esprit des nations* (1756) coined the phrase 'la révolution des ésprits': he thereby introduced the concept of a radical change in intellectual and moral outlook, but without any necessary association with revolt from below or popular involvement. Rousseau used the term to denote radical changes in society, but, again, without any necessarily positive conclusion, or large-scale involvement from below.[7] At the same time, the term acquired new scientific authority from the theories of astronomy, signifying the movement of the stars. While this was not a directly political meaning, it had the implication that such processes were inevitable, or as would later be said 'determined', and that they involved a large-scale reorganisation of the units in the system. This suggested, as did contemporaneous concepts of a world being transformed by the ineluctable but hidden hand of the market and free trade, a process *beyond* human control. By the latter half of the eighteenth century the term had begun to acquire a sense of something unavoidable and transformative. This meaning was captured in the saying of Louis Sébastien Mercier in 1772: 'Tout est révolution dans ce monde', and by Tom Paine's argument in his 1782 *Letter to the Abbé Reynal* that the American revolution was not, as the Abbé had argued, cyclical, but rather a fundamental change.

It was with the French revolution that these earlier anticipations were combined and the modern sense of the word came to be fully articulated.[8] As Krishan Kumar has summarised it so effectively:

> No other event in the history of modern times has so powerfully aroused the sentiments of novelty, transformation, and the creation of a new order. As Alexis de Tocqueville later wrote, 'no previous political upheaval, however, violent, has aroused such passionate enthusiasm, for the ideal the French Revolution set before itself was not merely a change in the French system but nothing short of a regeneration of the whole human race'. Edmund Burke, severely critical of its course as he was, was drawn to say that 'all circumstances taken together, the French Revolution is the most astonishing that has hitherto happened in the world'. 'How much the greatest event in the history of the world and how much the best', Charles James Fox greeted the fall of the Bastille. Goethe declared that the victory of the French revolutionaries at Valmy in 1792 marked a new era in man's history. And Hegel waxed ecstatic over the fact that the French Revolution had revealed the great secret of human history, as the progressive realization of Reason.[9]

The incident at which the old and new combined is said to be when the courtier of Louis XVI, Count de Liancourt, was advising his monarch about the disturbances of 1789: when asked by the king whether it was a 'revolt', he is said to have replied 'Non, sire – c'est une révolution'.[10] Unwittingly, perhaps, de Liancourt combined the earlier sense of a massive quasi-astronomical change with that of great political change; but he also initiated the association of the term 'revolution' with new ideas that were current in the political vocabulary of the time and which did much to constitute 'Revolution' as a central idea, or myth, of modern politics. In this process it was detached not just from its etymological but from its scientific origins. As Kosseleck has written:

Revolution congealed into a collective singular which appeared to unite within itself the course of all individual revolutions. Hence, revolution became a *metahistorical concept*, completely separated, however, from its naturalistic origin and henceforth charged with ordering historically recurrent convulsive experiences. In other words, Revolution assumes a transcendental significance; it becomes a regulative principle of knowledge, as well as of the actions of all those drawn into revolution. . . All further characteristics of the modern concept of revolution are sustained by this metahistorical background.[11]

Kosseleck may overstate the degree to which the earlier scientific association, not of a circulatory, but of an overwhelming natural event, was now lost; but he is right in his identification of an idea that was fundamentally distinct *and* mythic, at once descriptive and normative, or, as he terms it, 'metahistorical'. Its similarity in this respect to another idea emerging at this time, one that both described and prescribed 'nation', is striking.[12] Both terms acquired new meaning and resonance from their association with the political and socio-economic transformations of the late eighteenth and early nineteenth centuries: they were, in this way, inextricably linked to the onset of capitalist modernity.

This diversity of emphases accompanied the translation of the term 'revolution' into a variety of languages, through discursive internationalisation. The conception of revolutionary change was international in both its diffusion and its very meaning. While it arose from the French revolution, it soon spread throughout other languages as the ideas of the French revolution spread. Yet there was a choice, based on which aspect of 'Revolution' the translation wished to stress. Some sought an *etymological* rendering, based on a variant of the idea of 'turning' or 'circulation'. Others chose the *semantic* rendering, translating the word into equivalents denoting 'upheaval' and mass revolt. It is significant that even in European languages which strive to produce their own indigenously rooted terms for politics, such as German and Russian, variants of the same word – *Revolution, revolutsiya* – are used; the one notable exception is modern Greek, which retains the classical word, which captures the semantic import, *epanastasis*. The Finnish term, too, *vallankomous*, comprises the words for power and overthrow.[13]

As European political thought spread across the world in the nineteenth and twentieth centuries so very different languages and contexts yielded their own renderings, sometimes by using indigenous words partly in a new political sense and sometimes by producing new words believed to accord with the European term. Thus in Arabic there was a semantic rendering: the indigenous word *thawra*, meaning to revolt, was used to denote contemporary upheavals, blurring the distinction between revolt and revolution. *Thawra* too came to mean both event and post-revolutionary state. The word *daula*, which itself originated in a root *dwl* meaning to rotate, came to mean state: it thus prefigured the twentieth-century institutionalisation of the term 'the revolution', to mean a post-revolutionary regime, and a claim to the legitimacy thereof. In Persian, an Arabic word *inqilab*, derived from the root *qlb*, meaning to revolve or rotate, was used, but in Arabic was used for a coup d'etat.[14] The Iranian revolutionaries of 1978–9 had no problem in proposing an 'Islamic revolution' (*inqilab-i islami*) but they did object to the term 'revolutionary Islam', on the grounds that there could be no qualification of the faith.[15] Ottoman Turkish also used the *qlb* root rendering it as *inkilâp*, and also the term *ihtilal*, from an Arabic root *khll* denoting disorder, but in contemporary usage the favoured word is *devrim*, derived from another Arabic root, *dwr*, meaning to turn.[16] Maltese, a mixture of medieval Arabic and modern Italian, reflects both its origins: *taqlib*, for disorder, and *rivoluzioni*, for revolution.[17]

Classical Hebrew had at least four words denoting revolt or rebellion: *mered*, rebellion; *kom*, uprising; *marah*, revolt, in particular rebellion against God; and *kesher*, plot. For example, in describing the revolt of King David's son against him, the Bible uses the term derived from *kom*, *hitkommimut*.[18] In modern Hebrew these were not used: instead three modern words, based on the root for the word to change or turn around, *hpch*, were coined. One, *mahapecha*, implies a radical change by force, as in Russia in 1917 and in Iran in 1979; a second, *mahapach*, denotes a change by peaceful means, and came into use for the major Israeli electoral upsets of 1977 and 1992; the third, *haficha*, denotes a revolt. Another example of the incorporation of both the etymological and the semantic is to be found in one of the more obscure languages deployed by modern revolutions, Quechua, the Andean language used by the guerrillas of the Peruvian *Sendero Luminoso*: the word *revolución* from Spanish is alternated with the indigenous works *q'eqikuy* and *auqanchanay* meaning rebellion.[19] Hindi uses the word *kranti*, from Sanskrit roots denoting radical change and human agency, while Urdu uses *inqilab*. Of all the long-established languages Chinese is the one which has been the most consistent. In the *I Ching*, the Book of Changes, believed to have been composed about a thousand years BC, the term *ge-ming*, is applied to T'ang and Wu, the founders of the Shang dynasty in the seventeenth century BC. Its formulation of the problem contains advice that practitioners of the later modern concept could well comprehend:

> Heaven and earth undergo their changes, and the four seasons complete their revolution. T'ang and Wu led insurrections according to the will of Heaven and in response to the wishes of men. Great indeed is the significance of such a time.
>
> Change of any kind is generally viewed by people with suspicion and dislike; therefore it must be instigated gradually. When change is necessary, it will only be approved after it has been seen to work. A proven necessity beforehand, and a firm correctness throughout: these are the conditions under which revolutions can be successfully brought about.[20]

Ge-ming is a semantic rather than an etymological rendering: it combines the character *ge*, denoting change, and also removal from office, with *ming*, meaning life, fate, destiny, and the mandate of heaven.[21] For its part, Japanese uses the same characters as Chinese, pronouncing them *kakumei*.[22] However, as already noted, etymology has its limits: it is current usage, itself largely shaped by international factors, that has determined the meanings of 'Revolution' since 1789.

The Metahistorical Idea

The post-1789 concept of revolution partook of the broader democratic spirit of the times, but there were four constitutive elements in this new idea of revolution: popular involvement, progress, a new age, and a total transformation. The idea of popular involvement, later embodied in the idea that particular social groups, including, in the Marxist perspective, classes, could 'make' revolutions marked a break with both the astronomical and the purely constitutional associations of earlier conceptions. Equally, it brought to the fore something that had been present in much earlier political thinking and action, namely the legitimacy of revolt against the ruler. While classical and earlier modern European writings, and, in a different vein, Muslim political thought, had allowed for revolt under certain conditions, the predominant view had been that revolt was not legitimate. This was especially so where monarchs had supposedly divine sanction, as they had in both mediaeval Christian and Islamic societies. With the rise of individual and democratic political thought in the seventeenth and eighteenth centuries, this absolute right of the rulers had begun to be questioned, but in what was still a cautious and limited qualification. The idea of the sovereignty of the people, as distinct from their right *in extremis* to exchange one ruler for another, was very much a product of the latter half of the eighteenth century, expressed in the American revolution and, with greater impact in Europe, in the French.

The idea of progress, of history moving in a linear, positive, direction, not in a circle and not being static, was given greater force by the social and economic changes of the time – an increasing understanding of nature, the discovery of the Americas, economic change – by indeed the concomitantly named 'industrial' revolution.[23] So much of post-1789 thought was dominated by this concept of progress, whether phrased in liberal, revolutionary or purely scientific terms: it was symptomatic that in the language of communist orthodoxy of the twentieth century the word 'progressive' should have played such a central and vacuous role. With its ever unresolved combination of deterministic and voluntaristic elements, i.e. progress as something that happens *and* equally something that is achieved, 'Revolution' was to underlie much of the optimism, and justify many of the crimes, of subsequent 'revolutionaries'. The word 'progressive' and its contraries, 'conservative' or 'reactionary', became central to revolutionary legitimation.

The concept of revolutions as introducing a new age was, equally, a break with the earlier, circular or astronomical, conception even as it picked up on the Thucydides–Plato concept of *neoterismos*: revolutions were now the points of transition, or entry, into a new period. They marked not returns but movement along a line, a break with the constraints of the past, the traditional or established society. They allowed a new society, even a new world, to be constructed. This emphasis upon breaking with the past, the creation of something new, was to become a prominent strain in the appeals and self-justification of revolutions. Equally it was to form the basis of the opposition to revolutions. It was at the end of the eighteenth century that the terms 'reaction' and 'conservative' were coined to denote opposition, and at the end of the nineteenth, in 1891, Pope Leo XIII was to issue one of the most influential Papal Encyclicals of modern times, *Rerum Novarum*, 'About New Things': it advocated a Christian transformation of society against the three 'revolutions' – industrial, liberal capitalist and socialist – of the modern age.

This legitimation by reference to 'newness' did not preclude alternative, retrospective, historical legitimations and imitations. The Iranian revolutionaries of 1979 went further in invoking *sadr-i islam*, the 'golden age of Islam', in particular the Prophet Muhammad's government of the seventh century, as their model, but they were an exception only by degree. Marx had expressed the hope that modern revolutionaries would not be shaped by those that had gone before:

> The social revolution of the nineteenth century can only create its poetry from the future, not from the past. It cannot begin its own work until it has sloughed off all its superstitious regard for the past. Earlier revolutions have needed world-historical reminiscences to deaden their awareness of their own content. In order to arrive at its own content the revolution of the nineteenth century must let the dead bury their dead.[24]

Marx was, however, too precipitate, not least because, in a fine case of the reciprocity that characterises all revolutions, his successors would themselves look back to their own predecessors, international and national. All revolutionaries used at least some element of the past to justify what they were doing, be this as self-justificatory models for what they themselves were doing, or as part of an attempt to deploy a national and international past for current legitimation. Louis XIV's planners had termed Paris's main avenue the 'Elysian Fields', after the Isles of the Blest, mentioned by the poets Homer and Hesiod, where special heroes, exempted from death, are transported. The revolutionaries looked to classical Rome for their models, a process in which they were encouraged by the neo-classical artists of the time. The Bolsheviks admired earlier Russian radicals (Herzen, Chernychevski, Kropotkin), as well as the Jacobins of the 1790s – Lenin inclining to Robespierre, Trotsky to Danton.[25] The Chinese revolutionaries presented themselves as inspired both by the Bolshevik Revolution of 1917 and the warriors and heroes of classical Chinese antiquity and literature. The Latin Americans of the 1950s, 1960s and 1970s invoked earlier nationalist radicals, such as Simon Bolivar, Jose Martí and Augusto Sandino. The Viet Minh of the 1940s and 1950s combined Lenin and Robespierre with national heroes. This was evident, for example, in the nationwide uprising of August–September 1945 that first established communist power in Vietnam: in Hanoi, Ho Chi Minh declared independence on 2 September by invoking the 1776 US Declaration of Independence and the 1791 French Declaration of the Rights of Man; the leader in Saigon, Tran Van Giau, consciously imitated Petrograd 1917 in launching the insurrection in the south.[26]

These exemplars drawn from the past were used not only as a source of personal modelling and inspiration, but also as a public and popular legitimation to justify the particular radical and complete break being advocated. While this 'newness' was represented by the necessity, the 'inexorability', the inevitability of the changes which were taking place, 'Revolution' was a process that involved not just a change in the political or constitutional form of society, but also a change in economic structure, in values and beliefs, and even in dress, language, and systems of calculating time. We can gain some perspective on this concept by noting its two most common alternatives – 'reform', denoting change that is more cautious or limited, and 'evolution', suggesting change that does not involve a radical break with the past. Revolution was, to use another word that came to be associated with this process and its ideology, 'total'.[27]

Distinctive Events

The idea of 'Revolution' produced by the French revolution was to define modern political discourse for two centuries. It developed in the nineteenth and twentieth centuries through the work and actions of a range of thinkers. If this was most notably the case with Karl Marx and his theory of communist revolution, it was not specific to Marxism – anarchism staked an equally cogent claim.[28] It was in the mid nineteenth century that it came to be seen as an irresistible, immanent and historical force, like some suppressed tidal wave that would sweep all before it. One can indeed argue that while it was 1789 which gave the idea its 'metahistorical' content, it was in the 1840s that there took shape the idea of 'Revolution', an inevitable historical force. In a Europe dominated by five great powers, Marx termed it 'the sixth great power', the one that would overwhelm the other five. Marxism was to be the most pervasive embodiment of this, but perhaps nowhere was this better expressed than in the words of the Russian exile Alexander Herzen. Herzen was an aristocrat with a small following, but someone who in addition to reflecting the thinking of his own time was to influence later revolutionaries, notably Lenin. Herzen wrote in 1857:

> We do not build, we destroy; we do not proclaim a new truth, we abolish an old lie. Contemporary man only builds the bridge; another, the yet unknown man of the future, will walk across it. You perhaps will see it. Do not remain on this shore. Better to perish with the revolution than to be saved in holy reaction.
>
> The religion of revolution, of the great social transformation, is the only religion I bequeath to you. It is a religion without a paradise, without rewards, without consciousness of itself, without a conscience.[29]

In common with other Marxist ideas such as the critique of imperialism, this idea of revolution was to have a resonance far beyond the communist movement: as nationalism began to develop in the latter half of the nineteenth century, the ideas of national independence and of revolution came to be closely associated with each other. This was in part because it was argued that the very assertion of independence against entrenched foreign rule would itself be 'revolutionary', would introduce a new age for the people concerned, and in part because it was argued that only through a revolution, i.e. a mobilisation and a radical transformation, could such independence be attained. However, this association of revolution with nationalism did not remove, even as it conflicted with, the term's internationalist associations: such internationalist commitment rested on the idea of the new nation as the bearer of revolutionary and potentially universal ideas, which others should follow. Equally inherent in the ideology of these national upsurges was an international model, the Mazzinian idea of a harmony of nations, a family of independent states, that would be produced by the attainment of freedom. For these reasons, the nationalisation of the idea of revolution did not preclude a continued association with internationalism:[30] it was indeed the work of Marx and his comrades in the International Workingmen's Association, founded in 1864, which prompted the emergence of the term 'internationalism' later in that decade.

At the same time, and in part because of the attainment of power by revolutionaries, the very term 'Revolution' began to acquire different, if related, shades of meaning, some of which at least merit attention. If revolution initially came to be associated with a particular *event* – the overthrow of the monarch in France, or, later, the communist seizure of power in Russia – it eventually came to denote a much broader process. Thus movements or organisations that aspired to come to power, and which claimed legitimacy in terms of alleged or real popular and historical support, called themselves 'revolutionary' and their movement 'the revolution'. And regimes that had been established through revolutions used the term to denote not just the events but the whole post-revolutionary period, and indeed the regime itself – so that 'defence of the revolution' or 'counter-revolutionary' came to be defined in terms not of a particular moment, but of the interests of that state.

These shifts and multiple meanings also led to a devaluation of the term 'revolution', or at least to increasingly loose usage of the term. Thus, in addition to mass upheavals introducing major changes, the term was now used by any movement or regime wishing to proclaim its historical and international importance: military coups, changes of political system, local uprisings, all called themselves 'revolutions'. The Arab Ba'ath Socialist Party of Iraq, a dictatorial organisation which came to power in two army coups in 1968, designated these as *thawratain timuz*, 'the two revolutions of July'. In an equally inflated denomination of the 1980s the Republican Presidencies of 1981–8 were called by their proponents 'the Reagan Revolution'. Throughout the second half of the twentieth century, and across the world, political organisations with dubious resonance in the population entitled themselves 'revolutionary': dilution went hand in hand with diffusion.

The Communist Variant

The role of Marxism for the constitution of the modern concept of 'Revolution' in the 1840s was decisive. By far the most influential and diffused conception of revolution was indeed that established by the communist movement, first in the writings of Marx and

Engels in the 1840s and later in the writings of Lenin and his associates in the Russian revolution. Following the Bolshevik assumption of power in 1917 this idea came to be adopted by a range of movements across the world: at its height the communist movement counted eighty-one parties and was in power in over two dozen countries. This idea of revolution – as a seizure of power, as immanent social process, as international movement, as a regime to be defended and developed, and as a culmination of world history – was to dominate much of the twentieth century. If there were twentieth-century revolutions that were clearly separate from that of communism – most notably the Mexican revolution of 1910 and the Iranian revolution of 1979 – the great majority of revolutionary movements, successful and otherwise, saw themselves as in some way within this tradition.

For communists, revolution was the means to achieve a break with the existing capitalist and imperialist society and to enter a new post-capitalist world. In such a post-revolutionary order the capitalist system of oppression, based on private ownership of the means of production, would be superseded. This conception began in the work of Marx and Lenin with an argument about the direction of history, that capitalism itself was preparing the objective basis, through accumulating contradictions, for its own collapse and supersession. This was the message of the canonical *Preface to the Critique of Political Economy*. It was therefore inextricably linked both to the idea of progress, as something desirable and inevitable, and to the idea of ruptures in history, moments of transition from one society to another.[31] As Teodor Shanin has written, it was in the name of this progress that later Marxists, once in power, were to commit some of their most terrible crimes:

As to the dogma and the mask, of which we have already spoken, they are still to be found in the depiction of the future set out in the textbooks of Eastern Europe and the USSR. Socialism there is the beginning of the final state of unilinear ascent to an ultimate society of humans whose desires are all met and who, once the state has 'withered away', like gods run themselves. To be a socialist is therefore to recognize the inevitable and to speed it up with the help of a scientific outlook and of a disciplined admiration for the leaders and prophets of socialism who marked out the future road. To be a socialist is to help remove obstacles from the road of inevitable progress, that is, to fight into the ground backwardness in institutions, backwardness in humans, and humans who are backward. This is why, in the words of Kautsky, 'social development stands higher than the interest of the proletariat and of Social Democracy', an idea which Stalin executed according to his own lights. This is the frame in which the view that 'freedom is recognition of necessity' made perfect sense. Ethics becomes but a recognition of and service towards the inevitable progress. Any other attitude to morality is upon sentimentalism and/or a legacy of pre-scientific thought and hence, of course, 'petty bourgeois'.[32]

Progress was, in the Marxist as in the liberal and other progressivisms of the time, not merely a matter of determinism: human agency had its role. While only possible when objective conditions favoured it, this revolutionary process had none the less to be completed, and the construction of the new society begun, by a conscious elite, the revolutionary vanguard who would appropriate and mould the state they had acquired. The connection between the rapidly changing character of capitalism, and the conscious action of a new emancipatory subject, the working class, was well captured in the (often partially quoted) words of Karl Marx: 'All that is solid melts into air, all that is holy is profaned, and man is at last compelled to face with sober senses, his real conditions of life, and his relations with his kind.'[33]

Communist revolution was, in this perspective, not the rejection of modern society, but its culmination. Communism indeed defined itself as the most radical, and at the same time inevitable, expression of modernity, this latter understood as the social and ideological order associated with reason and with the emergence of industrial society.[34] Central to the idea of progress was the idea of totality, of all social and political activity being interrelated. Hence under capitalism all was linked, aesthetics to economics, religion to property. Equally, post-revolutionary transformation would be total – in aspiration and capability. Once in power the revolutionary vanguard, with the support of the proletariat, would set about transforming society, 'abolishing' the old society through expropriation, social engineering, ideological mobilisation and so forth and building a new social order. This was possible because communism was inevitable and in line with historical development: hence policy was designated as dealing with a set of 'questions', inherited from the old regime, which would be 'solved' definitively as the post-capitalist order developed. These included the economy, the agrarian question, the army, the law, education, religion, housing, hygiene and, at least, two other 'questions' that capitalism could not solve, the 'national question' and the 'woman question'.[35]

In its more confident mode, which lasted until the 1960s, communism saw itself as able not only to outbid capitalism, and 'solve' all these problems, but also to produce a distinctive natural science capable of assisting the emancipation of man. One of Lenin's least felicitous interventions was his attempt to intervene in debates on scientific method – *Materialism and Empirio-Criticism* of 1908. In Russia in the 1940s, for example, this took the form of Lysenkoism, the belief that a 'proletarian science' could alter and improve human personality.[36] In the 1950s this historic self-confidence appeared to receive confirmation in the successes of the USSR in space – sending the first manmade object into orbit in 1957 and the first man into space in 1961. In China, the success of the Communist Party in establishing control of a quarter of mankind led the leadership to believe it could radically short-cut even the Soviet experience of industrialisation and political change: the adventures, catastrophic in terms of human life and economic collapse for the Chinese people, of the Great Leap Forward (1958–61) and the Great Proletarian Cultural Revolution (1965–9) followed. In 1969 Mao's chosen successor, soon to die in an unsuccessful attempt to flee to the USSR, was to proclaim:

> As a result of Chairman Mao's call to 'grasp revolution and promote production', the great cultural revolution had promoted the revolutionization of people's ideology and spurred the rapid development of industrial and agricultural production and of science and technology.[37]

Such broad statements, combining vapid historical claims with exhortation to a passive mass audience, were common fare in the China of Mao as they were in Stalin's Russia. It is easy, post-1989, to see these beliefs as mistaken. This was *not* how they appeared to communists *and* their enemies, at the time.

The communist revolutions achieved much in the countries they ruled, most notably in terms of education and social policy. However, the costs of this gigantic human experiment were enormous in terms of human lives and in terms of the destruction wrought on their societies. While able initially to establish effective political control and galvanise economies, they were unable to continue these rates of economic growth, as will be examined in Chapter 10. They gradually became paralysed by the policy of central planning, itself a visionary rationalist myth, and by the incapacity to introduce technological and administrative reform. In a cruel reversal of the modernistic project of total transformation, the very goals of communism were themselves arrested and archaic – evident in the realm of design and art, as in attitudes to social problems and, most importantly, political rights. The vision of 'modernity' that communism aspired to was a frozen product of the imagination of radicals of the 1900s.

Most important of all, communism misunderstood capitalism: capitalism was, and is, revolutionary, but it revolutionises the means of production, and the technology and ideas associated with production, not the political system accompanying it. Not only was capitalism not digging its own grave, as the deterministic vision of Marx and Lenin had assumed, but it was itself changing and providing new forms of political, social and economic benefits to the populations living under it: the tide of history turned against communist 'Revolution' in 1848, as the combined political and industrial revolutions unleashed at the end of the eighteenth century began to have their effects on West European society. If it was to take enormous social suffering, decades of capitalist authoritarianism and two World Wars for that potential to be realised, the opportunities for 'Revolution', the myth, to become revolution, the reality, had begun to recede.

Although 1917 appeared to mark a new stage in world history, it did not: if the vision of a world-wide and complete communist 'Revolution' first ran into difficulties in the 1920s, with the failure of the Bolshevik revolution to expand to Germany and to the rest of Europe, and the consolidation of the Stalinist regime in Russia, it was to take another fifty years, until the 1970s, before the full import of this unrealism was to be realised within the communist regimes themselves. In the 1920s and 1930s millions turned to communism as the best antidote to the rise of fascism. While the majority of the population of the non-communist and developed countries later abandoned or never espoused faith in this alternative 'Revolutionary' vision, it was only in the late 1970s that the leaderships of the communist states themselves were to lose faith in that utopian project. The fading of the Soviet experiment in Brezhnevite *zastoi*, stagnation, and the Chinese Four Modernisations of 1978 which opened China to the outside world, marked the final recession of a tide that had begun to turn a century and a half before.

Explicit Criteria: The Responses of Social Science

The definition and analysis of revolutions was, of course, too important to be left to the revolutionaries. Semantic diversifications of the word 'revolution' were reflected in the response of the other body of writers on revolutions, social scientists. Historians were the first to chronicle revolutions as individual events – English, French, Russian – within specific societies. For all the claims of later writers, the classic historical accounts – Burke, de Tocqueville, or Trotsky – contain as much in insight as any of their more 'scientific' successors. The first comparative studies tended to be by historians, as in the work of Pettee and Brinton.[38] Griewank and Hatto traced the intellectual history of the concept. Here there was less concern with the theoretical analysis of the causes of revolutions, more with charting their course, discerning some regularities and identifying shifts of meaning. There is much in their work that remains perceptive and relevant. In the 1960s and 1970s a substantial academic literature began to emerge. Some sociologists analysed revolutions in terms of the breakdown of established norms of social behaviour, and looked in particular for the behavioural accompaniments of revolution: for such writers revolutions were part of a spectrum of violent actions and were seen in temporal sociological terms, rather than as moments in the historical evolution of societies. There was, however, always another body of literature in historical sociology that sought to link revolutions as social events with broader analysis of historical change in society: in the 1960s this yielded the work of Moore and Huntington, in the 1970s that of Skocpol and Trimberger, and in the 1980s that of Goldstone.[39]

In the work of these more recent writers on revolution three important points are underlined: first, revolutions are distinguished from other forms of political and social upheavals – from revolts, rebellions, palace coups and so forth; secondly, a distinction is made between political revolutions, changes in system of government or constitution, and the more profound social revolutions, which involve both political change and substantial alterations in economy, social relations and values; thirdly, revolutions are treated not as breakdowns, from which a society recovers by returning to normal, but as important, distinctive events in the ongoing history of societies. In the work of sociologists such as Moore and Skocpol, revolutions were to be understood above all as moments of rupture and transition within social systems: this reflected Marx's own view of them as the 'midwives of history'.[40] They were to be studied in a long-term time frame with regard to both the social structures that produced them, and the reasons for the breakdown of the political order, as well as in terms of the kinds of changes they introduced and the post-revolutionary systems they created. Most of the literature looked at causes, some, including Huntington and Skocpol, at the post-revolutionary consequences.

For all the differences of theory and emphasis, this historical-sociological approach ascribed revolutions to their central place in the study of society in general, as much as it located them in the history of the individual countries where the revolutions had occurred. The historical sociologists also sought to provide a social science definition of revolution on which to base their analysis. For Skocpol this was as follows:

> Social revolutions are rapid, basic transformations of a society's state and class structures; and they are accompanied and in part carried through by class-based revolts from below. Social revolutions are set apart from other sorts of conflicts and transformative processes above all by the combination of two coincidences: the coincidence of societal structural change with class upheaval; and the coincidence of political with social transformation. In contrast, rebellions, even when successful, may involve the revolt of subordinate classes – but they do not eventuate in structural change. Political revolutions transform state structures but not social structures, and they are not necessarily accomplished through class conflict.[41]

The criteria by which social revolutions are therefore to be assessed are laid out here: 'basic transformations' of political and social structures; mass-based activity from below; the coincidence of political with social change. In similar vein, albeit without 'structuralist' theoretical associations, Samuel Huntington defines revolution as 'a rapid, fundamental, and violent domestic change in the dominant values and myths of a society, in its political institutions, social structure, leadership, and government activity and politics'.[42]

Such definitions of revolution are, like all definitions in social science, conventional: revolutions are not – anymore than are nations, classes, even events or dates – objectively given 'things', waiting to be unearthed or identified like the objects of natural science. They are phenomena which human subjects choose to group, on the basis of criteria of significance and recurrence, into one category rather than another. The strength of this definition of social revolution is that it allows for the identification of a discrete set of historical events which can be studied in their own right: if the three great revolutions that Skocpol studies – France, Russia, China – are examples of such events the list may be extended to include the events that appear to qualify if not as social revolutions then as political ones, with social implications. A number of Third World revolutions of the post-1945 period, aside from that of China, would seem, without stretching the criteria unduly, also to be candidates: Vietnam, Cuba, Iran, Nicaragua.

Implicit Criteria: Challenges of History

So far, so good, it would seem. The list of candidates for the title 'revolution' is open-ended but certainly restricted. Yet there are other cases which pose difficulties not so much on the question of whether they do, or do not, merit inclusion in this group, but by the way in which they challenge the criteria themselves. They draw attention to the difficulty of criteria *implicit* in much discussion. The first such category are those events, subsequently termed revolutions, which preceded the French Revolution of 1789: the revolt of the Netherlands, the English Civil War, the American War of Independence. These involved mass revolt from below, including the use of violence, even if they did not carry out fundamental social change to the degree found in Skocpol's three classic cases. They were, however, far more than mere changes of political regime following on revolt, since in their political programme and in their social consequences they embodied very different principles to those of the regimes they overthrew. The shift in perspective following from 1989 may allow not so much for a depreciation of the importance of the classic revolutions of the preceding two centuries, as for a broader and more inclusive historical canvas: perhaps the main consequence of 1989 is not, therefore, the reduction in the importance of the Russian revolution, but the increased attention paid, as Hannah Arendt had urged in *On Revolution* (1963), to the American. Here she had, of course, been preceded by Tom Paine who in his *Letter to the Abbé Reynal* of 1782 had argued for the *universal significance* of the American revolution.[43] There is no need to deny the distinctiveness of the post-1789 revolutions by excluding consideration of those upheavals that preceded them.

A second category of uncertain location are what have been termed 'revolutions from above', that is transformations of societies carried out not as a result of mass-based revolts from below, but as a result of changes, often quite radical and violent ones, in the composition of elites.[44] Examples of this include the Meiji Restoration in Japan, the Kemalist regime in Turkey and, in the post-war period, the military regimes of Egypt, Peru and Ethiopia.[45] If the criteria of the degree, the profundity of the transformations is taken as the criterion, then there is strong reason for, in a suitably qualified way, characterising regimes that do bring about such changes as revolutionary: the difficulty with such regimes is, rather, of a different kind, namely that of endurance.

The third category of potential 'revolutions' that pose difficulties for the historical-sociological criteria are, by contrast, those that appear to carry out fundamental changes in the society, but in a manner that does not fit any progressivist perspective. In one sense this problem applied to all revolutions: proclaiming freedom, they established coercive states; espousing the new, they ruled with many of the practices of the old. However, this problem was posed most sharply by two twentieth-century upheavals that seemed to reject all or much of the French revolutionary legacy – the Nazi experience in Germany and the Islamic revolution in Iran. The Nazis certainly aimed to transform the political system of their country, and acted with the support of a mass-based movement from below.

One argument against admitting this regime to be revolutionary would be to say that, with the terrible exception of genocide, it did not carry out a fundamental change in the social, including economic, system of the country: in economic terms its changes amounted to little more than an increased level of state intervention, not that different from what the New Deal was accomplishing in the USA. But one cannot escape the sense that resistance to including the Nazis as 'revolutionary' also stems from two other, less enunciated, criteria. The first is that the goals the Nazis proclaimed and the changes they did introduce went against any idea of progress or historical development, of the kind implicit not only in revolutionary ideology but in the theory of social scientists. The other is that the Nazi accession to power was in part directed *against* revolution: that of the Bolsheviks in 1917 and that which was threatening in Germany after 1918, a response to the Bolshevik revolution and the fear of the communist movement in Germany; in this sense, in its counter-revolutionary import, it challenged an assumption of linear progress. As will be argued in Chapter 8, Nazism was a counter-revolution, a movement *against* a change that was feared in Germany itself. In other words, the case of the Nazis brings out into the open two possible but usually unstated criteria for revolution – the 'progressive' or otherwise character of the regime's goals and policies, and the degree to which it is consistent with, or opposed to, a teleological view of history and to other already established revolutions.[46]

These difficulties were posed with almost equal clarity in the case of a subsequent mass movement that abutted against the criteria for revolution, namely the Iranian revolution of 1978–9. This event certainly exhibited the features associated with other revolutions: the political system was transformed rapidly from monarchy to clergy-dominated republic; there was much mass involvement – indeed the largest opposition demonstrations ever seen in human history – and a political general strike that followed nineteenth- and early-twentieth-century European revolutionary models; there was a wide-ranging change in society, combining direction from on top with mass movement from below, and a pervasive 'Islamisation' of the society.[47] Moreover, for those who saw all revolutions, pre- and post-1789, as parts of a continuum of messianism, the expression of a vision with religious connotations and a religious goal, the Iranian might have appeared to be the least obscure of all revolutions: it embodied the call for a return to a religiously sanctioned past, and the proclamation of a new, divinely sanctioned, golden age.[48] As we have seen, all revolutionaries, not just the Iranian, certainly invoked the past and had elements of visionary self-importance about them: but to detect a common retrospective element in upheavals of different times is not necessarily to identify a continuous phenomenon. The very concept of messianism as applied to modern revolutions is of nugatory value. In the other cases, such as the French or the Russian, the references to the past were instrumental rather than determinant features of these revolutionary regimes. In the Iranian, the past, and a past all of fourteen centuries ago, appeared to be ideologically central.

Yet this question of messianism and retrospective legitimation aside, there was considerable reluctance to characterise the Iranian case as a revolution: as with the Nazi case, the first line of defence was to argue that it did not carry out wide-ranging socio-economic reforms, or, if these did occur, that they were the result of nationalising and redistributing the property of those who had fled after the revolution, or the ensuing eight-year war with Iraq. Another argument was to claim that it was not 'organised': but this mistook the absence of Western-style mass radical parties for the absence of clerical, mosque-based, mobilisatory structures.[48] Certain aspects of the Iranian revolution were indisputably in conflict with the legacy of 1789, namely their policies on gender which were, in the purest sense of the word, reactionary. There was, however, a deeper reason, echoing that of the German argument, namely that the Islamic upheaval in Iran could not be a 'revolution' since its goals were conservative – establishing a system of government modelled on the seventh century, denying the sovereignty of the people and the emancipation of women, and asserting clerical authority over politics, law and the economy.[50] Indeed, while other revolutions had betrayed the ideals they proclaimed and for which many people may have initially supported them, they had nonetheless held to some amalgam of the late-eighteenth-century goals: the Iranian was the first explicitly to reject these.[51]

There were, at the least, three broad lines of reply to this. The first was to argue that in domestic and foreign policies, and despite the appearance of rejecting the social and economic goals of other revolutions, the Iranian actually did much of what others had done – redistributing wealth, expropriating the economically dominant class, developing social services, mobilising the population and promoting revolution abroad.[52] In the early stages of the revolution, this was also the argument which socialist and communist elements in Iran put forward as to why they were supporting the revolution.[53] Secondly, the ideology of the revolution was not what it appeared to be: rather than being based on a seventh-century programme, it used texts and symbols of that foundational Islamic period to promote and deploy concepts all too familiar from the modern revolutionary tradition – revolution itself, popular revolt, redistribution of wealth, equality, anti-imperialism.[54] Levels of education and of women's employment rose.

It would, thirdly, be argued by supporters of the Iranian revolution that the Islamic revolution, in so far as it was distinctive, was more successful in promoting revolutionary change than the secular models to which it was being compared. Thus leaders of the revolution claimed their country was *more* independent, *more* democratic, and their women *more* free than in other countries. Long rivals of communist radicalism, the Islamic revolutionaries took heart from the collapse of communism in the late 1980s to proclaim that, atheistic revolution having failed, it was Islamic revolution which would now mobilise the oppressed of the world and present an effective challenge to Western capitalism. In the statements of the revolutionary leaders there was a strong teleological vision of a world increasingly turning to Islam and to their revolutionary values, as the Soviet Union entered its terminal crisis, Khomeini wrote to Gorbachev, urging him to embrace Islam, while he and others talked of *taraqi-yi islami*, 'Islamic progress'. To the economic anti-imperialism of most Third World revolutions, they added a strong 'moral anti-imperialism', denouncing the West for its corruption and double standards.[55] In sum, the Iranian revolution, for all its anomalies, was arguably a revolution on a par with other core cases.

The Collapse of European Communism

If these 'revolutions' appeared to present anomalies for the definition of revolution, an even greater challenge was posed by the collapse of Soviet communism in the late 1980s and, in less spectacular form, by the transformation of Chinese communism after 1978. 1989 challenged not only those who believed in 'Revolution' of a communist or related kind, and its concomitant theory of history, but also academic theorists of revolution. At one level, there did not seem to be a problem: a 'revolutionary' change had certainly taken place, at least in the former USSR and Eastern Europe.[56] There had been a dramatic change in the political system, followed by a comparable change in the economic system and in social values, and there was considerable mass activity from below. The fall of communism seemed to meet Skocpol's criteria. There was relatively little violence and this certainly posed problems for the *explanation* of why these militarised and autocratic states had collapsed: but this need not have disqualified the events from being characterised as revolutions. Others questioned the degree to which a real political and social change had occurred, how 'basic' in Skocpol's words the changes really were. Here too, while recognising that many communist personnel and even partly reformed communist parties remained in power, few could doubt that the communist system had been destroyed. Equally few believed it could be repaired or revived. Indeed, precisely because communism was an *international* phenomenon, in terms of the military and political alliance that sustained it, and in terms of its own ideological legitimacy, it was not possible to sustain individual communist regimes in Europe once the system in general had crumbled: its survival *and* demise were international. The key moment, if one there be, was as international as any event could be: a speech by Gorbachev to the General Assembly of the UN in New York, on 7 December 1988, in which, formally confirming what his press spokesman Gennadi Gerasimov had already hinted, he pledged not to use force to maintain communist regimes in Eastern Europe.[57]

The analytic difficulties with accepting the collapse of communism as 'Revolution' pertain more to other, less overt, aspects of the concept. First of all, there would seem to be a problem about categorising as a 'revolution' something that overthrew a system that had itself been established and extended through revolution. Moreover, revolutions had hitherto been seen and had presented themselves as introducing something 'new', this novelty being central to the French revolutionary conception of revolution. Yet the upheavals of Eastern Europe and the former USSR were not carried out in the name of anything new. They were, rather, carried out in order to reject the communist version of novelty and change, and in favour of conformity: instead of 'new socialist man', they wanted political freedom and 'new consumerist man, and woman'.[58] They aspired to conformity with what were presented both with degrees of nostalgia and with varying degrees of accuracy as the 'traditions' of the country in question, but equally conformity with what were seen as an international normality, as defined in the West. Time and again leaders and participants in the collapse of communism argued that they wanted their countries to be 'like the West', 'civilised', 'normal' states, i.e. they rejected any suggestion of political or ideological innovation or challenge.

There was certainly an idealist, even utopian, element in the movements, epitomised in the writings of the Czech leader Vaclav Havel and the Hungarian dissident George Konrad, and in aspirations in East Germany for a 'third way'.[59] There was, none the less, no new principle inherent even in the programmes of these movements, no challenge to the norms and ideas predominant in the rest of the world. The alternative and 'anti-political' tendencies were transitional to another normalcy. Hence the argument of Jürgen Habermas about the 'revolution of recuperation', *die nachholende Revolution*:

> The revolution of recuperation, in so far as it is meant to make possible a return to constitutional democracy and a connection with developed capitalism, is guided by models that orthodox interpretations consider the revolution of 1917 to have made redundant. This perhaps explains a peculiar characteristic of this revolution, namely its total lack of ideas that are either innovative or orientated towards the future. Joachim Fest has made a similar observation: 'these events gained their hidden, confusing centre . . . from the fact that they did not emphasize the element of social revolution that has governed pretty well all the revolutions in modern history'. This is particularly confusing because it seems to remind us of a vocabulary supposedly superseded by the French Revolution: the reformist picture of the return of political regimes following one after another in a continuous cycle like that of the heavens.[60]

It is easy to elude the implications of these difficulties by arguing that all will not turn out as those who led the anti-communist movements had hoped. There can be, and already have been, conflicts with the West over strategic and economic issues. The 'Western' model is neither as one-sided nor as exportable as many had originally hoped. Successor parties to the old ruling ones remain influential in former communist states and have returned to power. But these are qualifications; they do not diminish the political and theoretical import of the events of the late 1980s. What these events challenged were not merely the explicit assumptions of what is involved in a revolution, as expounded in the criteria of a Moore, Huntington or Skocpol, but also certain *implicit* criteria, in particular: (i) that revolutions form part of a historical continuum;

(ii) that they challenge prevailing international norms about politics and society; (iii) that, once 'made', revolutions in some form or another leave irreversible legacies on the society in question, 'gains' or 'advances' that cannot be eradicated.

Belief in the irreversibility of revolutions, linked to a teleological view of history, was not confined to practitioners. In the academic literature there was an echo of the belief of revolutionaries that their access to power is historically irreversible. It is because revolutions were seen as part of a continuum, 'moments of transition' or pathways to modernity, that it seemed inconceivable that another revolution could then reverse it. Even those most distanced from revolutions wrote as if revolutionary regimes were especially well-entrenched and long-lasting and relatively invulnerable to pressures from within or without. In the emphases on post-revolutionary state capabilities, be this in models of 'totalitarianism', in Huntington's association of revolutionary states with modernisation or in Skocpol's emphasis on post-revolutionary transformation, let alone in sympathetic literature on 'the transition' to socialism or communism, one unarticulated assumption was essential: communist revolutions were irreversible.

The lack of ideological originality or deviance in the revolutions of 1989 should not, therefore, conceal the conceptual challenge which they posed to our understanding of revolutions: what those of 1989 did was to force into the open hitherto relatively unacknowledged criteria – unilinear historical progress, international nonconformity, irreversibility. If 1917 had been the 'revolution' against *Das Kapital*, 1989 was the revolution against a nineteenth- and twentieth-century scientistic concept of progress and historical teleology, linked to mechanistic views of mass mobilisation. It did not, of course, preclude the retention of other, less utopian, concepts of progress, for which the evidence remained rather strong.

The myth of 'Revolution', as it was formed in the French revolution and has pervaded much of political thought and history since, would appear to have been confounded by the collapse of communism. Not only did revolutionary regimes fail to achieve their goals and fail to meet the aspirations of those who participated in, and also led, them, but the very regimes they established proved to be more vulnerable and transient than many, whether sympathetic or hostile, had imagined. Revolutions were a product of the tensions of a developing modernity, of the combined and uneven spread of that modernity across the world; but they were also constrained by that process and, in the communist variant at least, ultimately overwhelmed by it. To present revolutions as either one or the other – either the highest form of modernity, or as criminal aberrations from it – is to miss the contradictory character of that relationship.

Whatever the longer-run implications, the collapse of communism both identified and confounded some of the underlying premises upon which much advocacy and study of revolutions has been based. This collapse also poses an interesting challenge for all those concerned with the study of states and their capacities: they may have to revise their estimates of the strength of states in the light of the collapse of communism. Equally, the manner and speed of the collapse of communism raise interesting questions as to the factors, including those of international character, that led to this outcome. To revolutions as events, and their implications for the location of revolutions within the overall pattern of world politics, we shall return in later chapters. First, the story of revolution and the modern international system, in its ideal and real terms, has to be told.

3

Internationalism in Theory: A World-Historical Vision

Revolution and 'World History'

The previous chapter examined how the general idea of 'Revolution' developed in modern history. It charted how this conceptual development had itself an international character – in discursive, generative, and paradigmatic terms. The aim of this chapter is to look at the international dimension of the concept itself, to show how, within the idea of 'Revolution' and attendant ideas such as progress, an international component was repeatedly present. Such an international dimension was always present in modern thought, but largely implicit. One can, indeed, say of this international dimension what Robert Nisbet has said of the idea of 'progress' – that beyond being an idea it was something broader, a 'context', a set of assumptions that were so taken for granted that they were often partially and very generically articulated.[1] Many assumed that just as progress was comprehensive – in science as in economics, in arts as in politics – so it was to be accompanied by a transformation of the world: barriers between nations and peoples would come down; science and communications would bring peoples together; war, a relic of now outmoded social orders, would pass; the fraternity of mankind, increasingly racially fused and preferably all speaking a common language, was at hand. This was a core idea, a commanding myth, of liberalism as much as of revolutionaries. Yet it was no less effective a part of revolutionary thought for being so generic, and for being shared with those whose ideas, in other contexts, revolutionaries would have rejected.

To examine this thinking of revolutionaries on international affairs, and in particular on the international consequences of revolution, might, at first sight, appear to be a fruitless endeavour. The ideas of revolutionaries on international affairs, as much as, or even more than, their thinking on domestic issues, were marked by a rhetorical streak, bearing little relation to reality or their own policies, utopian when not instrumental. Here, as in much idealistic thinking about domestic politics, we can detect that romantic streak that E. H. Carr associated with the revolutionaries of the pre-'scientific' age.[2] Moreover, the international as such, while present, was almost always secondary or marginal in their thinking, and has indeed remained so in the analyses which subsequent writers have made of revolutionary thinking. In the texts of all revolutionaries there is mention and invocation of the international, but it rarely merits the systematic exposition characteristic of other questions.[3] This relative neglect is not so much because the international did not matter, as because of the very implicit, *contextual*, character of thinking on the subject, of the certitude with which a set of propositions are held, and asserted as being self-evident, such that extended assessment is not necessary. There were exceptions: Marx, Lenin and Guevara did develop their ideas on world politics and the world economy, but these were, significantly, men who had been forced, by years of exile, to confront this issue more critically. For others – Robespierre, Stalin, Mao Tse-tung, Khomeini – the international was invoked with a rhetorical flourish and a wave of the hand, without any focussed engagement, though none the less certainly for that.

This chapter aims to counter, and correct, that bias. For all the unreality or manipulation involved, the ideas of revolutionaries merit attention, both for what they can tell us about their aspirations and actions, but also because, even if 'utopian', they point to underlying premises about revolution. These ideas influenced the actions of leaders and mass movements alike. These premises are formed in the course of revolutions themselves and in the latter's interactions with the international. It is easy, for reasons of apologia or contempt, to dismiss what revolutionaries say and think about the international, but to do this is to ignore the framework within which they view international relations, and equally, the degree of confrontation which they anticipate in foreign affairs. It will be possible in the subsequent chapters, on the export of revolution and the foreign policy of revolutionary states, to chart how these ideas were converted into practice. Even where this was not so, the very fact that certain myths – the international

constitution of the oppressor and its global conspiratorial extension, the fraternity of the oppressed, the imminence of global
revolution, the ease with which war can be eliminated – recur in
the theory and rhetoric of revolutions may provide a means of
assessing the genesis and course of revolutions. All the great
mobilising forces of modern history have involved myth – those
of nation, or imperial destiny, as much as those of revolution. Their
ability to move people to act necessitates examination both of what
these influential ideas were, and of the consequences of such widespread espousal.

The content of this myth or context can easily be summarised.
The idea of 'Revolution' was as international in content as it proved
to be in diffusion. By the very conceptual underpinning of this idea,
it denoted changes that were universal, and part of a broader, often
global, process: hence it became common to talk of an 'age of
revolutions' or indeed, in the singular, of the 'age of revolution'. As
if by some immanent logic, it was part of the self-legitimation of
revolutionary ideas that they were valid not only for their country
of origin, but for all peoples the world over and were part of a
global historical trend; equally, revolutionaries appealed for support to fellow revolutionaries abroad, and mobilised their own
peoples on the grounds that the world was struggling with them.

Also, part of the new age being created by revolutionaries was the
removal of barriers between nations and peoples characteristic of
the old regime: if monarchs, or bourgeois or colonial rulers had
divided people, the new age would be of one of collaboration,
fraternity and, by implication, peace. Paradoxically, one can say
that the idea of revolution was international above all in that it
proclaimed the abolition of the 'international', in the sense of
differences between states or nations. This claim to transcend
differences between peoples, the latter seen as the creation of the
oppressors (kings, bourgeois, imperialists), was indeed part of the
vision, what Arendt has characterised as the 'pathos' of the revolutionary ideal. As we shall see in Chapter 4, the French revolutionaries, as the Bolsheviks were later to do, proclaimed peace to the
world and pursued, in a number of ways, policies that were
supposed to eliminate differences between peoples. That things were
not to turn out quite this way, and indeed that the very implementation of internationalist policies was to provoke national opposition, was, of course, one of the many disappointments of the
revolutionary project. If in the following chapter we shall be

concerned with the practical and political consequences of such connections, and of the internationalist commitment in general, this chapter will examine the ideas accompanying such an orientation.

The Necessity of an International Vision

Whatever their particular national or internal origins, all revolutions therefore produce an ideology that in addition to calling for the internal transformation of societies also proclaims itself as pertinent to the international sphere, as, in some sense, 'international' or 'global'. If this is so for the obvious exemplars of revolutionary internationalism – France, Russia, China, Iran – it was also true of the apparently more insular cases. Oliver Cromwell saw his Puritan revolution as an example to all Protestant peoples. The Founding Fathers in America regarded themselves as an inspiration to the world; this aspiration was to be given symbolic form a century later, when, in 1886, the State of Liberty was unveiled in New York, with the eight shafts on its head symbolising the transmission of the American revolution to the continents of the world. In 1983 Fidel Castro was to say: 'North Americans don't understand . . . that our country is not just Cuba; our country is also humanity'.[4] As Reinhardt Kosseleck has noted:

> If the declarations of the American, French, and Russian revolutions are taken literally, there is no doubt that their 'achievements' are intended to be to the advance of all mankind. In other words, all modern expressions of 'Revolution' spatially imply a *world revolution* and temporally imply that they be *permanent* until their objective is reached.[5]

There is virtually a *logic* within the *ideology* that leads to the affirmation of ideals that pertain to more than the country in which the revolution itself is taking place. This relevance is as evident to those in other societies who may be threatened or encouraged by such ideals as it is to those within the revolutionary countries themselves. The reasons for this are several. In the first place, revolutions legitimate themselves in terms of an appeal to general, abstract, principles, i.e. ones that are not, whatever their origin, specific to a particular country or nation: these may be reason, freedom, independence, proletarian power, the dignity of peoples, or 'true Islam'. The two, often contrasted, revolutions of the late eighteenth century, the American of 1776 and the French of 1789, both advocated *universal* theories of rights. Secondly, within the conceptual system of revolutionaries, whether clearly articulated or not, is a view of their oppressors or enemies as constituted internationally – as part of some global or at least multinational entity which conspired to maintain oppressors in power and which is now hoping to restore them. This conception has, in part, a national origin, in that these rulers are to be discredited *precisely because* they are linked to, dependent on, alien and 'anti-national' forces. But there is also a separate, more theoretical, logic at play here, insofar as the political perspective of the revolutionaries is one that posits an international system of oppression and resistance, within which their particular country is one part.

At the same time, revolutions posit, as part of their vision of a new world, the transcendence of inter-state boundaries and national divisions: the original late-eighteenth-century conception of revolution, and indeed of counter-revolution (as in Burke), was constituted before modern conceptions of nationalism gained dominance. Revolutionaries have thereafter tended to be blind or hostile to the inhibitions of national affiliation and sentiment, except where, as in anti-colonial revolts, such sentiment assists the revolutionary cause. Equally, overcoming the division between nations is, along with overcoming of social divisions within, very much part of the revolutionary vision. So too, and perhaps less noticed, is the revolutionary aspiration to abolish states, in the sense of distinct administrative entities. This is most evident in anarchism: immanent within the anarchist abolition of the state *within* countries is a vision of the abolition of the state-based division between them – once the 'state' has been abolished, then the divisions between societies will disappear and a single world community, more or less 'state-less', will emerge. As the example of Lenin was to show so clearly, the mistaken expectations of revolutionaries about the abolition of the state 'within' are compounded by the myth of so doing 'without'.

The internally generated logic of revolutionary thinking was noted by Arendt. The idea of revolution developed in the course of the nineteenth century into that of a single, universal process that would deliver mankind:

> Truth, in other words, was supposed to relate and to correspond
> not to citizens, in whose midst there could exist only a multitude

of opinions, and not to nationals, whose sense for truth was limited by their own history and national experience. Truth had to relate to man *qua* man, who as a worldly, tangible reality, of course, existed nowhere. History, therefore, if it was to become a medium of the revolution of truth, had to be world history, and the truth which revealed itself had to be a 'world spirit'.[6]

This was a point not lost on one of the most pungent critics of the French Revolution, Josèphe de Maistre. In his *Considérations sur la France* (1796) he opined that while he had often met Frenchmen, Italians, Germans and Russians, 'As for Man, I've never met one in my life'.[7]

If these are factors arising more or less from the 'logic of ideology', there are other, more practical, reasons for the adoption of such internationalist positions. Revolutionaries, as part of their mobilisation of support at home, assert the importance of what they have done not only in terms of changes or aspired-to changes within their countries, but in terms of the international attention and relevance they have aroused. Every revolution involves the announcement of foreign recognition and support – in the twentieth century the flow of delegations, telegrams, solidarity meetings – to the population of the home country. Self-importance, reassurance, even national pride can play a part in this.[8] The pronouncement that the revolution is 'not alone', 'has friends all over the world', is admired and imitated by struggling peoples elsewhere who are eagerly studying the 'lessons', 'thoughts' and 'writings' of the revolutionary leaders, runs through twentieth-century revolutionary rhetoric. Thus in the hagiographic paintings of revolutions, along with ones of the leader surrounded by adulatory workers, peasants and other members of the oppressed, there is the repeated genre of the leader surrounded by admiring representatives of the peoples of the world, typically holding a copy of his writings or in other ways signalling esteem.

Such motifs are modular. At the opening in the Kremlin of the Eighteenth CPSU Congress in March 1939 Stalin was hailed as the 'genius of toiling humanity' who 'tirelessly watches over the interest of the working class of the entire world'.[9] In 1967, during the height of the Cultural Revolution, the message from China was clear: 'The *Quotations from Chairman Mao Tse-tung* Lights Up the Whole World', 'Greetings the World's Advance Into the Great New Epoch of Mao Tse-tung Thought', 'Chairman Mao is the Leader of the

World Proletariat; the Chinese Communist Party is the Vanguard of the International Communist Movement'.[10] Ayatollah Khomeini was 'the hope of the oppressed of the world'. Others – Enver Hoxha, Kim Il-sung, Ho Chi Minh, Mu'ammar al-Qadhafi – were portrayed in similar vein, and appeared willing to be so portrayed. Among revolutionary leaders of the twentieth century only Fidel Castro, in other respects not resistant to the diffusion of his ideas, avoided such treatment.

This domestic rationale for international militancy is, of course, compounded by another factor, namely the practical need for support from similar or related revolutionary forces abroad, a need often accompanied by unduly optimistic expectations about such forces. In a situation of continuing domestic conflict, and with threats from abroad, real, exaggerated or imagined, revolutionary movements and regimes seek to strengthen their own position: they aim to weaken that of their enemies, by building international alliances, and, if possible, assisting such movements to come to power. 'Internationalist solidarity' therefore has an instrumental as well as an ideological character to it. This is all the more so when there is a real threat from abroad, either from foreign states or from exiles who have fled from the revolution and now seek to return. As will be discussed in Chapter 8, revolutions are inevitably accompanied by such a response in other states and by driving some of their own population abroad: such is the dynamic of the revolutionary process, an externalisation and internationalisation of domestic conflict.

There is, in conclusion, the reason which is most often cited by the enemies of revolution, namely that the revolutionaries themselves are in some way part of an 'international conspiracy', or that they are not really nationals of the country in which they are active at all – foreign agitators, 'anti-nationals', 'cosmopolitans' or whatever. Such anathemas reflect a reluctance to engage with the internal roots, or the legitimacy, of revolutionaries. But this should not prevent the examination of what are often international connections and inspirations, or specific revolutionary movements. When a revolutionary movement emerges, or comes to power, there certainly are often historical reasons for the internationalist character of revolutions: revolutionary movements, and their leaders, organisations and guiding principles, rarely have a purely national or country-specific origin.

This is true first of all in the realm of ideas. Long before late twentieth-century communications, ideas, images and models spread across boundaries. Indeed, the early history of revolutionary internationalism, before the emergence of mass nationalism, in some ways made this easier. Not only in the eighteenth century, but even earlier, with the ideas of the Reformation and of the Protestant rebellions of the seventeenth century, radical ideas moved from country to country. So too did individuals, for whom part of their emancipation from the constraints of rulers was their rejection of any particular local or national affiliation. It was only in the nineteenth and twentieth centuries, however, and more specifically in the socialist, later communist, movement that these linkages and inspirations took a clearly organised form. If the International Working Men's Association, the 'First International', had little organisational strength or international impact, seeking only to coordinate, the Second International (1889–1914) while lacking strong organisational strength over its members did encompass an international movement of ideas, personalities and groups that served to inspire and guide the Bolshevik Party. When it came to power in 1917, having broken with the majority of the Second International parties, the Bolshevik Party nonetheless owed a great deal to that organisation, even as it set up its revolutionary alternative, the Third, or 'Communist', International.

It was in the Comintern (1919–43), and in its more limited nine-party successor organisation, the Cominform (1947–57), that the international linkages between revolutionary groups were taken furthest: this involved a formal commitment on the part of the member organisations to assist each other. This entailed, in practice, subordination to the policies of the USSR, even as within each party social and political factors pertaining to that country continued to affect policy: the history of the Communist International is one of policy directed from Moscow, but also of social and ideological movements across the world. Later, other looser or weaker international organisations were established – the Trotskyist Fourth International, the Cuban OSPAAAL: they too served to inspire, coordinate, and link.

In the case of Latin America, ties of ideological and personal affinity linked revolutionaries in specific countries to the wider continental, anti-imperialist, context. In the nineteenth century and early part of the twentieth century free-masonry provided a liberal, transnational community. Augusto Sandino, the leader of guerrilla opposition in Nicaragua in the 1930s, had been radicalised by working in Mexico during its revolution.[11] Fidel Castro had participated in an attempted insurrection against Trujillo, dictator of the Dominican Republic in 1947, and had been in Bogotá, Colombia, in 1948 when that country plunged into its *violencia*. His 1953 speech, *History Will Absolve Me*, showed a commitment to the Latin American revolution, and also, in an extended philosophic and legal defence of the right to revolt, invoked a range of authorities from Milton, Montesquieu and Locke, to Paine and the American Declaration of Independence.[12] Even in the more constricted post-1989 context, revolutionary organisations sought such formal internationalisation: in Peru, *Sendero Luminoso*, which based much of its appeal on the interests of the indigenous population, sought to extend its influence to other native American peoples of the Andean region, in Bolivia and Ecuador. In the Mexico of the 1990s, the Zapatistas made much of the global network they had created, an anti-globalisation alliance that had already initiated 'the Fourth World War'.[13]

A parallel history can be observed in the Islamic context: the Muslim world has always had international cultural and theological networks, sometimes of a political kind, sometimes as in the *tariqat* or Sufi orders more mystical. Twentieth-century Islamist groups have replicated this, by creating interconnections, sometimes of inspiration, and sometimes of organised support. Those in power, who claim legitimacy from the Islamic religion, have also sought to organise their following – this being as true for the Kingdom Saudi Arabia as for the Libyan Jamahariyah and the Islamic Republic of Iran. To deny the efficacy of such linkages – intellectual and inspirational as much as material or organised – would be almost as inaccurate as to ascribe all revolutionary movements and triumphs as the result of 'external' and, by implication, imported and imposed, influences.

The Rise of Revolutionary Cosmopolitanism

The political term 'internationalism' first came into use in the 1860s, in regard to Marx's First International.[14] The concept is like that of revolution itself, in that, while in its modern form distinct, it draws elements from classical and early modern European thought.[15] At its core lie four interrelated theses: that the world is, in some senses at least, becoming more and more interconnected and unified; that this is accompanied by a growing interconnectedness of peoples; that this political internationalisation, while possessed of its own causes and dynamic, is in part a product of these 'objective' processes; and that these processes, separately and combined, are positive. In this sense 'internationalism' is part of the progressivist and deterministic view of history that emerged from the Enlightenment and the French Revolution. In common with other such concepts – be these freedom, democracy, independence – it has both revolutionary and other – liberal or even conservative – variants.

The classical ideas on which it draws include the ancient Greek, specifically Stoic, idea of the universal political community – the *cosmopolis* – and the conception of an educated citizenry sharing certain common values – of language, supernatural belief, political culture. Such an entity existed to some degree in both ancient Greece and Rome, and was reproduced in various forms in mediaeval Christian thought. There was nothing particularly radical, let alone revolutionary, about this: in early modern Europe, the first projects for the creation of a single state were based on the union of monarchs, directed against the external enemy, the Ottoman Turks. Ironically, the Ottoman empire itself practised a form of pre-modern, imperial, multiculturalism, drawing people from all over the empire into its ruling elite, and ordering its subjects into distinct ethnic and religious groups. However, with the rise of the early modern revolutions a variant of internationalism, tied to radical ideas, began to emerge: thus during the English revolution, itself inspired by the revolt of the Netherlands, the common cause of England with other peoples was recurrent. One commentator on the Parliament of 1640, Samuel Hartlib, thought it would 'lay the cornerstone of the world's happiness'. Cromwell and his associates drew inspiration from the struggles of other Protestants and in turn committed themselves to aiding them.[16] Cromwell expressed solidarity with the Hussites in Bohemia, and in an early version of the exaggerated international optimism of revolutionaries he eagerly anticipated the establishment of a Protestant republic in Spain.[17] An English Protestant preacher in 1645 was in fine internationalist form:

Methinks I see Germany lifting up her lumpish shoulder, and thin-cheeked Palatinate looking out, a prisoner of hope; Ireland breathing again, that not only lay bedrid, but the pulse beating deathward; the overawed French peasant studying his long-lost liberty, the Netherlanders looking back upon their neighbouring England, who cemented their walls with their blood, and bought their freedom with many, many thousands of good old Elizabeth shillings. Indeed, methinks, all Protestant Europe seems to get new colour in her cheeks.[18]

A radical thinker, George Fox, stole a march on all later revolutionaries by addressing a pamphlet *To all the Nations under the Whole Heavens.* No one embodied this internationalism more effectively than the poet John Milton:

Who knows not that there is a mutual bond of amity and brotherhood between man and man over all the world, neither is it the English sea that can sever us from that duty and relation.[19]

Milton's own work had an international resonance: his defence of regicide was read in the Netherlands, France, Germany, Sweden and Greece.

In the eighteenth century ideas that we would today associate with internationalism were common in the Enlightenment – interstate boundaries being presented as the creation of monarchs, war as equally the product of despots. It was confidently expected that the spread of enlightenment and its accompaniments, science and popular rule, would sweep away divisions between peoples. This enlightenment conception of internationalism was evident both in the thinking of Anglo-American liberalism and in that of the French *philosophes.* The proponents of this current were a cosmopolitan elite, intellectuals moving from country to country, in what they assumed was an anticipation of a broader historical trend. For some, this entailed general support for the progress of mankind, within which they assumed the fusion of peoples and states.[20]

The French revolution was to occasion an intense period of internationalist declaration and policy: the practical effects of this commitment will be examined in the next chapter. Suffice it to note here that through the early years of the revolutionary state the issue of solidarity, and indeed of fusion with other states, was to recur in the debates of the Assembly. The Girondins were to articulate the most militant internationalism in 1792: Brissot declared 'we cannot be at ease until all Europe is in flames'.[21] For their part, the Jacobins, above all Robespierre, adopted positions that suited their current domestic concerns – anxiety about the strength of the state at home and the readiness of French society for war, on the one hand, and concern lest the king use the occasion of war to re-establish his position, on the other. They were therefore initially more cautious. In January 1792 Robsespierre was to declare:

> No one likes an armed missionary and no more extravagant idea ever sprang from the head of a politician than to suppose that one people has only to enter another's territory with arms in its hands to make the latter adopt its laws and its Constitution. . . Before the influences of our revolution can be felt abroad, it must be fully established at home. To expect to give freedom to foreign nations before we have achieved it ourselves, is a sure way to slavery, both for France and for the world. . . The Declaration of Rights is not like the sun's rays, which in one moment illumine the whole earth; it is no thunderbolt, to strike down a thousand thrones. It is easier to inscribe it on paper, to engrave it on brass, than to retrace its sacred characters in the hearts of men, from which they have been erased by ignorance, passion, and despot-ism.[22]

But by April 1793 Robespierre too was advocating internationalist collaboration against the princes, aristocrats and other tyrants.[23] In that month he presented to the Jacobin Club a more radical version of the Declaration of Rights: 'Men of all countries are brothers, and the various nations must assist each other according to their resources, like citizens of the same State'.[24] Like Lenin, Robe-spierre, the most hard-headed of revolutionaries, swung from scepticism towards international revolution towards an instrumen-tal, but itself idealistic, advocacy of armed internationalism.

The most far-reaching internationalist views were articulated by a Prussian member of the Assembly, Jean-Baptiste Cloots (1755–94): in 1790 he brought to the Assembly an 'embassy of the human race', comprising thirty-six foreigners attired in theatrical 'national' cos-tumes and proclaimed that the whole world would adhere to the declaration of the rights of man. The Assembly invited them to sit in on its session, before proceeding to other business, which included the abolition of servants' livery, and of the practice of fumigating nobles with incense.[25] Entitling himself 'the orator of the human race' Cloots changed his name to Anacharsis, after one of the sages of antiquity. He called for the establishment of a single world republic, a proposal he introduced, without success, to the Convention in 1793.[26]

The most elaborated view of how this internationalism related to the general belief in human advance was to be found in the work of Nicolas de Condorcet, in his ten-part schema for the progress of humanity, written in 1795. Condorcet, who had earlier written an *Avis aux Bataves* encouraging the revolt of the Dutch, identified such cosmopolitanism as part of the ninth phase of progress:

> The philosophers of different nations who considered the interests of the whole of humanity without distinction of country, race, or creed, formed a solid phalanx banded together against all forms of error, against all manifestations of tyranny, despite their differences in matters of theory. Activated by feelings of universal philanthropy, they fought injustice even when it occurred in countries other than their own and could not harm them personally; they fought injustice even when it was their own country that was guilty of acts against others; they raised an outcry in Europe against the crimes of greed that sullied the shores of America, Africa, and Asia.[27]

Condorcet reproduces the themes of radical internationalism: the influence of the American revolution on Europe, the right of man being upheld 'in writings that circulated freely from the shores of the Neva to those of the Guadalquivir'.[28] In the tenth, final, stage of human perfection, mankind will overcome war, to be replaced by the brotherhood of nations;[29] a new universal language, based on scientific principles of observation, will further the enlightenment of mankind.[30] For others in the eighteenth century, internationalism involved what would later be termed solidarity: thus the revolt of the island of Corsica against Genoese rule inspired both Rousseau, who never visited it, and James Boswell, who did, to support its struggle for independence.[31]

This Enlightenment cosmopolitanism was replicated in the Anglo-Saxon world by the rise of liberal thinking. The American revolution was very much part of this intellectual ferment, inspired as it was by ideas of English liberalism, notably Locke, and conceiving of itself as part of a broader international process. The greatest impact of the American revolution was by example – the advocacy and implementation of a new social order, freed of the constraints of the European past.[32] The American republic did not try to expand its influence by active means. Yet it was widely assumed by the leaders of the American movement that the establishment of republics would introduce an epoch of peace and, by extension, open the possibilities of greater cooperation and federation between states.[33] Benjamin Franklin believed that there could be an equal federation between Britain and its colonies, and propagated anti-war ideas during his period as American ambassador to France in the 1780s; in 1787 he anticipated that the influence of the American revolution on Europe could be such as to open the possibility of an association of European states comparable to that which had been created in the USA.[34]

A cogent example of the Anglo-American conception is found in the writings of Thomas Paine, the English-born radical whose *Common Sense* (1776) was one of the most influential polemics in the American revolution, and whose *The Rights of Man* (1790) was a defence of the French revolution against Burke's critique in his *Reflections*. In 1792 he was to declare 'My country is the world and my religion is to do good.'[35] Paine was confident, first, that the events of America, and later those of France, marked a break, something fundamentally new, in human history. Writing of the American revolution, he argued that if independence was gained through the expression of the will of the people in Congress, then

we have every opportunity and every encouragement before us, to form the noblest, purest constitution on the face of the earth. We have it in our power to begin the world over again. A situation, similar to the present, hath not happened since the days of Noah until now. The birth-day of a new world is at hand, a race of men perhaps as numerous as all Europe contains, are to receive their portion of freedom from the events of a few months.[36]

Retaining some of the resonances of the astronomical, 'natural', conception of revolution, Paine regards the American and French revolutions as presaging a new era, not by force of arms, but of their example:

From the Revolutions of America and France, and the symptoms that have appeared in other countries, it is evident that the opinion of the world is changed with respect to systems of

Government, and that revolutions are not within the compass of political calculations. The progress of time and circumstances, which men assign to the accomplishment of great changes, is too mechanical to measure the force of the mind, and the rapidity of reflection, by which revolutions are generated: All the old Governments have received a shock from those that already appear, and which were once more improbable, and are a greater subject of wonder, than a general revolution in Europe would be now.[37]

In a pattern of argument that later thinkers were also to follow, Paine derives his view of the age from a set of other internationalist propositions. In the first place, he enunciates what I have termed above 'the logic of ideology', i.e. the derivation of an internationalist position from the assertion of some broad legitimating principles, in this case the rights of man:

> Every history of the creation, and every traditional account, whether from the lettered or unlettered world, however they may vary in their opinion or belief of certain particulars, all agree in establishing one point, *the unity of man*; by which I mean, that men are all of *one degree*, and consequently that all men are born equal.[38]

Secondly, Paine, in common with all radical democrats of the eighteenth and nineteenth centuries, linked conflict between peoples and war to the absence of popular sovereignty: monarchies and despotic governments use war to maintain their domination and raise taxes – the abolition of war therefore involves a radical change in the political system:

> Monarchical sovereignty, the enemy of mankind, and the source of misery, is abolished; and sovereignty itself is restored to its natural and original place, the Nation. Were this the case throughout Europe, the cause of wars would be taken away. . . As war is the system of government on the old construction, the animosity which Nations reciprocally entertain, is nothing more than what the policy of their Government excites, to keep up the spirit of the system. . . Man is not the enemy of man, but through the medium of a false system of Government. Instead, therefore of exclaiming against the ambition of Kings, the exclamation should be directed against the principle of such governments; and

instead of seeking to reform the individual, the wisdom of a Nation should apply itself to reform the system.[39]

Thirdly, Paine, in common with virtually all advocates of internationalism, asserts that this morally desirable goal accords with an objective process in the world. He argues, in particular, that in the new world of the Americas the barriers between social groups and peoples are broken down. In this way as in others, America can act as a model for the renovation of Europe: 'It is pleasant to observe by what regular gradations we surmount the force of local prejudice, as we enlarge our acquaintance with the world.'[40] Equally, he argues that in America the absence of the European political system allows it to pursue a different foreign policy and to express solidarity with the rest of the world:

> We fight neither for revenge nor conquest; neither from pride nor passion; we are not insulting the world with our fleets and armies, nor ravaging the globe for plunder. . . Perhaps, we feel for the ruined and insulted sufferers in all and every part of the continent.[41]

From this it is but a short step to the advocacy of international revolution coupled with the optimistic expectation that it will occur. The concluding words of *Rights of Man*, written in 1790, are an eloquent assertion of these classic themes within which, be it noted, the terms 'reform' and 'revolution' are synonymous:

> From what we now see, nothing of reform in the political world ought to be held improbable. It is an age of Revolutions, in which everything may be looked for. The intrigue of Courts, by which the system of war is kept up, may provoke a confederation of Nations to abolish it: and an European Congress, to patronize the progress of free Government, and promote the civilisations of Nations with each other, is even nearer in probability, than once were the Revolutions and Alliance of France and America.[42]

Two years later his optimism remains constant: 'I do not believe that monarchy and aristocracy will continue seven years longer in any of the enlightened countries in Europe.'[43] Like his other enlightenment predecessors, he envisaged the uniting of the peoples of Europe.[44] It was not armed action by revolutionaries, but the force of example that would achieve this: 'An army of principles will penetrate where an army of soldiers cannot', he was to write in *Agrarian Justice* (1797).

Marx's Reformulation: 'Proletarian Internationalism'

The internationalist themes found in the American and French revolutions were to be reproduced and given far more systematic expression in the ideas and activity of the socialist and communist movements, so much so that the very word 'internationalism' was introduced into political discourse as a result of the founding of the First International in 1864; the *Oxford English Dictionary* gives the date of the first occurrence as 1877. This conception, characterised as 'proletarian' internationalism, to distinguish it from other, liberal and presumably 'bourgeois', variants, was to be one of the core themes of the whole communist movement, alongside the need for, and legitimacy of, mass revolution and the dictatorship of the proletariat. It was equally to form the legitimation for the founding of the various workers' international organisations. It was also to prove the source of many of the most acute controversies in the history of the socialist movement, and to provide some of the bitterest disappointments to its leaders and those who participated in it. Its most succinct summary was the slogan coined by the Comintern and phrased in its official language: *Weltklasse, Weltpartei, Weltrevolution* – international class, international party, international revolution.

The early history of socialist internationalism, from the French revolution to the emergence of the communist movement in the 1840s, developed themes present in the French revolution itself. Saint-Simon writing in 1814 linked his analysis of the growth of a modern industrial society to that of a growing unity of peoples:

> There will no doubt come a time when all the peoples of Europe will feel that questions of common interest must be decided before questions of national interest. Then evils will start to decrease, troubles to abate, wars to die away. Towards this moment we strive unceasingly; towards this moment the progress of the human mind bears us along. . . The Golden Age of mankind does not lie behind us, but before; it lies in the

perfection of the social order. Our forefathers did not see it; one day our children will reach it. It is for us to clear the way.[45]

The early socialists assumed, in line with the general conception of internationalism, that objective processes – the growth of a world market, industrialisation, the migration and mingling of peoples – were accompanied by a growing political solidarity: Saint-Simon spoke for what others – Robert Owen, Charles Fourier, Wilhelm Weitling, Flora Tristan, Moses Hess – all articulated. Hegel's metahistorical theory, of the 'bacchanalian whirl' of the world spirit drawing more and more of human activity into its scope, was a dramatic representation of this same vision, in idealist terms. In many ways the internationalist perspective of Marx and Engels differed little from that of other liberals of the first half of the nineteenth century: capitalism was transforming individual societies but also breaking down barriers between them, national sentiments were on the decline, and cooperation and fraternity, above all an interest in peace, was growing.[46] The idea of an international *organisation* of workers was first put forward by the feminist cosmopolitan Flora Tristan in her *L'Union Ouvrière* (1843).[47] In Britain the Chartist movement contained a significant, if marginalised, internationalist component.[48] In this perspective, no country was exempt from the spread of the world market: as Marx wrote in his Preface to *Capital*, the less developed should look at the more developed countries and realise *de te fabula narratur* – this is a tale told for you.[49] What was distinctive about the communist perception of internationalism was, firstly, the linking of this broad moralistic and visionary approach to a specific analysis of society, in this case capitalist society, and, secondly, the move from a set of broad, and often residual, aspirations to the creation of an organised, disciplined, international movement.

The development of this distinctive approach to internationalism can be analysed in terms of the influence on Marxist thinking of those three strands which Lenin, with only some pedagogic simplification, later saw as constituting the communist approach – French communism, German idealism and English political economy. From French communism, beginning with Babeuf and running on through the socialists of the 1830s, Marx derived the idea of the working class as a force with not only distinctive social interests but as intrinsically international – without allegiance to, or interest in, a particular nation. Beyond any pragmatic calculations of solidarity and common struggle, the working class, albeit located in particular nations, was essentially without nationality. From German idealism, Marx derived the idea of a single world process, the Hegelian *Weltgeist*. The *Weltgeist* not only yielded a single, global, understanding of history, beyond any particularities of place or nation, but also drove humanity towards an ever-greater unity and towards changes which would take place on a world scale: in place of Hegel's conception of agency through the *Weltgeist*, Marx substituted the agency of the new world subject, the proletariat. All of this appeared to receive greater confirmation from the findings of the English (more properly Scottish) political economists, who showed both the reality and the desirability of growing international trade, the breaking down of frontiers and the creation of a single world market. Once again political process – proletarian solidarity – is accompanied by and reinforces objective processes, be these the growth of the market or the spread of the world spirit. As Lenin was later to formulate it: 'In place of all forms of nationalism, Marxism advances internationalism, the amalgamation of all nations in the higher unity, a unity that grows before our eyes with every mile of railway line that is built, with every international trust, and every workers association that is formed.'[50]

The fusion of German idealist philosophy with Marx's economic and political views is already evident in writings of the mid-1840s. The primacy of the material base determines the identity of the worker, not any supposed national character:

> the nation of the worker is not French, nor English, nor German, it is *toil, the wage slavery, the selling of oneself*. His government is neither French, nor English, nor German, it is *Capital*. His native air is not French, English nor German, it is the *factory air*. The land which belongs to him is not French, nor English, nor German, it is a few feet *below the earth*.[51]

The clearest exposition of the Hegelian-communist view of internationalism is given in *The German Ideology* of 1845–6. The main argument of *The German Ideology* is a critique of idealist German philosophers, in the Hegelian tradition, of those who, like Feuerbach, have inverted Hegel's philosophy but in so doing retain many of its structural weaknesses. It is in this context that Marx discusses both the development of the world market and the consequences of this for the creation of a world-historical emancipatory class. His purpose is not so much to argue for this world-historical class as to use what he takes to be an evident process as the example and context for his new revolutionary materialist approach. The arguments on internationalisation serve three functions in this elaboration of Marx's theory on the material determination of ideas and society: its *theoretical* function is to show how this world-historical material process, the growth of the world market, has political and ideological consequences; its *polemical* function is to argue that such a perspective will knock the German philosophers out of their national and idealist isolation; its *historical* function is to demonstrate that the universalisation of production destroys national illusions and creates an international consciousness.

Marx asserts that production is now being organised on a world-wide basis: 'this development of productive forces . . . implies the actual empirical existence of men in their *world-historical*, instead of local, being'.[52] As a concomitant, the class created by this system is itself a world-wide class:

> Communism is for us not a *state of affairs* which is to be established, an *ideal* to which reality [will] have to adjust itself. We call communism the *real* movement which abolishes the present state of things. The conditions of this movement result from the premises now in existence. Moreover, the mass of *propertyless* workers . . . presupposes the *world market* through competition. The proletariat can thus only exist *world-historically*, just as communism, its activity, can only have a 'world-historical' existence.[53]

Capitalist society creates a world market which is both the condition of most extreme oppression and the precondition for a revolutionary emancipation. Marx's primary concern here is not with the global or world-historical dimensions of this process, rather he takes the, for him, self-evident world-historical economic process as the material basis for his view of history and change, leading to revolution:

> In history up to the present it is certainly an empirical fact that separate individuals have, with the broadening of their activity into world-historical activity, become more and more enslaved under a power alien to them. . . a power which has become more and more enormous and, in the last instance, turns out to be the

world market. But it is just as empirically established that, by the overthrow of the existing state of society by the communist revolution . . . and the abolition of private property which is identical with it, this power, which so baffles German theoreticians, will be dissolved; and that then the liberation of each single individual will be accomplished in the measure in which history becomes transformed into world history.[54]

Later in this work, Marx provides a capsule history of the development of the world market, stressing in particular that the spread of large-scale industry served both to unify and homogenise the world: 'Generally speaking, big industry created everywhere the same reactions between the classes of society, and thus destroyed the peculiar individuality of the various nationalities.' From this Marx draws the conclusion that a new universal class was being created:

while the bourgeoisie of each nation still retained separate national interests, big industry created a class, which in all nations has the same interest and with which nationality is already dead; a class which is really rid of all the old world and at the same time stands pitted against it.[55]

Marx and Engels were active participants not only in the German socialist movement, but also in the broader opposition movement of contemporary Europe, and this involved support for struggles of national independence. Thus in speeches in December 1847, on the seventeenth anniversary of the Polish revolution of 1830, Marx and Engels make their – revolutionary – case for supporting Polish independence. Far from this involving some accommodation, tactical or otherwise, with a generic nationalism, Marx used this issue to draw the distinction between 'bourgeois' and 'proletarian' approaches:

The unification and brotherhood of nations is a phrase which is nowadays on the lips of all parties, particularly of the bourgeois free traders. A kind of brotherhood does indeed exist between the bourgeois classes of all nations. It is the brotherhood of the oppressors against the oppressed, of the exploiters against the exploited.

Such a brotherhood cannot, in Marx's view, lead to emancipation, since it rests on the root of the oppressive system, property relations: the conclusion is that the interests of nations can be guaranteed only by the abolition of existing property relations. Marx argued that the triumph of the proletariat would entail the ending of national oppression:

> The victory of the proletariat over the bourgeoisie represents at the same time the victory over national and industrial conflicts, which at present create hostility between the different peoples. Therefore, the victory of the proletariat over the bourgeoisie also signifies the emancipation of all downtrodden nations.[56]

For Engels there were also specific national, i.e. in his case German, reasons for supporting the Poles: 'It must be the concern of us Germans, above all, of us German democrats, to remove this stain from our nation. A nation cannot be free and at the same time continue to oppress other nations.'[57] This particular assertion of support for the Poles, is, however, followed by a restatement of the emancipatory dynamic of capitalism laid out by Marx in *The German Ideology*. The first blow to the oppression of peoples would come in England, because there the transformations of modern industry are most advanced, but this will also recur in other countries:

> because the position is the same for the workers of all countries, because their interests are the same and their enemies are the same, for this reason they must also fight together, they must oppose the brotherhood of the bourgeoisie of all nations with the brotherhood of the workers of all nations.[58]

Capitalism and Revolution: The Communist Manifesto

The clearest statement of the Marxist view of internationalism is given in the Communist Manifesto of 1848. Here the linkage between objective process and political movement, with a desired revolutionary culmination, is presented in the starkest terms. In the first section, 'Bourgeois and Proletarians', which lays out the historical perspective of the *Manifesto*, the growth of a world market is seen, first, as having hastened the end of feudalism:

The discovery of America, the rounding of the Cape, opens up fresh ground for the rising bourgeoisie . . . [markets and trade] gave to commerce, to navigation, to industry, an impulse never before known, and thereby, to the revolutionary element in the tottering feudal society, a rapid development.[59]

For its part the new class, the bourgeoisie, was compelled to establish its system on a global basis:

The need of a constantly expanding market for its product chases the bourgeoisie over the whole surface of the globe. It must nestle everywhere, settle everywhere, establish connections everywhere.[60]

This transformation of society on a global level is accompanied by a political change:

In place of the old local and national seclusion and self-sufficiency, we have intercourse in every direction, universal interdependence of nations.

In material, so also in intellectual production. The intellectual creations of individual nations become common property. National one-sidedness and narrow-mindedness become more and more impossible, and from the numerous national and local literatures, there arises a world literature. . . The bourgeoisie, by the rapid improvement of all instruments of production, by the immensely facilitated means of communication, draws all, even the most barbarian, nations into civilisation. The cheap prices of its commodities are the heavy artillery with which it batters down all Chinese walls, with which it forces the barbarians' intensely obstinate hatred of foreigners to capitulate. It compels all nations, on pain of extinction, to adopt the bourgeois mode of production; it compels them to introduce what it calls civilization into their midst, i.e. to become bourgeois themselves. In one word, it creates a world after its own image.[61]

But if in an earlier period this spread of trade and industry across the world helped the bourgeoisie, the contradictory character of capitalist development now produces a situation in which another revolutionary class, created out of and benefiting from this transformation, is able to assume power. Modern bourgeois society is 'like a sorcerer, who is no longer able to control the powers of the nether world whom he has called up by his spells'.[62] 'The weapons with which the bourgeoisie felled feudalism to the ground are now turned against the bourgeoisie itself.' Significantly, the *Manifesto* does not envisage a single world-wide revolutionary crisis:

> Though not in substance, yet in form, the struggle of the proletariat with the bourgeois is at first a national struggle. The proletariat of each country must, of course, first of all settle matters with its own bourgeoisie.[63]

These individual struggles were none the less seen as international, both in the sense that they reflected a process of global capitalist transformation, and because the working class, although located and struggling within specific states, was, as national differences disappeared, becoming more international in loyalty and character:

> The Communists are further reproached with desiring to abolish countries and nationality.
>
> The working men have no country. We cannot take from them what they have not got. Since the proletariat must first of all acquire political supremacy, must rise to be the leading class of the nation, must constitute itself as the nation, it is, so far, itself national, though not in the bourgeois sense of the word.
>
> National differences, and antagonisms between peoples, are daily more and more vanishing, owing to the development of the bourgeoisie, to freedom of commerce, to the world market, to uniformity in the mode of production and in the conditions of life corresponding thereto. The supremacy of the proletariat will cause them to vanish still faster. United action, of the leading civilized countries at least, is one of the first conditions for the emancipation of the proletariat.
>
> In proportion as the exploitation of one individual by another is put an end to, the exploitation of one nation by another will also be put an end to. In proportion as the antagonism between classes with the nation vanish, the hostility of one nation to another will come to an end.[64]

The *Manifesto* devotes no attention to the political implications of this process, laying stress on the shared, but separate, struggles of individual working classes in Europe, and laying its greatest hopes on the imminent bourgeois revolution in Germany. Yet in the final words it returns again to the international plane, linking the issue of property relations, and the proletariat's lack of property, to the issue of internationalism: 'The proletarians have nothing to lose but their chains. They have a world to win. Working men of all countries, unite!'[65]

The final lines of the *Manifesto* on internationalism have been often quoted, and form the basis of the subsequent orthodox communist theory of 'proletarian internationalism': when, as has often happened, socialists and communist have failed to live up to the expectations of others in this field, they are held to account in terms of the *Manifesto*'s appeal. Some of the arguments made have a striking validity: although written in the 1840s, before the onset of the 'New' Imperialism of the 1870s, it presaged the determination and force with which the industrialised countries would indeed set about subjugating the rest of the world through colonialism. The perspective on economic integration, indeed the very use of the term 'interdependence', sounds more like liberal internationalist literature of the 1970s and 1980s, with their stress on 'globalisation', than an analysis from a century and a half before.

In certain respects, Marx's view may have been mistakenly criticised. The most obvious misconception arises from the last lines, and from the interpretation put on them to the effect that Marx and Engels are calling for international union, i.e. solidarity and cooperation, between different working classes. Reading the lines in their context suggests that this is in fact a doubtful interpretation: the preceding discussion, part of the short final part 'Position of the Communists in Relation to the Various Existing Opposition Parties', is a list of the separate working-class parties now in action and of the importance of their organising, or to use the older word 'combining', to further these individual struggles. Just as the most outward-oriented term of the French revolutionary trinity, *fraternité*, was at the time used to denote solidarity *within* France, the 'unite' at the end of the *Manifesto* refers not to any international action, but to the organisation of workers within each state. The German original *'Arbeiter aller Welt, vereinigt euch'* could as well be rendered 'Workers of Each Country, Get Organised'.[66]

This is a rather more cautious message than subsequent interpretation has suggested, and is reflected in what Marx said when he returned to the question of internationalism two decades later, with the establishment of the First International in 1864. In his Inaugural Address Marx calls for the workers to educate themselves about general issues of foreign policy, just as they had prevented European states from supporting the South in the US Civil War: but what he talks of is something rather specific – 'fraternal concurrence', on foreign policy issues, a theme echoed in the 'Provisional Rules' of the Association. The preamble ascribes the failure of the working-class struggle to date to the failure of workers within countries to unite, and 'from the absence of a fraternal bond of union between the working classes of different countries'. Article 1 establishes 'a central medium of communication and cooperation between working men's societies existing in different countries, and aiming at the same end, viz. the protection, advancement, and complete emancipation of the working classes'.[67] If the First International can be taken as a realisation of the *Manifesto*, then the meaning of the latter's final words is clear: unite workers *within* countries, coordinate activities *between* them.

There are, however, other issues on which Marx and Engels' conception of revolutionary internationalism is more questionable. First, it is assumed that the objective process, of a growing world market, will indeed erode national differences. Since, they argue, these differences are transient, as are the sentiments – 'nationalism' – associated with them, the workers' movement need not concern itself with their legitimacy: insofar as the revolutionary crises will not occur simultaneously in all countries, communists will come to power in particular states, but this is a matter of deferred revolutionary unification, not an acceptance of the permanence, or legitimacy, of nations. Indeed elsewhere Marx and Engels spelt out more clearly their views on this matter: on the one hand, many nations would simply disappear, fused into larger ones in the process of capitalist development; on the other, nationalism was to be supported only insofar as it helped socialist transformation – the nationalism of pre-capitalist peoples was to be overridden by capitalist conquest, the nationalism of bourgeois governments was an instrument to distract the working class. This involved, among other things, a misunderstanding of the very year, 1848, that was to be so central to his theory: for while in Paris 1848 did indeed adumbrate a social upheaval, elsewhere it was nationalism that dominated. Secondly, it is assumed that the general process of capitalist transformation will produce a single and homogeneous world, a 'uniformity' which all countries are compelled to follow.

Thirdly, Marx seems to be believe that humanity as a whole is not only actually moving towards a single world culture but that this is desirable – the ultimate goal being a homogeneous humanity, a modern, communist, variant of *cosmopolis*. Above all, it is assumed that this world-historical process is inevitable, accompanied as it is by the growing and ultimately explosive contradictions of capitalist society. Without the teleology, and the sense of an all-encompassing world history, Marx's internationalist vision would lose much of its force.

In the Age of Imperialism: Lenin

Although never given systematic statement elsewhere in his work, Marx's ideas on internationalism continued to change, as is reflected in later writings. Indeed, some recognition of these problems can be found in what Marx later had to say, and, even more so, in the writings of his major successor, Lenin. If Lenin presented himself as the inheritor of Marx's ideas, he also found himself in a markedly different historical and intellectual situation. His actual policies will be examined in Chapter 4; here the focus will be on his use and development of Marx's ideas. Lenin presented himself as the unflinching defender of Marx's central ideas, and that of 'proletarian internationalism' was as central as its domestic correlate 'the dictatorship of the proletariat'. The argument about internationalism pervaded not just Lenin's conception of the foreign policy of the Bolshevik state after 1917 but also much of his work in the international communist movement prior to the seizure of power, and in particular the debate on the appropriate revolutionary reaction to the First World War. At the same time, before and after 1917, Lenin was preoccupied with the issue of nationalism itself. This was in regard both to the nationalism of colonial peoples, in various stages of resistance to Western imperialism, and the separate question of the 'nationalities question', i.e. of the rights of nations to self-determination and of inter-ethnic relations more generally, within Russia and, by extension, within other multinational empires. This sensitivity to nationalism was evident in Lenin's own person. A committed internationalist in politics, and an unrelenting critic of Russian tradition (one of his earlier writings was entitled *The Heritage We Reject*), he nonetheless retained not only much of the mindset of the Russian political tradition, but also a distinctively Russian taste in cultural matters, particularly music.

In sum, in the writings of Lenin and of those influenced by him the term 'internationalism' came to refer to several distinct questions – the international policies of revolutionary parties, the foreign policy of the socialist state, policies towards nationalist movements in Asia and Africa, and the handling of inter-ethnic relations within Russia and other states. It can therefore be said that Lenin introduced four major developments in the theory of internationalism inherited by Marx.[68] In the first place, he adopted a more consistently sympathetic attitude towards nationalism itself – accepting the legitimacy of colonial resistance to imperial domination and seeing in the struggles of colonial Asian and African peoples an ally in the struggle against imperialism. In regard to the multinational states, he advocated, and in some cases practised, the right of secession, on the grounds that only when nations had achieved their independence, or had ceased to oppress others, could they embark on the road to socialism. Secondly, Lenin developed a theory of *international revolutionary strategy* specific to his times, and based on the opportunities which the First World War provided for revolutionaries to seize power. While opposed to this war, as one between predator bourgeois and imperialist states, Lenin also saw in it the opportunity to, in his words, 'turn the imperialist war into a civil war', and hence to advance the revolutionary struggle. This theory, based on a conception of the world-wide imperialist system and of its contradictions, was developed into an international conception of revolution as beginning at the weakest point of the chain of oppression, before moving on to the stronger, more developed, capitalist states. Revolution, while the product of the contradictions of capitalist development, was not necessarily to take place first in the country where the capitalist system had most developed, where it was, in terms of the development of the forces of production, the most 'mature'.

These developments of Marx's theory were, however, posited on the basis of a more fundamental and central rethinking, one that went to the heart of Marx's conception of internationalism, namely the conception of capitalist development. Marx's whole emphasis had been on the spread of capitalism as something that produced uniformity between societies, and in so doing eroded national and other differences. From this it followed also that for Marx the

84 *The Internationalist Engagement*

bourgeoisies of different countries were less likely to go to war than previous ruling classes. By the time Lenin was writing, a very different picture had emerged: on the one hand, the spread of capitalism, whilst universal, had taken place in a strikingly uneven way, so that far from being uniform, societies were at different points of development and power; on the other hand, the most developed countries, far from being more peaceful, were in the grip of a nationalistic and militaristic competition that led first to the competition for colonies after 1870 and then to the explosion of the First World War itself. The central theme in Lenin's revision of the Marxist schema of internationalism was not so much differing attitudes to nationalism, or self-determination, or to war, but to the nature of *capitalist development* itself. It was on the basis of this new conception of the conflictual nature of capitalist development, one that Trotsky had also identified in the 1900s, that the other threads of Lenin's approach were developed – the inevitability of war within capitalism, the opportunities for a flexible international strategy based not on maturity but on the weakest link, and on the exploitation of inter-capitalist war for revolutionary purposes.

These ideas came together in Lenin's analysis of the First World War, and in particular in his work *Imperialism, the Highest State of Capitalism* published in 1916. From this general analysis Lenin drew one further set of conclusions that marked him off from Marx and which also reflected the evolution of this thinking, namely the importance of *organising* the international following of the revolution. For reasons both ideological and tactical Marx and Engels had downplayed the organisational question, and Engels had even in 1885 suggested that no international organisation was needed.[69] Lenin, who in the 1900s had developed a radically more organised conception of the proletarian party and of its vanguard, transposed this to the international plane in his construction of the Third 'Communist' International, founded in 1919. This organisation was to have the tightest of centralised controls, and was to constitute itself as one single international entity, a programme epitomised in the 'Twenty-One Points', or conditions of membership. It has been argued that this centralisation was a result of the failure of the European revolution to spread after 1917, but the roots of it lay in the very model of the Bolshevik party pioneered by Lenin since *What is to be Done?* of 1902. Although he had a clear idea of revolutionary organisation, Lenin was less prepared for the other major practical issue of internationalism in the post-revolutionary epoch, namely the formulation of a revolutionary foreign policy. Like Marx, Lenin had oscillated on whether the revolution would, or would not, be a relatively simultaneous affair, bringing about socialist transformation on a world scale. During The First World War Trotsky had envisaged a United States of Europe, even a united world. Lenin dissented. Yet even when he accepted that revolution would not come about simultaneously, he assumed that the broader conflagration would not be long delayed: his pages echo with the revolutionary optimism as much as do those of earlier, and later, visionaries of the global insurrection. There was no need to confront the issue of how such an interrupted, or incomplete, revolutionary process would affect the possibilities of socialist construction: this was, of course, to prove to be one of the central political and theoretical issues of dispute in the whole Bolshevik experience.

Following Lenin's death the history of 'proletarian internationalism' is one of fragmentation but continued vitality and sensitivity. On the one hand, the Soviet leadership, beginning with Stalin but continuing with his successors up to and including Gorbachev, argued *for* internationalism: this meant support by the international communist movement for the policies of the USSR. Stalin gave the most brutal and clear definition of internationalism, as unconditional support for the Soviet Union, and used Soviet foreign policy and the Comintern to this end.[70] Such indeed was his assumption of the right of the USSR to control the international communist movement that in 1943, as part of his campaign to cement the wartime alliance with Britain and the USA, Stalin dissolved the Third International altogether.[71] Yet the paradox was that despite this organisational dissolution, the Soviet leadership continued to proclaim and practise internationalism of its own kind. This was the basis on which Stalin occupied and installed communist regimes in Eastern Europe after the Second World War. The Cominform, set up in 1947, pledged loyalty to the USSR; internationalism justified the Soviet military interventions in Hungary in 1956 and Czechoslovakia in 1968; and as late as 1987, Gorbachev, even as he was setting in train the dissolution of the communist and Soviet systems, was to enjoin other communist parties and regimes 'to learn from the international experience' of the USSR. Nor was this solely a top-down policy: for millions across the world, emboldened above all by Soviet success in the Second World War, loyalty to the USSR was a spontaneous and deeply felt commitment.

Under Brezhnev two attempts at a theoretical reformulation or 'development' of the international conception of global revolution were made. On the one hand, the invasions of Czechoslovakia and subsequently of Afghanistan were justified by the theory of 'limited sovereignty' of states within the bloc of communist countries; on the other hand, a conception of world politics as dominated by a process of shifting bloc power, a 'correlation of forces', was produced, according to which the power of the Soviet bloc was gradually growing at the expense of the capitalist.[72] Yet the very extension of communist power after 1917 was to provoke crisis and fragmentation: at every point in the history of the communist movement when the movement divided, the issue of 'internationalism' was raised as one with which to denounce ideological opponents. When the Bolshevik party itself divided in the 1920s one of the issues on which the left opposition of Trotsky and his associates rested was that of 'internationalism' and Stalin's abandonment of it. Indeed, as we shall see in Chapter 11, Trotsky linked this issue, of the failure to spread world revolution, to the internal crisis of the Soviet regime: he saw this failure as both effect and cause of the 'degeneration' of the Bolshevik revolution.[73] Although the Comintern was dissolved in 1943, Moscow in effect kept control of the world communist movement, formally in the European Cominform, informally elsewhere. After the Second World War, communist states that defied Moscow saw in internationalism the disguise for Russian domination – first Yugoslavia in 1948, and then China in 1963.

If the Yugoslavs denounced internationalism itself, and made a strong and, for its time, original critique of the dangers of Soviet policy leading to war, the Chinese adopted the alternative strategy, upholding the principle of 'internationalism', and berating the Soviet leadership for its failure to pursue this revolutionary policy, and, in so doing, minimising the dangers of nuclear war.[74] The polemics of the Sino-Soviet dispute (1960–3) may read now like the archaic debates of an old scholasticism: at the time, they reflected real issues, of power, strategy and security, and international strategy.

In such disputes 'Internationalism' was not rejected by either side: rather it became, in the debates of the international communist movement from the late 1950s through to the early 1980s, an object of dispute, an emblem that each side sought to define and appropriate, even as it advanced its own specific national interests beneath this apparently broader banner.[75] Thus the Soviet invasion of Czechoslovakia in 1968 was justified on 'internationalist' grounds. In June 1976 when Moscow summoned a meeting of 29 European communist parties to a meeting in East Berlin, the Soviet party tried to reimpose its definition of the term, while the Euro-communist parties of Italy and Spain sought to redefine a 'socialist' variant that was opposed to the 'proletarian' version.[76] In the Eurocommunist break with Moscow 'proletarian internationalism' was officially and formally renounced as being, along with the dictatorship of the proletariat, one of the two conceptions seen as most redolent of the Stalinist past. The East Berlin summit recognised the 'sovereign independence of each party'.[77] Yet in the late 1970s the Italian party proposed a 'new internationalism' that incorporated not only communists, but also socialists, social movements, the churches and liberal opinion.[78]

The 1980s saw a further erosion of any lingering adherence of the communist movement to this concept.[79] When, in January 1979, two communist states, Vietnam and Cambodia, went to war, this caused a shock amongst the world's communist parties: this was an index of the continued vitality of the belief that revolution would abolish war. A shock of a more conventional kind came with the Soviet intervention in Afghanistan in December 1979, an event widely, if mistakenly, interpreted as re-run of the invasion of Czechoslovakia. When he came to rework Soviet doctrine in 1987, Mikhail Gorbachev rejected the old idea of an internationalism based on obedience to one line, let alone one state, and argued instead for a diversity within the recognition of the common interests and problems of mankind.[80] In April 1988, on the last such occasion, representatives of no less than ninety communist parties were convened in Prague to hear a speech by the head of the international department of the CPSU, Anatoli Dobrynin, on the need for an international discussion of the difficulties of the socialist experience.[81] When communism finally fell in Eastern Europe in 1989, one of the concepts most openly rejected and reviled, along with central planning, the emancipation of women and the abolition of religion, was 'internationalism': it had become a term associated both with the legitimation of Soviet domination and with the expenditure of large sums of money on politically motivated solidarity with other, mainly Third World, communist states.[82]

Challenge from the Third World

Lenin's reformulation of the concept of internationalism marked not only a transition within Marxist theory and communist policy but also served as the start of a much broader diffusion of ideas of an international revolutionary strategy to the Third World. The result was that in many of the anti-colonial revolutions of the latter half of the twentieth century the core elements of the Marxist perspective were reproduced, in altered or indeed wholly distinct theoretical and political contexts. What Lenin had done, through his formulation of an international perspective based on 'imperialism', was to provide a new basis for any international conceptualisation of revolutionary struggle: the unity of the oppressed peoples was given not so much by the workings of a world market, or by the property-less and hence nation-less character of the oppressed, but by the unity of the structure of oppression, namely imperialism, and the separate but convergent revolts of Third World peoples against it. The latter, by dint of the colonial experience and of the legitimation of their revolt, were national and often nationalist struggles. The early Marxist perspective on the *disappearance* of nations and national sentiment was set aside. Instead, nationalism itself, and what came to be termed 'national liberation', often expressed through revolutionary mobilisation and military challenge, came to be part of the international and internationalist movement against the global phenomenon of imperialism. In some ways this was a much more international perspective than that of the earlier, more 'proletarian', internationalism: from the start it stressed the common interests and struggle of different peoples against a single, globally extended, enemy. The dividing line in world politics ran not so much within each country, as *between* nations, and states.

The idea of the oppressed peoples as distinct from classes of the world constituting a definable and potentially mobilised force had arisen at several points in revolutionary thinking before 1945. In the nineteenth century, the theorist of the Italian revolution, Carlo Pisacane, had analysed the Italians as more oppressed and therefore more revolutionary than the more developed European countries.[83] In the Bolshevik revolution itself a fraction of the communist movement based in Central Asia, led by Sultan Galiev, articulated its own global theory of the oppressed peoples and nations.[84] In China, Li Ta-Chao, one of the earlier leaders of the Chinese party, saw the non-European peoples as the leaders of the world proletarian movement: Li saw the Chinese people as a 'proletarian' nation, not by dint of some nationalist unity, but because of their place in a world hierarchy created by capitalism.[85]

In the post-1945 period, however, when Third World revolution came to be a historical reality, first in China, and then in other continents, a number of formulations of this global strategy emerged. In China, Mao Tse-tung and his associate, Lin Piao, produced a theory, both of a world revolutionary process, within which China played a leading role as a state, and also of the generalisation on to a world scale of the Chinese 'model', with the countryside of the world, represented by Asia, Africa and Latin America, encircling the cities of the world, represented by the developed countries.[86] This projection of the Chinese experience was to take two forms at least: a radical 'left' variant, with the proclamation in 1965, at the start of the 'Cultural Revolution', of the theory of global revolution represented by Lin Piao,[87] and a subsequent 'right' variant, represented by the formulation by Teng Hsiao-ping of the 'Three Worlds Theory', in 1974.[88] While the former stressed the importance of guerrilla struggle in the Third World, the latter emphasised the need for a political alliance, a 'united front' including the governments of Third World countries and the countries of the 'intermediate zone', i.e. Europe and Japan, against the two 'imperialist' centres, the USA and the Soviet Union.

A parallel, and for much of the time rival, conception of the international struggle was articulated in Latin America. The original leaders of the Latin American revolutions, above all Simón Bolivar, had envisioned a union of all the peoples of the continent. In the latter part of the nineteenth century the Cuban revolutionary Jose Martí had also seen the revolt of his country as the first step in a second continental war of liberation. These ideas, echoed in the Mexican revolution of 1910–20, were revived by the Cuban revolution of 1959, and in particular in the work of two non-Cuban associates of that revolution, the Argentinian Che Guevara and the French writer Régis Debray. Guevara, upon his departure from Cuba in 1965 to promote revolution in Latin America, issued a call for the 'creation of two, three, many Vietnams', to over-extend 'imperialism' and to consolidate a new revolutionary front.[89] Debray, in his theoretical elaboration of the 'lessons' of the Cuban revolution, sought to generalise from the Cuban experience to produce a new more mobile conception of revolutionary struggle on a continental scale.[90] The political statements issuing from both Peking and Havana in the 1960s envisioned a global revolutionary front, in which the unity of Third World peoples would undermine the imperialist hold and, through promoting conflict in the more developed countries, lead to an overthrow of the ruling classes and their associated system of imperialism on a world scale.

This conception of a global struggle, linked to, but independent of, the policies of the Soviet Union was mirrored in the writings of many Western anti-imperialist writers of the 1960s and 1970s. Here too the system of oppression in First and Third Worlds was similar, the former relying on the profits generated by the latter, and on the ideologies of racial and economic superiority used to maintain support from the populations of developed countries for their system. The belief was both that the imperialist system was driven to oppress Third World peoples and that once this system had been broken or had cracked in the Third World there would be revolutionary upheavals in the developed countries. The political turmoil promoted in Europe and the USA during the late 1960s by the war in Vietnam appeared to lend credence to this view, one of a unified and systemic global oppression that would be countered by an alternative, revolutionary, front of oppressed peoples and classes.[91]

A very different, but in its own way confirmatory, perspective on this question was to come a decade later from another quarter, namely the Iranian revolution of 1979. As discussed in Chapter 2, this revolution appeared at first sight to diverge from other revolutions, in ideology as much as in policy; yet despite its hostility to all modern and particularly communist ideas, in international as in domestic matters it was to express many of the same ideas and implement many of the same policies as other revolutions. Thus in the language of Khomeini and his associates there was a conception of a world system structured by an oppressive system, 'world arrogance' (*istikbar-i jahani*), against which the oppressed (*mostazafin*) had to struggle. These 'oppressed' constituted not only Muslim peoples, but also non-Muslims peoples of the Third World, such as those in South Africa or Nicaragua, who were victims of the dominant system. Khomeini, as much as any other revolutionary leader, enjoined solidarity on his followers, and provided a particular Islamic rendering of the internationalist perspective of revolutionaries according to which the revolution was itself international: 'there are no frontiers in Islam', he proclaimed.

Khomeini articulated a message that, for all its distinct language, was very much in the internationalist tradition:

I hope that the general Islamic mobilization will become a model for all the meek and the Muslim nations on the globe and that the 15th century of the Hegira will be a century of the smashing of big idols and the substituting of Islam and monotheism for polytheism and atheism, justice and equity for injustice and iniquity, and of devoted men for cultureless cannibals.

   O meek of the world, rise and rescue yourselves from the talons of nefarious oppressors. O zealous Muslims in various countries in the world, wake up from your sleep of neglect and liberate Islam and the Islamic countries from the clutches of the colonialists and those subservient to them![92]

Equally, the Iranian revolution called for the promotion of revolution abroad, 'the export of revolution', as part of the consolidation of the revolution at home. It should not have come as a surprise to hear that the rhetoric of the Iranian revolution, like that of its more secular predecessors, hailed the imminence of revolution abroad and saw its own state as but the first in a series of revolutions that would sweep the Islamic world.[93]

A Contradictory Vision

The recurrence of internationalist revolutionary thinking of this kind suggests a division of such ideas into three general categories: the utopian, in the sense of those aspirations that corresponded little if at all to real potential; the calculated, where revolutionary aspiration and capability overlapped; and the instrumental, where internationalism reflected more the interests of one state than that of the movement as a whole. If the argument so far has established the recurrence and near-uniformity of revolutionary conceptions of internationalism and the international dimension of revolutions, it may also have given some indications of the limits and inherent contradictions in this global vision.

   First, there was the danger of instrumentalism: the greatest criticism of the internationalism of revolutions has been that the very intervention in other countries has been an extension of state interests. The best-known critique of revolutionary states is one of excess caution, of sacrificing others to their cause by inaction: thus did Trotsky denounce the USSR in the 1930s, as did the Chinese and, to a lesser extent, the Cubans in the 1960s. But equally important, if less articulated, is that of the revolutionary state using, and distorting, movements in other countries in a way that does violence to the needs of those states: the Bolshevisation of the communist movement in the 1920s, the obsession of the Chinese with a globalised mimetic Maoism in the 1960s, and the Cuban imposition of their militaristic *focismo* exemplify this charge. As we shall see in Chapter 5, the very idea of a revolutionary state as internationalist, in policy and model, contained within it the inevitability that this state would use its international influence to impose its will and policy on others, or that even if it sought not to, it would be so perceived by those in the countries where it was seeking to promote upheaval.

Secondly, this internationalist tradition had an uneasy relation to nationalism. As much as was 'Revolution' so was nationalism a product – as ideology and as movement – of the twin revolutions – political and industrial – of the late eighteenth century and early nineteenth century. If earlier eighteenth- and nineteenth-century conceptions of internationalism had assumed that nationalism would, through objective change, disappear, later thinkers, beginning with Lenin, sought to recruit nationalism to their cause. Yet neither perspective was to prove itself vindicated: for the earlier theorists, nationalism did not disappear; for the latter, revolutionary nationalism proved to be the source of much more international conflict and competitive focus on national interest, than an assumption of any revolutionary harmony of interests would have suggested. Trotsky's warning of 'national messianism', the belief in one's own nation's special role in a revolutionary world, was to be relevant to every revolution of modern times.

Thirdly, the very conceptual basis of this internationalist perspective, assuming a consonance of objective, political and moral dimensions, was suspect: objective internationalisation might promote not greater, but less, political understanding, while processes of internationalisation – or as it later came to be known, 'globalisation' – were often perceived not as positive, but as negative and destructive features of political change. Fourthly, the very perspective upon which these visions rested, namely of a continuous and inevitable world-wide revolutionary upheaval, was itself contradicted by reality: revolutions had their international effects, but they failed to spread in the manner that rhetoric suggested, leaving the revolutionary state with the need to conduct diplomacy and trade with the non-revolutionary world. Revolutions had to face the longer-term impact of such an outcome on their own revolutionary transformation. This entailed that the commitment to internationalism might be one that the revolutionary movements and the states themselves came to question, as the investment in upheaval abroad gave way to accommodation with the existing system of states and with the political orders they represented. The challenges to internationalism came not only in the realm of relations with *other* states and societies, but also *within* the revolutionary states themselves.

4

Internationalism in Practice: Export of Revolution

Transgressing Diplomacy: The Export of Revolution

The world of ideology and rhetoric, and the world of the real, have never coincided, in revolutionary or tranquil times. Yet to a considerable degree they did develop in some rough combination: the ideas of the previous chapter were to a remarkable extent realised in the practices of solidarity and more specifically in the export of revolution. 'Export of revolution' conventionally meant the active promotion of revolution in other countries by a revolutionary regime. Revolutionaries were caught, by dint of their own ideology, in the conflict between asserting their obligation to encourage change elsewhere, and their recognition of the limits which any such external assistance could have. Equally, they were divided by their desire to affirm solidarity, often far in excess of what they were capable of, and the wish to fend off the hostility of counter-revolutionary states. Hence, protestations to the effect that such states were not violating international 'norms' by assisting revolutionaries abroad, were accompanied by claims that such assistance in any case was not possible, since revolution could not be exported. From the French revolutionaries in the 1790s to the Nicaraguan Sandinistas in the 1980s, all such states have expressed innocence when accused of promoting revolution abroad. They have not, however, believed in such innocence, any more than have their enemies: the latter have taken such aspirations as a justification for their own counter-revolutionary interventions. In the words of one critic of the Russian revolution: 'By challenging the legitimacy of all foreign governments, the Bolsheviks invited all foreign governments to challenge theirs.'[1]

Initially, revolutionary regimes confronted the question of exporting revolution in the field of diplomacy. The critique of traditional, realist and secret diplomacy had been part of the Enlightenment critique of absolutist regimes.[2] Revolutionaries proclaimed a new method of foreign relations, that of relations with *peoples* rather than with states, of open rather than secret diplomacy: therefore even if embassies existed in foreign countries, they were there to relate to the popular and opposition movements within those states rather than to conduct negotiations with the governments in power. Upon coming to power the Bolsheviks published the secret treaties between the Czarist regime and the other great powers. In the negotiations at Brest-Litovsk, Trotsky sought to appeal over the heads of the German military negotiators to the peoples of Europe. In a famous example of the internationalist use of diplomacy, the first Bolshevik ambassador to arrive in Berlin, in April 1918, Adolf Joffe, refused to present his credentials to the Kaiser and instead began distributing revolutionary literature, money and some arms to German revolutionaries. Joffe was later to say that his embassy 'served as staff headquarters for a German revolution'.[3] Days after he was expelled from Berlin a rising of workers, soldiers and sailors toppled the imperial government against which he had been agitating.[4]

Revolutions proclaim a new form of diplomacy, in part in the expectation of a near-simultaneous set of insurrections in other countries. In practice, revolutionaries doubt the need at all for diplomacy, in the sense of regular inter-state relations. This theme, the denial of the relevance of diplomacy, recurs in many revolutions and has at least three different components: the belief in the near-simultaneity of the imminent world revolution and hence the opportunity to avoid any contact with non-revolutionary states; disdain for what is seen as a quintessential *ancien régime* and elitist practice; and a belief in the benefits and practicability of open, people-to-people relations as distinct from the 'secret' and anti-popular world of diplomacy. Thus Trotsky, when appointed commissar for foreign relations in the Bolshevik government, defined his responsibilities succinctly: 'I will issue a few revolutionary proclamations to the peoples of the world, and then close shop.' Although he later said he had exaggerated his point, he did so 'to emphasize the fact that the centre of gravity was not in diplomacy at the time'.[5] At moments of crisis in post-revolutionary regimes this has involved attacks on diplomatic immunity itself, if not by the actual regimes, then by forces close to them. In August 1967, during the Chinese Cultural Revolution, the British Embassy in Peking was burnt to the ground by Red Guards protesting at British policy in Hong Kong.[6] In November 1979, after the Iranian revolution, a radical faction within the regime, *daneshjuan musulmanan piramun-i khatt i-imam*, the 'Islamic Students Following the Imam's Line', seized the US embassy in Tehran: they regarded the hitherto prevailing conventions of diplomatic immunity and representation as objects worthy of attack. The over fifty US diplomats in the embassy were not entitled to immunity but were *jasusan*, spies, and the embassy itself the *jasuskhane*, or 'spy house'.

Diplomacy, however unorthodox or transgressive, was not however the sole, or often main, means by which revolutionary states promoted their goals abroad.[7] Such goals were promoted by the export, active and proclaimed, of revolution. The historical record shows that even if the rhetoric of solidarity is indeed often far in advance of reality, revolutionary states nonetheless sought in a number of ways to assist fellow militants abroad. This assistance could take a political form, involving assistance with propaganda, through radio and other forms of publicity. The French revolution promoted its cause initially in ideological form through the distribution of statements and the despatch of propagandists, and, later, by military means. In the twentieth century, political support was organised in a more formal manner, accompanied by the creation of international organisations in which both the revolutionary state and its allies elsewhere were members. The Third International (1919–43) was the most developed example of this, but in the 1960s the Cuban revolution created two organisations for coordinating, respectively, Third World (OSPAAAL) and Latin American (OLAS) movements.[8] Equally such assistance could be diplomatic – as in the provision of passports, hosting of representation of the revolutionary movement, and assistance vis-à-vis other states in international fora.

More substantively, solidarity could involve providing money, publishing facilities, transport and logistical support for revolutionary movements. Most importantly, such assistance could be military – the training of revolutionary troops, the provision of advisers to the military forces of revolutionaries, the provision of transit facilities and bases, protected by the revolutionary state itself. In the twentieth century there were many examples of this: the

Soviet provisions – through the Comintern – of arms, training and advisers to underground military units of their allied communist parties; Chinese communist support for Vietnamese opposition to France from 1950 to 1954; and Cuban aid to the Sandinistas in Nicaragua, especially from 1977 onwards.[9] The practice of military support was evident in even the more exposed, or marginal, revolutionary regimes: thus the People's Democratic Republic of Yemen, after its establishment in 1967, provided bases, training and arms to guerrillas in two out of its three neighbours, Oman and North Yemen, and engaged in sporadic border and propaganda clashes with the third, Saudi Arabia.[10] The most significant and risky form of such assistance was direct participation by the armed forces of a revolutionary state in another country. Examples of the latter, often occurring in a context of inter-state war, would include the French revolutionary promotion of the establishment of *républiques soeurs* between 1792 and 1794; and Bolshevik attempts up to 1920 to assist revolution in Poland, Iran and Mongolia. Iran, generically committed to supporting militant Islamic forces abroad, devoted particular attention to assisting armed opposition in three countries – Iraq, with whom it fought an eight-year war, Afghanistan, and Lebanon. Much of this assistance was covert: but the French, Bolshevik and Iranian attempts to promote revolution abroad were, in some instances, openly justified.

Such commitments were, of course, explained and legitimated in terms of the overall internationalist orientation of revolutions already discussed in Chapter 3. They were also, however, part of the policy of state consolidation at home, and were reflected in the propaganda directed by revolutionary states at their domestic audiences. Amongst all the other campaigns and appeals directed at their own populations, internationalist solidarity was to recur. The French revolution practised days of support for liberty. The Bolsheviks mobilised around days of proletarian solidarity: even in the 1970s the calendar of fifty-three official Soviet holidays comprised several such internationalist days:

8 March	International Woman's Day
18 March	Day of the Paris Commune
24 April	International Day of Solidarity of Youth
1 May	Day of International Workers' Solidarity
25 May	Day of the Liberation of Africa

8 September	International Day of Solidarity of Journalists
10 November	All-World Day of Youth
17 November	International Students' Day[11]

Mass meetings to denounce the crimes of imperialism, or to express support for struggling parties and movements, were a regular feature of life in other communist countries. In China, millions would be deployed on to the streets to protest against imperialist aggression, or support particular movements. In Iran, the regime began in 1982 to celebrate *hafte-yi vahdat*, the 'week of unity', i.e. a time of solidarity with oppressed Muslims the world over, coinciding with the birth of the Prophet; foreign delegations were invited to Tehran, amidst appeals for the unity of Sunni and Shi'a Muslims.[12]

Against this internationalist enthusiasm and the recurrent practice of revolutionary states, can be set the caution with which many revolutionaries have, in certain circumstances, viewed the possibilities of military confrontation with other states, including through 'exporting' revolution. The classic expression of this caution was that of Robespierre who in 1792 warned against the militancy of the Girondins. In the Russian case, Lenin had argued, in the face of the threat of renewed war from Germany in the early part of 1918, for tactical conciliation at Brest-Litovsk: decades later Fidel Castro was to question the wisdom of this concession.[13] Khomeini too advocated export of revolution, but replicated the concerns of his antecedents: 'It does not take swords to export this ideology. The export of ideas by force is no export.'[14] The reasons for prudence are self-evident: on the one hand, a calculation as to the risk to which such adventurist policies would expose the revolutionary state; on the other, an awareness that promoting revolution by external intervention would arouse not the support but the hostility of the people in the country concerned – such was indeed the reaction in Poland in 1920 in the face of the Bolshevik advance, as it was in Italy during the French revolutionary occupation, and in Iraq during the war with Iran of 1980–8.

To recognise these limits, and the failure of such attempts to 'export', is not, however, to settle the matter of how far it is possible to promote revolution abroad by deliberate state action. The very recurrence of this policy of active promotion of revolution abroad, up to and including the 1980s (Iran, Nicaragua), suggests that revolutionary states face strong and conflicting pressures, from their own ideologies and from within and from without their own societies, to pursue such initiatives. Against the limits and costs of such policies must be set both the domestic benefits, sometimes in the form of promoting national glory, and the opportunities which such assistance, if more or less rightly calibrated, can provide for the advancement of the interests of the revolutionary state. In some cases, such assistance can provide an important element in the success of revolutionaries: Russia in Mongolia, China in Vietnam, Cuba in Nicaragua are all cases in point. On the other hand, support for revolutions elsewhere, even in its diminution or abandonment, can provide the revolutionary state with a negotiating asset in achieving resolution of its conflict with interventionist powers. For all the costs and illusions involved, 'export' of revolution, seen as an accompaniment not a substitute for the upheaval within the state concerned, can be both a practicable policy for a revolutionary state and an element of the protection of its own state interests against those wishing to destroy it. Much as revolutionary states may deny it and liberal friends downplay it, the commitment to the export of revolution, i.e. to the use of the resources of the revolutionary state to promote radical change in other societies, is a constant of radical regimes.

France: 'La Grande Nation'

For all their internationalist intentions, the political revolutions of England and America did little to actively promote revolution abroad. Cromwell's support for anti-Catholic forces was frustrated; the Americans proclaimed universal principles, and, in their vast majority, applauded the French revolution, but did not become embroiled in the upheavals of Europe. By contrast, the record of the French revolution is one with which the commitment to, and implementation of, the export of revolution has a central place.[15] In a singularly inept attempt at a natural allusion, implying that the sun could light up both sides of the globe simultaneously, Robespierre was to declare: 'La moitié de la révolution du monde est déja faite; l'autre moitié doit s'accomplir.'[16] It was this which, amongst other factors, so alarmed the conservative powers of Europe. Burke in his *Reflections* talked of the 'malignant charity' of the French revolution, of a commitment, beyond the demonstration effect which he also deplored, to promoting change abroad. Sorel in his

L'Europe et la Révolution française spoke of 'zélateurs cosmopo-
lites'.[17] De Tocqueville wrote of the analogy between the French
revolution and religion:

> All mere civil and political revolutions have had some country for
> their birthplace, and have remained circumscribed within its
> limits. The French Revolution, however, had no territorial
> boundary – far from it; one of its effects has been to efface as
> it were all ancient frontiers from the map of Europe. It united or
> it divided mankind in spite of laws, traditions, characters, and
> languages, turning fellow-countrymen into enemies, and foreign-
> ers into brothers; or rather, it formed an intellectual country
> common to men of every nation, but independent of all separate
> nationalities . . . As it affected to tend more towards the regen-
> eration of mankind than even towards the reform of France, it
> roused passions such as the most violent revolutions had never
> before excited. It inspired a spirit of proselytism and created the
> propaganda. This gave to it that aspect of a religious revolution
> which so terrified its contemporaries, or rather, we should say, it
> became a kind of new religion in itself – a religion, imperfect it is
> true, without a God, without a worship, without a future life, but
> which nevertheless, like Islam, poured forth its soldiers, its
> apostles, and its martyrs over the face of the earth.[18]

Initially, the French revolutionary regime declared itself to be in
favour of peace. In its decree of 22 May 1790, the French National
Assembly insisted that the right to declare war belongs to the people
and that it 'undertakes not to undertake any war with a view to
conquest, and that it will never use its forces against the liberty of
any people'.[19] There is no reason to believe that its leaders
harboured other intentions: they were not committed, as subsequent
communist or Islamist revolutionaries would be, to the promotion
of an internationalist activity abroad. They had few links to foreign
revolutionaries, no commanding belief that their revolution should
be promoted by the export of arms or the training of insurrectionaries. The most evident action of this kind which was taken, a
product of ideology as much as of revolutionary calculation, was
that of according French citizenship to foreign citizens deemed
worthy of membership of the new revolutionary community.[20]

However, all this was to change under the dual impact of
increased confrontation abroad and radicalisation within. At first,

i.e. until 1792, the impact of the French revolution was indeed one of example, or, to put it another way, ideological: radicals in other countries, among them England, Ireland, the Rhineland, Holland and Geneva, sought to emulate the French revolution. Of the three other 'democratic' revolutions which occurred at the time, two – in Liège, and in Brussels – were defeated by 1790, with only a third, in Geneva, surviving. The radicalisation of the republic's relations with the outside world in 1792, signalled by the failed flight of the monarch and the outbreak of war with Austria in September, led to a sharpening of sentiment in the National Assembly, and to the expectation that French forces would advance into other countries where revolution might occur. The defeat of the Austrian counter-revolutionary intervention at Valmy in September 1792 was to play for France the ideologically radicalising role that the defeat of the CIA expeditionary force at the Bay of Pigs was to play for Cuba in 1961. The day after Valmy, 21 September, the Convention proclaimed France a Republic. It was in this context that what became known as the 'Propaganda Decrees' were proclaimed in 1792.[21] Thus in November the Assembly decided:

> The National Convention declares, in the name of the French nation, that it will accord fraternity and help to all peoples who shall desire to recover their liberty, and charges the executive power with giving its generals the necessary orders to provide help to these peoples, and to defend those citizens who may have been threatened or who could be in the cause of liberty.[22]

A month later they voted on precisely those instructions to be put into effect:

> In territories which are or will be occupied by the armies of the Republic, the generals will at once proclaim, in the name of the French nation, the sovereignty of the people, the suppression of all established authority, taxes or existing contributions, the abolition of the tithe, of feudalism, of seigneurial rights, be they feudal, quitrent, fixed or casual, of banalities, of real and person servitude, of the privileges of hunting and fishing, of corvées, of the nobility and generally of all privileges.
>   They shall announce to the people that they bring them peace, help, fraternity, liberty and equality and that they will summon immediately primary and communal assembly to create and

organise provisional administration and justice; they will watch
over the security of individuals and property; they will print in the
language or dialect of the country, post and carry out without
delay, in every commune this decree and the proclamation
annexed to it.[23]

In this latter proclamation the French people applied to those they
had conquered to join them in proclaiming the sovereignty of the
people: 'From this moment you are, brothers and friends, all
citizens, all equal in rights, and all summoned equally to govern,
to serve and to defend your homeland.'[24] The slogan of the French
revolutionary armies was *guerre aux châteux, paix aux chaumières*,
'war to the castles, peace to the cottages'.

The impact of these ideas was, however, determined not by
popular insurrection in these states, nor by a coincidence of such
insurrection with the advance of the French armies, but by the
course of the revolutionary wars themselves. The advances of 1792
and early 1793 were reversed, the *républiques soeurs* failing in the
process. The most radical period of the revolution at home, that of
the Jacobins (1793–4), was to involve a somewhat more cautious
foreign policy. Subsequent developments allowed, however, for the
proclamation of the Batavian Republic in 1795, and the Helvetian
Republic in 1798. But Belgium was simply annexed to France and
the Rhineland kept under a French military government: resentment at French domination grew. Later Italy, where pro-French
sentiment was strongest, was to fall under French rule following the
Napoleonic conquests.

The record of the French revolution in the export of its politics is,
in many respects, comparable to that of other revolutions: if it
lacked a coherent internationalist ideology, it made up for this with
a generic cosmopolitan radicalism that appealed as much as any
other doctrine was to do to rebel forces in other countries; if it
lacked an idea of a political party or comparable formal organisation it was able to attract, in a spontaneous way, an international
following of sympathetic groups. In three other respects, moreover,
its record was very similar to that of the revolutions which were to
follow. First, the development of an internationalist policy was
inextricably intertwined with the confrontation of the new state
with foreign powers – it was external hostility, as much as internal
intention, that brought the French state from the declaration of
peace of 1790 to the export of revolution in 1792–3. Second, this

evolution was interlocked with the factionalism in the revolutionary state itself – the conflict between radical internationalists, such as the Girondins or the Prussian radical Anacharsis Cloots, and more cautious forces was played out in faction fighting, even death, in Paris. Third, the overriding determinant became not the fate of like-minded radical parties, but the course of war, within which radical parties sought, with varying degrees of success, to maintain independence of manoeuvre from their French revolutionary patrons. In the end the revolution did not spread, nor was the French army able, in a lasting way, to establish or consolidate *républiques soeurs*. It was only a generation or two later, when conditions inside their own countries had ripened, that the revolutionary message, the 'malign charity', of the French revolution, was to take root in the broader context of Europe, and, even later, the world.[25]

Russia: The Communist International

Whatever else may have been in doubt, there could be no questioning the commitment of the Bolsheviks to a militant solidarity with comrades abroad, and their willingness, spurred on by a belief in the imminent collapse of hostile regimes, to support revolution in other states. At the moment of coming to power in October 1917 the Bolshevik leadership was convinced that it was both possible and obligatory for the revolutionary regime to do all it could to promote revolution on a world scale. On the very first day of power, October 24, a declaration of peace was made. In his *History of the Russian Revolution* Trotsky gives a dramatic account of the proclamation by the Congress of the Soviet Dictatorship of 'a just, democratic peace' to the governments and people then at war:

> Listen, nations! The revolution offers you peace, it will be accused of violating treaties, but of this it is proud. To break up the leagues of bloody predation is the greatest historic service. The Bolsheviks have dared to do it. They alone have dared. Pride surges up of its own accord. Eyes shine. All are on their feet. No one is smoking now. It seems as though no one breathes. The president, the delegates, the guests, the sentries, join in a hymn of insurrection and brotherhood. . . Everyone felt greater and more important in that hour. The heart of the revolution enlarged to the width of the whole world.[26]

The years after 1917 were ones in which, to a degree seen in no other revolution, the leaders of the new regime exerted themselves in promoting revolution abroad. They believed *both* that revolution elsewhere, in the aftermath of the war, was inevitable, *and* that if no revolution elsewhere occurred they would themselves be doomed. 'There are only two alternatives; either the Russian Revolution will create a revolutionary movement in Europe, or the European powers will destroy the Russian Revolution!', Trotsky declared on the very aftermath of the seizure of power.[27] In 1919 the Bolsheviks established the Third (Communist) International, the organisation that was to coordinate a world revolutionary struggle. In a manner seen at the time as inseparable from the consolidation of power at home, not least in the face of an Allied invasion in support of the White counter-revolutionaries, Lenin and his associates committed themselves to the realisation of their internationalist agenda.

The Bolshevik 'export of revolution' was not conceived of primarily in military terms, but it had a military component. The seizure of power in Petrograd had, of course, been through armed insurrection: this was to be part of the model of revolution that the Comintern promoted, in a dogmatic attempt to make the particular experience of the Russian revolution a model for all others. In 1928 the Comintern was, indeed, to produce a handbook on how such insurrections were to be conducted, making armed insurrection an 'inexorable necessity' for the proletarian movement.[28] Later the NKVD (People's Commissariat for Internal Affairs) produced a set of instructions on the conduct of guerrilla war, based in part on the Soviet experience in the Spanish civil war.[29] But following the example of the French revolution, there also emerged a theory of how the revolutionary state itself could assist in the promotion of revolution abroad. In the period 1920–1 the Red Army, in cases linked to the fight against intervention and counter-revolution, did send its forces into three countries – Poland, Iran and Mongolia. In the last of these a Soviet client state was indeed established: it was presented as a beacon for the Asian revolution as a whole but was in fact so remote from other countries that it had no impact whatsoever. In Iran a revolutionary republic was temporarily sustained in the northern province of Gilan: but it was abandoned after the Bolsheviks sought an accommodation with Tehran.[30] The Bolshevik representative Blumkin allegedly received a telegram from Moscow with the instructions 'Cut your losses, revolution in Iran now off'.[31] In the summer of 1920 Lenin, along with all the other members of the Bolshevik leadership, supported armed action against Poland, believing on the one hand that they were justified in so doing because of the support by Poland for the counter-revolution inside Russia, and on the other that a revolutionary movement existed inside Poland which, if properly used, could take the Bolshevik forces to the heart of Europe:

> Here stood the basic question of a defensive or an offensive war, and we in the Central Committee knew that this was a new, fundamental question, that we stood at a turning point of the whole policy of Soviet power. . . We faced a new task. The defensive period of the war with worldwide imperialism was over, and we could, and had the obligation to exploit the military situation to launch an offensive war. We had defeated them when they advanced against us; we would now try to advance against them in order to assist the sovietization of Poland. . . we said among ourselves that we must probe with bayonets whether the social revolution of the proletariat in Poland had ripened.[32]

In the event, Bolshevik forces were defeated in the Battle of the Vistula, 14–17 August 1920.[33] After that defeat Lenin and Trotsky reaffirmed their belief that no such export was possible.[34] Yet, as Isaac Deutscher writes:

> the 'error' was neither fortuitous nor inconsequential. It had its origin in the Bolshevik horror of isolation in the world, a horror shared by all leaders of the party but affecting their actions differently. The march on Warsaw had been a desperate attempt to break out of that isolation. Although it had failed it was to have a deep influence on the party's outlook. The idea of revolution by conquest had been injected into the Bolshevik mind; and it went on to ferment and fester. Some Bolsheviks, reflecting on the experience, naturally reached the conclusion that it was not the attempt itself to carry revolution abroad by forces of arms but merely its failure that was deplorable.[35]

In the aftermath of the Polish campaign, the military commander Tukhachevsky developed in 1921 a theory of the 'offensive revolutionary war', according to which the Russian revolution should have in preparation an expeditionary corps designed to assist insurrectionaries in other countries. Explicitly revising Marx's view, elaborated in the *Manifesto* that the working class must take power in its own country, Tukhachevsky argued that revolutionary struggle becomes international and that, therefore, external assistance to help is possible and legitimate:

> Thus, from the moment of insurrection, the proletariat joins battle not only with its own bourgeoisie, but also – unequally matched – with the bourgeoisie of the entire world. Thus, as it develops, the struggle between the working class and the bourgeois class ceases to be purely a domestic one, and becomes an international war in which the proletariat cannot restrict itself to a passive role. An attack by a working-class revolutionary army over the boundaries of a neighbouring bourgeois State can overthrow the power of the bourgeoisie there, and transfer dictatorship into the hands of the proletariat.
>
> In general, the seizure of power in a bourgeois country can take place in two ways; firstly by means of a revolutionary uprising of the working class within that country, and secondly by means of armed action on the part of a neighbouring proletarian State. The aim in both these cases is identical – to bring about a socialist revolution. That is why, naturally, they should be considered of equal value, for the workers of all countries.[36]

Tukhachevsky developed this theory in the wake of the defeat of a major attempt by the Bolsheviks to implement such a policy. Nonetheless, the history of the next sixty years and more, i.e. from the defeat in Poland in August 1920 to the advent of non-communists to power in that same country in June 1989, was to represent not the abandonment of this commitment, but a reformulation. On the organisational side, the Soviet Union continued for decades to support the Communist International as an instrument for the promotion of fraternal parties across the world. Even when the Comintern was dissolved Moscow continued to support, and to seek to control, the international communist movement. It committed large amounts of money to this venture and despatched advisers and agents across the world to further the Comintern's goals. The Comintern itself held seven international congresses, the last in 1935, and was, until the Second World War, a major factor in the politics of many European states and those of China and much of the colonial world. Although the Comintern was dissolved in 1943 in a move by Stalin designed to appease his British and US allies, Moscow retained control of the international communist movement as a whole, up to the moment of the split with China in 1963. Even thereafter, right up until the 1980s, the USSR retained control of a significant part of the communist movement. Only this can explain why, as late as 1988, ninety communist parties were summoned to Prague by the International Department of the Communist Party of the Soviet Union (CPSU).

There are two reasons for questioning how far this policy did, in reality, involve the export of revolution. The first is the historical record: in no country during the life of its existence, i.e. up to 1943, did a party member of the Comintern come to power. The second objection is one of political assessment: as argued by Trotsky and his followers, the Comintern was not an instrument for promoting revolution, so much as an instrument for containing it. The answer to both points is that the failure of parties to come to power did not necessarily mean that Moscow tried to prevent them from so doing: be it in Britain in 1926, in China in 1927, in Germany in 1933, in Spain in 1936–9, communist parties sought, and failed, to challenge regimes. Elsewhere it was not the conciliatory character of Stalinism that cost communism so dear, but rather its unwarranted sectarianism. Nowhere was this more true than in the Germany of the early 1930s where the division between communists and socialists facilitated the triumph of fascism.

When seen in a longer-term perspective, moreover, the record is more mixed. Like the French revolution, the Russian had more impact in the longer run, after the initial revolution itself had subsided. In his 1947 article 'The Sources of Soviet Power' George Kennan was to draw an analogy between revolutions and the merchant family in Thomas Mann's novel *Buddenbrooks*: it was when the family was already in decay within that its external influence appeared the greatest. For it was in the aftermath of the dissolution of the Comintern that, in the context of the very world war that had led to the Third International's dissolution, communist parties *did* come to power – be it through the intervention of the Red Army in Eastern Europe and the Far East, or through their own bids for power, in an international context where, as a result of the Second World War, the controls of former rulers, indigenous or colonial, had been weakened. In Europe the former comprised six 'People's Democracies' (Poland, Hungary, East Germany, Bulgaria, Rumania, Czechoslovakia), the latter Yugoslavia and Albania. In the Far East the aftermath of war led to the creation of one further

regime by Soviet occupation, North Korea, and, following protracted conflicts precipitated by the war and its outcome, to the
revolutions in China and Vietnam. Later communist regimes were
established through guerrilla war in Laos and Cambodia, through a
military coup in Afghanistan, and through the adoption by a radical
nationalist regime of Soviet models in Cuba. By 1982, at the death
of Brezhnev, there were eighteen communist states in the world.
None had been created through the export of revolution as envisaged by Tukhachevsky. All had, however, been created as a
result of the 1917 revolution and its impact on world affairs. The
Comintern and its successors, formal and informal, could therefore
claim to have played a significant role in promoting the spread of
revolutionary regimes across the world.[37]

The record of the use of state power proved also to be a mixed
one. Tukhachevsky's vision had involved a purposive use of Soviet
military power for the extension of the Bolshevik model: this was to
prove both more successful and ultimately catastrophic than might
have appeared possible in the light of the Polish events of 1920. The
stalemate of the 1920s and 1930s, when the expansion of communist
revolution appeared contained by the isolation of the USSR, was
broken by the Second World War. From the turning back of the
Nazi armies in 1942–3 it became possible to envisage, on a scale
indeed far beyond what Tukhachevsky had conceived, the use of the
Soviet armed forces to create allied regimes. This is what occurred
in the latter stages of world war: the result of these conquests was,
as we have seen, the creation of seven client states and the facilita-
tion of four others.

By the late 1940s the isolation and psychological defensiveness of
the Soviet Union had been broken. In the three decades that
followed, Moscow continued to use its military might to encourage
and, when established, protect allied regimes around the world. This
took the form of massive arms supplies to China and Vietnam in the
1950s, to Cuba and Vietnam in the 1960s, and to Angola and
Mozambique in the 1970s. The Cuban and Vietnam commitments
above all represented major involvements of equipment and personnel, and imposed a high cost on the USSR as far as relations
with the USA were concerned: the former, a running sore in US–
Soviet relations for thirty years, led to the brink of nuclear war in
1962; the latter occasioned the despatch of over half a million US
forces, and the death of over 57,000. These commitments were
neither casual nor trivial, but reflected an underlying ideological

commitment. Finally, following the seizure of power by the People's Democratic Party of Afghanistan in April 1978, Moscow, first through weapons and then through the despatch of forces in December 1979, sought to protect this ally from being overthrown by Islamist counter-revolutionaries.

Soviet policy throughout this period was marked by proclamations of innocence and non-involvement in other conflicts. Until the despatch of forces to Afghanistan it was claimed that Soviet forces had not been involved in combat in the Third World. But even leaving aside the significance of the very large military supplies, credit and training provided, this was simply false. As was to emerge after the end of the Cold War, Soviet military personnel had participated directly in combat in no less than nineteen states in the period since 1945: a hitherto unknown International Association of Internationalist Fighters was disclosed to the public.[38] Albeit tempered by the desire to avoid world war, by calculations of state interest and by the circumstances of the time, all of this can be seen as derived from the initial Bolshevik commitment to promote revolutionary victories or, in the event of their occurring, to defend allied regimes from attack.

The results of their internationalism were, in the short run, such as to confirm the confidence of the Soviet leadership in their global aspirations, and to pose a serious challenge to the West. Of all the leaders it was not Lenin, or Stalin, or the extravagant Khrushchev, but the apparently cautious Brezhnev who, long after the entropy of revolutionary sentiment at home, did most to challenge Western hegemony, and cause concern in Western capitals. This was, however, achieved not only at a price but with results that were, in the end, to undermine the Bolshevik revolution itself. While their impact was exaggerated by some, there is no doubt that the costs of the arms race with the USA, in both nuclear and conventional fields, played some part in lessening the growth of the Soviet economy and hastening the collapse of the late 1980s. More obviously, the commitments in Eastern Europe and Afghanistan proved unsustainable in the face of opposition within, and Western pressure without. The turning point came in 1987–8 when in separate, but ultimately convergent, announcements Gorbachev announced that Soviet forces would no longer be used to sustain regimes in the Warsaw Pact countries and in Afghanistan: the announcement of the former, at the UN in December 1988, was followed by the completion of the latter, in February 1989.

Not only did this change in Soviet foreign policy represent a strategic reverse, but it also hastened the process of dissolution *within* the USSR itself. A CPSU that could not retain its forward positions in Berlin and Kabul lacked authority to contain ethnic and political opposition forces within the USSR; a party leadership that abandoned one of the central legitimations of the whole regime, the 'gains' of the Great Patriotic War of 1941–5, was less able to command respect at home. Most poignant of all was Afghanistan. The direct costs of the war, in human lives and economic investment, could have been contained, as the USA had contained the costs of Vietnam; but by refuting the central historical claim of the Bolsheviks, that history was moving inexorably towards a progressive, communist future, the Afghan adventure dealt a serious ideological blow to the Soviet leadership, and this, amongst several other factors, contributed to the final collapse.[39] It was, therefore, this very commitment, a persistent even if warped continuation of Bolshevik internationalism, which was to do so much to weaken the Soviet Union itself. Gorbachev and his advisers spent much time after he came to power in 1985 questioning the concept of 'internationalist duty'. In this sense the argument of the left critics of Soviet policy is the reverse of the truth: it was not that the USSR did so little, but that, for all the constraints, and the apparent prejudice to state interests involved, it did so much that it was forced into a defensive and ultimately self-destructive path.

China: The Dialectics of 'Anti-Hegemonism'

At first sight there could be no greater contrast between the records of the two great communist powers, the USSR and China, on the issue of export of revolution. For the first eleven years of the post-revolutionary period China was formally allied with the USSR: it pursued no independent policy vis-à-vis other communist parties. Whether in war, as in Korea in 1950–3, or in diplomacy, as in its participation in the Geneva conference on Indo-China in 1954, China, while articulating independent emphases, did not contradict the overall line of Soviet policy. With the Sino-Soviet dispute of 1960–3 – initially a public exchange of polemics about the 'general line' of the communist movement, then a complete breach between Moscow and Peking – China espoused a line of independence for all communist parties, rejecting any claim of the USSR to be the centre of a world movement. As early as November 1960 China was putting forward qualifications about internationalism and the export of revolution:

> Marxist-Leninists have always held that revolution cannot be imported, nor can it be exported. To say that revolution can be imported or exported is entirely wrong. Precisely this is the slander the imperialists and reactionaries in various countries hurl against the people's revolution in any country, but such slanders can in no way check the advance of the revolutionary movement in any country or prevent the rise of revolution in any country.
>
> The socialist revolution cannot triumph at a single stroke in all countries of the world simultaneously. It will come, separately and gradually as a result of the inherent factors of society in the various countries and the political awakening of the people themselves, their own efforts and their preparations for revolution.[40]

After the break with Moscow, China never sought in a sustained way to organise an international following of any kind, or even regular gatherings in Peking of like-minded 'anti-revisionist' communist parties. They did try to rally support from other Third World states through their membership in the Afro-Asian People's Solidarity Organisation (AAPSO), a body founded by the Bandung Conference in 1955 and based in Cairo. In the period leading up to a tenth anniversary conference of AAPSO heads of state, planned for Algiers in June 1965, China made particular efforts to rally support. However, the Algiers conference was cancelled following a military coup against President Ben Bella, and subsequent divisions within the organising committee. Chinese interest in AAPSO waned thereafter, as Egypt, which controlled the movement, sought to align it behind a more pro-Soviet policy.[41] Other communist parties, or factions therein, did follow China's line, espousing the thoughts of Mao Tse-tung and repeating China's current line on world affairs: but these acted very much in an individual way, paying an ideological tribute to Beijing. With the exception of Albania, from 1961 to 1980, and of a handful of parties around the world, there was not, even in this minimal sense, a 'movement' of pro-Chinese parties.[42] For China, secure in its demographic and strategic position, the absence of an organised revolutionary following was not a matter of life and death, as the Bolsheviks had believed it was for them in 1919. Instead, Peking resorted to broad appeals to the peoples of the world, thus circumventing the need to work in a systematic way with communist parties, even as it went beyond these parties to form alliances with states and nationalist movements.

The ideological reasons why China did not found a 'Fifth International' might appear evident enough: on the one hand, China based its revolutionary legitimacy, in contrast to Moscow, on non-interference in the affairs of other parties; on the other, there were simply not enough parties, let along ruling parties, to comprise a credible pro-Chinese bloc. Confident in its own self-sufficiency, and scarred by decades of Soviet interference before and after 1949, China therefore seemed to avoid the temptations of promoting revolution abroad. In addition to these general considerations, it would seem plausible that at the moment when China might have created such an organisation events conspired to frustrate this. In the late 1940s there were signs that some in the Chinese leadership were concerned to organise an Asian communist movement, possibly on the lines of the European Cominform: China would have had the leading role, as the USSR did in Europe. Moscow had set up the new communist international, the Cominform, one that encompassed only European parties and thereby appeared to downgrade the importance of the former Asian components of the Comintern.[43] A conference of trades unions in Shanghai in 1949 may have been intended to further this; but Soviet opposition and the belief of Mao Tse-tung that nothing should be done to challenge the Soviet leadership appear to have prevented these plans from proceeding.

In the mid-1960s when China did break from Moscow other developments strengthened China's reluctance to proceed along this course. On the one hand, the destruction of its close ally, the PKI, the Communist Party of Indonesia, in the months after September 1965, robbed it of its greatest ally in Asia. On the other, China was plunged from mid-1965 onwards into the vortex of the Cultural Revolution, an event that preoccupied and divided the Chinese leadership for four years at least and precluded any effective engagement with the outside world.[44]

During this Cultural Revolution period factional and interpersonal issues played a key role within Chinese leadership politics: the defeat of the PKI was used as one of the issues with which to castigate inner-party opponents, notably President Liu Shao-chi and Mayor of Peking Peng Chen. Mao had little in his background to give him an internationalist orientation comparable to the Bolsheviks or Latin American revolutionaries. He had never been outside China until his visit to Stalin in 1950, and in his writings and statements showed no detailed knowledge of, or interest in, developments outside China. Never greatly concerned with international affairs, beyond airy evocations of the general direction of world struggle and lofty acknowledgements of the respect the peoples of the world felt for him, Mao launched a Cultural Revolution that in effect severed China's relations, diplomatic and otherwise, with the outside world. The not-so-militant foreign minister Chen Yi provoked the anger of the Red Guards for casting doubt on the international relevance of Mao's thoughts, but what he said reflected what the leadership as a whole seemed to think: 'These thoughts of Mao Tse-tung are really a Chinese product, we mustn't take them abroad.'[45]

These limitations notwithstanding, there can be no dispute that in the first three decades after the Chinese revolution of 1949 it did, systematically and consciously, seek to promote and sustain revolution abroad, even while distancing itself from the 'hegemonist', later 'social-imperialist', policies of the USSR. As discussed in Chapter 3, China espoused a world-view, in which revolution and nationalist struggle had a central part. In the 1950s this was muted, contained by the relationship with the USSR. As the latter eroded China took up a more and more combative stance. In direct opposition to the Soviet Union, China gave the appearance of denying the need to temper revolutionary rhetoric or strategy because of nuclear weapons. At the same time, China made a series of statements encouraging revolutionary movements. In December 1963, in a speech to the cadres of the Algerian National Liberation Front, foreign minister Chou En-lai had hailed the prospects for revolution in Asia, Africa and Latin America. Revolution was 'a powerful tide of history that no reactionary force on earth could resist'.[46] Early in 1964 while in Somalia, continuing a ten-state tour of Africa, Chou En-lai declared 'Revolutionary prospects are excellent throughout the continent.'[47] In 1965 there followed the appeal by Lin Piao for a people's war to encircle the cities of the world. It was only in the early 1970s when, maintaining its opposition to Moscow but seeking to find a rapprochement with the USA, China began to back away from support for revolutions abroad: its support in 1971 for the Sri Lankan suppression of an armed insurrection, and for the Pakistani attempt to crush the nationalist movement in Bengal, marked a turning point in reputation, if not policy. There followed a series of situations in which China in effect sought to endorse not revolution, but counter-revolution: its backing of right-wing guerrillas in Angola, and later Afghanistan, and its support for the military coup in Chile in 1973 were the culmination of this shift. Days before the right-wing coup that overthrew the Popular Unity government in Chile the Chinese ambassador was warning the Chilean foreign minister Almeida of the dangers of a *pro-Soviet* coup.[48] The dramatic nature of these changes only served to underline, however, the degree to which, in the previous decade above all, China had acted to use its state power to further revolutionary movements abroad.

In the first place, China used its military power to assist revolutionary forces in neighbouring states Korea and Vietnam. China's role in the *outbreak* of the Korean war, in June 1950, may be a matter of dispute, but it would seem incontrovertible that China, like Russia, was informed in advance of Kim Il-sung's plan to invade the South and gave at least implicit support to it. Quite indisputable is the role China played once the war had begun and, in particular, had started to turn against its North Korean allies: in November 1950 an estimated 900,000 Chinese troops entered the war, pushing American forces back from near the Sino-Korean frontier on the Yalu river to the starting point of the war, the 38th parallel. This large-scale, decisive and costly intervention saved the North Korean regime and contributed to the return to the *status quo ante* in 1953. On its southern frontier, in Vietnam, China did not intervene directly: but throughout the years from 1949, when communist Chinese forces were established on their side of the frontier, the Vietnamese communists benefited from the assistance China gave, not only in terms of supplies but also in terms of deterring a direct US attack on the North. On the other hand, China's direct military role was confined to the Far Eastern region. Unlike the USSR it could not offer serious defence commitments or supplies to Third World states elsewhere. But in the 1960s above all, this did not stop China from supplying arms in significant quantities to states and movements around the world. Thus in the Middle East it gave arms to South Yemen, and arms and training to guerrilla movements in Oman, Eritrea and among the Palestinians. In Africa it armed opposition groups in South Africa, Zaire and Angola.

As far as intra-party relations were concerned, China sought throughout the 1960s, as much as did the USSR, to cultivate sympathetic leaders in neighbouring states. While it never swung the entire regime behind Peking, as it was to do in Albania between 1961 and 1978, it did exert enough pressure on Vietnam to prevent Moscow from establishing its dominion, as Moscow had in the Mongolian People's Republic. Elsewhere in South East Asia, the Chinese had an impact both successful and catastrophic. In Indonesia they were able to dominate the PKI until its elimination in late 1965, ironically after that party had pursued collaboration with the nationalist forces akin to the disastrous line which Stalin had imposed on the Chinese party in 1927. In Cambodia, China developed close relations with the Khmer Rouge who came to power on the back of the Vietnamese victory in 1975, only to be ousted four years later by Hanoi's invasion. On its south-western frontier, with India, another curious outcome was to occur: China's defeat of India in the 1962 border war did not consolidate Indian communism behind Moscow, but was followed by a three-way split, into pro-Soviet, pro-Chinese and independent groupings.

The costs for China of this internationalist policy were in most respects much less than for the USSR. China did not seek to compete with either Moscow or Washington in the strategic field, nor did it noticeably distort its domestic economy in an arms race. When it did find a rapprochement with the USA, after 1972, this in no way impeded the continued modernisation of its armed forces, including its nuclear weapons. China did suffer losses when it sought to use military force to 'punish' Vietnam, for its invasion of Cambodia, in early 1979, but it had no commitments comparable to those of the USSR in Eastern Europe or Afghanistan. Yet in certain other respects it also faced a crisis of internationalism which contributed to the change of its internal system, in a way different from, but potentially convergent with, the USSR. The greatest cost of Chinese radicalism in the 1960s was paid internally, in the ravages of the Great Leap Forward of 1958–61 and the Cultural Revolution of 1965–9: in both cases China suffered greatly not only by the extremism and impracticality of the policies, but also by the way it associated these policies at home with rhetorical and often self-defeating militancy abroad. The later swing to the right, after 1972, culminating in the Four Modernisations of 1978 and the opening of China to foreign capital, reflected a failure not only of the domestic radicalism but also of the policy of confrontation with the outside world, above all the Soviet Union *and* the USA simultaneously. It was ironic indeed that the country which had most vigorously pursued the concept of 'self-reliance' now opened its door to foreign investment even as it pursued a strategic alliance with the leading representative of the 'imperialist camp'.

Cuba: The Tricontinental

The Cuban revolutionaries who came to power in January 1959 were, as much as any others in modern history, imbued with a sense of their international mission. They were faced on the one side by a hostile United States, which in one form or another had sought to dominate Cuba from the 1890s. On the other hand, they were familiar with the lessons of their fellow revolutionaries in Latin America – inspired by the Mexican revolution of 1910, enraged by the overthrow of the Arbenz reformist government in Guatemala in 1954, and inheritors of the more radical legacy of the liberal and masonic traditions of the nineteenth-century independence and anti-oligarchic movements. The figure of the Latin American internationalist, the fighter who wanders from country to country supporting radical causes, is familiar not just from history but also from literature.[49] There were those within the Cuban revolutionary leadership who from the start were conscious of this dimension of the revolution: Fidel Castro's involvement with Latin American radical movements went back to the late 1940s; Che Guevara had been in Guatemala when the CIA overthrew Arbenz in 1954. Any uncertainties Castro and his associates might have had about this internationalist, and Latin American, dimension were dispelled in the first three years of their regime as the crisis with the USA worsened.

The turning point, and the commencement of Cuba's internationalist action, was Fidel Castro's speech of 4 February 1962, officially termed *The Second Declaration of Havana*. Ostensibly a reply to the expulsion of Cuba from the Organisation of Latin American states, it was also directed at the – for Cuba – equivocal stance of the Soviet leadership, then concerned to develop a policy of 'peaceful coexistence' with the West. After reviewing the history and character of imperialist exploitation of the Third World, and particularly Latin America, Castro turned to the two themes that were to dominate Cuba's external policy in the coming decades: the need to *make* revolution, and the *common struggle* of all Latin American peoples:

> The duty of every revolutionary is to make the revolution. It is known that the revolution will triumph in America and through-out the world, but it is not for revolutionaries to sit in the doorways of their houses waiting for the corpse of imperialism to pass by. The role of Job doesn't fit a revolutionary. Each year that the liberation of America is speeded up will mean the lives of millions of children saved, millions of intelligences saved for culture, an infinite quantity of pain spared the people. Even if the Yankee imperialists prepare a bloody drama for America, they will not succeed in crushing the peoples' struggles, they will only arouse universal hatred against themselves. Any such drama will also mark the death of their greedy and carnivorous system.
>
> No nation in Latin America is weak – because each forms part of a family of 200 million brothers, who suffer the same miseries, who harbour the same sentiments, who have the same energy, who dream about the same better future and who count upon the solidarity of all honest men and women throughout the world.
>
> Great as was the epic of Latin American Independence, heroic as was that struggle, today's generation of Latin Americans is called up to engage in an epic which is even greater and more decisive for humanity.[50]

Events following the *Second Declaration* were to confirm the Cuban leadership in their commitment to support Latin American and broader Third World revolution. Cuba developed a strategy term, *Defensa Revolucionaria Activa*, 'active revolutionary defense': this meant responding to US attacks by internationalising the struggle, supporting guerrilla movements in Latin America and preparing for covert operations in the USA itself. On the one hand, relations with the USA deteriorated further, leading in October 1962 to the missile crisis. On the other hand, Cuba was caught up in the vortex of disputes in the communist world, attracted to China yet unable to form an alliance with it, repelled by and critical of Moscow but bound to it for reasons of military and economic security. Cuba thus sought, within the constraints of these two global powers, to pursue its own independent revolutionary path, at once to strengthen defiance of the USA and to challenge Moscow's commitment to peaceful coexistence and a peaceful road to socialism.

The zenith of this commitment came in the middle 1960s. In January 1966 the Tricontinental Conference, attended by 512 delegates from eighty-two countries, met in Havana to found OSPAAAL.[51] This had been inspired by the Moroccan revolutionary Mehdi Ben Barka, who had been abducted in the centre of Paris and murdered the previous October. In August 1967 there convened the conference of the Latin American Solidarity Organisation, attended by five thousand delegates from Cuba and other Latin American countries. The general themes of both conferences were the same – the predatory and aggressive nature of American imperialism, the common condition of all Latin Americans, the impossibility of a peaceful transition to socialism, the role of guerrilla struggle. The slogan of the OLAS conference was 'The history of Cuba is the history of all Latin America', displayed beneath portraits of Simón Bolívar, Maximo Gómez, José Martí and Che Guevara.[52]

OSPAAAL and OLAS were also occasions for Cuba to present itself both as a model of revolution for other countries to learn from, and as the source of aid. This latter commitment was spelt out by Castro in his closing speech to the Tricontinental Conference when he promised unconditional aid 'to any revolutionary movement in any part of the world'.[53] The final declaration asserted:

In the face of the growing struggle of the oppressed peoples to shake off the yoke of imperialist exploitation, the imperialists, especially the North Americans, use the incredibly cynical argument that this fight constitutes a foreign aggression, when it is their own bloody repression that brings on a brutal armed intervention against the rights of peoples to independence and social progress. . .

In opposition to this arbitrary norm of international conduct announced and carried out by imperialism, the conference must proclaim and carry out the right of each subjected country to solidarity; the right and the duty of all countries to assist by all means within their power those peoples who are fighting for their national liberation in every corner of the world. . .

The drawing together of the revolutionary movement of Asia and Africa has proven its extraordinary value, surpassing the test of time, surpassing barriers and difficulties, to emerge as a force which not only represents a contemporary historic reality, but is able to grow and join the revolutionary forces of Latin America to make possible the creation of what may one day be one of the greatest historic movements of the world.[54]

At OLAS the Cubans distributed a 159-page report or *Informe*. Beginning with an invocation of the battle of Carabobo of June 1821 in which Bolívar's forces confronted the Spanish, it laid out the Cuban revolutionary line, distinct from both the Soviet and Chinese variants.[55] In 1976, when a new Cuban constitution was finally promulgated, a commitment to the principles of proletarian internationalism and of the combative solidarity of peoples was formally included in Article 12.

What, in practice, did all this amount to? The international revolutionary organisations themselves that Cuba founded amounted to little: within two years of the OSPAAAL conference in 1966, its public face was reduced to one office in Havana, a journal, and some official representatives from other countries.[56] Neither OSPAAAL nor OLAS ever convened again. But, as with the Comintern, OSPAAAL and OLAS had a later life more effective than the organisations themselves. In the course of the ensuing two decades individual organisations represented there were to take power through victory in guerrilla war – in South Yemen (1967), the former Portuguese colonies of Africa (1974–5), Vietnam, Cambodia and Laos (1975), Nicaragua (1979), Zimbabwe (1980) and, much later, South Africa (1994) and Palestine (1994). Cuba's own commitment also came to mean a great deal. From the triumph of the Cuban revolution in 1959, revolutionaries from Latin America, and countries from all over the world, came to visit, participate, discuss with Cuban officials. It was not therefore difficult for the Cuban government to begin organising an international network of support: political in some cases, intelligence in others, and, in regard to certain kindred organisations, military.

Cuba did not create the Latin American guerrilla movement, but from the early 1960s onwards it sought to control and assist it, in pursuit of revolutionary goals. The key person in this internationalist effort was the Deputy Minister of the Interior, in charge of intelligence operations, Manuel Piñeiro, also known as Barbaroja, 'Red Beard'. Based in the early years in the Ministry of the Interior, his Dirección General de Inteligencia was responsible for internal security, and also for training Latin American guerrillas.[57] In 1974, following an agreement between Cuba and the Soviet Union on relations with the Latin American communist parties, Piñeiro left the Ministry of the Interior to head the America Department of the Central Committee of the Communist Party, a position he held until March 1992. Responsibility for contacts with the Latin American left, and for training guerrillas at the Nico López Political School, was now shared with the Departamento de Operaciones Especiales (DOE), another branch of the Ministry of the Interior.

Piñeiro's task was to train and coordinate the activities of Latin American guerrilla groups: he was the organiser of *Defensa Revolucionaria Activa*. The first operations were carried out in 1962, in Argentina and Venezuela, and in the years that followed, Cuba was in one form or another to back guerrillas in almost every Latin American country, except Mexico. The fortunes of guerrilla struggle appeared to decline in 1967, following the death of Che Guevara in Bolivia, and the success in democratic elections of Cuba's ally Salvador Allende in Chile three years later. But the 1970s and 1980s brought a revival of such internationalist activity: Allende's overthrow in September 1973 scotched hopes of a peaceful path, and, in 1979, a guerrilla movement armed, trained and inspired by Cuba came to power in Nicaragua. The Sandinistas had received Cuban support ever since their establishment in 1961; their final military push in 1977–9 owed much to Cuban arms supplied via Panama and the Costa Rican town of Liberia. At least 500 tons of arms were supplied by Cuba to the Sandinistas; Cuban special forces from the DOE accompanied the Sandinistas, and were in direct radio communication with Havana. One of Piñeiro's men, Fernando Comás, the Cuban consul in the Costa Rican capital San José, was on the tarmac at Managua airport on the day the Sandinistas arrived, armed with an M-16 rifle. Following the victory in Nicaragua, the Sandinistas, and Cuban advisers, proceeded to increase their support for guerrilla movements elsewhere in Central America, in El Salvador and Guatemala. The Sandinista victory, and the broader Central American war that followed, were arguably the most successful and intense period of Cuba's militant internationalism in Latin America since 1959.[58]

Support for guerrillas in this form, carried out from a small island off the coast of the USA, represented an extraordinary logistical and political feat. Yet Cuba's internationalist actions in pursuit of Third World solidarity went beyond the actions of Piñeiro in two major respects. One was the most famous of all Cuba's Third World guerrilla initiatives, the despatch of Che Guevara and a group of Cuban guerrilla personnel to Bolivia, with the aim of first weakening the regime there and then spreading the revolutionary movement to other parts of Latin America. The Guevara mission was not, it would seem, carried out by the Ministry of the Interior but by a separate apparatus controlled by Castro. Its aim was, as Castro told the Cuban personnel before they were despatched, to overstretch the USA and in so doing to fend off pressure on Cuba itself. In the words of one of those present:

> Fidel brought us a historical and military explanation of what we represented: from where we had come, at what social and other level we found ourselves. It was at one and the same time a work of consciousness raising and an evaluation. He explained to us the need to prepare ourselves with great force and determination, for if Cuba had to spend ten thousand dollars to create a fighter like one of us, it cost imperialism more than a hundred thousand to destroy him. . .
>
> In carrying the struggle to Latin America, we would also have the effect that imperialism, which at that moment was concentrating all its efforts against Cuba, would immediately release 50% of the pressure exercised on that country and relocate it towards South America. That would benefit the island, would give us the possibility of bringing our teachers back to the classroom, and our workers to the factories.[59]

Such was the logic of *Defensa Revolucionaria Activa*. It was a highrisk, carefully planned and in the end fatal venture, one that not only resulted in the death of Guevara and many of his associates, but also marked the ebbing of the first tide of Latin American guerrilla revolution.

The other dimension of Cuba's internationalist activities was not guerrilla war, and not in Latin America, but the despatch of regular forces to support allied regimes in Africa: first, in support of Algeria, in its border war with Morocco in 1963, then in Angola in 1975 and Ethiopia in 1977. In Angola the aim was to back the MPLA (Popular Movement for the Liberation of Angola) against rival Angolan factions, supported by the CIA, Zaire, China and South Africa,[60] in Ethiopia to defend the revolutionary military regime of Mengistu Haile-Mariam against a Somali invasion,

carried out with some Arab support and at least tacit US backing.[61]
The defeat of South African forces at Cuito Canavale in 1986 was
perhaps the most signal achievement in Cuba's military record
abroad. Even more than the support for guerrilla activity in Latin
America, these military expeditions to Africa had been a striking
achievement for Cuba which gambled, successfully, on US paralysis
at a time when the fall of Saigon was fresh in the minds of US
Congress and President alike. It is said that when taking the
decision on whether or not to send troops to Angola, Castro asked
his advisers for a prediction of how each member of the US
Congress would vote if faced with the question of an American
response.

This record of more than thirty years of commitment, from 1962
to 1992, ranks as one of the most extraordinary and sustained
engagements by any state to the export of revolution.[62] Cuba not
only inspired radicals in much of the world, well beyond Latin and
North America, but amidst pressure from Washington and Moscow
alike, it exerted itself to match that verbal, ideological commitment
with actions, in the form of assistance and, in some cases, troops.
Yet no more than other states Cuba was unable, in asserting this
engagement, to abstract itself from the constraints of the international system, and of the links between that system and its own
internal development. In the first place, the internationalist commitment of Cuba was a product above all of the difficulties to which
the Cuban state itself was subjected: the launching of armed
struggles in Latin America in 1962 was a response to the attempted
US invasion of 1961. The sustained US blockade and political
support for the Miami-based opposition provided a lasting motive
for solidarity with those opposed to the USA elsewhere.

At the same time, the ideological tone of Cuba's statements and
its fraught relations with other Latin American revolutionaries, and
with China, reflected the entrapping necessity of Cuba's relations
with the USSR. No history of the Cuban revolution can omit the
impact in the 1960s of the tectonic conflict between the two leading
communist states, not least in the ways in which it repeatedly
affected disputes over policy and leadership conflicts within Cuba
itself. The internationalist commitment of Cuba was designed to
augment Cuba's independence *vis-à-vis both* the USA *and* the
USSR.

The balance sheet of Cuba's efforts also reflects the realities of
international relations and the limits of Cuba's power. In Latin

America it did assist numerous guerrilla movements, but for twenty years none came to power. When one did, in Nicaragua, it found itself embroiled in a war with the USA more destructive than even that to which Cuba had been exposed, and which, ultimately, in the elections of November 1990 that removed the Sandinista National Liberation Front (FSLN) from power, engulfed it.[63] In Cuba's case we can chart that slippage, seen in other cases, through the dimensions of internationalism: what was, in earlier moments, utopian or principled, became, in the hands of a beleaguered state, instrumental. Many are those who argue that, idealistic as Cuba's campaigns may have been, they ultimately led large sections of the Latin American left into lethal adventures that only served to lessen the possibilities of alternative, less militaristic, political strategies.[64] The failure to balance the two forms of opposition, revolutionary and reformist, evident in the European history of Bolshevism in the 1920s and 1930s, was to replicate itself in the Latin America of the 1960s and 1970s.

The Cuban expeditions to Africa had paradoxical outcomes, as do so many internationalist ventures. The regimes in Angola and Ethiopia were, in the short run, saved by the Cuban interventions. But in the longer run the Cuban investments appeared to have brought little benefit. Mengistu's regime in Ethiopia succumbed in 1991 to another guerrilla movement, that of the the EPRDF Ethiopian People's Revolutionary Democractic Front (a far left movement inspired by Mao and Enver Hoxha and paradoxically adopted by Washington), while the Angolan regime, forced into compromises with the UNITA (National Union for the Total Independence of Angola) opposition, severed cooperation with Cuba and took to firing on Cuban fishing vessels working, under prior agreement, off the Angolan coast. Where the Cuban expedition did, however, have an impact was where it had never set foot, namely in South Africa itself. Cuba's support for the MPLA enabled that regime to survive, and involved the halting and, on one occasion at least, defeat of the South African army; it thus made a distinct contribution to the turning of the tide in South Africa itself. No wonder that when Nelson Mandela was inaugurated as president of South Africa in 1994 Fidel Castro should have been a particularly honoured guest, at official and popular levels, in Pretoria. Three years later, in 1997, another Cuban involvement of earlier times was to have an unexpected confirmation when the forces of Laurent Kabila, a Marxist guerrilla leader who had worked with Che Guevara in 1964, succeeded in the space of a few weeks in sweeping across Zaire and ousting the dictator of over three decades, General Mobutu.[65]

The toll of this commitment on Cuba itself was, however, enormous: money, time, personnel were expended sustaining these commitments. It is estimated that up to 4,000 Cubans died in Angola. But the very complexity of the organisational arrangements made for these external operations, and the need to preserve their clandestinity and deniability, bred within the Cuban state an element of suspicion and subterfuge that, combined with the overall bureaucratic ossification of the regime, was to cost it dearly. In the 1960s Castro had used the cause of Latin American guerrillas to attack his domestic communist opponents. In the 1980s it was the turn of those who had been involved in foreign operations, notably the war in Angola, to face charges of drug-running and illegal activities. The trial in 1987 of leading military personnel involved in such activities, Arnaldo Ochoa, and the brothers Antonio and Patricio La Guardia, marked a decisive turning point in the history of the Cuban state. The Ochoa trial represented a disingenuous victimisation of individuals who had been associated with some of the most heroic episodes of the Cuban revolution's international commitment, but were sacrificed, possibly tricked, by Fidel Castro and his associates. The wounds created by that trial, and by the winding down of the internationalist stand, were seriously to weaken the legitimacy of the regime at home, and represented a cruel rebound within Cuba of the militant policy it had pursued abroad.

Iran: Muslim Solidarity, the *Umma* and the *Mustazafin*

For all its apparent exceptionalism, the Iranian revolution of 1979 followed, in many respects, the pattern of other modern revolutions, in its domestic as in its foreign policy.[66] As discussed in Chapter 3, the Iranian revolutionaries saw themselves in an international context of two kinds – a historically constituted *Islamic* tradition, within which they were the bearers of a new revolutionary spirit, and the contemporaneously constituted *anti-imperialist* context, in which they appealed to Muslims and other 'oppressed' (*mustazafin*) to rise up against their oppressors. Consequently, in the years after coming to power, they did what other modern revolutionaries did:

issued internationalist proclamations, organised meetings and training for radicals from other states, and provided, within the constraints of resources and inter-state relations, assistance to 'strugglers' in other states. Most importantly, they became involved in a costly war with a neighbouring state, Iraq, in which they sought to promote revolution.

The ideological commitment of the revolution was clear from the beginning. Visiting Tehran in the summer of 1979 I could see the slogans proclaiming support for the struggles of fellow Muslims the world over: in Palestine, Kashmir, Tajikistan, Afghanistan, Eritrea, the Philippines. In July the Foreign Minister Ibrahim Yazdi echoed the words of his predecessors in other revolutions when he proposed 'a federation of Moslem countries'.[67] In the charged atmosphere following the seizure of the US embassy in Tehran on 5 November 1979, the leader of the revolution Ayatollah Khomeini declared:

We hope that all Muslim nations may join in this struggle between infidels and Islam. This is not a struggle between ourselves and America; it is between Islam and the infidels . . . I call on all Muslim nationals, all Muslims, all Muslim armies, all Islamic security forces and all Muslim countries' presidents to cooperate with our nation; the Muslims must rise in this struggle between infidels and Islam.[68]

The Constitution of the Islamic Republic of Iran, adopted by referendum in December 1979, lays out this internationalist approach. The preamble states that the revolution 'was a movement for the victory of all oppressed people over the arrogant', and that the Constitution 'provides the basis for trying to perpetuate this revolution both at home and abroad'. It illustrates its argument with a quote from the Koran:

This is especially so with regard to expanding international relations with other Islamic movements and people to pave the way to form the world unity of followers (Your community is one community, and I am your lord who you are to worship) and to perpetuating the struggle to save the deprived nations under tyranny throughout the world.

The Constitution proclaims in article 3 as one of its goals a foreign policy of 'brotherly commitment to all Muslims, and unsparing support to the underprivileged and oppressed peoples of the world'.[69] Article 11 restates that all Muslims belong to one community and that the Islamic government 'should exert continuous efforts in order to realize the political, economic and cultural unity of the Islamic world'. Later, in article 154, it expresses, as clearly as any other revolution, a contradictory combination of goals – noninterference and internationalist solidarity:

> The Islamic Republic of Iran considers its goal to be the happiness of human beings in all human societies. It recognises the independence, freedom and rule of right and justice for all people of the world. Therefore, while practising complete self-restraint from any kind of influence in the internal affairs of other nations, it will protect the struggles of the weak against the arrogant, in any part of the world.

After the Iranian revolution, diplomats of Iranian embassies abroad were openly to proclaim their commitment to using embassy facilities and resources to promote groups sympathetic to the Islamic revolution. This led to an explicit commitment to what was termed *sudur-i inqilab*, the 'export of revolution': the official position was that this referred only to the moral or exemplary promotion of change abroad, but, as with other revolutions, this was an equivocation, the term encompassing everything from propaganda and the provision of literature to armed assistance to groups abroad.

As with their secular predecessors, the Islamic revolutionaries did not, initially at least, conceal their goals. Ali Khamene'i, later to be Imam Khomeini's successor as spiritual leader, addressed this issue in 1981:

> our revolution has been exported to the world in spite of all the opposition the trend has encountered. . . The Imam has said: Do not say that our revolution must not be exported. . . The Imam has himself reiterated several times that the revolution's concept is the same as the soft Spring weather. It does not recognise borders and frontiers, it will go through them.[70]

The speaker of the Islamic Consultative Assembly, Rafsanjani, later to be president, declared in 1984:

The thing that no-one could conceal or have the intention of hiding is the export of Islamic revolution. The Islamic revolution does not confine its true and noble nature to geographical borders and deems the conveying of the message of revolution, which is the self-same message of Islam, as its own duty.[71]

For his part, Khomeini often repeated that in Islam there were no frontiers and no divisions. The internationalist obligation was now restated, in religious form:

We are dutybound to respond to the cries of 'O Muslims help me' from a Muslim in any corner of the world. . . By Muslims I do not mean Iranians, I mean all Muslims. He who ignores the cries of a Muslim for help, is not a Muslim. This is deviation. . .Islam did not come to serve Iran alone. Islam has come to cover the whole world. The Prophet's divine mission was for everyone and everyone should obey it.[72]

In practice, the Islamic Republic of Iran did as much as any modern revolution to spread its message abroad. It organised conferences in Tehran to which representatives of opposition Islamist groups came from a range of Muslim countries. Radio Tehran broadcast messages of support for struggling Muslims, from Algeria to Afghanistan. Within months of the revolution, Tehran was calling on the people of Iraq 'to topple the regime of tyrants in revolutionary Iraq'.[73] In terms of concrete export, four countries in particular were supported: Afghanistan, Iraq, Lebanon and Bahrain. In each of these cases Iran provided military assistance. In the case of Iraq this led to the eight-year (1980–8) war with Iraq, during which Iran hoped to use the inter-state war to promote a revolution in Iraq itself. In the case of Lebanon, Iran sent several thousand Islamic Guards, and considerable financial resources, to support the Shi'ite forces there. Iran also supported smaller groups in a range of other countries, some overtly, some less so.

In addition to prosecuting its policies through the conventional means of 'export of revolution' Iran made use of some particular mechanisms to promote international support. One was the seizure of the US embassy in Tehran in November 1979: Iran presented this as an act of defiance of the global enemy, 'world arrogance', i.e. the USA, on behalf of all oppressed peoples of the world. Secondly, the

Iranians used the *hajj* or annual Muslim pilgrimage to Mecca and Medina to transmit a political message and to appeal to struggling Muslims everywhere. Thirdly, in an assertion of transnational defiance of established legal and political norms, Ayatollah Khomeini, in February 1989, condemned to death the British writer Salman Rushdie, for his novel *The Satanic Verses*. The purpose of this action was, in part, to mobilise support amongst other Muslims and to reaffirm Iran's claim to be the leading state in the Islamic world. Like the hostages affair, it was a crisis created by Iran to project a message across the Muslim world. As with the other forms of internationalist intervention specific to the Iranian case, Iran's policy on *The Satanic Verses* combined particularly Islamic forms of political appeal with others, of the kind deployed by secular, post-revolutionary, regimes.

This internationalist commitment was, however, as was the case with other states, related to, and usually subordinated within, relations between states. First of all, the ability of Iran to play such an internationalist role was to a considerable degree determined by the opportunities provided by inter-state conflict. Its ability to push for an overthrow of the regime in neighbouring Iraq was given, primarily, by the inter-state war that broke out between the two regimes in September 1980. Iran held on even after reasonable settlement terms were offered by Iraq in July 1982, in the hope that, through pressure on the Iraqi state, it could provoke an uprising in that country. It was forced in the end, in July 1988, to accept that this, an extreme form of export of revolution, had failed, at the cost of several hundred thousand Iranians killed. In the whole annals of the export of revolution and its frustration, none was as bloody and miscalculated as that of Khomeini against Iraq over these eight years: little wonder that when he did finally accept the UN's proposals for peace he said it was worse than drinking poison. The other area of greatest Iranian involvement, Lebanon, was also made possible by the Syrian–Israeli conflict in that country, and the very weakness of the Lebanese state itself.

Secondly, although Iran continued its broad internationalist commitment, it became more selective about how and where it pursued it. While it initially supported an uprising in Bahrain, by the mid-1980s it had come to accept the regime in that country. It continued to criticise Turkish secularism, and Iranian diplomats declined to honour the grave of Kemal Ataturk, choosing instead to visit that of the mediaeval Sufi poet and saint, Jamal ad-Din Rumi, at Konya. But rhetoric and symbol aside, Iran avoided any direct involvement in Turkey's internal affairs.

Thirdly, as with other revolutions, the relative balance between internationalist militancy and diplomatic accommodation shifted: the former was not abandoned, but it was toned down. Thus in 1984 the Iranian foreign ministry set out to remove radical elements from embassies abroad. The discussion of 'export of revolution' itself was altered, to focus on political and cultural work. In one of those involutions of revolutionary internationalism within the factionalism of the state that were evident in other countries, the leader of the unit of the Revolutionary Guards responsible for military links with groups abroad, and over three dozen of his associates, were arrested and charged with corruption, subversion and counter-revolutionary activities: Hashemi himself was executed in September 1987.[74] A commitment to international militancy did, however, remain, and was to continue to foster conflict between Iran and the West, particularly the USA. Thus in the 1990s Iran was cast as one of the 'outlaw' or 'rogue' states with which the United States in particular was in confrontation.

Solidarity and its Limits

The commitment to export would therefore appear to be a recurrent feature of revolutionary states, for reasons of ideological commitment, domestic advantage and international calculation alike. Time and again revolutionary states engaged in public declamations and clandestine actions in support of radical forces abroad, often with their own leadership believing, to a far greater degree than even a sober current evaluation would suggest, that their allies elsewhere were on the brink of coming to power. From Cromwell and Tom Paine, to Lenin, Mao, Castro and Khomeini, ideological commitment was matched by voluntaristic delusion in the commitment of their states to such policies.

The outcome of such commitments has to be seen at both the internal and the international levels. For just as the commitment to exporting revolution served, in part, domestic purposes, to isolate factional rivals in the leadership, to mobilise support and silence critics amongst the population, so the actual course of such policies, akin in this regard to wars, rebounded on the domestic situation. Success abroad meant success at home. Even here, however, the costs of successful internationalism, as of wars, could be high. Failure abroad meant, however, that those most associated with the policies had to compensate: Lenin was forced into retreat after the failure of the German revolution, Stalin resorted to factional manoeuvres after his defeat in China, Mao launched the Cultural Revolution amidst the embers of the Indonesian party, denouncing the PKI's Chinese supporters in the process, Fidel Castro was forced by the death of Che to accommodate Moscow's communist allies in Cuba, and Khomeini's vision of an expanding Islamic revolution foundered in the latter part of the 1980s – the result, the bitter peace with Iraq.

The politics of export of revolution had, moreover, another domestic consequence as enduring and universal as any other. It arose from the fact, denied by rhetoric but self-evident to anyone familiar with the realities of such a policy, that this most high-minded of policies, an expression of the brotherhood of humanity and the selflessness of the revolutionary state, was in the hands of the most low-minded of state apparatuses, the intelligence services. Those responsible for training, arming, and deploying agents, clandestine advisers and guerrillas abroad had to act in secret. They were, at the same time, those responsible for maintaining the security of the regime in its military *and* political dimensions at home. Revolutionary regimes tended to fuse such organisations, although in theory functionally separate: the export of the Bolshevik revolution was in the hands of the NKVD and its successor, the KGB. Other states exhibited a similar association of international solidarity and domestic repression. The result was not only that the internationalist mission was directed by men with a cast of mind suspicious and cruel, but that the very activities carried out abroad were subjected to the priorities of the intelligence services and their political masters. The hardening of authoritarian politics within post-revolutionary states, in part a product of the fear of counter-revolution from abroad, was then re-exported via the conduct of internationalist activities.

Assessment of the impact of such policies of 'export' abroad leads to the heart of the paradox of the revolutionary record. For, in a simple historical verdict, from Oliver Cromwell in the 1650s to Ayatollah Khomeini or Daniel Ortega in the 1980s, few cases of export of revolution succeeded. Success here is defined in the terms in which those involved would define it at the time, namely in the provision to revolutionary forces in other countries of such assistance that they would then, by their revolutionary efforts, come to, and for a reasonable amount of time, stay in, power. The victory of the Laotian and Cambodian guerrillas in 1975, following the fall of the regime in Saigon, may be one case. Nicaragua in 1979 may be another. No such cases can be found in the French, Russian or Chinese revolutions. The reasons for this will be discussed in Chapter 5: the limits of resources which revolutionary states could deploy; the differences of culture and history and social structure between 'exporting' and 'importing' state; the very resistance which such export involved. Revolutionary foreign policies are enduringly shaped by a set of contradictory relations or 'antinomies'.

Yet this verdict, of four centuries of failure, is only a partial one. The argument that such activity served its purposes, in deflecting pressure from a revolutionary state that might otherwise not have survived, is dubious: it may, however, have some validity. More pertinent is the fact that, over longer time frames, revolution did have an influence, if not in the way that the revolutionary state initially envisaged, yet in part as a result of the endurance and activity of the revolutionary state: Khomeini's 'spring rain', which passes across borders, is an apt idiom. The French revolution influenced world history for a century after 1815. The Russian had effect after 1943, with the dissolution of the Comintern. The Cuban took effect in Latin America twelve years after the death of Guevara, that in Africa in the early 1990s after all Cuban forces had withdrawn. The longer-term impact of the Iranian revolution remains, at the time of writing, to be assessed.

It is too easy, and from a variety of standpoints, to deny the force of this ideological commitment and the practical consequences that it had. Revolutionary states, manoeuvring in the conflict of conventional and revolutionary foreign policy, sought at the very time when they were conducting such export to deny that this was what they were doing: if it was admitted to, it was only as a response to prior, counter-revolutionary, aggression. Subsequently, such states, however continuous, found it easier to reduce, if not abandon, the international engagements of the immediate post-revolutionary years, even as critics at home blamed earlier privations on the state's involvement in other countries. Orthodox students of international affairs, remote from the emotional and ideological context of revolutionary regimes, and over-zealous in their identification of state interest and realist calculation, downplay the importance of such ideological commitments altogether. Those sympathetic to such regimes present all talk of external activity as propaganda. Curiously compounding this denial are radical critics of revolutionary states who, bent on discrediting any claims of such states to a revolutionary legacy to which they themselves aspire, see the international policies of such regimes as one betrayal after another. What is forgotten in all of this is that revolutionary states, their leaders, and many of their officials, believed much of what they were saying. They *did* want to change the world: this is a fact which, whatever its disappointments, had, as this chapter has sought to show, significant consequences. The difficulties which it encountered, despite belief and practice here analysed, form the subject of the chapter that follows.

5

The Antinomies of Revolutionary Foreign Policy

The distinctive character of foreign policy in a revolutionary state lies not just in the goals it sets and in the ideology it expresses, but in the recurrence of certain tensions within the making of foreign policy itself. It is the aim of this chapter to identify and explore these recurrent conflicts. It will be argued here that revolutionary foreign policies are, in several important respects, distinct from those of status quo powers. At the same time they are *contradictory*, i.e. riven by conflicting forces and rival considerations, what are termed here 'antinomies', that combine to produce the policy of the state in question. Neither idealistic declamation of a complete rupture nor 'realist' denial can do justice to these policies, which are the product of these underlying and contrary forces. The foreign policies of revolutionary states are, it is argued, constituted over the long run by six tensions, or antinomic relations.

Revolution and Diplomacy: The 'Dual Policy'

In his history of the Bolshevik revolution E. H. Carr describes the process by which, after the initial months of expectation of a revolutionary breakthrough in Europe, the Bolsheviks came to realise that they would have to conduct relations with other states. By the spring of 1918 they were therefore committed to what Carr terms a 'dual policy' combining support for revolution abroad with diplomatic relations with other states. The immediate factors leading to compromise were powerful enough: the failure of revolution elsewhere to follow immediately that of Russia, and the threat of military attack by Germany and Japan. In the longer run, other factors were to enforce this for Russia and for other revolutionary states – the need to trade and secure technology and investment, the pursuit of mutually beneficial international agreements on areas of common concern.

The adoption and pursuit of a dual policy leads rather too easily to the conclusion that the revolutionary part of the state's foreign policy has been abandoned. There is much in this. Above all, the history of the international communist movement is, from the early 1920s on, one in which the Soviet Union subordinated the communist movement to its own needs. But the simple conclusion is misleading: the policy remained dual, the primacy of each component rising and falling in response to events within the revolutionary state on the one hand, and developments in the outside world on the other. The Soviet example is clear enough. The accommodations of the early 1920s were to give way to the radicalism of Stalin's 'Third Period' of 1928–35 and to the military advances of 1944–5. In China, Cuba and Iran a similar enduring duality occurred. The record is not one of movement *from* internationalist conflict *to* diplomatic and/or strategic accommodation: rather it is of the maintenance – with shifting emphases – of both, of a dual commitment that is the overriding antinomy of the foreign policy of revolutionary states. The particular *formula* of this duality may vary from case to case, and can indeed be represented in a schematic way for each of the major revolutions: for France, diplomacy and *revolutionary war*; for Russia, diplomacy and *the Communist International*; for China, diplomacy and *support for national liberation*; for Cuba, diplomacy and *guerrilla war*; for Iran, diplomacy and *ideological mobilisation*.

To recognise this conflict between internationalist and diplomatic or statist concerns is not, however, to say that the latter was simply a disguise for the former, and that revolutions were ultimately just national or imperial projects. Whatever their hegemonic content and consequences, revolutions, by their ideas and example, generated changes in other societies very different from their pre-revolutionary antecedents. Revolutionary states also, through their actions, contributed to upheavals in other countries way beyond the initial period of revolutionary optimism. A closer examination of the actual record of revolutions demonstrates, once again, that if the declarations of revolutionaries and of their opponents must be

qualified, it is inaccurate to conclude that revolutions easily abandoned their internationalist orientation. The confrontation between
revolutionary states and their opponents lasted far longer, even as it
changed, than either the realists, or the critics of revolutionary
'betrayal', allow. Herein lies the most pervasive of the revolutionary
antinomies.

The conventional picture of the course of revolutionary foreign
policy is that it proceeds in two stages, from contestation of other
states and societies to acquiescence in the international system. The
historical record is rather different, indicating not two, but four,
stages of development. Even more importantly, it suggests that as
long as there is significant divergence between the domestic constitution of states an element of confrontation continues. This was
Burke's great insight, to be examined later in this chapter: the
central issue was not the conduct of foreign relations, but the
internal and contradictory diversity of societies. Therefore the
central question is not whether the revolutionary state is 'socialised'
in its external relations, but whether in the longer run the pressures
of the external context lead not just to changes in foreign policy but
also to an internal change, whereby the commitment to an alternative path of social development is abandoned.

Contrary to received opinion, revolutions tend not to begin by
immediately confronting the international system. Rather, for
reasons born of their own internal evolution, and from the very
unexpectedness with which they occur, revolutions tend at first to
enjoy good relations with external forces, a 'period of grace', and
only after some time to enter into full conflict. Thus, the French
revolution enjoyed a period of relatively cordial relations with
Britain and other European powers from 1789 to 1791, matters
only worsened after the flight of the king and the revolution's
perception of itself as threatened by an alliance of exiles and
European monarchs. The Russian revolution also began by entering
into negotiations with the German high command, and seeking to
establish relations with Britain and France. Only in the second half
of 1918, after the strategic context had altered to allow the British,
French and Americans to counter-attack, did it enter into outright
confrontation with the Entente powers and proceed to the civil war
in which external forces intervened. In the case of the Chinese
revolution, the period immediately after the accession of the Communist Party to power in October 1949 saw the establishment of
relations with Britain and some dialogue with the USA. It was the

outbreak of the Korean war in June 1950, an event which China did not precipitate but into which she was drawn, that led to the onset of China's strategic confrontation. In subsequent Third World revolutions, a parallel 'period of grace' can be observed. Castro's confrontation with the USA took over a year to mature, and he initially enjoyed goodwill in the USA. The Iranian revolutionary regime had relations with Western powers including the USA when it came to power in February 1979, until the seizure of the US embassy in November 1979 and the ensuing 'hostages crisis'. The conflict between Washington and the Sandinista regime in Nicaragua, which came to power in July 1979, only escalated into a military form in 1981, after the accession of Ronald Reagan to the US Presidency.

Two responses to this incidence of the 'period of grace' are worth nothing. On the one hand, it may be argued that such confrontations are in some sense inevitable, and that the 'grace' period is one of illusion, a calm before the ineluctable storm which revolutions produce. On the other hand, critics of those opposed to revolutions frequently argue that such an escalation is *not* inevitable, and that it is policy mistakes, misconceptions and automatic reactions which produce aggressive responses. In both cases the argument appears to focus on the dimensions of the conflict that appear liable to compromise. This underplays the domestic structural factors at work in both camps, and the ways in which these structural factors, while initially at bay, impel both sides towards confrontation.

The second period, of confrontation, leads to the standard image of revolutionary foreign policy: military clashes with interventionist forces, support for revolutionary forces abroad, appeals to the oppressed of the world to rise up, and a commitment to the 'export' of revolution. The instances of this period are recurrent: France in 1792–4; Russia from 1919 to 1921; China during the Korean War (1950–4) and again during the Cultural Revolution (1965–9); Cuba in the period from the break in relations with the USA through the Bay of Pigs invasion to the missile crisis (1960–2) and through the period of revolutionary internationalism and *Defensa Revolucionaria Activa* that ended with the death of Guevara (1967); Iran during the hostages crisis and the early part of the war with Iraq (1979–81); Nicaragua during the confrontation with the US-backed *contra* (1981–90). It is certainly not the case that in all revolutions the period of confrontation is as extreme as it was in, say, the Russian or Iranian cases: obvious counter-examples would be England,

America and Mexico. But even in these latter three cases elements of both international militancy on the side of the revolutionaries and of counter-revolutionary intervention can be noted. Cromwell was committed to the spread of Protestantism and republicanism to continental Europe. The American revolutionaries had a broad internationalist view of the importance of their revolution for the Americas and the world, and were, in the main, sympathetic to the French revolution even as their Loyalist opponents fled to Canada, from which they counter-attacked in the war of 1812–13. The Mexicans clashed with the USA, leading to forays into the southern USA and limited US interventions in Mexico.

This period of confrontation on both sides yields in time to a form of accommodation: intervention, revolutionary and counter-revolutionary, subsides; diplomatic and trade relations are restored; propaganda by both sides decline. It is in this context that the revolution, beleaguered economically, is able to devote more attention to development at home and to 'normalise' relations with the outside world. Such a process occurred in France, with the access of the more moderate faction to power in 1794, in Russia, with the normalisation of relations with Britain in 1921, and in China, with the opening of relations to the USA in 1971.[1] In the international relations literature, it is these changes above all which lend credence to the argument that, in the end, revolutions are 'socialised', tamed, by the international system. In the writings of revolutionaries, on the other hand, these changes are often associated with the Thermidor at home that combines domestic regression with an abandonment of internationalism abroad. In one sense, and beyond the differing ethical standpoints, there is a difference between these two approaches, insofar as the 'realists' recognise the constraints operating on revolutionary states that revolutionary critics themselves tend to deny. However, there remains a common and mistaken assumption in these analyses, namely that the period of accommodation marks the end of a revolution's international impact. In fact, the reality, paradoxical as it may appear, is that despite such accommodations, and the containment of a militant revolutionary foreign policy, the longer-run confrontation between revolutions and the international system continues.

In the case of the French revolution, this was true not only in the Napoleonic period, but even after the restoration of the monarchy in 1815. The ideas and social changes, of which the French revolution was the high point, continued to affect many European, and some non-European, countries throughout the nineteenth century. The subsequent upheavals in France – 1830, 1848, 1871 – had their own international impact. The case of 1848 is even more striking: none of the upheavals succeeded, in the sense of overthrowing existing regimes, yet, over the coming decades, the tide of nationalist and social ferment unleashed in that year was to bring democratisation to Germany and Britain, and lead to the unification, in a radical nationalist revolt, of Italy. In the case of the Russian revolution, and despite Stalin's manipulation of the international communist movement, indeed despite his dissolution of the Comintern in 1943, communism spread to Eastern Europe and the Far East as a result of The Second World War; right until the early 1980s, the USSR continued to encourage, and arm, radical forces around the world, most notably in the case of Vietnam's war with the USA. Cuba, apparently 'contained' in the late 1960s, was to see its greatest international successes a decade later – with the military expeditions to Angola (1975) and Ethiopia (1977), and with the triumph of the Nicaraguan revolution in 1979, which was the result of substantial Cuban military support. As for the Iranian revolution, despite its apparent failure to promote Islamic revolution in its neighbours during the 1980s, it continued to inspire Islamist radicals in a range of countries long after the initial expectations about its potential had faded.

This periodisation of revolutionary foreign policy cannot be explained solely by reference to the diplomatic decisions of the states involved. While these certainly played a role, two other dimensions are relevant. On the one hand, the international consequences of revolutions need to be seen as much as a reflection of the constitution of states as in anything specific to international politics as such. It is precisely because, irrespective of the wishes of the revolutionary states or of their opponents, upheavals within states have international effects, and these states are drawn into confrontation with their status quo neighbours. On the other hand, and in part because of this domestic political dimension of power, the reactions of both revolutionary regimes and their opponents are to a considerable, but not total, extent products of domestic politics. The escalation of revolutionary foreign policy in, say, the French or Iranian cases, owes much to factionalism within the regime, and the desire of one group to outbid the other in regard to the external dimension. Equally, status quo powers, even when not directly threatened in any security or serious economic sense, react because of the benefits in terms of domestic legitimacy, or in regard to their alliance systems.

What is perhaps most striking, however, about the foreign policy of revolutionary states is how the conflict between inter-state relations remains governed by the issue of domestic constitution. What this means, on the one hand, is that despite the rhetoric and conflict involved in the most acute, second, phase, it is rare that either side scores significant advances. Revolutions do not succeed in exporting themselves by supporting others, only by direct military actions. On the other hand, counter-revolutionary policies designed to overthrow revolutionary regimes rarely succeed in military terms. Both the advance of revolution and that of counter-revolution are governed by change in another dimension, namely in the internal constitution of states – hence the phenomenon identified here in terms of the fourth phase, of longer-run heterogeneous conflict, where revolutions continue to conflict with other states in the international system until or unless their domestic system so changes that the revolution itself, as defined within the country itself, is terminated. The reasons for this longer-run confrontation are several. In part, changes in the international situation allow a revolutionary state to alter its foreign policy and pursue goals that had to be avoided in the period of accommodation. But, equally important are two other factors.

One is that, irrespective of what the conscious diplomatic priorities of the revolutionary regime may be, the ideas it generated, and the example it sets, continue to encourage people in other states. To assess the impact of revolutions involves viewing this matter in a much longer time-scale than that of conventional diplomatic manoeuvre. The other factor is the pressure of homogeneity itself. As long as a state feels itself, and is felt by others, to be founded on a distinctive political and social basis, then it will also feel itself to be threatened by others and will hence act to reinforce its position in a competitive way: the case of the USSR in the Brezhnev period is a striking example of this. Although the Soviet leadership had long abandoned the revolutionary perspective and optimism of the Lenin period, it was still drawn into competition with the West in the military and economic spheres. The contradiction born of heterogeneity of political and socio-economic systems had its effects despite the greater degree of accommodation evinced by the subsequent leaderships. In probably the most extreme case, that of France after 1815, the impact of that revolution continued even after the regime itself had succumbed not only to the imperial distortions of Napoleon but even to the restoration of the Bourbon monarchy.

Continuity and Rupture

In international as in domestic policies, revolutions claim to represent a break, a rupture, with the past: as discussed in Chapter 2, revolutions are, above all, projects that claim to introduce something 'new' and which legitimate themselves by this. Yet, as was noted, revolutions also seek to legitimate themselves by reference to pasts – on the one hand, to the past of an international revolutionary culture, on the other, by reference to national pasts, so that they become the vindicators of rights long denied, be these social rights within the country or rights of national self-determination against external domination.

In the latter vein, the argument about restoring a 'national' past reaches its most explicit development in the nationalist revolutions of the post-1945 Third World. This recourse to the past is, however, only one part of the continuity within revolutionary ideology and practice. The argument that revolutions represent continuity rather than rupture was classically formulated with regard to the French revolution – in contrast to Michelet for the domestic and Godechot for the international, both of whom stressed the changes brought about by revolution, the argument for continuity was made by de Tocqueville with regard to domestic politics, and by Sorel with regard to external.[2] For all these changes in the substance and style of foreign policy, revolutions are no more able to break completely with the past in international policy than they are in the domestic sphere. To some degree revolutions justify themselves by arguing that they have realised a potential that was previously latent, but unrealised. Moreover, whatever a new regime may do internally, there are many features of its international environment which are unalterable: its economic endowment, and the trading needs that follow from it; its strategic location; its demographic strength. In the field of politics it inherits the antipathies which neighbouring peoples may feel towards it, just as within the country, attitudes of fear, sympathy or superiority may endure. Moreover, as the revolutionary regime consolidates at home, and faces limited success abroad, it is forced in some measure to adopt the mechanisms of interaction characteristic of the pre-revolutionary regime – economic, diplomatic and military. As much, therefore, in the international as in the domestic spheres, revolutionary regimes remain entrapped by the old, even as they are impelled towards the new. Revolutionary states both continue elements of the pre-revolutionary state *and* pursue foreign policies that are in important respects different from those of status quo powers. Such changes in foreign policy can be better understood in the context both of the domestic structural dimensions of revolutions and of the ways in which international relations not only affect relations *between* states, but also politics *within* states.

Revolution and Counter-Revolution: The Chimera of Primacy

The third antinomy is that between revolution and opposition to it. As already noted, one of the most common disputes about the international consequences of revolutions, a dispute conducted as much by those who support as by those who oppose revolutions, concerns the issue of whether revolutionaries do, or do not, seek to spread revolution abroad. In the context of political polemic, i.e. in the immediate aftermath of revolutions, this has often taken the form of arguments as to who bears initial responsibility for a deterioration of international relations. The revolutionaries claim that they are concerned with transforming their own country: it is forces opposed to them, 'counter-revolutionaries' of various kinds, who intervene in their internal affairs to crush the revolution. Equally, they claim that whatever assistance they provide to sympathetic groups elsewhere is legitimate: it cannot be a substitute for the internally generated movement within the country concerned. In a meeting with US politicians in January 1992 Fidel Castro defended Cuba's policy in this regard:

> Of course we wanted revolution. Of course we were prepared to help the revolutionaries. And if we became interventionists in Latin America, it might have been because we had a great teacher: the United States. Which country has violated more international standards: the US or Cuba? . . . Yes – we admit it. We supported the revolutionary movements, and we believe that a country assailed and harassed as Cuba was had every right to do so.[3]

On the other side, those opposed to the revolution claim that while the revolutionary state itself may be entitled to its particular revolutionary transformations, it is unacceptable for it to 'export' revolution to other countries.

Both parties to the argument make a historical and moral claim: the historical claim is that it was their opponents who initiated this conflict, and the internationalisation of the revolution; the moral claim, based on principles of national sovereignty and self-defence, is that it is the opponents who have violated these principles. In the academic literature, this argument is reproduced: those opposed to revolutions stress the destabilising, aggressive, expansionist character of revolutions and hence the obligation of other states in the system to react; those sympathetic to revolutions tend to play down the international consequences of revolutions, and the practical import of revolutionary ideology, and to show how it was the hostility of other powers, and the refusal to accept legitimate change within individual countries, that led to the ensuing confrontation. Revolutionaries mean much of what they say. This does not mean that they always, or ever, attain what they want.

As the record analysed here shows, this debate on cause or responsibility with regard to the international consequences of revolution is misconceived. It rests on a misinterpretation of the foreign policy of revolutionary states, derived in part from political standpoints, and in part from the misrepresentation of how and why revolutions are international events. There is no point in trying to establish a historical record of who bore initial responsibility for the internationalisation of revolutions: revolutionary states do seek to promote revolution abroad, while other states, and above all status quo powers, do react – in both cases largely irrespective of what the opponents may do. In other words, there are factors which impel both to become involved. Equally, the moral debate is misconceived: allegedly about sovereignty and respect for the principle of non-interference, it is actually about something else, namely the legitimacy or illegitimacy of the revolution in question. For those who accept the legitimacy of the revolution, its foreign policy is also legitimate and, as a consequence, defensive and reactive. For those who support counter-revolution in some form, an international and, at times, interventionist response to revolutions is justifiable and desirable. The way out of, or beyond, this counterposed debate on revolutions is therefore to address the underlying *structural* factors at work, and, secondly, to focus the moral argument where it actually originates, namely in the evaluation of revolution itself. Once this has been done it becomes possible to examine, without exaggeration or apologia, the question of how revolutionary states do conduct their foreign policy.

State and Society: An Internationalised Conflict

The fourth antinomy concerns the role and development of the state. Revolutions are, above all, attempts to take control of the state. In this they act in a contradictory direction – they weaken and destroy state power but, despite rhetoric to the contrary, result in the creation of stronger post-revolutionary states.[4] If this is true in domestic politics, it is equally so in international relations and in at least three senses. First, revolutions challenge the state internationally in that they claim, in the name of a new revolutionary fraternity of peoples, to deny and break down the frontiers that states have established. Second, they challenge the state by denying the right of governments and their associated apparatuses to monopolise relations between peoples. Third, in the name of an internationalism of the oppressed, they defy the reality and the claims of nations themselves. However, while this challenge to the state is made, the two-sided process that occurs within states also operates in relations between them: hence revolutions both challenge the state at the international level and in a more effective form reconstitute it.

The international challenge of revolutions to the system of states takes, as noted, three forms. Beyond the actual commitment of revolutionary regimes to weaken the effectivity of state boundaries and create a new transnational community, revolutions, by dint of their example and the ideas they diffuse, undermine the control of established states and social orders. It is this which leads to the illusion, found as much amongst revolutionaries as amongst their opponents, of a rapid transnational spread of revolutions. But if revolutions have their international effects, including and beyond the actions of the new state, they also encounter limits, in the form of the very entities they seek to defy, namely states and nations. For all their international causes and aspirations revolutions occur within a system of separate social units, which serve to limit the impact of revolutions beyond the frontiers of the state in question.

In the first place, states limit the impact of revolutions by the very fact of there being separate apparatuses of control and repression. If one such apparatus is overthrown the others remain in power. Contrary to the revolutionary image of a chain of domination, one link of which needs to be broken for the system as a whole to collapse, this fragmentation of states acts to stabilise the system. A fragmented, parcellised, inter-state system is in this way more effective than a unitary one. In the second place, the bases of all revolutions, the social systems and forms of domination, vary from country to country, so that even in broadly similar countries the success of revolution in one country does not entail its reproduction in another: the contrasts between, say, France and Britain in the 1790s, Russia and Germany in 1918–21, or Nicaragua and Guatemala in the 1980s, illustrate this. Thirdly, and again contrary to the more optimistic internationalist expectations of revolutionaries, systems of domination include as part of their mechanism of control ideologies that legitimate this domination within which such hegemonic ideologies as that of national identification, and hence of separation from others, is significant. Far from peoples automatically identifying with their social and political counterparts in other societies, there may be a rejection of any comparison or solidarity as a result of this ideologically constituted fragmentation of peoples. No modern politics is thinkable without relation to states: hence one ideological and social component of modernity, that of revolutionary universalism, confronts another, that of nationalist particularism.

Such identification of the ways in which states act to limit interaction between societies serves to present only part of the picture; for states, in addition to their enduring capacity to limit the impact of exogenous changes, are also capable of reacting, pre-emptively or subsequently, to changes in the international environment. Nowhere indeed is this more clear than in regard to revolutions: once a regime believes that its own interests and survival may be threatened by changes elsewhere, it can take measures within, as well as internationally, to counter this. Such measures may be towards greater repression at home, to limit the possibilities of any repetition of the revolutionary challenge seen in other countries, but may equally take the form of pre-emptive changes, to lessen or remove the causes of internal conflict. In a famous phrase concerning the response of Latin American regimes to the Cuban revolution, Régis Debray wrote that 'the revolution revolutionises the counter-revolution'.[5] If this referred in part to the carrying out of more effective counter-guerrilla activities, it also referred to the US programme, the 'Alliance for Progress', the promotion of land reform programmes and other measures of social intervention designed to undercut the appeal of the Cuban revolution.[6] Strikingly, the most effective case of where the fear of revolution promoted radical change was in the Far East itself. Beginning in the 1960s a range of countries embarked on dramatically successful industrialisation programmes that were to lead to the successes of the New Industrialising Countries. While much of their success lay in their economic policies, the impulsion to embark on these paths of rapid growth had much to do with the political context in which these states found themselves: the one thing that South Korea, Taiwan, Hong Kong, Singapore and, later, Thailand and the Philippines, had in common was the political and strategic fear of the communist regimes they adjoined.

It is here that the concept of the revolutions as 'combined and uneven', an idea developed within the Trotskyist tradition, has particular relevance, once shorn of its teleological associations:[7] for the international system is a system of interlocked units 'combined' by the world capitalist market, but the spread of change within it, including revolutionary change, does not follow any simple time-scale or dynamic. In this sense the fragmentation or 'unevenness' of the system confounds not only the internationalism of revolutionaries, but also the anxieties of their opponents. The latter's concern has often been expressed in terms of the 'domino theory'. This 'theory', i.e. the belief that if one state falls to revolution a series of others will too, was much cited in Indo-China in the 1960s during the revolutionary war in Vietnam, and again in the 1980s during the war in Nicaragua. It assumes, as much as does revolutionary internationalism, that the state system can simply or easily be swept aside by revolutions. As the above discussion has indicated, it is mistaken to underestimate both the capacity of states to inhibit the consequences of revolutions, and their ability to take counter-active measures to lessen the potential for revolutionary upheavals.

Therefore, revolutions can be seen as reproducing on the international plane what they achieve on the domestic. The initial challenge to states, and to the link between states and societies, leads to a reconsolidation of these instruments of domination and of the barriers between them. Just as the revolutionary project to destroy state power within a country and substitute for it a more devolved and democratic system leads to the emergence of a new, more centralised state, so on the international level, states, revolutionary and counter-revolutionary, are led by the dynamics of the revolutionary challenge to reinforce the fragmentation, administrative and ideological, of the inter-state system. It is one of the challenges to the foreign policy of revolutionary states that they have both to advance and to maximise the opportunities, which revolutions provide, for challenging the state internationally, and adjust to the new, enhancedly statist, environment that revolutions then produce.

Internationalism and Nationalism

Amongst the most striking and constitutive antinomies of revolutionary foreign policy is that between internationalism and nationalism, i.e. between an ideology that stresses an identity above nations and the common interest thereof, and one that places emphasis or priority on the people who have made the revolution in question, and on their 'national' interest. This is the fifth of the recurrent conflicts in revolutionary foreign policy. There can be little doubt about how, in their own minds at least, revolutionaries envisage their place in international relations. The previous two chapters addressed the question of how revolutionaries viewed the international system and identified a set of recurrent, indeed virtually universal, ideas that they articulated prior to, and subsequent to, attaining power. It also identified a set of factors that lead to this – from the logic of ideology, to the history of international contacts of revolutionaries, through to the exigencies of maintaining and consolidating state power subsequent to a revolution. This brought out the degree to which revolutionaries thought in terms of an international, when not global, significance of their particular revolutions. They believed that their struggles were part of, and could encourage, similar movements elsewhere. The point at which such an approach became a practical possibility was, of course, when the revolutionaries came to power, involving the transition from rhetoric and unofficial solidarity to the use of state power for internationalist purposes.

To identify a revolutionary commitment to promoting revolution on an international scale is not, however, sufficient to assess the actual policies which revolutionary states pursue. This might be taken to be one of the areas, along with the establishment of a higher form of democracy, or the withering away of the state, where rhetoric and reality not only diverged, but also where the rhetoric, by promoting one form of illusion and legitimacy, concealed a very different, indeed contrary, practice. The most commonly held view of the foreign policies of revolutionary states is that, beneath a rhetoric of internationalism, they pursue national interests, as much by betraying those they claim to support as by using their international support for tactical, 'cynical', ends. The history of revolutionary movements, and in particular that of the communist movement, has been replete with debates about this question. If some such debate has taken the form of arguing, on pragmatic grounds, for the reduction of internationalist goals and expectations, much has involved vituperation and accusations, concerning the 'sacrifice' of revolutionary internationalism to the interests of specific states. As noted in Chapter 4, every major split in the international communist movement, from that between Marx and the anarchists in the 1870s to that between Moscow and the Eurocommunists in the 1970s, has involved a dispute on this issue.

Within the literature on the foreign policy of revolutionary states, two important arguments recur which seek to limit the claim of any distinctive or revolutionary variant of foreign policy. The one, common within the realist literature, stresses the limits on what individual states can do, and the restraining or 'socialising' impact of the international system.[8] The other, while appearing to accept a distinctive form of foreign policy specific to revolutionary states, locates this distinctiveness in such states' pursuit of abnormal diplomatic and international practices, an ideological foreign policy or a use of terrorism, and in so doing confines the novelty to the apparent break with what is otherwise conventional diplomatic behaviour.[9]

Each of these approaches, however, raises problems. The apparently commonsense view of revolutions as guises for national interest understates both the impact of ideas as such, on revolutionaries and those opposed to them, and the actual history of the impact of revolutions on the international system. The literature on the 'betrayal' of revolutionary internationalism presupposes that revolutions can and do maintain an internationalist commitment; but it too often ignores the actual constraints on what these states can do. The converse critique, as in the work of Franz Borkenau or Jorge Castañeda, of the internationalised instrumentalism of revolutions may have more validity to it. The academic literature, be it realist or behaviouralist, is also inadequate: neither approach seeks to relate the question of foreign policy to that of the social roots of revolution and of the structural reasons, within revolutionary and non-revolutionary states, why revolutions have international consequences.

What occurs in practice is easy enough to relate. On the one hand, revolutions, when they come to power, put into practice their range of 'internationalist' policies: proclamations of peace to the world, support for kindred movements abroad, provision of citizenship to foreign nations sympathetic to the revolution, announcements of the brotherhood and common interests of humanity. Going beyond this, revolutionary states see practical support for other revolutionaries as the appropriate implementation of their internationalist commitment. Over time, however, it becomes clear that this simple approach of internationalist solidarity does not produce the consequences anticipated, and the policy of the revolutionary regime becomes more 'national' in character, as much in theory as in practice.

To explain this, several factors can be adduced. In the first place, the mobilisation of support at home requires revolutionary states to stress their nationalist character and invoke symbols of national legitimacy. While it may be logical and beneficial for revolutionaries to promote their own importance at home by proclaiming an internationalist perspective, the rigours of socio-political change and the frequent attacks from outside lead to the assertion of a patriotic theme to sustain domestic support. Thus Stalin invoked the great fighters of Russian history in November 1941 when the Germans were at the gates of Moscow, and Khomeini turned to using the term *mihan* or motherland after the Iraqi invasion of 1980. Secondly, the commitment to an internationalist policy, while initially serving domestic purposes, may over time produce antagonism within the revolutionary society: popular opinion may associate the costs of external involvement with the shortages or difficulties of everyday life, and in broader terms may blame the country's difficult relations with status quo powers on the policy of confrontation pursued by the government. Susan Eckstein has discussed the domestic costs of Cuba's internationalism in economic terms and in human life: the international costs – economic, diplomatic, military, and their domestic repercussions would add to the toll.[10] Ryszard Kapuściński's account of the conflict between

revolutionary internationalism and domestic scarcity in post-1962
Algeria epitomises this clash:[11]

> Algeria became the pivotal Third World state, but the cost of its
> status – above all, the financial cost – was staggering. It ate up
> millions of dollars for which the country had a crying need.
>   Gradually, the gap between Ben Bella's domestic and foreign
> policies grew wider. The contrast deepened: Algeria had earned
> an international reputation as a revolutionary state; its policies
> were brave, decisive and dynamic; it had become a haven for the
> struggling and the oppressed of the world; it was an example for
> the non-European continents, a model, bright and entrancing:
> while at home, the country was stagnating; the unemployed filled
> the squares of every city; there was no investment; illiteracy ruled,
> bureaucracy, reaction, fanaticism ran riot; intrigues absorbed the
> attention of the government.
>   This gap between foreign and domestic politics, typical of
> many Third World countries, never lasts for long. The country,
> even if of the politician's making, always drags him back down to
> earth. The country cannot carry the burden of these policies. It
> cannot afford to; and it has no interest in them.[12]

One of the important factors underlying the shift in Soviet policy
away from its Third World commitments in the 1980s was the
widespread sense in Soviet society that support for Third World
revolutionary regimes was the cause of the material difficulties
being experienced inside the USSR. Indeed, those who argued for
greater democratic control of foreign policy inside the then USSR
did so in part by claiming that the country had suffered from its
international and internationalist aspirations. In the words of one
Russian commentator writing in 1990:

> Soviet foreign policy has always been burdened by ideological
> dogma. The Soviet Union's conversion to a superpower further
> distanced its international course from reasonable national inter-
> ests. The preparedness to sacrifice this enormous ideological and
> 'supranational' ballast has been the main reason why the Soviet
> Union managed to improve its relations with the Western powers
> in the past few years. Soviet diplomatic efforts have been
> successful because this country rejected its traditional approaches

to international politics. The national interests of the country were not damaged.[13]

Within the ideology and practice of revolutionary internationalism itself there are, moreover, strong anti-internationalist factors. At the ideological level, this is a consequence of the very proclamation of a particular country as being a model, or leader, of others. The very assertion of internationalism also has a potentially hegemonic element, not merely suggesting but urging others to follow the lead of the victorious revolution. The French *philosophes*, for example, for all their cosmopolitanism, repeatedly expressed patriotic sentiments:[14] Lenin had decidedly Russian provincial tastes in culture, and Mao had, in formation and outlook, some of the characteristics of a Chinese autocrat, and on occasion compared his own record to that of the cruel emperor Qin Shi Huang Di. Hence, there emerges both the idea of the revolutionary state as the particular model which others should, indeed must, follow, and the link between revolution and the abolition of differences between nations.

This theme of the abolition of nations often involved the subordination of smaller states and cultures to that of the revolutionary state. The French revolutionary concept of *la Grande Nation* is a clear instance of this ambivalence. In one sense, it was an internationalist concept, stressing that the French were but part of a larger community of democratic people, citizens of a *nation* (the contemporary meaning of the term 'nation' had a political rather than ethnic connotation), and indeed that revolutionary France has international obligations. On the other hand, it carried with it a suggestion both of French greatness and of its right to expand territorially and strategically at the expense of others.[15] This hegemony of logic was compounded by the legacy of history. Without overstating the importance of this, it is evident that in case after case, revolutions, *in their very proclamation of an international significance*, evoke and reclaim elements of the pre-revolutionary aspirations of their countries. Thus the French played on the greatness of France, not least as a cultural and intellectual centre of Europe – there was talk of 'the new Athens' and the 'Vatican of reason'. The Russians in the nineteenth century had presented Moscow as a religious capital, a 'Third Rome', separate from either Catholic Rome or Orthodox Constantinople, an idea originally coined by a sixteenth-century cleric Philotheus of

Pskov.[16] China had presented itself as the centre of the world, *chung-kuo* or the 'Middle Kingdom', a state superior to others. And despite Khomeini's association of his movement with the struggle of all Muslims, there was a strong element of Persian cultural and national pride in the Iranian revolution, combined with the particularly Shi'ite character of the revolution and subsequent state. Even were these factors not to operate, the perception of other peoples, the historic neighbours of the revolutionary state, could all too quickly be that the internationalist claims of the revolutionary states, whatever their new or internationalist form, were but a continuation of the expansionist and hegemonic aspirations of the state in question. Hence the dilemma of all of those who sympathise with the goals of a revolution and wish to change their own society, but do not wish to become the instruments of a revolutionary state: the Dutch, German and Swiss radicals of the 1790s; the Polish, German and Spanish communists of the 1920s and 1930s; the Latin American radicals of the 1960s and 1970s; and the Iraqi opposition of the 1980s.

The almost universal reaction of peoples to attempts to liberate them from outside, from the French revolution onwards, has been inimical. The contradictions of this internationalism were well expressed in the question of two French historians: 'Peut-on aimer la révolution et refuser la France?'.[17] In the words of the French writer Albert Sorel:

> The French republicans believed themselves to be cosmopolitans, but they were that only in their speeches; they felt, they thought, they acted, they interpreted their universal ideas and their abstract principles in accordance with the traditions of a conquering monarchy. . . They identified humanity with their homeland, their national cause with the cause of all the nations. Consequently and entirely naturally, they confused the propagation of new doctrines with the extension of French power, the emancipation of humanity with the grandeur of the Republic, the reign of reason with that of France, the liberation of peoples with the conquest of States, the European revolution with the domination of the French revolution in Europe . . . they established subservient and subordinate republics which they held in a sort of tutelage. . . The revolution degenerated into an armed propaganda then into conquest.[18]

Heterogeneity and Homogeneity

The counterposing of heterogeneity and homogeneity refers to the role in international relations of differences in the domestic constitution of states. The argument from heterogeneity would suggest that, whatever the differences between states internally, this does not entail enduring conflict internationally. That from homogeneity would suggest that, while some elements of normal relations are possible, including tactical alliances against a shared enemy, the very diversity of internal constitution compels states with diverse domestic political systems to conflict. This is the issue that Raymond Aron saw as underlining the Cold War and which a purely inter-state or international analysis obscures.[19] While most evident in the Soviet case, this tension is found in all revolutions.

The specific historical question of the collapse of communism illustrates, perhaps more than any other case, the overall interaction of revolutions with the international system, and of internal and external change. It highlights, first of all, the limitations on rupture, of insulating one society, within a project of post-revolutionary consolidation, from the internal system as a whole, a subject to which I shall return in Chapter 10. The historical pattern appears clear. In the initial period, lasting perhaps for decades, it was possible for revolutionary states to defy the international system, placing whatever contacts with the outside world that were deemed desirable by the leadership under state control and insulating the broader population from contact with the outside world. Not only was this administratively and technically feasible, but it also had clear *political* benefits: at home, in that it severed potentially destabilising influences from across the frontier: abroad, in that it presented the post-revolutionary state as an alternative model around which other potential revolutionaries could rally. A defiant Stalin, Mao, Castro, Khomeini pursuing a separate path within, and confronting imperialist foes without, acted to mobilise a following. But such a policy presumed not just the technical ability to seal frontiers and prevent economic and social links, but also the willingness of a population to accept such insulation, and of the political leadership to pay the prices of autarky: over time neither self-sacrifice nor insulation could be sustained. A period of accommodation began, which, as the processes developed, created further difficulties for the revolutionary state. At some point in the Soviet case the process became uncontrollable, and amidst a combination of popular movement from below and leadership accommodation from above the revolutionary state succumbed to external pressure.[20]

This gradual erosion of post-revolutionary autarchy was, in part, driven by the very needs of the revolutionary state. But it was accompanied by something else, too easily omitted from broad macro-economic and social accounts of the collapse of the revolutionary state, namely continued pressure from outside by states opposed to revolutions. A related issue raised is therefore how far and in what ways differences in internal socio-political organisation played a role in foreign policy itself. Ironically, international relations theory in its orthodox geostrategic or 'realist' form has a split response to this question. Realism recognises forms of state pressure on other states – sanctions, economic sabotage, encouragement of opposition, propaganda. This played a role throughout the Cold War and was significant, but not, it can be argued, decisive, in the final collapse of communism. However, such conflict is subsumed into a view of international relations as essentially a conflict for power conducted by states. What this denies is the importance of non-state factors – of social, ideological, economic processes.[21]

But there is another tradition in social theory which asserts that beneath clashes over territory or power those over internal structure do matter and may constitute conflicts more intractable than orthodox strategic ones. In contrast to geostrategic or 'realist' approaches, which focus on changes in the balance of power, this alternative would imply that where states are structured on different, heterogeneous principles, the conflict will continue until and unless one side prevails over the other. Heterogeneous conflict is not settled by arms or by changes of territory but by the ending of that fundamental ideological heterogeneity which underlies the conflict.

Much of early sociological theory rests on this presumption of structural forces, subsumed under the term 'modernity', which affect states and societies in broadly similar ways. In this perspective, international relations contribute, along with domestic change following upon the industrial revolution, in leading to an internal homogeneity of states: from Comte and Saint-Simon, through Marx to Fukuyama, this has been a recurrent theme. One of the most cogent formulations of homogeneity, predating that of sociology, is in the unlikely form of Edmund Burke. A classic statement of this was in his *Letters on a Regicide Peace*, written in 1796–7 against those who wanted to negotiate a compromise with revolutionary France. Burke's argument was that there could be no peace between two conflicting sets of values and that the very existence of a France organised on a radically different basis would be a threat to the established monarchies of Europe. Burke formulated a 'law of neighbourhood' according to which '*No innovation* is permitted that may redound, even secondarily, to the prejudice of a neighbour.'[22] In complementary vein, the pro-revolutionary Abbé Gregoire was to state two years later a similar law: 'When my neighbour keeps a nest of vipers, I have the right to smother them lest I become their victim.'[23] Burke's conclusion, as comprehensible to any revolutionary as to a conservative, was:

> I never thought we could make peace with the system; because it was not for the sake of an object we pursued in rivalry with each other, but with the system itself that we were at war. As I understood the matter we were at war not with its conduct, but with its existence: *convinced that its existence and its hostility were the same*. (my emphasis)[24]

The conclusion Burke drew was that war, and pre-emptive war if possible, against revolutionary states was legitimate. But this approach can equally entail what became the logic of US policy in the post-war period – containment. In this sense, the classic formulation of US foreign policy, Kennan's long telegram, sent in February 1946, and reprinted in revised form in the 1947 *Foreign Affairs* 'Mr. X' article, bears careful re-reading. The Kennan telegram calls for military action, but only to stop the USSR from advancing further, in Europe or elsewhere. Its main argument was that the West should avoid the, in Leninist terms, final crisis of capitalism. It should build up its political and economic systems, to break the myth of capitalism's ultimate collapse and to compete successfully with the Soviet system:

> If, consequently, anything were to occur to disrupt the unity and efficacy of the Party as a political instrument, Soviet Russia might be changed overnight from one of the strongest to one of the weakest and most pitiable of national societies.

Thus the future of Soviet power may not be by any means as secure as Russian capacity for self-delusion would make it appear to the men in the Kremlin . . . who can say with assurance that the strong light still cast by the Kremlin on the dissatisfied peoples of the Western world is not the powerful afterglow of a constellation which is in actuality on the wane? This cannot be proved. And it cannot be disproved. But the possibility remains (and in the opinion of this writer it is a strong one) that Soviet power, like the capitalist world of its conception, bears within it the seeds of its own decay and that the sprouting of these seeds is well advanced.[25]

In the longer run, Kennan argued, the ideological self-confidence of the other side would be broken, and they would give way:

The palsied decrepitude of the capitalist world is the keystone of Communist philosophy. Even the failure of the United States to experience the early economic depression which the ravens of the Red Square have been predicting with such complacent confidence since hostilities ceased would have deep and important repercussions throughout the Communist world.[26]

This was more or less what happened. The Cold War was a contest of ideology, but of ideology embodied in social and political systems, and ended with one side prevailing very much as Burke and Kennan would have expected it to.[27]

This raises a third broad issue in social theory, that of how far it was external factors themselves that account for the evolution and ultimate failure of the communist and other revolutions. The argument advanced here has identified ways in which, throughout the various phases of post-revolutionary construction, the external – as threat, opportunity, pressure – affects developments within. But this is not the same as saying that such internal development is in any simple sense a result or product of the external. If a purely 'internal' focus has its limits, so too may its opposite, a purely 'external' one that lays all the explanation on international factors. Such 'externalism' may provide not so much an explanation, as an obfuscation of the progress and unravelling of post-revolutionary consolidation. To this question we shall return in Chapter 10.

Calculations of Deviation

Chapters 3 and 4 laid out the ways in which, in theory and policy, revolutionaries sought to promote change beyond their frontiers. In part this argument was designed to counter the arguments of those who denied the significance of this commitment, be they apologists of revolutionary innocence on the one hand, or proponents of inter-state 'realism' on the other. By contrast, this chapter has sought to show how, whatever the aspirations of revolutionaries in the ideology and practice of foreign policy, they have been constrained by the limits of their own societies, of the inter-state system, and of the broader world context in which they find themselves. These constraints are reflected both in the antinomies that characterise the foreign policies of such states, and the manner in which, over the longer run, the pressures of heterogeneity affect the domestic constitution of such states. Recognition of these constraints does not entail that the emphasis on revolutionary internationalism is misplaced: rather it has analysed the antinomial construction of foreign policy, in which aspiration and constraint enduringly interact.

Revolutionary states conduct foreign policy within the space defined by two constraints – the impulsion to promote conflict and revolutionary change abroad, and the necessity of preserving and consolidating the revolutionary state at home. As the foregoing discussion has indicated, policy cannot be analysed as the product of one *or* other of these, *simply* a product of utopian perceptions of the potentiality of change and of ideological commitment, *or* of the socialising realities of an already constituted system. Precisely because of the contradictory pressures operating on such states, and because of the multiple levels at which revolutions affect the international system, such policies both challenge and yield to the constraints of the system. Revolutionary regimes neither espouse a revolutionary challenge to the system irrespective of the costs, nor do they abandon their challenge once a set of initial expectations has been confounded or diplomatic truces with their opponents achieved. Throughout the different periods of revolutionary foreign policy, calculations born of domestic and international considerations affect the form and degree of the challenge to the system.

If, initially, the goal of a revolutionary foreign policy is the intensification of support abroad, this later yields not to a simple accommodation but to a less dramatic but enduring conflict of heterogeneity, a product as much of social and ideological trends in the international system as of any identifiable diplomatic priorities. Such an accommodation is conventionally accompanied by a change within the revolutionary state towards a more established – in the Soviet context 'bureaucratised' – political leadership. The seductions of the revolutionary phrase and the benign hopes of an international upheaval yield to more cautious domestic concerns and to a harsher view of the international system. An insistent 'Internationalism' becomes less a form of solidarity, more a cover for hegemony. Nationalist legitimation at home is used to consolidate domestic support.

However, even this apparently more stable reconciliation of challenge and realism is itself not a prelude to a permanent interrelationship with the external environment. For, despite changes within the revolutionary state, its system remains divergent from the international norm, and with different forms of legitimation and aspiration. Whatever diplomacy may achieve is itself subject to the consequences of heterogeneity, to the pressures on the revolutionary state not only to modify its foreign policy, but to alter its domestic order. In the broader context of inter-societal relations, of which diplomacy is, at best, a partial regulator, revolutionary regimes remain in conflict with the prevailing international order until one or other has yielded in its internal constitution.

Part II
Revolutions and the International System

6

The International as Cause

Conceptual Reassessments: State, Ideology, International

The first half of this book has been concerned with how *revolution-aries* themselves have conceived of the international system, how they have analysed it and what they have done, or tried to do. The focus of this second part is on how *revolutions* interacted with the system. Of all the implications of explaining the international dimensions of revolutions, there is one that transcends all others: the permeability, the limited nature, of the boundaries between states and societies. This is not a recent, perhaps transient, feature of globalisation, but a permanent and historic characteristic of the international system. That system is both an inter-state system *and*, in varying ways, a *transnational* one, i.e. one in which interactions other than those of the state affect societies, polities, economies.[1]

This is not how it initially appears, or how it is conventionally presented. In the conventional perspective, the world is constituted by states and societies, and, with varying degrees of fabrication and loyalty, by nations. These states and nations appear to have separate histories and separate characters. Most history is that of particular countries, most sociology is the study of what happens *within* societies, most political science is about domestic politics. The same applies to the history of revolutions – these are French, Russian, Chinese or Nicaraguan. If they have international dimensions this is very much as a result of something additional, i.e. decisions and policies formulated within these countries: states interact, but from an initial position of separateness. In that sense the standard approaches that do seek to locate states and societies in an international context do so on the assumption of an initial, historically prior, division: comparative politics, or sociology, looks at how different systems may be similar; international relations has conventionally taken the state, a distinct if not sealed entity, as its starting point. So too does the prevalent ideological view of international affairs reflected in everyday speech, the press, politics. We talk of a 'Britain', a 'Russia' a 'China: what begins as convenience of speech or denotation easily becomes an ideological given. The reality that states and societies are constituted by each other, is obscured.

The study of revolutions suggests a very different approach, one that retains the state, and the specificity of society, but which locates them within a broader international system that operates to shape, even as it is influenced by, the domestic constitution of states. Four dimensions of this interaction underpin this study: the role of international factors in *causing* revolutions; the role of internal factors in the *foreign policies* of states; the role of the *domestic constitution* of societies in determining the impact of revolutions; the impact of the international on the *post-revolutionary development* of states.

Such a perspective, of the interaction of the international and the social, is certainly not confined to the study of revolutions. For example, the economic history of any individual country is one of changes brought about to a considerable extent by international factors, of competition, imitation and homogenisation, even as, on the other hand, international economic history is a result of changes within specific leading countries. The histories of taxation, or of administrative centralisation, reflect this process. To take another example, the causes *and* diffusion of the industrial revolution, from the late eighteenth century onwards, bear much similarity with that of political and social revolutions. Equally the study by historical sociologists of the relations between international war and the domestic character of states shows an enduring interaction. One cannot study the development of the state in history without taking the international context into account, just as one cannot study the development of war without regard to the domestic dimensions – politics, demography, economic and technological change – within specific states.[2] Equally, cultures – languages, religions, forms of art and literature, cuisines – are the product of transnational interactions and, later, formalised separation.

What this suggests is a study of both revolutions and international relations within a context of a unified, if diverse, system, comprised of states, social and economic structures, and ideologies and cultures: for want of a better term, an *international sociology*. Such an approach would take as its starting point neither the bounded state/society, nor an undifferentiated global or world system, nor the inter-state system itself, but rather an international system constituted by the interactions of states, on the one hand, and by that of the broader civil society – economic, social, ideological, cultural – factors on the other. In this way the intentions and influence of states, the dominant actors, may be combined with the impact of other factors that states may seek to control or promote, but which may act against them.

Within such an international sociological perspective, it is the growth, and contradictions, within modernity that provide the overall context. Both the interstate system *and* the transnational socio-economic context are products of that modernity. Yet particular events, be they wars or revolutions, cannot be explained solely by this context of an expanding capitalist modernity. In explaining such particular events there can be no presumption in favour of the primacy of the state or against it, not only because factors other than the state operate, but also because the state itself is to a large extent subject to these factors. The range of enquiry would be sufficiently broad and differentiated to allow for the question of the role of states, as of other factors, to be posed. When it comes to causes, the role of states in promoting revolution would be taken into the picture: but, as the evidence suggests, this state role is far less than those seeking to promote revolution initially hope. The international causes of revolution lie much more in the economic, social and ideological fields than in the narrowly political: if states do directly cause revolution, it is by defeating their rivals in war rather than by export of revolution. The same would go for outcomes. When de Tocqueville compared the impact of the French revolution to that of a religion, or when later writers examined the demonstration effect of the Russian or Iranian revolutions, this highlighted the combination of state *and* transnational factors in determining the international consequences of revolutions.

The starting point for this *explanatory* section is the issue of cause. It is a relatively easy matter to establish that revolutions have international causes, but somewhat more difficult to establish precisely how this is the case, how these factors apparently external to a particular society can influence or determine a domestic outcome. To some extent this difficulty is a result of a polarisation present in much discussion of the question involving the twin dangers, alluded to in Chapter 1, of internationalist dilution and analytic fragmentation.

Those opposed to revolutions and seeking to derogate from their legitimacy or roots in the society in question, tend to ascribe radical change to the external – the foreign, the alien, the imported, the subversive. In extreme cases this takes the form of blaming 'foreigners' for the revolution itself – Jews and Armenians in the case of Russia in 1917, Afghans, Arabs, the BBC Persian service in the case of Iran in 1978–9. In this way a statement about international causes serves to deny either just reason or internal causation – there is nothing 'within' a society that accounts for such a process, it is all imposed or infiltrated from outside. Theories that stress disequilibrium or the destruction of hitherto functioning orders also treat the external as something disruptive. From a different starting point revolutionaries may also reinforce this position in operating with a view of the international system as but one homogeneous and transnationally structured society. They can deny the specific features of societies and the fire-breaks between domestic and international politics. On the other hand there is the distortion associated with fragmentation. Here much of the literature on the causes of revolutions, or on particular histories, tends to place international and broader external factors very much in a secondary place, as a marginal addition to what is primarily or almost wholly an intra-societal account. Revolutions in such a perspective are *of* particular countries and are located in analysis of specific societies or of the history of particular nations.

To develop an alternative approach to this issue involves not just the identification and listing of what external factors have contributed to specific revolutions: it involves a degree of conceptual rethinking about the categories that are associated with that of revolution. The prime instance of these is the concept of the state. In one of the most important developments of the theory of revolutions, writers such as the American historical sociologists Theda Skocpol and Walter Goldfrank showed, through their attention to the concept of the state and to its international linkages, how the external actions of a state could, by weakening it at home, contribute to a revolutionary situation.[3] The conclusion of their work is that without a concept of the state it is not possible to have an understanding either of revolutions in general or of the contribution of the international to revolutionary outcomes. There is, however, another dimension in which a reassessment of concepts can contribute to the explanation of the international causes of revolutions, namely through a reassessment of the role of ideology in the stability and instability of states. In particular, this examination of ideology involves an assessment of two dimensions of social and political life. On the one hand, it necessitates an account not only of how the international may operate if and when a revolutionary situation arises, but also of how international factors operate when there is no revolutionary situation; states and the societies they preside over are part of an international system in times of 'normality' as much as when 'abnormality' or revolution occurs. On the other hand, a revised and more general perspective on ideology permits a recognition of the power in domestic and international affairs, not only of conventionally accepted forms of power – military and economic – but also of the influence of ideas, and of assumptions about what is and is not possible. There are, however, more all-encompassing contexts than either state or ideology, namely that of the system itself and historicity. Whether phrased in Marxist terms or in a looser structural idiom, the concept of a world system, or of a specific world-historical conjuncture, allows revolutions to be located in their broader spatial and temporal context. At the same time it is the growth of modernity, with its globalised contradictions, that provides the historical context, ideological and sociological, for the incidence of major revolutions.

Causes of Revolution: (i) Theories in Social Science

No issue in the study of revolutions has received remotely as much attention as that of cause, not least because embedded within that discussion lie other issues: of the theory of social change, the legitimacy of revolutions, and indeed the definition of revolution involved. Understandably, as we have seen, those opposed to revolutions tend to minimise the causes, whilst those in favour tend to ascribe to them historical and social depth. Paradoxically, in the context of a study of the international causes of revolution, invocation of external factors tends to be the choice of those who wish to deny the validity or social depth of revolutions. This, of course, presupposes exactly what a study of revolution questions: the discrete character of societies, and the introduction of the international as something imported, artificial, 'foreign' or 'alien' to a particular society. A re-examination of theories of revolution, with an eye to their views on the international causes of revolution, implicit or explicit, may enable the identification of these causes freed from the internalist illusions of much social science.

Much of the richest literature on revolution, including that written by participants and contemporary witnesses, is written as history, or a commentary thereon: Burke, de Tocqueville, Trotsky, Arendt. All contain, explicitly or implicitly, ideas as to cause. It is, however, in the more recent academic and theoretical literature that most of the explicit discussion of cause, above all in a comparative perspective, is to be found. Academic theories of revolution have conventionally been divided into three broad schools: the first, based on the comparative study of regularities in the history of revolution; the second, involving concepts of conflict derived from psychology, sociology and political science; and a third, derived from macro-historical and structural concepts.[4] The evolution, content and relative merits of these theories have been well discussed elsewhere: what may be drawn out here is the way in which a recognition of the international is, or is not, present in each, and the way in which, in each case, the presentation of international factors involves preconceptions about state and society.

The aim of the first school of writers such as George Pettee and Crane Brinton was to write the histories of individual revolutions, and to seek common characteristics and phases within them. No one reading them can fail to notice the power of comparisons between apparently disparate situations and periods, and the stress which they lay on the fluidity and uncertainty, the haphazard ebb and flow of personality and event, within revolutionary situations.[5] Whatever their theoretical advances later, more 'scientific' accounts have lost some of the verve, the lived drama, of these narratives. The problem was that while the international was recognised in such 'natural history' accounts, it was set in a context that inhibited the analysis. Although presented as in some way exercises in objective comparisons, as studies in the 'natural history' of revolutions, these analyses had a clear bias against them: they regarded revolutions as regrettable interruptions in the history of countries, and in the pejorative sense, as 'unnatural'. Thus for Brinton revolutions are like periods of 'illness', their international diffusion a form of contagion.[6]

This was a view with significant relevance for comprehending the international dimension. What had to be explained was why and how hitherto healthy and stable societies broke down, and in this the international appeared as a suitable candidate – invasion, subversion, disruption of some kind. Equally, once revolutions became conceived of as analogous to diseases, then the mode of transnational or international transmission was inevitably characterised in medical terms, as 'infection' or the spread of a virus. It is hardly surprising that beyond the literature of social science it should be this viral or disease image of revolutions that should predominate in much of the literature.[7] This is so not least because, through the conventional association of revolutions with violence, the international spread of revolutionary influence is seen as the spread of a particular disease, namely violence. Yet this focus on the violence of the oppressed ignores the violence of the dominators and, not least, the international dimensions of the coercive potential they possess. A stable hierarchical society may rely just as much on violence and on the international sustenance of that violence as a society in the midst of mass revolt.

In the second, more 'scientific', school of theorists – writers such as Chalmers Johnson, Ted Gurr, Charles Tilly and S. N. Eisenstadt – the emphasis is above all on why previously stable forms of social order break down. The explanations range from psychological, in terms of dissatisfied individuals and groups, to sociological, in terms of dysfunctions and disequilibrium in the society, to political explanations, in terms of the tensions of modernisation and of conflict between groups over resources. In each case a significant international dimension is, or can be, identified. Thus any analysis in terms of dissatisfaction of individuals or groups can examine how international factors – in the first instance, awareness of, or believed perception of, different conditions elsewhere – can have effects within a particular society. If dissatisfaction is constituted by the gap between what is available and what is perceived to be possible or due, then nothing could be more striking a cause of such dissatisfaction than information or images from abroad. This perspective of a distance between the reality and aspiration applies to the rise of dissatisfaction in general, but also to the theories that stress a reversal in economic and social change after considerable improvement.[8] No account of the demise of communism in the Soviet bloc, for example, can ignore the impact of this factor, in both its forms.

Theorists of dysfunction and disequilibrium point to a range of conservative factors within a non-revolutionary society: revolutions then represent a challenge to this otherwise stable society.[9] Thus

Chalmers Johnson identifies two broad causes of disequilibrium – value-changing, and environment-changing; each has its endogenous and its exogenous variants. In regard to the latter he writes:

> Exogenous influences on the pattern of adaptation to the environment are obvious. They include the introduction of modern medical knowledge into underdeveloped countries, which often rapidly alters birth and mortality rates; market stimulation as a result of foreign trade; imported technologies and skills; the migration of populations; and intersystemic diplomatic relations. One particularly important exogenous source of change is military conquest, which introduces new actors, who automatically fill the status of authority, into a division of labor.[10]

If Ted Gurr and Chalmers Johnson focussed on social and psychological factors, comparable analysis was to be found in the work of other second-generation theorists, notably Samuel Huntington, Charles Tilly and S. N. Eisenstadt, who elaborated theories of political change and breakdown.[11] They located the onset of revolution in the process of modernisation, and allocated some significance to external challenges, notably war. The revolutionary situation resulted from the inability of previously established elites to maintain control. Clearly, therefore, such theories allow for, and in some degree recognise, the international context of such changes, be it through the long-term transnational process of modernisation or the impact of specific events such as war or dramatic changes on the international economy.[12]

The advent of the third, structural and comparative historical, generation of theorists allowed for much greater recognition of the role of international factors. Accepting as central the concept of the state, which the second generation in particular, beguiled by behaviouralist rejection of the concept, had avoided, Skocpol, Goldfrank, Kimmel and others could incorporate both the effects of inter-state conflict on state–society relations and, by implication at least, the role of intervention as the mechanism by which states could affect the state–society relation in other societies. At the same time, and taking much further the emphasis on modernisation found in some second-generation theorists, third-generation writers more effectively located the process of internal social and political change within an international context. They examined developments in the world economy, shifting demands for raw materials and products, and alterations in the international division of labour.[13] They drew on an earlier literature on peasant revolts and resistance, not necessarily of a revolutionary kind. This had identified the social conflicts within societies leading to peasant revolts as the results of the uneven impact of modernisation and, in large part internationally generated, economic change on these societies.[14] In a parallel work, focussing also on agrarian structure and state–society relations, Jack Goldstone produced a comparative study of revolutions in the early modern period, concentrating especially on the rise of tensions within the rural sector as a result of demographic change and taxation. Goldstone's 'demographic/ structural' model is critical of the resort to external factors, notably war, in explaining revolutions in early modern Europe: he argued that many states have been weakened in war *without* this leading to revolution. Yet while he concentrates on internal demographic and financial questions, Goldstone places such changes within a broad, comparative and transnational, context, comprising international trade, inter-state competition and changes in population.[15]

By focussing on the cohesion and power of elites, the third-generation theorists drew attention to the ways in which international events may affect this cohesion, not least that of the armed forces. International events may also lead to the elites adopting policies with contradictory implications – ones designed to *strengthen* the power of the state, through taxation or control of economic activity, but which provoke responses from society that *weaken* this power. This impact of international factors may be such as to weaken the cohesion of the armed forces, leading in the extreme case to revolt; but it may also provoke the emergence within them, allied to civilians, of radical reforming groups.

It is this latter group which Ellen Trimberger, examining the cases of Japan, Turkey, Egypt and Peru, analyses in her *Revolution from Above*.[16] In each case it was the perception of an external threat, military and economic, combined with the model of a more advanced society as perceived by a section of the elite in these countries, that led to the drastic changes at the top and the ensuing social and economic changes. Some of the most extreme cases of such attempted 'catching-up' have occurred in Third World countries that were not incorporated into the European empires and where the elites, belatedly aware of their own failure to develop compared to advanced and colonial countries, introduced programmes of rapid change. If, prior to the First World War, this was evident in both Turkey and China, similar belated modernisation, born of both competition and self-preservation, was to be seen in the 1960s and 1970s in several of the non-colonial countries – North Yemen (1962), Ethiopia (1974) and Afghanistan (1978).[17] Such processes were the product of transnational factors – of ideas, education, strategic pressures, economic challenges, and, not least, the supply of arms – all the more so because they were detached from and to a large measure imposed on their own societies.

If the preceding discussion is sufficient to show that within the sociological literature on revolutions some concept of the international is present, it is none the less striking that this recognition has, in the main, been tangential to the main line of enquiry. What consistent recognition of the international entails is a more general revision of the theoretical work on revolutions. Hitherto, such revision has taken the form of a critique by different political and sociological approaches, of general theories of revolution. Such a critique has been broadly derived from reassessment of general conceptions of society and social change and the implications of these for theories of revolution. Thus the second generation introduced concepts of change – psychological, social and/or political – that derived from more general conceptions of social and political order. The third generation, in addition to broadening the analytic scope, criticised the underlying assumptions, not least those on the role of 'violence', of the second generation of theorists, and, as they put it rather immodestly, brought the state back in.

These debates have their implications for international relations: behind every conception of the role of revolutions in international relations lie assumptions about society, state, social change. However, to these general critiques may be added a further one, based on an alternative conception of how the international itself constitutes, rather than just intermittently affects, social and political systems. In the first instance, and despite the interests of some theorists of revolution in the state, the role of inter-state relations, the core of international relations, as such plays a small role in the overall conceptualisation of how revolutions occur: structuralists are not interested in the international *political*, including ideological, causes of revolutions, any more than they are in the foreign policies of revolutionary states. Secondly, even where external factors are seen as important, these are, as it were, irruptions *into* an otherwise endogenously constituted entity, the society or nation: the change is not from one kind of external relation to another, so much as from insulation to vulnerability. This is as true of the Skocpolian structural conception of society as it is of the comparative historian's view of a discrete nation, or of the functionalists and their Parsonian view of a society moving from 'equilibrium' to 'disequilibrium'.[18]

Thirdly, what is suggested here as an important factor, in reinforcement and in challenge, namely ideology in the broad sense, is not treated systematically: the role of ideology – itself in part internationally constituted – in maintaining social systems, is downplayed. Not only are the international intentions of revolutionaries themselves, at the level of ideas, solidarity or state support, not taken into account, but the transmission of ideas through a transnationaly constituted society, the product of modernity, is omitted. The result of the double exclusion – of the international from the analysis of society, and of ideology from the study of revolution – is to constrain the external to the level of diffuse social and political events. The insights of these theories may nonetheless be recuperated for the analysis of the international dimensions of revolution, but only within a broader rethinking of conceptual underpinnings.

Causes of Revolution: (ii) Axes of Debate

If the preceding discussion has focussed on the international dimensions implicit in established theories of revolution, what follows is an examination of different axes along which historical analysis of revolution and its causes has proceeded. While these axes do not necessarily posit exclusive alternatives, they do provide different emphases and focuses of analysis that pervade much of the historical literature. At least four such broad axes of debate can be identified on theories of revolution: as between long-term and immediate, voluntaristic and deterministic, political and social, state-weakening and mass-mobilising. A study of the international dimensions of revolution can resolve none of these arguments even if, in many cases, it may inflect the analysis in one direction or another. Nevertheless, throughout these four debates, and in the competing theories within them, international factors are present to a more or less explicit extent.

The debate on long- versus short-term causes can be applied to every political or social change, but it is, because of their tendency to be unexpected, particularly acute in the case of revolutions: hence a prosperous France in the 1780s or Iran in the 1970s can explode in popular upheaval a short time later. The CIA was berated after the event for having reported in 1978 that Iran was *not* in a pre-revolutionary situation: but strictly speaking they were right, just as were those who saw France in 1788 as a stable country.[19] Everyone – CIA, KGB, political scientists of all stripes – was taken unawares by 1989: hence the saying of the Israeli political scientist Yehoshafat Harkabi: '1989 marked the end of two ideologies, in the east Marxism-Leninism and in the west political science'.[20] It would seem plausible that any change of this kind must have longer-run causes, but this need not preclude analysis that stresses the importance of particular, more immediate, causes. As de Tocqueville was to say of 1848:

> The Revolution of February, in common with all other great events of this class, sprang from general causes, impregnated, if I am permitted the expression, by accidents; and it would be as superficial a judgement to ascribe it necessarily to the former or exclusively to the latter.[21]

The events that lead from a general social unease to the fall of a regime may involve personalities, judgements, chance economic changes, external actions that turn a potentiality into an inevitability. Equally, the debate on determinism versus voluntarism need not be settled by exclusive answers: while revolutionaries and their opponents have long advocated a voluntaristic view, stressing the role of human will and organisation, few deny that such action cannot succeed except where objective factors enable them to do so. Moreover, the very process by which revolutionary leaders are themselves consumed by revolutions – the latter seen in the natural science sense as like tidal flows or earthquakes – confirms the strength of deterministic factors. On the other hand, while Skocpol rightly stressed that revolutions happen, that they are not made,[22] such deterministic analysis understates the importance of voluntaristic factors, not least those of the late 1970s in Iran and Nicaragua: organisation, ideology, leadership, sacrifice, timing, judgement all play a role in the outcomes. A purely structural account of revolutions, as a collective human process, is deficient.

This debate on cause and will is reinforced by that on the balance of political and social factors. This is especially so when the political dimension encompasses not only the question of constitutional and governmental power, but the very play of political forces and calculations, autonomous of social or economic constraints. Revolutions certainly do involve political change – of government, constitution, ideology – and are, like wars, situations in which political chance enjoys an especially free play. Yet these political processes and outcomes occur within a context of broader social and economic change and reflect, for all their autonomy, the strength of this context. The task of the student of revolution is not to deny one dimension, the political or social, at the expense of the other: it is to give to both their weight and to establish, in so far as is possible, the way in which the one interacts with the other.

The last of the conventional polarities, state weakening or mass mobilisation, is equally pertinent. The former draws attention to the capacity of states to rule society and therefore asks why and how states lose that capacity. The latter stresses the more commonly upheld view that revolutions occur as a result of revolt from below. If Skocpol has given this particular attention in her study of how states are awakened, it is in the words of one of the practitioners of revolution, Lenin, that the question has been most sharply phrased:

> The fundamental law of revolution, which has been confirmed by all revolutions and especially by all three Russian revolutions in the twentieth century, is as follows: for a revolution to take place it is not enough for the exploited and oppressed mass to realise the impossibility of living in the old way, and demand changes; for a revolution to take place it is essential that the exploiters should not be able to live and rule in the old way. It is only when the *lower classes do not want* to live in the old way and the upper classes *cannot carry on in the old way* that the revolution can triumph. This truth can be expressed in other words: revolution is impossible without a nation-wide crisis (affecting both the exploited and the exploiters).[23]

If, in reaction against uniquely bottom-up accounts of revolution, theories of the weakening of states lay special emphasis on the former of the two criteria, the approach that Lenin adopted, stressing both preconditions, has more to recommend it.

It is not difficult to see how international factors can play a significant part in each of these four dimensions of causation. If a focus on the international factors cannot resolve these debates themselves, it can certainly compel awareness of how no resolution of the causes of revolution in general, or of any particular revolution, can operate with a bounded concept of nation, policy or society. Much of the literature on long-term causes has been concerned with changes in the social and economic structure of societies, subsumed in the literature under the concepts of modernisation, industrialisation and capitalist development. It is at once evident that while these take particular forms and proceed at particular paces within individual states, the overall context for such changes is an international and indeed global one: first, because the processes have, over the past two centuries, taken place in a number of different countries and have spread to encompass much of the world, constituting, in all their contradictions and imperfections, an inescapable condition, that of 'modernity'; second, because one of the preconditions for the economic development of countries has precisely been the incorporation of their economies into a broader pattern of international trade, under varying degrees of inequality and coercion; third, because the very process of inter-state competition itself has been a major spur to economic and social change, leading states to intervene in the economy to direct resources towards national goals, and to imitate others for fear of being left behind in the economic and political competition. For all their specific 'national' form, the very conflicts within society that lead to upheavals are therefore, in a long-term sense, the results of international processes, the development of modernity in its dual, combined and uneven, character.

The Weakening of States

Within the context of this modernity perhaps nowhere is the international of more political significance than in regard to the last of the four causal interactions mentioned above, the combined weakening of the rulers and mobilisation of the ruled. If the latter, mass resistance, is the dimension to which most commentators pay attention, it is the former which may in many cases be crucial to the particular form that the revolution takes. It is not essential that the state be destroyed in external combat, i.e. completely defeated in war, for weakening of a significant and possibly decisive kind to occur. Such a weakening may take place in at least three ways: the stretching of a state's resources as a result of inter-state competition, such that it imposes greater burdens on the society it rules; the defeat of a state in military confrontation with others; and shifts in the international balance of power which may deprive a state of previously assured external support, military or ideological. In regard to the first of these, there could be no better example than the consequences of the Seven Years' War of 1756–63. Britain won and France lost in this war, but both were compelled, by the financial burdens they had incurred, to increase taxation over their subjects. In the British case, this was a significant factor in provoking the revolt of the hitherto more loyal American colonists. In the French case it was the monarch's attempt to impose taxation on the nobility which led to the revolt of 1789 and the secession of the assembly.[24] The outbreak of the popular revolution in the summer and autumn of 1789 came against a backdrop of social and political change *within*, exacerbated and developed by the aspirations of the French state to compete abroad. As Bailey Stone, critically developing Skocpol's approach, has shown so well in his geopolitical or structural account of the French revolution, no accidental or purely internal account of 1789 is possible:

> a structuralist explanation of the gestation of revolution pivots on the prerevolutionary state's growing inabiltity to compete suc-cessfully with other 'potentially autonomous' states in the con-temporaneous international state system and to harmonize its relations with prominent elements in its 'home' society.[25]

The Young Turk revolt against the Ottoman Sultan in 1908 and, to be discussed below, the Chinese revolution of 1911 were similarly inextricably bound up with the attempts of central governments, caught in rivalry with other states, to mobilise greater resources.

The role of war in weakening states may seem self-evident but repays closer attention. The absolute defeat of a state in war may not be a prelude to revolution since the opportunity to take power from it will, by dint of the outcome of war, be in the hands of the military victor not the insurgent population: Germany 1945. What is more conducive to revolution is not the absolute defeat of a state, but its comparative weakening in war, such that both its coercive capacity and its legitimising authority are eroded: Germany 1918. Given that the power of a state rests both on its ability to defeat challenges and on the prestige it gains from its successful security role, a defeat, even if it has limited impact on the mass of the population, can undermine a state's authority and embolden its opponents. It is defeat as an ideological discrediting as much as defeat as an absolute diminution of repressive capability that matters.

The Russian revolutions, that of 1905 and the two of 1917, exemplify this. The prelude to the revolutions of 1917 was the crisis in the Russian state produced by the losses and setbacks of the First World War. It is not necessary to show that the Russian army had disintegrated completely, which was not the case, in order to argue that the defeats on the front, combined with widespread dissatisfaction in the armed forces and economic difficulties for the population as a whole, produced the revolutionary challenge to the monarchy in February and then served to discredit the subsequent Kerensky regime. The Bolsheviks appealed for support as much because they promised peace as because they promised land. The earlier case, that of the Russo-Japanese war of 1905, is even clearer: a defeat at sea and in the remotest regions of the Empire produced a major political crisis that for a time undermined the power of the Czar. In the words of one historian: 'Tsushima *symbolized* the bankruptcy of a state structure already assailed by workers' strikes, peasant unrest, growing liberal calls for reform and, finally, revolution'[26] (italics added).

Other cases of the weakening and/or discrediting of states in war were to follow. The defeats of the Chinese state by the Japanese and by other external powers was an element in the onset of the revolution of 1911, while the balance of forces between the Kuomintang and the Chinese Communist Party, favourable to the former on the eve of the outbreak of war with Japan in 1937, had decisively shifted in the latter's favour by 1945, paving the way for the communist victory in 1949. Opinions vary as to how far the advances made by the Chinese communists resulted from their apparently more energetic and effective espousal of the *national* cause, resistance to Japan, and how far it was a result of their *social* programme. Even if the latter case is deemed to be the stronger, however, there can be little doubt that the weakening of state by the external conflict with Japan provided the context within which the communists were to consolidate their position.[27] Three decades later, and in a replay of the Russian experience of 1905, there was to be another case of an already discredited state being weakened by setbacks in distant wars, when the Portuguese fascist state, under guerrilla attack in three of its African colonies since 1961, was overthrown in the political revolution of April 1974.[28]

Shifts in international alliance, and the reduction of support by hitherto hegemonic allies, may also play a role, if often of a more immediate kind, in the fall of regimes. Here the importance may be as much at the symbolic and ideological level, in the very perception by regime supporters and opponents of what is involved, as in any direct removal of previously available military or economic support. Indeed regimes that appeared to be reliant on external support may here be victims of their own myth, in that the actual significance of such a reduction in external support may be much less than the perception thereof. But in a period of unchallenged domination, what may be a factor for the maintenance of a regime may also, in a period of rapid change and uncertainty, act to undermine it. Two significant cases of this were Cuba and Nicaragua, in 1958 and 1978 respectively. Both the Batista and Somoza regimes had enjoyed support from the USA and were then, to a degree far beyond the reality, perceived as mere instruments of Washington within their own countries. Under pressure of events, and as criticism grew within the USA, the Eisenhower and Carter administrations, respectively withdrew support from their erstwhile allies and suspended military aid. Whatever the material importance of this withdrawal of support by Washington (the regimes in question could have acquired weapons from elsewhere), it was perceived by opponents *and* supporters as a decisive weakening of the regime. It thus hastened the triumph of the revolutionary guerrilla opposition.[29] The titles of the memoirs written by the fallen dictators tell their own story: Fulgencio Batista wrote *Cuba Betrayed*, Anastasio Somoza *Nicaragua Betrayed*. In similar vein, the memoirs of the Shah of Iran, *The Shah's Story*, focus more on supposed US betrayal than on internal cause.[30]

Conjunctural Crises

Such a weakening of states on a bilateral basis may apply more broadly to the shifts in the international distribution of power brought on by, and also assisting, revolutionary change. Within the conventional international relations framework based on the theory of balance of power or of the maintenance of international order, a particular place is reserved for the hegemonic or regulatory power, who intervenes to restore balance or prevent destabilising upheavals within states. A reduction in the ability of such a state to act, be it in terms of real capability or of perceived willingness to act, can enable opposition forces to advance, and even take power, where previously they would have been deterred by the threat of intervention. Thus the crisis of the international political system and the changes provoked in it are less to do with the conventional issues of change and dispute, e.g. territory, or military strength. They reflect instead a conjunctural crisis, one of the international system as a network of political power: such a crisis is both the product of particular, specific and temporary, upheavals in the system, and a crisis *of the international system as a whole* that weakens particular states.

The idea of a 'general crisis' was first developed in regard to the extraordinary coincidence of wars and revolutions in the seventeenth century.[31] For Parker and Smith the 'general crisis' of the seventeenth century consisted of two separate but contemporaneous developments: a set of political upheavals, and a broader, global, demographic and economic crisis.[32] In the work of the historian Arno Mayer dealing with the period 1870–1945 there is another variant of this idea, a *theory* of general crisis – such a crisis embodying both inter-state and intra-state dimensions. Such *conjunctural crises* were evident in the aftermath of the French revolution, (arguably) in the 1840s, and after the First World War (in Europe) and the Second World War (in the Far East). In such cases, these were situations where pre-established international forms of control were not operative, and a series of other revolutions and parallel upheavals challenged existing social and political orders. These were crises of the system as a whole, specifically ones where the weakening of an internationally constituted hegemonic system undermined particular states.[33] As in the 1640s, the general *political* crisis developed against a backdrop of generalised *socio-economic* crisis.

A later, and striking, example of such a conjunctural political crisis occurred after the US withdrawal from Vietnam in 1973. The perception of US weakness, stimulated both by the successes of the Vietnamese communists and by opposition within the USA itself, at both popular and Congressional levels, emboldened opponents of US-backed regimes the world over. The result was the cascade of Third World revolutions between 1974 and 1980. Whereas there had been no such successful upheavals in the period after 1962, in the years 1974–80 there were no less than fourteen Third World revolutionary successes.[34] While not all were in a direct sense linked to the US defeat in Vietnam, they occurred in a context where there was a general belief that the USA would not act to support its allies. Two of the most dramatic examples of these were Operation Carlota, the Cuban intervention to assist the MPLA in Angola in 1975, and the supply of Cuban arms to the Sandinist guerrillas in Nicaragua, in particular from 1977 onwards. Both involved the transport by air and sea of arms and, in the case of Angola, men; both were perceived in Washington, and rightly so, as challenges to US hegemony. The Cuban leadership calculated that in neither case would the USA respond to interdict supplies, or retaliate – such was the conjuncture at the time.

A decade later it was the Soviet Union that was to face a hostile international conjuncture, with the collapse of the regimes in Eastern Europe. Against a backdrop of Soviet withdrawal from Afghanistan, and following on from a Soviet commitment in 1988 that it would no longer use force to maintain communist regimes in power in Eastern Europe, the reform and opposition forces in Eastern Europe pushed their cause, and in the space of a few months, from June to December 1989, all six of the pro-Soviet (or in the case of Rumania, dissident but pro-Soviet) regimes in Eastern Europe were overthrown. The removal of the hegemonic guarantee, relayed from the centre and from the example of each country, constituted the crisis of the system as a whole, and enabled oppositions, in some cases relatively weak and recently constituted, to come to power. The solidarity, verbal and material, of disparate revolutionary forces was in each of these cases significant. Yet what was more important was the shift in the hegemonic power and the accompanying crisis of the system. The old system of international domination and hegemonic relations could not go on in the old way.

The Impact of Ideas

So far the discussion has focussed on how international factors affect the capacity of states to rule. The role of international causation is equally evident with regard to an element that is central to the issue of intention and will, namely ideas. For within the polemical argument about 'alien' ideas and subversion, there is an important element of truth regarding the role that intellectual change on an international scale can have on particular societies. The subjective, imagined dimension of ideas has been examined in Part I of this book: it is worth recalling that from Tom Paine to Ayatollah Khomeini revolutionaries have argued for the ability of ideas to cross frontiers. The objective impact is evident from the spread of such influential ideas as Protestantism in the sixteenth century, or of nationalism, socialism, anarchism and Islamic radicalism in the nineteenth and twentieth centuries. Equally significant has been the spread of specific radical and revolutionary ideas in the past two centuries. This applies to very general principles – the equality of men, or the rights of workers and/or peasants, or of women's suffrage – and to principles of organisation, such as the 'vanguard party' or guerrilla war. The impact of ideas acts upon the supposed leaders of revolutions, who may be inspired and instructed. It also acts on those who follow them and who, while adjusting and changing ideas from other contexts, may be galvanised into believing that something different within their own societies is possible.

Those who look for the international influence of revolutions primarily in the actions of states, or in material support of a revolutionary state to insurgents abroad, may therefore miss the most important dimension of all, namely that of inspiration and ideological example. Social upheavals involve something at once nebulous and decisive, what Rudé has termed 'revolutionary psychology', a combination of political beliefs, prejudices and fears that predispose a people to act.[35] This involves not the introduction of ideology into politics but the challenging of an assumed set of values by an explicit alternative; ideology is the dimension of social and political power that is as essential in the preservation of order as much as in the challenge to it. Jacques Necker, Louis XVI's minister of finance, talked of 'that invisible power which, without treasure, without guards, and without arms, imposes its laws on the city, on the court, and even in the palaces of kings'.[36] Mao Tse-tung understood that the very fact of a revolution being consolidated and responding verbally to upsurges elsewhere was a form of action: 'Whenever a liberation struggle existed, China would publish statements and call demonstrations to support it. It was precisely that which vexed the imperialists.'[37] As Chalmers Johnson has argued, revolutions are, in part, intentional and ideological projects, for whom myths, paradigms and examples have an importance.

The question of the impact of the American revolution on the French revolution cannot be resolved by looking at what the newly independent United States did to help overthrow the Bourbon monarchy: the answer is, very little, not least because the Bourbons had helped to defeat the English armies in the War of Independence. In the words of de Tocqueville:

> The French Revolution has been frequently attributed to that of America. The American Revolution had certainly considerable influence upon the French; but the latter owed less to what was actually done in the United States than to what was thought at the same time in France. Whilst to the rest of Europe the Revolution of America still only appeared a novel and strange occurrence, in France it only rendered more palpable and more striking that which was already supposed to be known. Other countries it astonished; to France it brought more complete conviction.[38]

Or as Hannah Arendt was to put it, in reference to the equality of social conditions in the new world:

> Not the American Revolution, but the existence of conditions in America that had been established and were well known in Europe long before the Declaration of Independence, nourished the revolutionary *élan* in Europe. . . Not the American Revolution and its preoccupation with the establishment of a new body politic, a new form of government, but America, the 'new continent', the American, a 'new man', 'the lovely equality', in Jefferson's words, 'which the poor enjoy with the rich', revolutionized the spirit of men, first in Europe and then all over the world.[39]

The history of the two hundred years from 1789 was evidence enough of the role of ideas in stimulating revolution, even as each movement used, and often distorted, examples and ideas in international discourse for its own special purposes. Thus the French were inspired by a wholly recreated and transformed set of classical ideas, and the Bolshevik revolution was to have its greatest impact through the ideology of 'anti-imperialist' nationalism. The very adaptation, and exaggeration, of struggle elsewhere played its part in mobilising movements: the facts may play little role. With regard to the crisis of the seventeenth century Parker and Smith write:

> There is no way in which a 'revolutionary spirit' could connect the revolts in England, France, Austria, Naples, Muscovy and the Ukraine, except that the extreme events in one area made those elsewhere appear more serious.[40]

In his account of radicalism in early-nineteenth-century Britain, Edward Thompson gives an example of a meeting of rebels in 1817 where 'the recent news from the Brazils seemed to cheer them with greater hopes than ever'.[41] That there was no direct connection between conditions in Britain and in Brazil, and indeed that the English radicals had probably little idea of where Brazil was, was of less significance than that an apparent encouragement could be derived from elsewhere. A similar disjoined example can be seen in regard to the Iranian revolution: in countries with no Islamic movement, such as South Africa and Grenada, the fact that an unarmed mass movement had overthrown an autocratic regime was, in the aftermath of 1979, studied with interest. The history of every revolution is replete with such internationalist evocations.

Mobilisation of the Oppressed

Mention has already been made of two ways in which international factors may contribute to the growth of a revolutionary movement: social and political change induced by international factors, and the transnational impact of ideas and examples. This leaves the most controversial issue of all, namely direct assistance or input into the growth of revolutionary movements. Chapters 4 and 5 addressed the issue of the foreign policy of revolutionary states; what will be examined here is the story from the other end, what the role of such assistance in the triumph of a revolution may be.

In assessing the international contribution to revolutions, the literature of support, invoking solidarity, common struggle, and internationalism, tends to deny that material support is forthcoming. Yet the recognition of ideological solidarity is matched by that of opposition and derogation, focussing on 'subversion', 'infection' and 'alien' influence. The purpose of this latter delegitimation is to deny the validity of revolutions by focussing on the provision of support, including weapons, from outside. Such a focus can, however, be used not only for delegitimation but also for clarification. Only when external support, this other, equally important, dimension of the success of revolutions, is analysed does it become possible to address the question, posed first and foremost in most discussions of the causes of revolutions, of how the revolutionaries did organise themselves and the international dimensions thereof. The international must be taken from the realm of the mythic and put into that of the real. Such external assistance *does* play a role.

Polemic aside, it would, indeed, be surprising if assistance provided from abroad did not have some effect. This is not a question of according the conscious or voluntary aspect of revolutions a romanticised priority, but of a grounded and, in each case, specific assessment of what role external assistance provided to a revolutionary outcome. In purely material terms, this can take the form of money, weapons, military training and even troops. The claim by revolutionaries that these forms of assistance do not have an effect, a claim masked as an assertion of the need for internal preconditions and for self-reliance, is idealist, on a par with other purely moral conceptions of revolution: that these should *never* affect the outcome of a conflict is most improbable.

The simplest variant of such assistance is that provided by one revolutionary party to another prior to either coming to power, whether in the context of formal international organisation or on a less explicit, bilateral basis. The spread of revolutionary ideas and individuals across the Atlantic in the latter part of the eighteenth century, the growth of the communist movement prior to the First World War, and of militant Islamic groups in the 1960s and 1970s are examples of this. Even less organised, but no less effective, was the global spread of nationalism in the nineteenth and twentieth centuries. In no case of transnational social movements can states be said to have played a *decisive* role, but they contributed to the spread of radical movements. The issue of external support becomes far more significant when the assistance does come from a state. Striking cases of this include the actions by revolutionary France in support of kindred republican movements, the actions of Russia to assist communist parties right up to the early 1980s, and the support given by Third World states to anti-colonial and other Third World movements in the 1960s and 1970s. Thus in the case of Third World states, Cuba, Algeria and Egypt helped to finance, train and arm guerrillas from other countries. In his autobiography the South

African leader Nelson Mandela gives graphic detail of how Arab and Africans helped his movement in the early 1960s.[42]

Such assistance need not, however, come only from revolutionary states, acting out of a combination of interest and solidarity: it may also come from status quo powers at war or in competition with the state which the revolutionary forces are challenging. Examples of the latter would include the French monarchical support for the American War of Independence: France shipped 30,000 muskets and large quantities of gunpowder to America before the battle of Saratoga,[43] as well as helping the insurgents in the form of a naval blockade of US ports. Wilhelmine Germany provided assistance to Lenin, enabling him to cross from Switzerland to Russia in 1917 and so be able to organise, in place, the Bolshevik seizure of power. The US inability to *win* in Vietnam owed a lot to the fear that a land invasion of North Vietnam would trigger a Chinese intervention, as it had in Korea in 1950. Such external factors do not, notoriously, constitute causes of revolutions, in the sense of being necessary *and* sufficient conditions for the eventual triumph of the revolution: they are never sufficient, and may not always be necessary. It is a matter of historical judgement, counterfactual and contingent as this may be, as to what role exogenous factors played in the eventual outcome.

Appearances of Insulation: England, Iran

If the argument so far has made a general case for accepting international factors as a major contribution to revolution, and has given examples from a range of cases, this is far from having proved either a general theory of the international causes of revolutions, or that in every case revolution has a degree of international determination at all. The former aim, a general theory of the necessary international *and* domestic preconditions for revolution has long been a goal of social scientists. But one may question whether, beyond some very general statements along the lines of Lenin's two conditions, themselves tending to tautology, such a goal of a *general theory* is attainable or indeed desirable. While social science aims to compare and to produce general theory, it would be mistaken to assume that all political phenomena, be they nationalism, war, imperialism, or, in this case, revolution, allow of such a general theory, if by this is meant a set of conceptually elaborated preconditions for any such event to take place. What is being made here is a much more modest claim: that in all revolutions there is, in one significant manner or another, an international dimension. Since, in the end, the purpose of theory is to explain events and particular cases, this is by way of being the more important conclusion. In sum, the goal is to provide a perspective, itself backed by comparative and theoretical reflection, with which the better to explain individual cases.

There are, in this sense, some striking cases where *contra* Skocpol there is little if any sign of a major international contribution, where, indeed, the revolution appears to be largely a product of domestic causes: the state was not weakened by international competition nor was the elite split by disagreements over the response to external challenge; there were no dramatic external blows to the economic and social system or the expectations of people, no major exogenous transformation of the socio-economic system and no significant external support for a revolutionary challenge to the existing state. Two such cases, apparent exceptions to the rule of an international causation, are England in the 1640s, and Iran in 1979.[44] A closer examination may reveal, however, not only that in these particular cases external factors played a major role, but also that the very factors contributing to these revolutions allow us to broaden our general understanding of revolutionary causation.

There is an extensive literature on the origins of the English revolution and indeed on the character of this, the second – after the Dutch – 'bourgeois' revolution. The overwhelming majority of this literature focuses on changes in the social and economic structure of Britain prior to the 1640s and on variant interpretations of the social character of the parliamentary cause. One can, indeed, say that virtually the whole of this literature is written as if England was not just an island, but was a closed entity, separate from the political, economic and intellectual world of the rest of Europe. In a recognition of the absence of discussion of the international, the historian Lawrence Stone gives as one of the causes of the revolution the very *absence* of any external threat:

Men of wealth and property allowed this problem to reach the state of open conflict between Parliament and the King in the early years of the seventeenth century, primarily because they were no longer afraid, or rather were no longer as afraid as they had been. During the whole of the last half of the sixteenth century the ruling elites had been held together by a triple fear of a *jacquerie* of the poor, a civil war over a disputed succession linked to religious division, and an invasion by foreign enemies. By the early seventeenth century, however, all these fears had considerably abated. . .Men undoubtedly worried about the progress of the Catholic forces in the Thirty Years War, but the victories of Gustavus Adolphus made a stalemate seem to be the most likely outcome, and after the early 1620s few thought that England was directly threatened. As it turned out, the English Civil War was one of the very few in modern history whose outcome was not powerfully influenced by foreign powers (except Scotland). It was fought in one of the rare periods when the neighbouring states of continental Europe were too preoccupied to intervene.[45]

Note that what Stone says is that the *war* was not significantly affected by outside powers. There is, of course, nothing improbable about arguing that, precisely as Stone phrases it, the *lack* of an external threat was a contributing factor. If there is ever validity in the claim that states foster the idea of an external threat in order to control, divert or suppress domestic challenges, then the converse must apply, namely that when such a threat disappears the cohesion of the system declines – such, indeed, was one of the factors that contributed to the collapse of Soviet communism after 1985. It has, indeed, been argued that the rise of a militant, Puritan, anti-Popist sentiment in England in the early seventeenth century, itself a form of proto-nationalist hostility to French and Spanish influence, was facilitated by the decline in conflict with the external world.[46] In this way, it would be significant enough to show that there was an external *permissive* condition of the English revolution. There are at least several other ways in which the very material discussed by Stone, and framed in a predominantly *domestic* context, can be re-examined within an international perspective.

In the first place, the sequence of events leading to the outbreak of the Civil War in England, in 1642, was itself international. On the one hand, there was the British context. With Britain at that time composed of three kingdoms – England, Scotland and Ireland – the crisis in England, which was the decisive site, was preceded and precipitated by the clash with Scotland in 1639 and the rising in

Ireland in 1641. On the other hand, the specific issue on which the Stuart monarchy clashed with a Parliament it had been forced after eleven years to recall was the need to finance the war with Scotland.[47] This tension between absolutist state and recalcitrant society were by no means specific to England or Britain: they were characteristic of the crisis that was evident in several European countries.[48] So too were the longer-run changes that underlay the events of the 1640s. In England the process of social change, associated with the rise of the bourgeoisie and changes in agriculture, whatever its precise impact on the revolution, was itself a result and part of an international process, involving foreign trade, changes in intra-European relations following on from the discovery of the Americas, and the rivalry of rising mercantile powers in Europe. The changes in land tenure, and rural social relations, accompanying this, the stuff of the historiographers' strife, took place within an internationally stimulated and determined context. This was also true in the realm of ideas: the ideological processes that led to and accompanied the English revolution were equally international – a result of the rise of Protestantism, the conflict with an enemy both political and religious (Spain), and the emergence of new secular and radical ideas in Europe. For all that Cromwell and his associates saw themselves as Englishmen, they were part of a European religious and intellectual milieu. This is particularly so for the emergence of radical ideas, challenging monarch and church, which formed so important a part of the parliamentary and Puritan ideology.[49] Ideology played a role in another significant respect, one discussed by Stone, namely in the way in which the Stuart monarch was delegitimised: in a proto-nationalist reaction, the monarchy were seen as in various ways 'un-English', degenerate and too close to Spain.[50] To this was added a more diffuse hostility of the rural gentry to the cosmopolitan and hedonistic life of the city.[51]

Finally, and as Stone also recognised in his discussion of the lack of a foreign threat, the English revolution took place simultaneously with upheavals across Europe, accompanying the end of the Thirty Years War: it was very much part of the 'general crisis' of the seventeenth century. The year 1648, in which the English revolution reached its climax, was also a year of upheaval in several European states, and of the signing of the formative documents of modern international politics, the Treaties of Westphalia. It could be argued that this involved nothing more than a coincidence: as was always the case, simultaneity of upheaval concealed diversity of social and political conditions. The least one can say is that the conjuncture comprised of monarch–parliament conflict, social change, ideological challenge and inter-state conflict, produced, together with local causes, explosions in a range of European countries, England amongst them. What appears initially and in much of the literature to be a singular English event, turns out to be markedly international, in cause and character.

The Iranian revolution of 1978–9, beyond its other apparently unique features, also posed significant problems for any general theory of the international dimensions of revolution. In this and in other respects, such as the question of human agency and the role of modernisation, it seemed in particular to be a brisk contradiction of Skocpol's work, published in the months preceding the onset of the Iranian upheaval. If human agency, contrary to Skocpol, did indeed seem to play a role in the revolution, in the mass movement led by Khomeini, this was one which, despite the claims of its detractors, had no external support. It was organised, in a very material sense, with funds, organising officials, and communications networks. Yet these were generated by the mosque network in Iran and raised from bazaar merchants and other sympathisers, not provided by a foreign state. Insofar as Iraq had given shelter to Khomeini in the years preceding the revolution it could be said to have played a role: but this permission to reside in Najaf was more by way of being a counter in inter-state negotiation. There is no evidence that Iraq actively envisaged or encouraged a revolution that was to bring it considerable difficulty.[52]

Skocpol herself has tried to meet the apparent problems for her theory by pointing to two other aspects of the Iranian situation – the vulnerability of the state due to its rentier character, and the role of Shi'ism as an ideology of political mobilisation.[53] This response has not, however, addressed the question of the apparent absence of an external weakening of the state or of external support for the opposition. The collapse of the Iranian state, and not least its 400,000-strong armed forces, in the face of a relatively brief set of political mobilisations in late 1978, was indeed both unexpected and, by any historical standards, striking. The Iranian armed forces had been involved in some limited-scale external interventions: but these had been successful and played no noticeable role in the crisis of the state in 1978. That the state did collapse as it did, was above all a result of an internal factor, the very success of a mass political movement under a revolutionary leadership and ideology.

External factors did, however, play a significant role. In the first place, the conflicts generated within Iranian society were a product of the pattern of modernisation in the country, itself a response both to the economic incorporation of the country into the world economy, belatedly since Iran had not been colonised, and to the Shah's sense of the need to promote Iranian development for strategic, inter-state, reasons. This pattern of integration not only prompted political and ideological change and tensions within the society, but also provided a vulnerability that was to be one of the short-term, or accidental, stimulants of revolution; the oil price rises of the early 1970s, which fuelled both state expenditure and the rise in popular expectations, began to tail off after 1976. This reduction in the increase of expectations, combined with growing bottlenecks and resentment at corruption, produced precisely by the pattern of growth, led to a widespread crisis of confidence in the system, a striking example of the theory of rising expectations.[54]

Secondly, the ideology that Khomeini articulated, while phrased in religious and transnational terms, was, in addition to being a very Persian interpretation of Islam and one that no other Islamist movement espoused, also replete with nationalist and 'anti-imperialist' connotations. The Iranian revolution was far more nationalist than either Khomeini or his critics accepted.[55] In his statements on economics, Khomeini spoke in standard Third World populist terms of the need for an independent industrialisation programme. It can, indeed, be argued that the main political content of the ideology was similar to that of other Third World populist movements, not least in its hostility to the corruption of foreign influences at the cultural level, and in the delegitimation of the Shah as being dependent on the USA and tied to Israel.

Thirdly, while the state apparatus was not weakened in foreign conflict, the legitimacy of the Iranian state and its credibility were weakened in the period preceding the revolution, as a result of criticism within the USA of the Shah's human rights record. The very process that affected Batista and Somoza also undermined the Shah. The Iranian monarch was perceived initially as being strong but illegitimate because of his relations with the hegemonic power, but he was then seen as being weakened, or even doomed, as a result of criticisms, often unconnected with the US government, that appeared in Iran as marking the removal of US support. The perception, realistic enough, that the USA would not send troops to help the Shah, and especially so in the years after the withdrawal from Vietnam in 1973, was compounded by an unrealistic but effective myth about his abandonment by the USA. This myth emboldened his opponents, and demoralised his supporters.[56] The Iranian revolution therefore provides considerable difficulties for any general theory of the causes, international or other, of revolutions; it is equally a striking example of how attention to international factors, variant as these may be, can help to illuminate the genesis and course of such upheavals.

The 'International' Revisited

It has already been argued that to reassess the issue of causation in the light of international factors involves not just identifying, historically and comparatively, such factors, but also re-examining what is meant by two of the central concepts in any such discussion – 'state' and 'society'. The implications of such reassessments do not, however, end with thinking about the state and society: they lead to a rethinking of what is meant by the 'international' itself. The conventional picture of the international as a set of discrete societies linked by 'external' relations makes it difficult to gain an adequate picture of the international causes of revolutions: for this concept of society would suggest examining how such inter-state relations contribute to revolutionary change within – war, state-directed subversion, use of diplomacy to undermine other states, financial support from one state to another's enemies. This concept of the international, as a set of relations between distinct units, closely mirrors that in most accounts of revolutions, of society as a bounded unit, occasionally intruded on by the extraneous, the international.

An alternative picture of the international system would be that of an interlocked set of social and political units, partially fragmented or separated by state frontiers, but between whom state-to-state relations in the stricter sense would form only one part of a broad set of interrelationships. Thus the concomitant revision of the concepts of both 'society' and 'international' produces a very different picture of how the 'international' may operate – not just, or even mainly, as the actions of states upon each other, but of the interaction of societies, via a range of channels.

This interaction operates as much when societies are stable as when they are in periods of revolution. To put it in an idiom of housing more familiar to urban dwellers in Europe or Asia than in North America: societies are not separate, detached houses, but are rather like houses in terraces, or a line; while they have a discrete identity and number, they are part of a continuum with others, and liable to be affected by what happens in the others. History is not irrelevant, rather it is constitutive, both in the shared historicity of the state system itself and in the ways that historical context produced the discrete formation of states and societies: these were built at the same time and of roughly comparable materials. If there is a fire, or a flood, let alone a crack in the foundations in one, this will affect the others. Burke realised this two centuries ago with his 'law of vicinity'. At the very least, noise in one will reach and influence the other. The proprietors of each individual house, in this case the state, may take measures to insulate themselves, and reduce dependence on the other house if the influences that come from the other are not to their liking. By analogy, this is what states do in periods of conflict, be they revolutionary or counter-revolutionary. Indeed one part of the intensified state-building of revolutionary regimes is designed precisely to keep out such influences from outside. But in the immediate revolutionary period, and in the longer interaction of revolutionary and non-revolutionary states, such insulation by revolutionary states can be only partly successful, as also with non-revolutionary states. The challenge is not only that of analysing how revolutions have international causes and effects, but also that of identifying how the fragmented state system operates to limit their internationalisation.

7

Revolutions and International History

Hannah Arendt's formulation of the *twentieth* century as that of wars and revolutions needs revising only in that *previous* centuries have also, to varying degrees, been influenced by such upheavals. Reformulated, Arendt's observation could read: *the whole history of the modern international system is one of wars and revolutions.* Underlying each is the shifting, irresolvably contradictory, character of modern social and economic evolution itself: they are both products of the conflicts of modernity. Wars *and* revolutions are the defining crises of modernity, the products and punctuation marks of the process of international history. A survey of that relation in historical narrative terms may serve as a prelude to examining both the general impact of revolutions on international relations and the ways in which this impact has hitherto been analysed. If the subject of the previous chapter was the international as cause, this chapter seeks to analyse consequence, how revolutions have affected relations between states and the course of international history in general.

Revolution and International History

At first sight, revolutions appear to receive little recognition in theories of the international system. For example, in the listing of the five mechanisms, or 'institutions', of international society Hedley Bull excludes revolutions.[1] Relations between states are conventionally seen as based on calculations of power and national interest. In this international sphere, as in the domestic, revolutions may easily be classed as, at most, interruptions, departures from the conventional, in international affairs. Part 1 of this book examined the ideas of revolutionaries and the foreign policies of revolutionary states. Here the argument will be based on an historical overview, on an identification of the ways in which revolutions, as political and social events, have affected relations between states, and on variant explanations of this impact. Chapter 11 will address the implications for theories of international relations of this historical reorientation.

The importance of revolutions in international history has certainly been recognised, but more as a factor of abnormality, and interruption than of sustained influence. Just as in discussion of the role of revolutions *within* individual societies, where they are seen as breakdowns in an otherwise enduring norm, so in the international sphere the periods of revolutionary politics are seen as interruptions of 'normal' – by which is usually meant non-ideological and manageable – relations between states. Yet in a perceptive aside on the role of revolutions in international affairs Martin Wight observed that for roughly *half* of the history of the modern international system relations between states have been determined by issues of ideological conflict.[2] This certainly suggests how important revolutions and their consequences may be in shaping the course of international relations. Indeed, taking this as a starting-point it can be suggested that there have been three broad periods in which revolution has played an especially central part in relations between states: the period of the Reformation and the wars of religion, 1517–1648; the period of the 'Atlantic Revolution', 1760–1815; and the long wave of twentieth-century revolutions, 1905–91. 1848, although marked by no revolutionary success, was, as a link between the second and third of these periods, to have its own transnational and long-term impact. What emerges from a survey of these periods is, however, that the impact of these periods of upheaval is even more extensive than the listing of these years alone would suggest. For, through the changes they provoked, and the settlements arranged to conclude them, these periods of revolution can be said to have laid the foundations for the subsequent, supposedly 'normal', periods that ensued. Martin Wight's periodisation, revealing as it is, can therefore be revised to take account of the longer-run, constitutive impact of revolutionary periods on the whole evolution of the international system, at both the international level itself, i.e. the pattern of relations between states, and the level of domestic politics, which itself did much to determine these subsequent inter-state relations. Each revolutionary period was accompanied by international upheaval. Each ended – in 1648, 1815, 1948, 1989 – with the reconstruction of a new international system.

(i) 1517–1648

The crisis of the sixteenth and seventeenth centuries predates the later age of 'Revolution'. It spans the period from the original Protestant challenge to Rome, represented by Martin Luther in 1517, to the restoration of the monarchy in England in 1660 and the 'Glorious Revolution' – in the sense of a return to Protestant legitimacy – of 1688. Much attention has been paid to the remarkable coincidence of revolts in Europe in 1648 when in no less than six different states insurrections or revolution occurred: Catalonia, Portugal, Sicily, England, France, Naples. Around the same time, there were revolts in the Ottoman empire, Moscow, Bohemia, and, indeed, India, Morocco and China. As Voltaire was to observe a century later, the first part of the seventeenth century 'was a period of usurpations almost from one end of the world to the other'.[3] While the coincidence of any world-wide political crisis must, at the most, be laid at the door of those factors that could be argued to operate globally, namely climate and, possibly, population, within the European context it is possible to identify certain common political influences. 1648 was accompanied by a degree of mutual inspiration and linkage, and by the sense amongst some contemporary observers of an internationalised political and social crisis. While the particular interconnectedness of these revolts of 1648 can be debated, they occurred in the context of a broader social and political crisis attendant upon the emergence of the modern state system in both its domestic and international forms.

At least two, very different, sets of transnational factors contributed to this change. On the one hand, changes in population, accentuated in the 1640s by climactic deterioration, increased pressures on states and prompted social unrest. While there was no automatic interconnection between these long-term trends and political events, it would appear that they provided important, and shared, impetus to radical opposition.[4] On the other hand, with its rejection of universalistic and religiously sanctioned authority, Protestantism provided the ideology both for the rejection by the rising middle classes of the claims of monarch and aristocracy, and for the acceptance of different states, each sovereign in its own domain. The emerging social forces across Europe articulated their grievances through this set of beliefs, leading both to challenges to authority within states and to the wars of religion of the seventeenth century. The moment of recomposition, associated with the treaties of Westphalia of 1648, involved the establishment of new rules of sovereignty, between *and within* states.

(ii) 1760–1815

The thesis of the 'Atlantic Revolution' encompasses the period from the Seven Years' War through to the end of the Napoleonic wars, and links, within one international context, the American and French revolutions, as well as the other upheavals that occurred in Europe in the latter part of the eighteenth century – in Ireland, Poland, and, subsequent to the French revolution, in Holland, the Rhineland, Switzerland, Italy and the Iberian Peninsula.[5] Marxist writers, intent on giving a unique status to the French revolution, long resisted this thesis. Yet the French uprising of 1789 was only possible because of broader trends – inter-state competition, ideological ferment – in the international system. It was preceded not only by the rising of the Americans, but by insurrection in Eastern Europe, in Poland.[6]

There can be little doubt that this period of tension, represented above all by the American and French upheavals, constituted a crisis of the international system as a whole, leading to both the first internationalised war of revolution and counter-revolution and indeed to the first global or 'world' war.[7] Yet it was also a period in which the examples of these two revolutions spread to other societies, in which new ideas were introduced into the political life of different countries, with consequences that were to reverberate through the nineteenth and twentieth centuries.[8] Thus among the ideas that emerged from these two revolutions were those of popular sovereignty, national self-determination, socialism and individual human rights. Less expansionist than the French, although embodying some of the tendencies to hegemony that were to become evident a century or more later, the American revolution represented a set of political ideas that were to affect Europe and Latin America and were, even when US hegemony emerged most clearly in the mid-twentieth century, to have a radicalising impact on other societies. The strategic impact of the American revolution, combined with the weakening of the monarchical systems in Spain and Portugal by the Napoleonic invasion, was to lead to the decolonisation of much of Latin America. The political impact of the French revolution was even greater. Even in countries where incipient national opposition to French rule was provoked by French occupation, such as Germany and Italy, the ideas of the French revolution were to inspire further political change. Indeed the ultimate paradox of the French revolution was that while the regime it produced was defeated in 1815 and the Bourbon monarchy restored, the political and intellectual influence of the revolution, in France and elsewhere, was to continue to have effects throughout the nineteenth century. The return of Louis XVIII in 1815 was followed by the revolt of 1830, the 'year of revolutions' of 1848, and the Parisian communist insurrection of 1871. 1848 was indeed a 'watershed' in the history of Europe, short-term resistance to change yielded to longer-term accommodation and, in the case of Italy, to a radical popular and nationalist mobilisation for unification.[9]

(iii) 1905–1991

This impact of revolutions on the international system was even more evident in the twentieth century, the historical period above all in which social and political upheaval dominated relations between states. Indeed if it is legitimate to speak of a general crisis of the twentieth century, this is not just one of militarised rivalry between great powers, resulting in two world wars and in the long post-1945 Cold War, but of the interlocking of this strategic rivalry with conflict within states and of that rivalry's internationalised aftermath. It was indeed revolution, rather than war, which began the century. In a range of countries, broadly termed 'semi-peripheral', the years after 1900 saw political and social upheaval. This was a dramatic replay, in a world made more united and conflictual by the advance of modernity, of 1648 and the late eighteenth century. These upheavals testified to a generalised set of economic and social conflicts resulting from the development of the world economy over the preceding decades, but also to a renewed belief, found in different ways in each country, of the need and possibility for radical change. In Russia, China, Mexico, Turkey, Persia and Portugal these revolutions reflected economic and inter-state conflict, but preceded the explosion of war in 1914.[10] In one case in particular, that of Turkey, there was a direct link between the political upheaval, the 'Young Turk' revolt of 1908, and the subsequent world war. The new regime in Istanbul, espousing a more assertive Turkish nationalism, became embroiled in the Balkan wars, the direct prelude to August 1914.

The First World War, of course, ushered in a series of upheavals, by far the most important of which was the Russian Revolution of 1917. This created a regime that was, in internal constitution and external orientation, in confrontation with the West for the subsequent seven decades and more. The response of the status quo powers was clear: purposive, if half-hearted, military intervention to contain, weaken and, if possible, overthrow the Bolshevik state; mobilisation of diplomatic resources to isolate the new regime, not least in the context of the new League of Nations;[11] political mobilisation within the developed countries and their colonies, to counter this new challenge. If immediately after 1917 it appeared as if the Bolshevik revolution already constituted a world-wide threat, this apparent menace had by the late 1920s receded. It would, in this sense, be a simplification to say that from 1917 onwards the confrontation with Soviet communism was *the* dominant factor in the foreign policy of status quo powers. Yet it remained an enduring concern, and was a major factor in provoking what did become the major challenge to the established states, namely the rise of fascism. For, while in each case these right-wing authoritarian movements drew on particular internal social and national grievances, the combat with communism was an ideological justification common to all.

Not for nothing was the alliance of Germany, Italy and Japan named the 'Anti-Comintern Pact'. In Italy, Mussolini justified his seizure of power in 1923 on the need to fight communism, as did Franco in 1936 when he launched the civil war in Spain. This connection between fascism and counter-revolution was most evident in the case of Germany. As will be discussed in Chapter 8, in the German case both the challenge of communism domestically and the eastwards-oriented drive to fight Russia internationally were to be central to the Nazi programme. While the conflicts of the inter-war period and of the Second World War took the form of a conflict between capitalist powers, authoritarian and democratic, a major factor in the development of this conflict was the response, in the fascist form, to the Bolshevik revolution.[12]

After the Second World War there was no longer any doubt as to the underlying division line in world politics, that between the Soviet and Western blocs. While direct military confrontation was almost wholly avoided,[13] this conflict, represented in the term 'Cold War', involved both an extensive arms race, in both nuclear and conventional weapons, and the competitive involvement of the great powers in a range of Third World conflicts, in which many millions died. Rivalry and confrontation with the West became the dominant concern in the communist bloc, even as different approaches to this provoked divisions, while in the West itself the predominant security concern was the containment of communism and of Soviet military influence. This confrontation was, moreover, fuelled by the continuing incidence of revolution in Third World states after 1945, most notably in China but also in other countries across all three continents of the Third World. These Third World revolutions, beyond their immediate consequences for the states and regions in which they occurred, provoked responses in the West, of counter-revolutionary action on the one hand, and of the development of new strategic approaches on the other. In this way the conflict between the Bolshevik revolution and the capitalist West, explosive immediately after 1917 and a major contributing factor to the rise of an aggressive authoritarian capitalism in the inter-war period, became the dominant feature of international relations from 1945 until the collapse of Soviet communism at the end of the 1980s. The greatest single element in the course of the Cold War was not diplomatic confrontation between Washington and Moscow, or the process of nuclear arms race, but the repeated incidence of Third World revolution.

Cold War Conflict and Third World Revolution

The history of the post-1945 world was therefore to a considerable extent that of the clash between the Bolshevik revolution and the West, at the level of strategic nuclear confrontation, and of the extension of that conflict into the wars of the Third World. What was perhaps understated was the degree to which, far from being separate processes, these two levels of international conflict were in fact interrelated. Thus for the West the extension of Soviet influence in the Third World appeared to be part of a strategic expansion designed to strengthen the overall communist 'threat'. In Soviet perspective the 'advance' of nationalist and revolutionary movements in the Third World was part of the broader shift in world politics. That these Third World revolutions had their own indigenous, and to a considerable extent nationalist, roots did not prevent them from being perceived as part of, and having considerable influence on, the overall balance of international relations.

It would be mistaken to say that revolutionary upheaval in the Third World was the sole influence upon the post-1945 strategic conflict and upon the nuclear arms race, but it played an important part in it. In the first place it heightened the sense of confidence, or alarm, felt in both blocs. At the same time the state of the nuclear balance was seen as one of the mechanisms by which crises between the blocs could be regulated. The victory of the Chinese revolution in 1949, and attendant crises in Korea and elsewhere, fuelled the sense of US concern at the Soviet 'threat' that resulted in the formulation of a new US strategic doctrine embodied in NSC 68 of 1950. The US sense of a 'missile gap' in the early 1960s was in part a reflection of concern at Soviet overall strategic intentions resulting from the upheavals of the Third World. In the early 1980s, when the US administration was engaged in a renewed attempt to 'restore' its previous position vis-à-vis the USSR, the Third World upheavals of the latter half of the 1970s were an important part of the overall argument.[14]

Vietnam, especially during the period of US deployment of ground forces (1965–73), was the most acute crisis of US hegemony at the military, economic and political levels, of the post-1945 period; conceived of as an indication of US credibility, it had to be abandoned when the strains became too high.[15] The loss of all three allied regimes in Indo-China (Vietnam, Laos, Cambodia) was followed by the triumph of revolutionary forces in Africa; other allied regimes fell in Ethiopia and Iran; and in 1979 the Sandinistas took power in Nicaragua, the first successful revolutionary insurrection on the Latin American mainland in the Cold War period. The symbolism of these defeats, epitomised in such episodes as the chaotic flight of US personnel from the roof of the US embassy in Saigon in 1975 and the detention of US diplomats as hostages in Iran, combined with the real involvement of Soviet and Cuban forces in a number of conflicts, produced a sense of strategic threat within the US government and, to some extent, within the US population.

The Most Dangerous Moment: October 1962

The moment at which the link between the two levels of competition, nuclear arms race and Third World revolution, was clearest was in October 1962: this is what in the USA is termed the 'Cuban Missile Crisis', is known in Cuba as the October crisis (since none of the missiles were 'Cuban' in any sense), and in the USSR as the Caribbean crisis.[16] In one perspective, this was a clash over military issues, the stationing of missiles near the USA by a Soviet Union intent on compensating for a strategic inferiority. The crisis was hence essentially part of the nuclear competition between the two powers; its aftermath, whereby the Russians withdrew their missiles after a confrontation with the USA, and the US redeployed missiles from Turkey, reflected a return to the military *status quo ante*. But this strategic military interpretation is, in three respects, inadequate: it is to ascribe to the Russians a purely military reasoning in their decision to put the missiles there; it obscures the role of the Havana government in the development of the confrontation; it ignores the broader political consequences of the crisis.

Strategic calculations did certainly play a role in the Soviet decision: Khrushchev talked of 'putting a hedgehog in Uncle Sam's pants'. There was, however, another dimension to the missile deployment, one that goes to the heart of the formation of foreign policy by revolutionary states: this was the fear, shared by both Soviet and Cuban leaderships, that the USA was preparing a second invasion of the island, to remedy the failure of the Bay of Pigs attack of April 1961. The prelude to the Soviet decision to station missiles on Cuba was international counter-revolution: the spur was not, therefore, just Soviet inferiority in the deployment of missiles nor the political conflict between Cuba and the USA following on the revolution of 1959, but the particular threat posed to the revolutionary regime by US attempts to invade; the instructions given to the Soviet military on Cuba, and the Soviet–Cuban treaty of 1962 under which the missiles were stationed, made this intention, defence of Cuba from invasion, explicit.[17]

While the attempt of April 1961 had failed, there were many signs that Washington was planning to invade again. No attempt at an actual invasion was made after April 1961, yet the CIA organised an intensive campaign of sabotage inside Cuba, designed to weaken the economy and provoke an uprising against the Cuban government. Operation Mongoose, initiated in November 1961, aimed to

'use our available assets . . . to help Cuba overthrow the Communist regime'.[18] The Kennedy administration was determined to
destroy the revolutionary regime in Cuba, and also made several
attempts to murder the Cuban leader Fidel Castro.[19] Despite
denials by many prominent US officials, and the absence of any
specific invasion decision, the balance of evidence now suggests that
the US government was prepared, if necessary, to back up any
uprising with direct armed intervention. The date set for such an
uprising had, by coincidence, been set at October 1962.[20] On their
side, the Cubans were divided. The initial request concerning missile
installation came from the Russians, and Cuban intelligence
doubted that the USA was planning an invasion.[21] The leadership,
however, its anxieties increased by information from Soviet sources,
saw the missiles as something that would inhibit another US-
organised invasion.[22] Far from being a product of a strategic logic
alone, specific to nuclear weapons, the decision to station missiles
was more a response to the conflict between revolutionary Cuba
and its opponents.[23]

The conclusion of the crisis also takes on a different meaning
when seen in this political context: while the Russians were compelled to withdraw their missiles, they did so with the understanding
that the USA guaranteed not to promote another invasion of Cuba.
Therefore, what at the purely military level appeared as a victory for
the USA became at the political level a gain for the Cubans: the
problem was that neither Washington, nor Moscow nor Havana
saw it this way. Washington had originally countenanced a formal
non-intervention pledge in response to Khrushchev's letter of 26
October to Kennedy, but only in return for the right to inspect
Cuban sites. This the Cubans refused to do: no US non-intervention
pledge was therefore given.[24] Yet, in practice, and despite a
commitment made by Kennedy in December 1962 to the Bay of
Pigs prisoners that Cuba had released – that Castro *would* be
overthrown – the campaign against Cuba declined during the course
of 1963. In the weeks before his death, Kennedy was engaged in a
back-channel negotiation with Castro on reducing tensions.

In retrospect, it can be said that the Cubans got their non-
intervention commitment. They, for their part, denounced the
Russians for betrayal and embarked on a sustained campaign of
promoting revolution in Latin America. This had, as discussed in
Chapter 4, the *dual purpose* of, on the one hand, placing pressure on
the USA and thereby, so Havana believed, lessening the ability of

Washington to intervene (*Defensa Revolucionaria Activa*), and, on the other, of dividing the pro-Cuban radical left in Latin America from the pro-Soviet communist parties. In the event, therefore, and despite Cuban protests, neither Washington nor Moscow got their way. The prospect of any invasion receded and this gave the Cubans a freer hand to promote revolutionary movements elsewhere in Latin America and in other parts of the Third World.[25] Although Fidel Castro himself did not see it this way, and denounced the Russians for giving in to US pressure, his was a political victory none the less.[26] The strategic defeat of the Cuban revolution was to come not through the timidity of a Soviet leader in 1962, but five years later, with the adventurism of Castro's closest comrade, Che Guevara – supported, in a manner as yet obscure, by Castro himself – in Bolivia in 1967. It was this defeat which more than any other event sealed the fate of the Cuban revolution, placing it on the defensive in Latin America, and pushing it more and more into the arms of the USSR.

Legacies of Communism

The Cuban missile crisis was therefore part of a broader internationalisation of social conflict in a context of great power rivalry. To chart the course of the relation between interstate conflict and revolution in the twentieth century does not, however, adequately identify the impact of the Bolshevik revolution and of other twentieth-century upheavals on international relations. As in the case of the French revolution, the apparent collapse or defeat of the revolutionary regime itself contrasts with the longer-run impact of this upheaval on the international system. In three ways in particular, it can be said that the challenge of communism affected the international system as a whole and in ways which outlasted the actual confrontation between the two blocs. In the first place, communism, by positing a revolutionary challenge in the Third World to Western imperialism, especially in the post-1945 period, helped to bring about the end of colonialism. It therefore played an important part in the independence of the one-hundred-odd Third World states, and in ending this particular form of political domination. Secondly, as a result of the challenge posed by communism, the opposed capitalist states were compelled to introduce reforms into their own systems as a means of pre-empting challenges from within. The spread of universal suffrage, the rise of the welfare state and the increase in civil liberties within capitalist states in the decades after 1917 and, most spectacularly, after 1945 were in part a response to the external revolutionary challenge.[27] Finally, the threat of revolutionary communism was to lead to a reassessment by Western economists of the need for economic development; the most famous such response published in 1960, Rostow's *Stages of Growth*, had an apt sub-title – *A Non-Communist Manifesto*.[28] Such considerations, strategic, national and intellectual, were to have a galvanising economic impact in the East Asian region as part of the outlook guiding authoritarian 'neo-Confucian' states. The rapid changes in South Korea, Taiwan, Hong Kong, Singapore and Thailand from the 1960s onwards reflected not so much a set of technical and economic management policies as a response to the strategic and political challenge posed by the advances of revolutionary communism in China, North Korea and Vietnam. In one of the stranger outcomes of world history, this challenge from Far Eastern communism led not to the collapse of capitalism, as many communists and anti-communists had anticipated, but to its reinvigoration. It was a revival that in the end was to contribute much to the failure or transformation of communism itself.

The Impact on International Relations

Abstracting from these particular cases, it is possible to identify several more general ways in which revolutions within particular countries can affect the international system. However, understanding this impact involves not just looking at the ways in which states relate to each other, bilaterally or within the broader international system, but also at the ways in which domestic factors within revolutionary and non-revolutionary states affected foreign policy. It is only possible to specify how and why revolutions have an international impact if the question is broadened to include these internal dimensions of state power and policy.

In the first place, as discussed in Chapter 5, revolutionary states to a considerable extent do pursue distinct foreign policies. While these embody elements and ideas from the pre-revolutionary era, the foreign policies of revolutionary states, for reasons of ideology, interest and strategy, depart in important respects from those of their predecessors. This is often misleadingly presented as a matter of these states adopting distinct *methods* in their foreign policies, and in particular their espousal of *ideology*: but the question of methods is at best secondary to that of goals. The focus on the ideological content of the foreign policy of revolutionary states obscures the fact that all states have such an ideological content, but one that in periods of homogeneity is implicit and unstated. Moreover, revolutions, by dint of the uncertainties they occasion, both within their own societies and as to their broader intentions, produce an international precariousness that provokes countervailing action. Such a response may, in particular, lead to actions designed to contain or even overthrow the revolutionary state, the subject of Chapter 8. It is never possible to ascertain in the initial stage what the international effects of a revolution are, and they may well be exaggerated by revolutionaries and their opponents alike. But for this very reason, and in order to cater for unexpected eventualities, status quo powers mobilise against the revolutionary state. There follows the policy of counter-revolution and intervention.

There are three ways in particular in which revolutions affect status quo powers. First, and whatever the proclaimed goals or actual policies of revolutionary states, the very fact of upheaval in a particular state has consequences elsewhere. Social and political movements respond to the fact, or perception, of revolution for domestic reasons. Such responses, in the consequences they have as much as in the reactions they provoke, affect the policies of other states, which will seek to prevent the spread of opposition within their own boundaries. In this sense, counter-revolution, be it that of 'pre-emptive' reform or that of repression, begins with the domestic policies of the state affected. Secondly, beyond the mobilisation of dissent within states, the challenges posed by revolutions, and not least the costs and strains of counter-revolutionary policy, produce fissures within the status quo powers, at both popular and elite levels. The examples of Spain and the war of Cuban independence up to 1898, of France and Algeria to 1962, of the US and Vietnam to 1973, and of the USSR and Afghanistan to 1989, show how – movements of emulation or solidarity aside – a state's protracted confrontation with insurgency elsewhere may weaken it.[29] Thirdly, revolutions destroy pre-existing alliances, and hence weaken the foreign policy of states. The Russian revolution disrupted the wartime alliance against the Central Powers, the Chinese revolution broke up the Sino-American alliance that had endured the Second

World War, the Iranian revolution ended the Central Treaty Organisation in 1979 (CENTO having, in its earlier incarnation as the Baghdad Pact, been weakened by the Iraqi revolution of 1958), the triumph of the communist forces in Vietnam in 1975 marked the end of the South East Asian Treaty Organisation, and the overthrow of communism in 1989 led to the dissolution of the Warsaw Treaty Organisation.

Challenges to the System

This summary history suggest the importance not just of a narrative that links international politics and social upheaval, but also of the international sociology discussed earlier. As some of these instances themselves suggest, to identify the impact of revolutions on the international system it is not sufficient to look at the policies and responses of states: equally significant are the responses at the level of the system as a whole. On the one hand, revolutions involve not just changes in one country and the reaction of other states to these, but, by dint of the very international character of the factors that cause revolution, a set of crises, of varying intensities and forms, in a range of countries. These interrelated upheavals are often misrepresented by those who endorse them as evidence of a single and ineluctable global process – the Comintern usage of 'conjunctures' – and by those opposed to them as 'international conspiracies', i.e. as the workings of some unspecified transnational agencies. The simultaneity of upheavals, in the seventeenth century as much as in the twentieth, reflects the remarkable systemic character of revolution, even if it poses a set of analytic questions as to what constitutes this simultaneity and how far common factors account for it. On the other hand, if there is an international character in the crisis of the system, there is equally one in its recomposition. Faced with the spread of revolution, and with threats to order both domestic and international, states seek to go beyond the mere resistance to upheaval and to establish new international mechanisms that will prevent the incidence of upheaval and conflict in the future. The history of the establishment of the institutions of the international system is to a considerable degree that of the response to periods of revolutionary upheaval.

The end of the first phase of international upheaval came with 1648, and the Treaties of Westphalia, at which in the first constitution of the modern inter-state system the principles of sovereignty and respect for religious difference were established.[30] The Atlantic revolution and the Napoleonic wars concluded in 1815 with the Congress of Vienna and the creation of the Concert of Europe and the modern diplomatic system. The revolutionary period of the twentieth century has involved a series of attempts to reinforce the existing order by mechanisms to avoid both war and revolution. The League of Nations, established in 1920, had the goals both of preventing war and of containing the Bolshevik revolution. The United Nations, founded in 1945, was equally seen as a means of preventing wars, something which throughout the remaining four decades of Cold War it signally failed to do, precisely because of the deeper, unresolved fissure in world politics. Yet it was precisely when the Cold War ended, with the collapse of the Soviet system, that it became possible to speak of making the UN work for the first time. The symbolic conclusion of the Cold War came in December 1990 with a new moment of international recomposition, the signing in Paris of the treaty that set up the Organisation for Security and Cooperation in Europe. The dissolution of the USSR came a year later. The history of the international system is therefore marked by a cycle of dissolution and recomposition, attendant upon the incidence of internationalised revolutionary crises and their supersession. In their incidence as in their demise, revolutions therefore mark the path of the international history of modernity. The evolution and character of the international system are inextricably linked to the incidence of revolutions; if other factors played a formative role, none was greater than that of political and social upheaval within states.

8

Counter-Revolution

Reaction Across Frontiers

If revolutions are international in their causes, programmes and consequences, the same is equally true for attempts to overthrow or prevent them. The fear of such an overthrow haunts all revolutionaries. Two months after the Bolshevik seizure of power, Lenin wrote to Trotsky 'This is a moment of triumph. We have lasted a day longer than the Paris Commune.'[1] Counter-revolution, a universal accompaniment of all revolutions, is as international as revolution itself: it is, as much as revolution, a constitutive element in the modern history of international relations. Like revolution, counter-revolution often has international causes. Moreover, it is international in that it seeks to affect politics across state frontiers. It is international above all because, like revolution, counter-revolution is both product and further stimulant of a generalised crisis of the state system that engulfs a range of countries and that forms the focus for international politics in a particular epoch.[2]

The term 'counter-revolution' refers to a policy of trying to reverse a revolution, and, by extension, to policies designed to prevent revolutionary movements that have already gained some momentum from coming to power. It denotes, therefore, both reversal or overthrow, and what has been referred to, variously, as suppression and containment. Like so many terms in the modern political vocabulary, it has its origins in the French revolution, in the movement that developed in the early 1790s, partly within France, in such areas as the Vendée, and partly amongst royalist emigres outside France, and which sought to restore the monarchy to power.[3] Counter-revolution cannot turn the clock back, it cannot restore in full measure that which was there before: the passage of time, the very impact of revolution, prevents replication. Just as revolution claims to reject the past, but cannot entirely do so, so counter-revolution cannot realise its claim to restore that which was overthrown. The restoration of Louis XVIII in 1815 did not re-establish a stable Bourbon monarchy in France. The suppression of revolt in 1848 did not stem the political currents that had emerged in that year. Counter-revolution can, however, overthrow the political system created by the revolution and restore the main political and social elements of the previous order.

This response to the French revolution was to produce not just the term 'counter-revolution' but many of the other concepts and policies that have in the subsequent two centuries been associated with the reaction of conservative powers to revolutions. The ideology of conservatism, indeed the very term itself, was formulated in response to 1789, in the writings of Edmund Burke and Josèphe de Maistre above all; so too was the association of the term 'reaction' and 'reactionary' with conservative policies. In the end the French revolution was defeated in battle at Waterloo and the monarch restored, an event followed by the Congress of Vienna of 1815. It was there, in the work of the Austrian chancellor Clemens von Metternich, the so-called 'doctor of revolutions', that the most explicit theories of counter-revolutionary order were elaborated.[4]

If the French revolution served as the originator of the modern conception, and policy, of counter-revolution it also exemplified how this phenomenon has a necessarily international character. The first such international dimension, as true of France as of all later cases, is, as already discussed in Chapter 5, the necessary accompaniment of revolution by counter-revolution: all revolutions provoke a response, within the country and without, that lasts as long as the revolution itself. No study of the international dimensions of revolution can afford to neglect this topic, both for what it tells us about the consequences of revolution, and for the broader development of international relations.

Yet this impact, and the response to it, are never solely or predominantly a matter of the policies of states. Just as revolutions provoke responses of admiration or anxiety beyond those which the revolutionary states themselves envision, so does counter-

revolution. Like revolution, counter-revolution generates an internationalised ideological and psychological atmosphere that goes
beyond the policies of states.

Secondly, the French, like later counter-revolutions, involved
both domestic *and* international forces: the first stirrings of counter-revolution came from *within* France, from dissatisfied politicians
and conservative peasantry; the course, and success, of all counter-
revolution involves a combination of these two aspects. Of particular relevance here is that a purely externally generated movement
is much less effective, and even if substantial, involves another
condition, the weakening of the revolutionary state. As we shall see,
the record of attempts to overthrow revolutionary states short of
inter-state war or, in the case of Soviet communism, a radical
weakening of the state, is meagre.

Thirdly, whatever its programme, the counter-revolution, like
revolution, challenges the established values of states. For if the
central values of the established states system are sovereignty and
the principle of non-interference, counter-revolutionaries, as much
as revolutionaries, argue for a right of interference, indeed of
intervention, in other states. As with revolutionaries, the arguments
are often mixed – claims of self-defence and response to aggression
combining with the need to respond to appeals from opponents
within the revolutionary states and the need to defend universal
principles. From Edmund Burke in the 1790s to Ronald Reagan in
the 1980s, this is a recurrent feature of the ideology of counter-
revolution. As much as revolutionaries, counter-revolutionaries see
international politics as a form of internationalised civil war, in
which divisions of frontier or nation may, for a time at least, matter
less than those of ideological and social interest.

Finally, we see in revolutions, as with counter-revolutions, the
limits which the international poses. For as much as the rhetoric
and aspiration of revolutionaries exceeds the constraints of reality,
so, in many cases, does that of counter-revolution. As far as the
explicit intentions of states are concerned, the record of exporting
counter-revolution is as long on rhetoric, and short on achievement,
as is that of revolution itself. The established divisions of states tend
to prevail over the cross-border appeals of either revolutionary or
counter-revolutionary. Only when longer-term social and ideological processes have taken hold does the internationalisation of
revolution and counter-revolution become more possible.

Varieties of Counter-Revolution

Counter-revolution is not, however, a single phenomenon, any more than is revolution, and the rhetorical, almost mystical, use of the term conceals a variety of possibilities. In the first place, 'counter-revolution' may refer to the overthrow of a revolutionary regime by opponents working within the country and with external support. This is the original French revolutionary meaning of the term, and it is this phenomenon which revolutionaries, ever vigilant about domestic threats, seek to eliminate. On the other hand, it may refer to what in revolutionary parlance is referred to as Thermidor, the event named after the French month of July 1794 when the radical Jacobin dictatorship was overthrown. 'Thermidor' is said to denote the end of the revolutionary period, the seizure of power not by representatives of the old regime but by a counter-revolutionary faction within the new. Thus left Bolshevik critics of Stalin accused his regime of being from 1923 Thermidorean, because of the suppression of political debate at home and the curbing of revolutionary activity abroad.[5] 'Counter-revolution' also refers to movements or policies that are not designed to overthrow or corrupt an existing revolutionary regime, but rather to prevent a revolutionary movement from coming to power. Thus *coups* designed to prevent revolutionary groups from coming to power, or to prevent reforming regimes from pressing on to more radical measures, can be termed 'counter-revolutionary' – the Spanish nationalist coup led by General Franco in 1936, or the Chilean coup of Augusto Pinochet in 1973, being cases in point. By extension, social and political measures, including reforms, that have as their goal the blocking of more radical policies can qualify: the land reforms carried out by the USA in the post-1945 period, first in the Far East, then in Iran and Latin America, were designed to pre-empt peasant revolution.[6]

All of these forms of counter-revolution have their international dimension. Internal oppositions look for and receive support from abroad; Thermidorean coups respond to external pressures and seek to placate external foes; policies of repression and pre-emptive reform are encouraged by status quo powers. But the most direct international involvement in counter-revolution is that of states who deploy their resources to oppose revolutionary regimes. This is conventionally presented, in the literature on international relations, as 'intervention', a term that denotes something more than diplomatic or military pressure, but usually something short of outright invasion; it suggests at least the principle that the sovereignty and separate identity of the state in question will endure. Intervention is coercive: it involves military activity of some kind and violation of the orthodox norm of sovereignty, and has a goal of altering if not the regime itself then at least its policies.[7] Thus the military involvement of the Allies in Bolshevik Russia in 1918–20, of the USA in Vietnam from 1965 to 1973, are cases of intervention. In such cases troops from the counter-revolutionary power were directly and publicly involved in military activities in another state. However, intervention can take indirect forms – support for guerrillas and sabotage, harassment along the frontiers, financial backing for opposition groups within the revolutionary state. More broadly, it may involve the deployment of propaganda resources and of economic sanctions designed to undermine the revolutionary regime and lessen its ability to meet the aspirations of its people.

Such intervention, overt or covert, accompanies almost all revolutions. As discussed in Chapter 5, intervention is justified by the counter-revolutionary state on the grounds that it is a response to the international activities of the revolutionaries. On the other hand, it is used by revolutionaries to justify their own international activities. Thus the Bolsheviks presented themselves as responding to the Allied intervention, the Chinese to US imperialist encirclement, the Cubans and Nicaraguans to CIA-backed sabotage, and the Iranians to an Iraqi invasion allegedly backed by the USA and Israel.

So central is this recurrence of both revolution *and* counter-revolution that it has come to be one of the dominant themes of modern international history. Time and again states have sought to limit, 'contain' and overthrow revolutions using a variety of mechanisms, and often against initial calculations of what a purely 'national,' i.e. statist, calculation of interest would be. To comprehend the ways in which the revolution/counter-revolution interaction interacts with the international system, it is necessary to grasp both the extent of this interaction and the limits which the international system places upon each. The history of the two centuries since 1789 is, to a considerable extent, that of the workings out of these conflicts on an international scale, in ways that go beyond the intentions of states, and, at the same time, of the ways in which the states system directs and limits that interaction.

The Compulsion to Intervene

The international upheaval unleashed by the French revolution brought into being, after a pause, a coalition of counter-revolutionary forces: the Austrian monarch, Leopold II, encouraged by royalist emigrés was by 1791 committed to reversing the revolution. From 1793, even Britain, which had at first remained aloof from the continental conflict, became involved, giving naval support to a royalist uprising in the port of Toulon in the latter part of 1793, and in June 1795 landing 3,000 emigrés on the Brittany coast at the Quiberon peninsula in the hope of encouraging a counter-revolutionary uprising.[8] Given the inequality of power of the revolutionary and counter-revolutionary forces *within* France, and the ability of the revolutionary regime to turn foreign hostility to nationalist advantage, these first attempts at counter-revolution failed. There followed years of formal military conflict, culminating in the defeat of Napoleon in 1815. Therefore counter-revolution came not through internal uprising but through the defeat of the French state in conventional war.

The Congress of Vienna, convened by the anti-French alliance of Russia, Prussia, Austria and Britain, sought to draw the lessons of the French revolution for the future management of Europe. Vienna was, quintessentially, a conference designed to restabilise order in Europe, to repair the damage 1789 had done to 1648. It did this in three ways – by redefining the frontiers of the European states, by organising a system of formalised relations between the major powers, and by laying down policies for preventing further revolutions. It was therefore concerned to legitimise counter-revolution, to prevent any recurrence of the French revolution, a commitment reflected in two agreements. First, and despite the belief of the British in particular in the principle of non-interference, the four victorious allies agreed, in a treaty signed after the main Congress was over, to remain on guard in case 'revolutions should again convulse France. . .and to take the measures necessary for the safety of their respective states'.[9] The very fact of revolution, not any aggression it might commit, was thus considered to be a legitimate cause of intervention. This commitment to a cooperative internationalised counter-revolution was taken further in an agreement between four powers, but not Britain, signed in 1816 – the Holy Alliance.[10] What this alliance represented was a commitment not just to security *between* states, to what has been termed 'vertical' security, but also to security *within* states, to 'horizontal' security. In his 'Confession of Faith', a memorandum sent secretly by von Metternich to Tsar Alexander I in December 1815, he wrote:

> A league between all governments against factions in all states . . . union between the monarchs is the basis of the policy which must now be followed to save society from total ruin. . . The first and greatest concern for the immense majority of every nation is the stability of the laws, and their uninterrupted action – never their change. Therefore, let the governments govern. Let them maintain the groundwork of their institutions. . . Let them maintain religious principles in all their purity, and not allow the faith to be attacked and morality interpreted according to the social contract or the visions of foolish sectarians. Let them suppress secret societies, that gangrene of society. In short, let the great monarchs strengthen their union . . . paternal and protective, menacing only the disturbers of public tranquillity.[11]

There could be no absolute division between the maintenance of international peace and the maintenance of the stability of legitimate states. Change there might be, but it would have to come through cautious constitutional change.

It is conventional to argue that the commitments made at Vienna were soon abandoned in the face of the rise of nationalism in Italy and Greece and, more broadly, in the spread of revolutionary upheavals across Europe – in 1830, 1848, the Italian *risorgimento* of 1859–61 and 1871. But this is to downplay the central achievement of the European states in the nineteenth century, which was to prevent not only upheavals but that such upheavals should lead to war. There were no general inter-European wars for ninety-nine years; those wars that occurred were independent of – or in the case of the Franco-Prussian war of 1870, anterior, rather than subsequent to – revolutionary upheavals. The system, looser but none the less effective, lasted for close to a century. It was to be torn apart only in the vortex of the crisis that swept Europe in the first two decades of the twentieth century.

The crisis of 1900–20 was, as already noted earlier, a dual one – a crisis of the inter-state system *and* of the political system within states, the greatest generalised crisis of the international system. From 1900 onwards the fatal combination of revolt from within and war from without returned to convulse Europe. Preceded by revolt in a range of semi-peripheral countries – Russia, China, Persia, Turkey, Mexico, Portugal – the crisis then exploded in the Balkans in 1914. The crisis of 1914 was itself then to produce greater upheavals, in the great wave of uprisings and collapsed empires that was unleashed by the inter-state war. The years from 1916 onwards were ones of generalised revolution *and* counter-revolution across Europe. Risings, mutinies and oustings of monarchy were accompanied by repression, civil war and military rule.

The task confronting those who convened at Versailles in 1919 was, therefore, in some large measure, to replicate Vienna a century or more ago. Boundaries were to be defined and guaranteed; hitherto unfree peoples were to acquire their states. New institutional mechanisms for regulating inter-state relations, in this case the League of Nations, were set up. But as important as any of these was the prevention of revolution. Here, as at Vienna, opinion varied: the French, under Clemenceau, were the most determined to use the new international machinery to crush the Bolshevik revolution; Woodrow Wilson, the US President, was to demonstrate a fascination with crushing revolutions that characterised later Democratic presidents; the British under Lloyd George were more cautious. Versailles did, however, take the containment and destruction of Bolshevism as one of its central tasks, one that was to be continued by the individual states in the two decades that followed. The USA did not recognise the new Soviet regime until 1933; the League of Nations was to delay more than a decade before inviting the Bolsheviks to join. From their perspective, the sentiments were reciprocated. The Communist Party Congress of 1919, in a programme drafted by Lenin, had seen the League as a new form of international consolidation of capitalists, a League of Robbers, 'directing their first efforts toward the immediate suppression of the revolutionary movements of the proletariat of all countries'.[12]

The First World War, however, was to unleash counter-revolution in a rather different and, ultimately, more extreme form than any gathering of states at Versailles. The war had not resolved the generalised crisis of European society, but only brought it to a more explosive point. The turmoil of European societies provoked by this war, in political, social and economic terms, was in time to foster a movement for revenge and for authoritarian, militaristic rule that was to bring the European states system, and its revolutionary movements, to their greatest crisis. The containment of the wave of revolt after 1918, in Germany and elsewhere, was contained by suppression. For a few years it appeared as if the European system had been normalised: democracy developed, the states participated in the League. But from the late 1920s things began to change. The economic crisis and the rise of radical right-wing movements presaged a much more ferocious right-wing onslaught than any hitherto imagined.

In Germany, the crisis following the war had created a mass social movement of embittered former soldiers, brutalised by their experiences in the war around which the Nazi leadership could mobilise. The aims were multiple, incoherent in expression, but focussed on a composite three-part enemy – foreigners, Jews, Bolsheviks. Out of the cauldron of this dislocated world emerged the fascism of Hitler. Hitler saw his movement as a counter to Bolshevism. Borrowing elements from it in ideology and organisation, he argued in *Mein Kampf* that his ideology was the alternative to Marxism, itself the culmination of the Enlightenment: instead of class and equality, Hitler proposed race and hierarchy as organising principles of his new politics.[13]

As Arno Mayer has argued, Hitler's ideology was above all a syncretic one, in which the three major themes were combined. His hatred of Bolshevism was fused with anti-semitism in attacks on 'Judaeobolshevism', on Marx as a Jew and on the Jewish character of the Bolshevik leadership. If it is impossible to disentangle, in the protean flow of Nazi rhetoric, the geostrategic, racial supremacist and specifically anti-Bolshevik elements, the latter is a recurrent and important part of the whole. Mayer shows how in Hitler's *Mein Kampf* these three different elements combine: the geostrategic need for Germany to expand to the east, for reasons of *Lebensraum;* hatred of Jews; and hostility to Bolshevism. Since Russia was the main opponent to the east, and since 1917 was presented as the outcome of a 'Judaeo-Bolshevik' conspiracy, the three elements were combined.

Yet in the early 1920s there was a discernible gap between the predominance in his *rhetoric* of anti-semitism, and the wider *appeal* of his anti-Marxism, the latter becoming especially strong in late 1922.[14] Anti-semitism itself fed on counter-revolutionary fervour; the most notorious of all anti-semitic tracts, *The Protocols of the Elders of Zion*, was brought to Germany and diffused there by White Russian emigrés after 1917. Anti-Marxism continued to be central to Hitler's ideology and was accentuated by world events. At the National Socialists German Workers' Party (NSDAP) congress in September 1936, two months after the outbreak of the Spanish civil war, he delivered a particularly strong anti-Bolshevik tirade; at a speech in early October 1941, a little over three months after the invasion of Russia, he declared Bolshevism broken.[15] His invitation to Italy and Japan to join the Anti-Comintern Pact was no idle one.

That this fusion of themes was no mere ideological concoction was to be evident in the course of the Second World War itself, when the different ideological elements coalesced. The elimination of Jews in Eastern Europe coincided with the campaign to eliminate Bolshevism, and the extermination of large numbers of Slavs (over 50 per cent of Russian POWs died in captivity); from 1941 onwards, the great majority of the Nazi war effort was directed to promoting the Eastern Front. On the basis of what Hitler said, and, even more, on the basis of what he did, the conclusion can be drawn that, beyond the rejection of the Weimar Republic and of Versailles, and the elimination of the Jews, the final goal of Nazism was the destruction of Bolshevism.[16]

The onslaught of fascism was in the end checked by the Second World War, an alliance of liberal capitalist and authoritarian socialist states that, at great cost, destroyed the Axis powers. It was followed, as in 1815 and 1945, by international conferences that settled frontiers and created bodies for institutionalised international cooperation; there was no single conference, in this case, but a succession, at Tehran (1943), Yalta (February 1945) and Potsdam (July 1945). Yet the issue of revolution and counter-revolution was as present as it had been in the previous epochs. For this very victory set the stage for another conflict, one that was to dominate the world for the ensuing four and a half decades. In this conflict between liberal capitalism and authoritarian socialism, the two sides sought within their spheres of influence to maintain their own regimes in power while provoking revolt in the other.

For three decades at least, the initiative appeared to be with the Soviet Union, as nationalist and socialist revolt swept much of the Third World. In this context, the USA and its allies were the proponents of counter-revolution. Within the Soviet system itself, however, the control and suppression of mass movements was equally central. In some degree against his bureaucratic instinct, Stalin benefited from the upsurges of the Second World War, in Eastern Europe and even more so in the Far East. But far from using these upsurges to liberalise his own regime, Stalin sought to impose control over them: Russia was the only country affected by the Second World War which did not experience significant political change afterwards. In Eastern Europe an authoritarian revolution from above was imposed, crushing and dispiriting those who had believed in an alternative socialist model. In those countries where indigenous revolutionary forces had triumphed out of the Second World War, Soviet policy, intrusive and hegemonic, provoked in time revolt – in Yugoslavia in 1948, China in 1960, Albania in 1961. The loss of these states, above all that of China, was to weaken the Soviet Union strategically. But the defiant regimes, by dint of maintaining their own indigenous authoritarianisms, did not challenge the Soviet political model. Titoism, and later, Maoism, had some appeal in the Soviet bloc, but this was contained. In the end, and decades later, it was the pressures of the West, above all the demonstration effect of capitalist economic success, which brought the Soviet system, and that of its defected allies, down.

The Cold War can therefore be seen as a global conflict involving at least three different elements: a military confrontation, focussed on the arms race; a competition between two models of social and economic achievement – what the Soviet Union came in the late 1950s to term 'peaceful coexistence'; and the suppression by each side of revolt within their spheres of influence. Both the US and Soviet systems had, therefore, a counter-revolutionary element in their foreign policy. Within this, the apparently separate, technologically determined, field of nuclear weapons was, in the main, driven by political concerns, the desire to maintain a credible deterrent such that each would be able to conduct other offensive and defensive operations in contested zones.

On the Soviet side there was a rhetoric of freedom and liberation, one that masked the imposition of authoritarian role at home even as it supported revolutionary and nationalist movements abroad. The first phase of the consolidation of this authoritarian rule, in the immediate aftermath of 1945, was carried out without great apparent difficulty, thanks to the presence of the Red Army on the territory of the countries concerned. Where the Red Army and the intelligence services could act they suppressed independent social and political movements, as they had in the areas of the Spanish republic in the 1930s. Where they could not, as in China and Vietnam, they sought to win influence through elements in the political and security apparatus sympathetic to them.

Over time, however, the challenges began to emerge, not only at the popular level, but also within the ranks of the Eastern European communist parties themselves – in Germany (1953), Poland and Hungary (1956) and Czechoslovakia (1968). In each case resistance was crushed by military force, with the support of factions within the local parties. The justifications for these interventions shifted: in the 1940s the logic of the construction of the socialist camp; in the 1950s the need to crush counter-revolution and 'revanchism'. It was in the context of the suppression of the movement in 1968 that the most explicit justification of such actions in counter-revolutionary terms was based, in the form of Brezhnev's theory of 'limited sovereignty'. When confronted by challenges, those opposed to change placed the defence of kindred regimes – their horizontal security – above that of respect for state sovereignty and boundaries – vertical security – just as much as did revolutionaries.

On the US side the incidence of this commitment to an inter-nationalised defence of established regimes is most striking, if a simple test is applied: that of the topic on which US presidents were to stake their reputations. There had, of course, been precedents for this. President Monroe (1817–25), in his doctrine, proclaimed in 1823 the right of the USA not only to exclude other, European, powers from influence in the Americas, but also to intervene in that region when regimes allied to it were under threat. A policy initially designed to prevent the European powers from re-establishing their colonial power in the Americas became a legitimation of US assertion of its newer hegemony. President Theodore Roosevelt (1901–9) had proclaimed a similar doctrine in 1904, a 'Corollary' to the Monroe Doctrine declaring the USA to be 'an international police power'; it was Roosevelt who popularised the adage 'Speak softly and carry a big stick; you will go far'. In the period after 1945 it might have seemed self-evident that the most important issues facing US presidents were, first, the nuclear balance, and, second, the health of the advanced industrial economies. These were certainly central preoccupations, but it was not on these issues that US presidents staked their names. That issue was the suppression of revolt in the Third World.

Thus Truman (1945–52) in 1947 proclaimed a US commitment to preventing a communist victory in Greece and Turkey, and, by extension, Iran. Eisenhower (1953–60) in 1957 announced a doctrine of support for US allies in the Arab world. Kennedy (1961–3) in 1961, faced with the revolution in Cuba, launched a campaign to shore up US allies in the Third World by a combination of pre-emptive reform and counter-insurgency. Lyndon Johnson (1963–8) proclaimed his doctrine on 1 May 1965 with the invasion of the Dominican Republic in response to an uprising there; only a month later, and without invocation of the doctrinal name, it was to develop into a catastrophic commitment, with the despatch of over half a million US combat troops to Vietnam. The setbacks in Vietnam led Johnson's successor, Richard Nixon (1969–74), to proclaim in 1969 the 'Nixon Doctrine': contrary to Johnson's, this advocated the withdrawal of US forces from direct involvement in Third World conflicts and the delegation of responsibility to power-ful Third World states. Nixon's successor, Ford (1974–6), did not have a doctrine, but in practice it was one of strategic caution, in particular, one in which no action was taken to defend US allies in Saigon and Vietnam or to prevent Cuban forces from intervening in Angola. Carter (1977–80) may have hoped to avoid involvement in Third World conflicts, but in the aftermath of Iran and Afghanistan he too proclaimed a doctrine – defence of the Arabian Peninsula and Persian Gulf states (1980). It was to take effect in an increasing US role in support for Iraq's war with Iran, and, later, in the mass intervention to reverse the Iraqi invasion of Kuwait (1990–1). The years of Ronald Reagan (1981–8) were marked by perhaps the most activist and explicit counter-revolutionary campaign of all, the aim to oust Soviet allies in the Third World by arming their foes – in Cambodia, Afghanistan, Angola and Nicaragua.[17]

The dénouement of the clash between these two contradictory counter-revolutionary logics was to come at the end of the 1980s. As we have seen, it involved the prevailing of one bloc over the other, in a combination of conflict levels. However, the very out-come was itself to reveal complexities that, in retrospect, cast the rival endeavours of the two powers in a different light. On the Soviet side, the commitment to revolution abroad was to produce, or to assist in, the transformation of several parts of the Third World, from Korea to Cuba. Yet the price of this commitment was not only the sharpening of relations with the USA, and a nuclear arms race, but the imposition on these countries of authoritarian regimes that replicated in many respects the system in the USSR itself. Moreover, while at the strategic and military levels the Soviet Union appeared able to advance to its peak in the early 1980s, this consolidation was simultaneously undermined by the erosion of the domestic bases of the system itself, culminating in the crisis of

1989–91. The Soviet Union *was* able to prevent revolt from within its own ranks, by dint of arms, first in Eastern Europe and then in Third World allies. It could not prevent the defection of nationalist communist regimes from 1948 onwards. Most important of all, and on the terrain it had itself chosen as that on which it would compete with the West in 'peaceful coexistence', the Soviet system gradually eroded and collapsed. Once the guarantee of force to the Eastern European regimes and, later, to the constituent republics of the USSR was removed (in 1988 and 1991 respectively), the USSR succumbed not to the counter-revolution of imperialist agents or revanchists, not even to that of *mujahidin* or *contras*, but to that of living standards and popular aspiration.

In the US case, the terms were almost exactly reversed. The most important US military commitment, NATO, had almost no direct counter-revolutionary role at all. It was established in 1949, after the suppression of the communist and other post-liberation mass movements in Western Europe. The uprising in France in 1968 did not pose a major security challenge. The only case where this did occur, from a radical popular and military movement, was the Portuguese revolution of 1974; there can be no doubt that US diplomatic and security personnel played a role in the turning of the tide from this radicalism, but it is to misunderstand the main dynamic of the Portuguese revolution to see it as one inspired by radical socialism.[18] US attempts to contain revolutionary movements in the Third World by force were for a long time only partly effective. From the late 1940s in China, through to Vietnam, Iran and Nicaragua in the 1970s, US allies, with varying degrees of military backing, were ousted by popular movements. The presidential doctrines were, in large measure, attempts after the event to prevent further erosion. Eisenhower did not prevent the fall of Iraq in 1958, and nor did Kennedy, Johnson or Nixon prevent the fall of Vietnam in 1975.

The counter-revolutionary insurrections of the 1980s had themselves mixed outcomes. In no case did they succeed in their proclaimed goals, that of ousting the regimes in power. Nor, despite much talk of 'eroding the Soviet system at the margin', did they play a major role in the collapse of the Soviet system itself.[19] In Cambodia and Angola, the USA and the international community in general ended by accepting the established communist regimes in power, formally as coalition partners with their former enemies, practically as the dominant parties in those coalitions. In Nicaragua the years of *contra* harassment, which had failed to capture a single city, did, combined with other factors, lead to the elections of February 1990, in which the FSLN were voted from power. In Afghanistan, the Soviet troop withdrawal of February 1989 was followed by the collapse of the communist regime in April 1992. But in these two latter cases the shift in regime was, as much as anything, a result *not* a cause of the shift in Moscow itself.

The Incoherences of Counter-Revolution

The mixed record of such attempts to maintain 'horizontal' and 'vertical' security suggests ways in which, beneath the appearance of an internationalised commitment to counter-revolution, other, less detectable, forces may be at work. Indeed this record points to ambiguities in the process of counter-revolution itself. In the first place, for all the commitments of states to counter-revolution, and their arguments against state sovereignty, they are constrained as much as revolutionary states by that system. Unless it can be carried out swiftly and at acceptable cost, the commitment to counter-revolution is a limited one. Indeed, on closer examination, what one sees time and again is the *incoherence* of the counter-revolutionary commitment.

This is first evident in the uncertain reactions of status quo powers to revolutions. In retrospect it may appear inevitable that such powers would come into conflict with revolutionary regimes: their own conceptions of order, national and international, and the very commitment of revolutionary states to a radical internationalism, would alone have ensured that. But this is not what the historical pattern indicates. Mention has already been made of the interlude, the 'period of grace', which revolutionary regimes enjoy once they have come to power. The whole world does not rush to suppress them, but rather waits, gives them some tentative benefit of the doubt, and hopes for an accommodation. It was precisely this caution which, in 1790, and even more directly in 1796, Edmund Burke sought to denounce. For Burke, it was not a question of waiting for the revolutionary state to attack others, it was the very fact of ideological challenge, posed by the existence of a society based on radically different foundations, to which the status quo powers *had* to respond.

Even when they do respond, however, the counter-revolution is less directed, less mobilised, and in the end less effective than might appear at the time. For what recurs time and again are attempts at counter-revolution that are, in many ways, half measures. They are enough to show something is being done, enough certainly to antagonise the revolutionary state, but well short of what is required to destroy the revolutionary regime, and certainly well short of the full mobilisation of resources and power which the status quo powers are capable of. In the aftermath of the French revolution, the status quo powers, Austria, Prussia and Britain, did go to war with France and, in the manner that was to become familiar in later times, did support counter-revolutionary exiles: arms, training, money, propaganda were provided, but to little avail. Only in 1815, after Napoleon had sought at Waterloo to reverse the historical verdict, were the full mechanisms of military defeat and occupation achieved.

The twentieth century gives many examples of this incoherence. Certainly, there were cases of successful counter-revolution. Some of these were decisive military interventions to crush revolutionary regimes – Hungary in 1919, the Dominican Republic in 1965, Grenada in 1983. Others, equally decisive, and in the short run 'successful', were the Soviet interventions in Hungary in 1956 and Czechoslovakia in 1968. But the examples of incoherence are equally, if not more, compelling. Thus the Allied intervention in Russia in 1918–20 ended with the withdrawal of the armies of the eighteen states that had sent troops on to Russian soil, and the defeat of the White armies backed by the Allies. The eighteen states sending troops into Russia deployed only a fraction of their available military resources, and were divided in aim. While there were those in the British state, as in France, who wanted to overthrow the Bolsheviks, the main aims were to support continued war against Germany and to prevent military supplies sent by the Allies from falling into German hands.[20] In Vietnam, in 1954, and in Algeria, in 1962, a militarily overwhelming France was forced to yield to nationalist opponents and withdraw.

In the Indochinese wars of the 1960s and 1970s the USA, with backing from some allies, sustained heavy losses in trying to stem the Vietnamese revolutionary movement, but in the end withdrew, and after an interval of two years saw its allies in Saigon defeated. It is not clear what, in retrospect, were the aims of the US intervention in Vietnam. At one level, they were obvious: to prevent the victory of the communists in the south and the reunification of Vietnam under communist rule. But for all the commitment of troops, money and prestige, the USA was far from deploying its full might in this endeavour. It never invaded North Vietnam, or bombed northern cities, nor could it sustain its allied regime in the south which, for all its shared anti-communism, was riven with factionalism, military and political. In Vietnam the USA was not defeated *militarily*, yet it sustained the greatest *political* defeat in its international history.[21]

Four years later, the USA faced equally striking, and even more absolute defeats, when it was unable to help its beleaguered allies in Iran and Nicaragua. The rise of a popular revolution against the Shah in the last months of 1978 prompted debate in Washington about what to do. But there was sharp division between Carter's advisers about how to respond; no one seriously thought any form of direct US intervention could save the Shah's regime. A few months later, the same dilemmas played themselves out in Managua, as the Somocista National Guard, retreating in the face of the Sandinista uprising, crumbled and fled.

When it came to the fight back, to the 'Reagan Doctrine', a similar incoherence prevailed. In the 1980s the USA began to undermine the Sandinista regime in Nicaragua. But throughout this period of US counter-revolution in Nicaragua there was no clarity as to what the USA was doing. Large sections of the US state – including Congress and the State Department – were against the US policy, and the President was forced to resort to devious and illegal means to fund the *contra* effort. At the time there was widespread uncertainty, and debate, about what the US agenda and its goals were. We know from subsequent reports that in Washington there was no clear agenda: no centre of decision, no clarity of purpose, no common policy on this issue.[22] In one sense, this may not have mattered: it did not take much for the powerful and proximate USA to inflict damage on a nation of three million people. It did matter, however, in the 1980s, in that a war was fought for which no clear objective existed and which had as its central goal the weakening of Soviet power, something that it played no significant part in achieving. It certainly mattered to those who wanted a more committed US intervention, and who resented the limits to a direct US role which political conditions imposed.

A similar incoherence could be detected on the Soviet side, with the case of Afghanistan. The decision to send troops to Kabul in December 1979 was taken by a small group of leaders, without even the processes of consultation among military and civilian leaders that had become practice on some other issues. Clarity of goals, information, and discussion of options were absent. The regime it was committed to supporting in Kabul was, as much as that which the Americans had sustained in Saigon, riven with factions: the emergence of one group on top entailed the antagonisms of other military and political forces. When, six years later, in November 1985, a decision in principle to withdraw was taken, it exposed the lack of a clear strategy: to protect the regime, crush the rebels, insulate Central Asia, prevent a US takeover. There was no clarity of purpose in intervention, or in withdrawal.[23]

Limits on Power

The record of counter-revolution is therefore one in which the almost universal incidence of attempts to prevent revolutions is matched by the comparatively limited, and often unsuccessful, outcome of such endeavours. In the whole period from 1789 to 1989, counter-revolution defined as *the coercive overthrow of an established revolutionary regime* was only achieved on two occasions: once, through defeat in inter-state war, at Waterloo in 1815; secondly, through the use of overwhelming military power against a state that had lost the support of its people, in Grenada in 1983. Counter-revolution defined as *violent suppression of revolutionary movements* had a more successful record, but even here what is striking is the limitation, as much as the success, of such policies.

The reasons for this limited response, and for the incoherence, are several. Indeed the incoherence, the mixture of goals and the disputes between officials responsible for the policy, points as much as anything to a frustration with the limits which the international and domestic political systems place upon those committed to counter-revolution. In the first place, counter-revolutionary states have to deal with opinion within their own countries. Patriotic sentiment may be strong when a state is confronted with an attack on its own territory, or allied territory; it is generally less willing to sustain loss of life, and expenditure of money, when it comes to intervening to change the regime in another state. If this is generally so, it is all the more so if the potential counter-revolutionary power is itself exhausted after earlier conflicts – characteristically so in the case of the Allies and Russia in 1918–20.

Even where this is not so, however, the general presumption is that counter-revolutionary interventions, precisely because they involve transgressing a broad conception of sovereignty, are harder to justify to public opinion. If they are rapid and successful they may succeed in getting public support. If not, as the Americans found in Vietnam, then such support erodes. Nor is it merely a matter of public support: prolonged and unresolved confrontation can have two other, related, effects – it can affect the morale and cohesion of the armed forces themselves, and it can incur other costs that alienate significant constituencies within the society. In the case of the US intervention in Vietnam, both occurred: discipline and morale declined in the army, and significant sections of the US business community came to oppose the war. The question of how, and when, the USA decided to pull out of Vietnam may never be answered; what is clear is that, at a certain moment in 1968–9, the weight of opinion turned against continued involvement, and led to a revision of official policy.

Intervention also entails costs at the international level. Other states not directly involved in the conflict may oppose the intervention, and, while not intervening themselves on the side of the revolutionary state, may provide assistance to it. The more the counter-revolutionary power intervenes, the more other states will be likely to increase their own commitment. France aided the USA in its War of Independence, Russia aided Vietnam. In Vietnam too, the US anxiety was to avoid a repeat of what had happened in Korea, when, as US forces advanced towards the Chinese frontier, on the Yalu River, China itself intervened directly to push back the US forces. By the late 1960s, moreover, China had acquired nuclear weapons; the US could not 'go to the source', even if it had been willing to sustain the troop casualties, because there could be no certainty that China would not use its nuclear weapons in an ensuing confrontation.

The restraints on US involvement in the 1970s and 1980s were of a comparable kind. Intervention in Iran was, in addition to everything else within the country, precluded by the country's proximity to the USSR. A direct attack on Nicaragua, or for that matter Cuba, was constrained partly by fear of a Soviet counter-move – against, for example, Berlin – but partly by the alienation which it was believed would follow in Latin America and Western Europe. Again, there may not be any one reason why the USA did not invade Nicaragua; nonetheless, the outcome, a result of several pressures, was such that Washington was constrained from using the military power which it undoubtedly had to oust the FSLN.

These constraints, whether domestic or international, have been *political*, and this applies equally to the very relation involved in a conflict of revolutionary and counter-revolutionary powers. Such a relation is, in military and economic terms, profoundly unequal, or *asymmetric*.[24] The counter-revolutionary power has the advantage. Yet in political terms it is the revolutionary power which has, or potentially has, superior assets. This is so in three respects. Within the country at war, it can mobilise large numbers of people in long, demanding, conflict situations in a manner that the counter-revolutionary power cannot. Moreover it can, in both political *and* military terms, turn the asymmetry to its advantage, wearing down the political will of the opponent in the field, and eroding the political constituency for counter-revolution in the metropolitan state itself. It can, moreover, mobilise international support and, beyond that, opinion in its favour.

As in any conflict, the outcome of such asymmetric wars is not pre-ordained. The strategy of guerrilla war, propagated at various points in modern history, has had, as will be argued in Chapter 9, as much myth as reality about it. Examples abound of the failure of rebellions, guerrilla wars and the like. Yet the recurrence of cases in which rebellion *has* succeeded, against states much more powerful in military and economic terms, draws attention to a potential for victory that conventional assessments of power may not comprehend.

Why States Intervene

The difficulties associated with counter-revolution pose a question that might initially appear to permit of an easy resolution, namely *why* states act as they do. As far as internal counter-revolution is concerned, there would seem to be an obvious answer: fear of a revolutionary victory, or reaction to it. This seems a plausible explanation in many cases. Yet, as Arno Mayer has shown, it cannot be a sufficient explanation. For what Europe witnessed in the late nineteenth century and early twentieth century was a counter-revolutionary wave *far greater* than anything confronting it from the revolutionary left. In a situation of generalised crisis, Europe underwent a crisis of overreaction, where right-wing forces, threatened by the social tension and disruption of war, launched a drive for the restoration of authoritarian rule and a return to pre-modern political and social values. This crisis was, Mayer argues, as much a reflection of a weakening and division within the ruling elites as of any rational response to a real revolutionary threat. The cycle was not one of revolutionary challenge producing counter-revolution and then war, but rather of elite overreaction leading to domestic counter-revolution and war, a process which, in turn, destroyed those elites and unleashed the very forces they had tried by overreaction to contain.[25]

In the case of the international counter-revolution a similar reinterpretation is needed, since the reasons that may initially seem to explain the incidence of attempted counter-revolution do not adequately explain what occurred. The obvious answer as to why counter-revolutions occurred is because revolutions, by their activist foreign policies and by promoting the export of revolution, threaten the security of other states. But if this was so, the states thus threatened would sustain their counter-revolution as long as the revolution in question remained committed to its foreign policy, something that is not the case. The question of why states embark on counter-revolution is more complex than that, and there have indeed been many who have doubted the rationale of such actions. The one group of people who have no doubts about the rationale of counter-revolution are revolutionaries: they see themselves as threatening the status quo powers, and, within their internationalist ideology, they see their own revolution as a blow against an *internationally constituted* structure of oppression. For others, however, the picture has been less clear. Liberal writers have long argued that revolutions should be left alone, that confrontation only makes them more authoritarian: the whole trend of post-1945 liberal critiques of US policy in the USA has been to make this point. But conservative writers, too, have in some cases come to a similar conclusion. George Kennan, father of containment, argued *against* US involvement in the Third World, as did the 'realist' international relations theorist Hans Morgenthau.[26] The argument *for* intervention, an aggressive Liberalism rather than a calculated realism, was never that clear, or that compelling.

There are certain general reasons for the compulsion that status quo powers feel to intervene. One is the credibility of their own power. Hegemonic powers maintain alliance systems, of clients and junior allies, to whom they guarantee some degree of security, horizontal and vertical. Failure to support one therefore threatens the viability of the system as a whole. It may, indeed, provoke, through demonstration effects, an internationalised *conjunctural* crisis of the kind identified in Chapter 7; such was the crisis that befell the US hegemonic system in the mid-1970s, and, even more dramatically, the Soviet system in Eastern Europe in the late 1980s. What appears as a paradox from one perspective – that great powers worry about revolution in small states – now appears, conversely, to have a logic – that the system of influence and alliance sustained by such a power requires its guarantees of support to be credible; the smaller the ally that is overthrown, the greater the challenge to the prestige of the great power. Nor are such pressures solely international. Within hegemonic powers the possession of overseas commitments, be they formal, as with colonies, or informal, as in the post-1945 US alliance system, has an important place in the minds of public opinion; a government which easily abandons such an overseas commitment is vulnerable to such internal attack. It is this combination of strength and exposure which Philip Windsor has most aptly termed 'the vulnerability of great powers'. The greatness consists in the power available to these states, and the range of their influence; the vulnerability is, simultaneously, produced by the commitments this power entails *and* by the unity of the very hegemonic system they seek to maintain.

To these factors must, however, be added another, one that revolutionaries both assert and deny, and which liberal critics of counter-revolutionary intervention too easily avoid, namely the impact of the revolution itself. This impact has necessarily two parts: one the one hand, the policies of the state, on the other, the broader impact of example, the demonstration effect, of the revolutionary process. The former, as discussed in Chapters 3 and 4, is not negligible: France, Russia, China and the post-1945 revolutions *did* seek to promote change abroad. But even had they not, they would have had a demonstration effect. The very fact that they challenged a regime and overthrew it has impact elsewhere. The changes introduced, and the new principles of legitimacy proclaimed, have their impact. This is what Burke so rightly identified in the 1790s, in words that echo down the history of counter-revolution thereafter. What regicide and atheism were for the 1790s,[27] land reform, emancipation of women and literacy campaigns were for the 1950s and 1960s. Equally, within the Soviet bloc the threat of the mass oppositions in Eastern Europe in the 1950s and 1960s was not that if they came to power they would launch territorial aggression against the Soviet Union. It was that by showing that communist parties could be challenged, and then changing their own societies, they would encourage others to do the same. What Burke said of the French revolution, that its *existence* was its *hostility*, could be said equally by the USA of Fidel Castro and the USSR of Alexander Dubcek. As discussed in Chapter 6, all international systems of legitimacy and hegemony therefore involve a high degree of homogeneity. The international system is not just one of sovereign states related to each other, but also one which sustains the international preconditions for the stability of particular societies, social and political. The international norm is not only that states should in a conventional way cooperate, but also that other states and societies should be similar in domestic constitution. In other words, there is a presumption towards homogeneity in the international system *both* in the mechanisms of interaction *and* in the ordering of domestic affairs. The precondition for international order is domestic order. The precondition for domestic order is a broad homogeneity in the composition of states.

This discussion has so far touched little on the explanation which revolutionaries themselves provide, namely the threat which revolutions pose to the economic interests of the status quo powers. For Marxists, the reason for counter-revolution was the threat which these upheavals posed to the capitalist system, as embodied in investments and related interests in Third World countries – in oil, plantations, industry, finance, services. Much of the critical literature on US intervention in the Third World in the post-1945 period emphasised this point, and sought an identifiable economic rationale for interventions. As has been argued, this is not the whole story, yet it is far from being a negligible one, affecting not only the policies of states and major business interests, but also broader popular attitudes. In a narrow sense the book value of investments expropriated in a particular state cannot explain all interventions: the USA did not intervene in Vietnam primarily to protect its control of rubber plantations. But in economics as with strategy, the very existence of an internationalised system of hegemony entails that an individual challenge, real or anticipated, will be assessed in terms of what it can do for the system as a whole.

The great revolutions of the twentieth century did, without exception, expropriate foreign economic interests: even the

Mexican, which at first was cautious about so doing, proceeded in the 1930s under President Lazaro Cardenas to nationalise foreign oil investments. In some cases, this was *the* issue around which confrontation developed: it was Cuba's nationalisation of the Standard Oil of New Jersey refinery in April 1960 that led to the final break with the USA, and the start of military subversion by the USA of the Cuban revolution. More generally, and with wide resonance in the countries concerned, the failure of revolutions to respect private property, and international private property in particular, has served as a rallying cry for counter-revolution. Nowhere, it may be added, are the issues of credibility and pre-emption more striking. For even when it appears unlikely that the property expropriated can be recovered, the argument for acting in order to deter others remains compelling.

The Domino Theory: A Second Look

Just as in assessing the impact of revolutions, assessing the record of counter-revolutions involves distinguishing between rhetoric and myth on the one side, and actual processes and outcomes on the other. Status quo powers feel compelled to act, and do so in a variety of ways. To mobilise support, at home and abroad, and to justify what they are doing, they tend to overstate the threat which, in any concrete sense, revolutionary states pose. Speaking in 1954, US President Eisenhower sought to draw attention to the threat of communism in South East Asia by an analogy that later defined this approach:

> You have broader considerations that might follow what you might call the 'falling domino' principle. You have a row of dominoes set up. You knock over the first one, and what will happen to the last one is that it will go over very quickly. So you have the beginning of a disintegration that would have the most profound influences.[28]

This counter-revolutionary internationalism was, however, to prove an unsteady guide to policy. On the one hand, the success of revolution in one state did not necessarily lead to the fall of others, as Vietnam was to show – Thailand, Malaysia and Indonesia did not fall. On the other hand, the commitment to counter-revolution, and the resources which status quo powers deployed, did not produce the specific result intended. The record of counter-revolution is more mixed and far less successful than assessment on the basis of capability would suggest.

Yet a focus on this aspect, the incoherence and constrained character of counter-revolution, is to miss the place of this response in the broader pattern of international relations and the outcomes of revolutions. Counter-revolutionary powers cannot overthrow established revolutionary states: in this, the explicit goal of their actions, they fail. But this does not mean that the broader insight that underlines counter-revolutionary internationalism and the strategy of containment, as it does revolutionary internationalism, namely the interlocked character of social order in distinct states, is without validity.

Enough has been said elsewhere to indicate that the proposition underlying the domino theory, that revolutions have, wittingly and unwittingly, international effects, is to a substantial extent true. The expansion of the revolution from the three Indochinese states to others was blocked, not by military intervention on behalf of the USA, but by something more effective – pre-emptive transformation of the other regional states. Thus, as in a north-east Asia faced by communist China, in South-East Asia states faced with the revolutionary challenge from Vietnam and China embarked on a dramatic reorganisation of their own economies in order to offset domestic discontent. The origins of the East Asian boom lay, as much as anything, in the imperatives of development resulting from the very real challenge of communism, as well as in the exclusion of China as a competitor in export markets. By the mid-1990s, moreover, they were increasingly exerting pressure on Vietnam and the other Indochinese states, and even on China, in a reversal of the revolutionary domino effect.

By contrast, in southern Africa and in Central America the spread of revolution, countered by its opponents, was to transform the politics of the whole region. In the former, the triumph of revolutionary nationalism in the Portuguese colonies of Angola and Mozambique in 1975, followed by that in Zimbabwe in 1980, unleashed a decade of war, not least between South African and Cuban forces, that was to culminate in the early 1990s in the collapse of the apartheid regime in South Africa itself. The conflict was internationalised, all states were transformed. In Central America, the verdict, although less absolute, was in many ways similar: the impact of the Nicaraguan revolution was to stimulate the guerrilla movements in El Salvador and Guatemala. If the Sandinista regime ceded power after over a decade in office, it had through its example and assistance helped to promote the guerrillas in the other two states. The result was that by the mid-1990s, while the FSLN remained a legal party, in opposition in Nicaragua, the wars in both other countries had been concluded and the guerrillas had been able to enter the democratic political process. The contrasted outcomes of these three cases suggest that while the domino theory, as a simple model of international impact, was mistaken, it was more accurate in the broader reality it pointed to, the internationalised linking of horizontal security.

The containment strategy espoused by George Kennan in 1946 rested on a two-sided proposition. One argument was that the USSR, a state which *did* wish to establish its system on a global scale, could be contained by military means, i.e. it could be prevented from expanding into Europe. But to this, apparently defensive, proposition was attached another, offensive, one, according to which such a containment accompanied by the continued success of the West would, in the end, produce the collapse of the Soviet system. That system rested upon an ideological imperative, the belief in the world-wide progress of the revolutionary wave. If checked, the system would erode from within and, ultimately, faced with a more successful and stable West, collapse.

The counter-revolution envisaged by Kennan was therefore one brought about not so much by military pressure on Soviet society, let alone by attempts to mobilise revolt from within, but rather by a management of the enduring ideological rivalry of the two blocs. Containment in the first sense, i.e. the bottling up of the Soviet Union in its zone of influence, would permit a longer-run weakening and collapse of the system. Kennan was in large measure right, even if he underestimated the vitality of the communist system in the Third World context in the intervening decades. What his insight rested on was the perception that in revolution as in counter-revolution it is the ideological and exemplary, as much as force of arms or diplomatic pressure, that enables one side to expand its influence internationally. Revolutionaries and counter-revolutionaries both seek to defy the states system and national sentiment: as against the principle of non-interference, they explicitly invoke higher obligations, and act accordingly. Insofar as they rely on the state system to prosecute these international goals, they tend to fail. Yet in the longer run the links between societies, and the demonstration effects of one on the other, do transcend and undermine states. They do so in a manner and over a time-scale that neither revolutionaries nor counter-revolutionaries may have anticipated.

9

War and Revolution

It has already been argued that war and revolution are the two formative processes of modern international history. The history of revolutions is repeatedly combined with that of war. This was never more so than in the twentieth century. It was the upheavals accompanying two world wars that provided the context for revolutionary triumph and counter-revolutionary reversal alike. A survey of the relationships between war and revolution can therefore serve to bring together some of the themes of earlier chapters, and to examine more closely some of the ways in which this phenomenon, political as well as military, relates to revolution. Revolutions, in addition to precipitating wars, guerrilla or conventional, are themselves often caused by wars. Perhaps most importantly, wars in many ways *resemble* revolutions, and are indeed, in some approaches, assimilated to them. That they are interrelated, but distinguishable, is one starting point for an overall assessment of how these two formative processes interact.

It is in part this resemblance between war and revolution which explains the contradictory attitude of revolutionaries to war. On the one hand, revolutionary thinking, and in particular the internationalism of post-1789 radicalism, has been associated with opposition to war, with pacifism in the broad sense of being in favour of peace. One of the central promises of revolution has been that it, and only it, can abolish war. This was the claim of the French and Russian revolutions, just as Mao Tse-tung in 1938 envisaged, in visionary terms, a coming epoch in which, after the defeat of fascism and capitalism, there would be no more war.[1] On the other hand, revolutionary leaders have been drawn to war, fascinated by its mobilisatory potential and by its moral challenge, and, both before and after coming to power, shaped by it. Trotsky argued that war was 'the locomotive of history', Che Guevara that 'There is no deeper experience for a revolutionary than the act of war.' It is worth noting, however, that while most revolutionary leaders have talked and written of war, and some, such as Trotsky, Mao and Tito have commanded wide-ranging military campaigns, only Fidel Castro is known to have had direct battlefield exposure, dodging bullets in a sugar-cane field as Batista's forces tried to eliminate the guerrilla force that had recently landed on the eastern coast of Cuba.[2]

For revolutionaries, the most immediate relationship between war and revolution is that of war as the *instrument* for the revolutionary attainment of power. It was guerrilla war – that form of irregular revolutionary warfare – which was so central to revolutionary movements in the latter part of the twentieth century. However, while guerrilla war does merit attention in this context and will be discussed later in the chapter, it is far from being a sufficient approach to the subject. Guerrilla war is by no means an exclusive instrument of revolutionary movements: it can equally be the instrument of those opposed to revolutionary regimes, as indeed it was in its original form, as a method of resistance to the Napoleonic occupation of Spain.[3] Moreover, guerrilla war is not the only means by which revolutions use violence in pursuit of their ends. Revolutionary states use war, i.e. their conventional armies, for foreign policy purposes, particularly to extend the influence of revolution to other states. This too merits attention.

Similarities, Distinctions

The similarities between war and revolution are significant for both. In the first place, war and revolution share the characteristic of being resorts to violence in the context of breakdowns of hitherto prevailing patterns of political interaction, be they of political life within a state or of diplomatic and other interaction between states. Both war and revolution involve this use, or threat, of violence as the means for defeating the opponent and imposing acceptance of the victor's will when other forms of policy have broken down: hence Lenin's fascination with von Clausewitz's *political* understanding of war. Secondly, both involve the application of intention, of conscious political purposes, towards the attainment of a

236 Revolutions and the International System

goal, even as any such application takes place within objective constraints, a structure, that limits the effect of these intentions and may well confound them. War and revolution are also unpredictable, involving a high degree of chance and uncertainty, within which factors that might otherwise be of minor importance – the personality of a leader, accidents of politics, chance coincidences – come to play an important and possibly decisive part. For all that structural and objective factors do limit outcomes, in wars as in revolutions there is a heightened element of contingency; von Clausewitz wrote of the 'free play of the spirit' in war,[4] and this has been noted in revolutions as well, not least by Lenin. In broader historical terms, wars and revolutions involve certain analogous processes and consequences. In both, large numbers of people are mobilised in collective projects which, whatever their outcome, have longer-run effects on the societies in question. In both, too, subsequent patterns of political and social power, and the very boundaries of states, are shaped by the particular outcomes of these two variants of collective struggle. Both are, in this sense, *formative* processes.

It is not therefore surprising that some theorists have seen war and revolution as similar processes, be it in behaviouralist conceptions of revolution as 'internal war', or Marxist theories of 'class war'. The Bolsheviks and their successors, up to 1956, asserted that war between their revolutionary state and the West was inevitable, that while distinct the two phenomena were historically conjoined. Yet the distinctions between them, theoretically and analytically, are significant. In the first place, wars involve a symmetry, a conflict between two constituted states, each with its own territory and delimited population. Revolutions, by contrast, are based on the asymmetrical conflict between a political movement and a state, each contesting the same territory and population. Secondly, while ideological differences may and do enter into war, the justifications for war may be other – disputes over territory, or economic issues. In revolutions, the two sides differ above all because of the varied and contrasting ideological programmes they offer, combined with the different social interests embodied in them. Revolutions are, initially, conflicts over the bases of power and legitimacy *within* states; wars about power between them. Neither in theory nor in their historical impact are these two processes assimilable.[5] What we are left with are two major historical and political phenomena, similar and overlapping in some respects but conceptually and historically distinct. The task is to specify how they interrelate.

Four forms of interconnection suggest themselves. In the first place, wars can be seen as the *precipitant* or *cause* of revolutions. The weakening of states in inter-state conflict, through outright defeat or over-extension short of defeat, may so affect the state–society relationship that forces opposed to the state are able successfully to challenge it. Secondly, revolution precipitates armed conflict. Most obviously war may be seen as the *result* of revolutions. As seen in Chapter 7, successful revolutions frequently lead to war with status quo powers, the dynamic in the direction of war being evident in both camps. However, war may be seen in a different, indeed contrary, way to be a *product of particular state–society contradictions*, of domestic crises in which ruling groups resort to war to manage internal political conflicts. The most obvious argument here would be that such wars are launched to prevent revolutionary challenges, but the relationship may be different. As Arno Mayer has suggested, the onset of wars may reflect not the deflection of a pre-revolutionary situation, but the confidence of an elite that revolution has been contained and that it is possible to resolve domestic questions without running the risk of a social explosion.[6] Finally, war may be seen as the *instrument* of revolution. This is exemplified in conceptions of war as a means of attaining power, as in theories of armed insurrection and guerrilla war, or of the revolutionary offensive war.

Wars as Precipitant

Wars have acted as precipitants of revolutions most evidently by weakening the power of states. The forms of this weakening have been mentioned in several contexts above: wars weaken the coercive powers of states, by reducing the strengths of armies; they delegitimate states by denying them the supreme claim to loyalty, that of defenders of the security of the nation; they weaken the ability of the state to provide goods required by citizens; they weaken the cohesion of society by sharpening social conflicts. In all three of the major general crises of the international system – the seventeenth century, the Atlantic revolution, the twentieth century – it can plausibly be argued that revolutions were encouraged by, and not merely chronologically followed from, the incidence of inter-state war. War so altered the political and ideological situation within countries and exacerbated state–society conflict that social upheaval ensued.

The third wave of international revolution, that of the twentieth century, provides striking illustration of this connection. After the First World War and the Second World War the general 'world' war was followed by an almost equally widespread incidence of political upheaval, within states hitherto involved in the conflict. The First World War led, whilst still being fought, to the Bolshevik revolution in Russia, in the aftermath of the armistice of November 1918 political upheaval engulfed many of the former combatant states: Germany, Italy, Hungary and Austria in Europe; Mongolia, China and Korea in the Far East; Egypt, Iraq and Iran in the Middle East. Each of these had their specific national roots, but their occurrence was more than just a coincidence, a product not only of the spread of particular ideas of socialist and nationalist insurgency but also of the international political situation, the weakening or destruction of hegemonies, provoked by the First World War. On an even greater scale, a 'world' revolutionary upheaval was to follow the Second World War, which, in most of the victor states as in the defeated, was to promote a crisis of hegemony at both the ideological and coercive levels. Thus the defeat of the Axis powers in 1945 was followed by the triumph of revolutionary guerrilla movements in Yugoslavia and Albania, widespread social unrest in France and Italy, and, most strikingly, the emergence of revolutionary communist regimes in the Far East – in Korea, Vietnam and China. The Second World War was thus a conflict that developed on several levels – that of inter-state conflict on the one hand, that of exacerbated social, nationalist and political conflict within states on the other.[7] It led, after a brief pause, to its aftermath, forty years of Cold War, a global political conflict, regulated by nuclear weapons and the arms race.

This connection between war and revolution applies not only to situations of actual combat, but also to the effects of long-term strategic competition between states, the result of which is to place greater strain on the state–society relationship in the countries concerned. An earlier example of this, discussed in Chapter 7, was that of the Seven Years War on both Britain and France: the strain on state finances, leading to increased taxation, was a precipitant of, respectively, the American and French revolutions. A later example was that of the effect of the Cold War and the attendant arms race upon the USSR. Most discussion of this military competition was in terms of the necessities and dynamics of the arms race itself. The main public justification within both camps was that the accompanying expenditures were necessary to counter the policies of the other side; the main political argument was that military competition and the maintenance of some concept of 'balance' were inescapable parts of the global competition for influence and power between the blocs. But there was a third dimension to this, namely the Western belief that the arms race itself, by placing unsustainable burdens on the Soviet Union would precipitate a crisis within it. This could never be said to be the sole or dominant consideration in Western strategy; the main *political* goal of the Western arms buildup was to reduce Soviet influence in crisis situations. But the belief that such forms of rivalry would weaken the USSR was on occasion articulated, as Kissinger was subsequently to indicate:

Arms control had become an abstruse subject involving esoteric fine points that, even with the best intentions, would take years to resolve. But what the Soviet Union needed was immediate relief, not simply from tensions but from economic pressures, especially from the arms race. . . In this manner, arms control negotiations were becoming a device for applying pressure on the rickety Soviet system – all the more effective because they had not been designed for that purpose.[8]

Near the end of the Cold War, this approach was to receive belated comparative confirmation in the work of Paul Kennedy, which located the decline of hegemonic systems in overextension, i.e. in situations where military expenditure and dominion were expanded to protect economic and political interests, but in so doing went beyond the capabilities of the state.[9]

None were more cognisant of this relationship, of war as a stimulant to revolution, than Lenin and Trotsky who, after August 1914, saw in the outbreak of the 'inter-imperialist' war the opportunity for a revolutionary breakthrough in Russia. This, not the analysis of north–south relations, was the central message of Lenin's 1916 work *Imperialism* as it was of Trotsky's *The War and the International* published in 1914.[10] In many cases of war between states opponents of one or other have hoped that this will provide the opportunity for them to take power. Thus during the First World War it was not only the Bolsheviks but also the Irish nationalists of *Sinn Fein* who took what they saw as the insurrectionary option. The 1916 Easter Rising in Dublin failed because, in contrast to the situation prevailing in St. Petersburg in October 1917, the old regime, in this case the British state, *could* go on ruling in the old way. During the Second World War, a range of nationalist movements in the Middle East and in Asia saw in the beleaguered condition of the imperial powers – British, French, Dutch – an opportunity for asserting their programmes. One of the most striking instances of this dialectic occurred in the context of the Iran–Iraq conflict of 1980–88, the longest inter-state war of the post-1945 period. While opponents of the Iranian regime sought aid from the government in Baghdad for military and political actions against the Islamic Republic, Iran provided substantial assistance to the Kurdish and Shi'ite Muslim oppositions operating within Iraq.

However, such support had drawbacks which, beyond their implications for this particular kind of political alliance, point to limits in establishing any simple relation between wars and revolution. The great danger run by those who seek such alliances in the midst of inter-state war is that they discredit themselves in the eyes of their own population: the charge of 'treason' is easily levied. This indicates that for states involved in such wars, conflict with another state can be two-sided, weakening it in some respects but providing it with legitimation for more effectively mobilising the population and containing opposition. States may initiate wars precisely in order to pre-empt opposition within: here war serves not to weaken but to enhance the powers of states. Equally, once involved in war, states will find it easier to control and suppress opposition. Such was the experience of, for example, the British state in the 1790s and 1800s, when the outbreak of war with France was used to control domestic sympathy for the French revolution, or of the Polish state in 1920 when, faced with an 'internationalist' military intervention by the Bolsheviks, it mobilised nationalist sentiment against a threat seen in national, i.e. anti-Russian, terms. Hence it cannot be argued that, in any universal sense, wars serve to weaken the state and so facilitate the work of its opponents: the impact of wars is contradictory, a product of the more general interplay of political and social factors with the ever uncertain fortunes of war itself.

Success and Failure: War as Consequence

The incidence of revolution as a precipitant of war is as common as
that of war as a prelude to revolution. Indeed, while avoiding
suggestions of any *laws* of history, it is an almost universal generalisation that revolutions lead to wars between the revolutionary state
and other states, involving some combination of the use of war by
the revolutionary state and contrary counter-revolutionary war by
status quo powers. Chapters 3 and 4 have examined the ways in
which revolutionary states envisage themselves as in conflict with
their neighbours – the former through a perception of themselves as
the promoters of internationalised revolutionary change, the latter
through their belief that revolutionary regimes threaten the stability
of other states. For its part Chapter 8 analysed the place of war in
strategies of counter-revolution.

The historic sequence of revolution and war is striking. In the
sixteenth and seventeenth centuries, the revolutions of Holland and
Britain led to inter-state conflict, the former involving the Habsburg
empire and its opponents, the latter pitting Cromwellian England
against Holland and Spain. The American revolution, a conflict
between the insurgents and the English crown, was followed by the
Anglo-American war of 1812–13 in which counter-revolutionary
Loyalists who had fled to Canada returned to combat their American opponents. The French revolution was followed by over twenty
years of war between France on the one side, and a changing
alliance of opponents on the other. In the twentieth century the link
has endured: as discussed in Chapter 7, the outbreak of the First
World War was preceded by a range of revolutionary upheavals,
expressions of the growing social and political tensions accumulating during the late nineteenth century. The Bolshevik revolution
was followed immediately by the war of intervention, which lasted
from 1918 to 1921, and by armed interventions in Poland, Iran and
Mongolia. In a less direct but none the less definable way, 1917 was
a major precipitant of the Second World War.[11] In the post-1945
epoch the pattern has continued: the triumph of the Chinese
revolution in October 1949 was followed by the outbreak of the
Korean War in June 1950; the Cuban revolution of 1959 led to the
attempted armed invasion of April 1961 and the missile crisis of
October 1962; the Iranian revolution of February 1979 was followed by the Iraqi invasion of September 1980 and an eight-year
war; that of Nicaragua in July 1979 was followed by a decade of

conflict in Central America, involving not only the already present civil war in El Salvador, but also the creation of a new opposition force, the Nicaraguan *contra*. One partial exception to this pattern might appear to be the Mexican revolution of 1910–20. Largely contained within Mexico, and marginal to world politics after the outbreak of the First World War in 1914, this nevertheless led to significant international military action, with Pancho Villa's forays into Texas and the despatch of US expeditionary forces to occupy areas of Mexico.[12]

The relationship suggested here is that revolution serves as a cause of war because of the impact it has on the international system, through changes in the policy of the revolutionary state and through the response of status quo powers. One example given has been that of the period prior to the First World War, one of widespread social and political crisis in much of the world. The period from the 1890s onwards was indubitably one of 'general crisis', involving a move towards war on the one hand, and social and political upheaval in many states on the other. It can plausibly be argued that the rising tide of revolution contributed to the general crisis and so to the outbreak of war. Yet there is another explanation of this period which stresses not *revolution as a cause of war* but *of counter-revolution as a cause of war*. This is the theory of counter-revolution developed by Arno Mayer and already mentioned in the previous chapter. Mayer has argued that war is a response by elites to strengthen their position when faced with challenges from below that they feel they can contain, and with divisions within the ruling bloc:

> Not pre-revolutionary pressures but cleavages in the hegemonic bloc and unsettlement or stalemate of government are the womb of crisis and of crisis-generated war. This is not to say that these political distempers have no deep socioeconomic roots and that pressures from below are of no consequence. But the impact of these pressures is not a function of their high intensity and their imminent explosion into revolutionary unrest. If anything, the opposite holds true: the insufficiency and decline of social rebellion favors divisions in the hegemonic bloc which, in turn, foment war.[13]

The 'general crisis' of the early twentieth century was 'a crisis of *over*-reaction, whose main expression was the politics of unreason and domination at home and the diplomacy of confrontation and war abroad'.[14] Such crises, and the wars they lead to, do not necessarily lead to revolution: indeed they only do so if defeat so weakens the incumbent regimes that they are challenged or over-thrown by revolutionary oppositions. The conclusion would be that wars may well lead to revolutions, but that these wars are not caused by revolutions so much as by the attempts of elites to enhance their positions against oppositions domestic and interna-tional, and that revolutions ensue only when these elites fail in such an endeavour. It is this which marks out the contrast between the Russian and German elites after the First World War. The former faced such a crisis of society that they succumbed to a revolutionary movement; the latter, despite insurgent challenges, survived, only to launch an even more ferocious war two decades later. In neither country were revolutionary forces on the brink of taking power in 1914. It was the war which provided the opportunity for the Russian opposition to seize power; no comparable opportunity of a disintegrating state was offered to the numerically and politically much more influential German socialist movement.

War as Instrument: (i) Armed Insurrection

The pursuit of a specifically 'revolutionary' theory of war, be it in the understanding of combat and violence or in the moral positions adopted, has been a recurrent theme in the thinking and practice of revolutionaries. This has, in part, reflected changes in the character of war which have themselves been part of the changes in society and politics that revolution itself has reflected. 'War' is no more a constant than 'revolution': both have been transformed by the political and industrial changes associated with modernity. The interaction of the two is not therefore a static one, but rather of how changes in society and ideology together have altered the conception of war as an instrument of politics and the very manner of its organisation.

The French revolution saw in the mass mobilisations of the *levée en masse*, and in the new tactics of Napoleon, an alternative to the military practices of the eighteenth century. The co-founder of historical materialism, Friedrich Engels, envisaged the development of a new science of war, distinct from the bourgeois doctrines hitherto prevailing.[15] Lenin made a careful study of Clausewitz, and tried to produce a synthesis of Clausewitz and Marx, based on a development of Clausewitz's analysis of the *political* goals of war.[16] In the twentieth century two particular theories of war have been associated with the development of the communist movement: in the aftermath of the Bolshevik revolution; a concept of armed insurrection, in the post-1945 period, a concept of guerrilla war as in some sense the apposite, and distinctive, mechanism for the revolutionary seizure of power.

Both theories of war as instrument – those of armed insurrection and of guerrilla war – involved the generalisation of the 'lessons' of particular upheavals and the specification of a supposedly distinct kind of revolutionary strategy. If guerrilla war was a generalisation from the Chinese, or later Cuban, cases, armed insurrection was a generalisation of what had occurred in Petrograd in October 1917. In a letter to the Central Committee in September 1917 Lenin wrote: 'at the present moment it is impossible to remain loyal to Marxism, to remain loyal to the revolution *unless insurrection is treated as an art*'.[17] The Comintern handbook was clear:

> For the proletariat, armed insurrection is the highest form of political struggle.[18]

> Armed insurrection, as one of the forms taken by the class struggle of the proletariat, is central to the system of Marx and Engels. The utilization of this form by the proletariat, at a determinate historical stage in the evolution of the class struggle in any given country, is an absolute, inexorable necessity. This necessity derives immediately from the entire Marxist conception of the development of Society; of the revolutionary role of violence in history; of the role of the State, as the instrument of a single class's domination; and finally of the dictatorship of the proletariat. *Denial of the inexorable necessity for armed insurrection or, more generally for armed struggle against the ruling classes on the part of the proletariat, means automatically denial of the class struggle as a whole. It means denial of the very foundations of revolutionary Marxism and its reduction to an idious doctrine of non-resistance.*[19]

The central tenets of this theory of revolutionary war comprised the arming of a proletarian militia which, together with dissident units of the armed forces, would seize power. It was to be based in cities, involve the choice of the apposite and 'correct' moment for the attempted seizure of power and to be accompanied by widespread mass mobilisations. Armed insurrection was to become the main form of attempted revolutionary seizure of power in the inter-war years; following the successful revolution in Russia, other attempts were made in Germany, Estonia, and China.

The theory of armed insurrection might appear to be a matter of purely internal politics, a tactic for use where the domestic corre-lates of conflict favoured revolutionaries. However, that these later attempts were unsuccessful was a result of something that, for all their invocation of Lenin and the 'international lessons' of the Bolshevik revolution, the theorists of this practice understated, namely the *international* context. This was so in two ways. First, in any contest between the forces of the established state and of an armed proletarian force, the advantages were overwhelmingly with the former, in terms of arms, training and resources, except where the former had been decisively weakened in international competi-tion. The precondition for the success of the Bolshevik revolution lay not just in those elements which subsequent theories of insurrec-tion identified – arming the workers, intelligence, timing, selection of buildings – but also in the very international conjuncture that had so undermined the Czarist state. What was therefore presented as an *internationally valid* theory of revolution was in reality a strategy fatally devoid of international perspective: the fate of earlier insurrections – Paris 1848 and 1871, Dublin 1916 – was equally evidence of this truth.[20]

Even more fundamentally, the 'international' character of the theory masked what was in fact *a failure of international analysis*, namely that of recognising the difference between societies, not least with regard to the possibilities of assuming power through insurrec-tion. For behind the theory of armed insurrection lay a failure to recognise that such forms of taking power were appropriate only to some kinds of society. At the very moment when the dogmatic 'internationalists' of the Comintern were producing such a general theory of insurrection, another revolutionary thinker, the Italian Antonio Gramsci, was identifying precisely why what had hap-pened in Russia could not recur in Central or Western Europe. Gramsci took as his starting point the contrasted forms of strategy developed in the First World War – the 'war of manoeuvre', allowing of quick and decisive advances in the East, and the 'war of position', involving much slower advances in the face of a better entrenched and armed enemy in the West, this including much of Central Europe. His argument was that the political systems of East and West were, equally, contrasted, that of the West having a much denser 'civil society' and entrenched power that made sudden attacks, characteristic of the 'war of manoeuvre', impossible. Hence by dint of a closer study, combining that of war with that of society and politics, Gramsci produced an international analysis, and specification of strategy, far more perceptive than the theorists of the Comintern.[21] In the case of the uncompleted bourgeois revolution in Italy itself, with its great differences between north and south, he had a powerful example of the impact of combined and uneven development. His awareness of the workings of Western European society alerted him to the inappropriateness of applying Bolshevik insurrection to a Western Europe transformed, if incompletely so, by modernity. The Western and Central European 1848, and the Italian 1861, offset the platitudes of the Russian 1917.

War as Instrument: (ii) The Politics of Nuclear Weapons

In the period after 1945, revolutionary states and movements faced a situation very different from that which had preceded the Second World War. On the one hand, the traditional argument on the inevitability of war between capitalism and communism continued to prevail in the USSR. On the other, the advent of nuclear weapons meant that the risks of war were recognised as far greater. In response to this situation two conflicting responses can be identified. One was accommodation to the new strategic reality. Most importantly, the USSR and, after the breakdown of its nuclear defence pact with Moscow, China sought to acquire their own weapons: Stalin in 1949, Mao in 1964. In each case this *de facto* acquisition of nuclear weapons was followed, with a delay of some years, by a recognition that war was indeed *not* inevitable. Khrushchev espoused 'peaceful coexistence' in 1956, and the Chinese, who for a decade and a half afterwards denounced this as a betrayal of Marxism-Leninism, decided by 1971, when opening contact with the USA, to do the same.

On the other hand, there was a recurrent streak of verbal rejection of the strategic stalemate which nuclear weapons, by making war impossible, had apparently created. In the Soviet case at least, theorists continued to speculate on the possibility of nuclear war and the application of Marxism to this.[22] The will-o'-the-wisp 'proletarian' or 'scientific' theory of war, applying historical materialism to inter-state conflict, never entirely died in the Soviet Union. However, the most potent, and irresponsible, views were expressed in countries with a less developed military capability. One element in this rejection of the nuclear impasse was a romantic, and potentially reckless, denial of the potential destructiveness of nuclear weapons. In 1946, Mao had declared that the atom bomb was a 'paper tiger'. He meant by this not only that nuclear weapons could not guarantee the USA victory, but also that the Chinese and other revolutionary peoples should not be terrified by the mere fact of US possession of them, two arguably rational propositions. However, through the 1950s and early 1960s he continued to go further, to make grotesque projections of how, after a nuclear war, it would be easier to build socialism.[23] In Cuba an analogous recklessness was also detectable in the context of the 1962 missile crisis. In a secret speech published in the aftermath of the crisis Castro stated: 'We defended these missiles with affection, with an incredible love. . .We were transported by this new situation. . .by this extraordinary international proletarian spirit which we had dreamed about.'[24] At one point in the crisis Castro wrote to Khrushchev asking him to launch a nuclear strike against the USA in the event of an American attack on Cuba.[25] Guevara was to reinforce this: 'We must proceed along the path of liberation even if this costs millions of atomic victims,' he wrote, portraying the Cuban people 'advancing fearlessly towards the hecatomb which signifies final redemption'.[26] These revolutionaries therefore did adjust to the reality of nuclear weapons but with some difficulty.

War as Instrument: (iii) Guerrilla War

The impasse produced by the nuclear stalemate was, however, to see a very different generalisation, that of guerrilla war, in effect a substitute for strategic or inter-state war. Raymond Aron described the nuclear epoch as *paix impossible, guerre improbable*: the margin of freedom to wage war offered by this 'improbability' was filled by guerrilla war. This acquired great prestige as a result of the victory of the Chinese revolution in 1949, after which it was propagated through the writings of Mao Tse-tung.[27] It was also to acquire apparent validation from the success of the revolutionary movements in Vietnam and in Cuba. In the former case this was above all codified in the writings of the military commander General Vo Nguyen Giap; in the latter case in the writings of two non-Cubans, the Argentinian Ernesto Che Guevara, a leading participant in the revolution,[28] and the French intellectual Régis Debray.[29] Here it appeared that a new and distinctive revolutionary strategy had been discovered, combining a record of success with a new 'scientific' discovery of the mechanisms of war itself.[30]

Much of the 'theory' of guerrilla war rested on a set of prescriptions for irregular warfare against a conventional military foe: manoeuvre, mobility of bases, concentration of weaker forces for sudden attack, use of terrain and local resources. But it also rested on two broader political concepts, of relevance to the overall issue of revolutionary strategy: popular mobilisation, and political undermining of the opponent. Guerrilla war theory evoked forms of reliance on 'the people', usually on the rural population, who would provide a reserve for the recruitment and support of the military units. Infused as it was with a high ethical tone, and with the thesis that material advantages on one side could be countered by the moral and ideological advantages of the other, this strategy served both to legitimate the guerrilla movement and to provide a resource with which to offset the conventional military advantages of the enemy. The victories of guerrilla war – in China, Vietnam, Algeria, Cuba and elsewhere – provided an apparent vindication of this strategy.

Guerrilla war was an 'international' phenomenon in several respects. First, from its relative obscurity prior to the Second World War, it became the formula for popular and national resistance throughout the Third World from the 1950s to the 1980s, encompassing not just the Far East, but also Palestine, the resistance to Portuguese rule in Africa, and a range of movements in Latin America. In the aftermath of the Cold War it persisted or erupted in numerous countries. The reasons for this success are several. The weakening of the colonial empires during and after the Second World War encouraged subject peoples to revolt and weakened the resolve of the dominant powers. The changes in economic and political organisation within Third World countries created forces more prone to revolt – a radicalised intelligentsia and an often uprooted rural population. The incidence of guerrilla war also corresponded to the defining feature of the international situation, namely the stalemate produced by nuclear weapons. Since the latter inhibited outright war between states in the two blocs of the Cold War, guerrilla war became a means of pursuing military conflict without this leading to an outright nuclear confrontation. It was not only revolutionaries and their sympathisers, but many in power in Western states who, in the 1960s and 1970s, believed that the Third World guerrilla wave of those times represented a harbinger of the future.

Guerrilla war was an international phenomenon in another, ideological and organisational, sense in that it contained within it a theory of conflict, military and political, on the international level. On the one hand, it projected its conception of the political undermining of conventional powers on to the international level, with the strategy of weakening the domestic and international political base of its opponents. On the other, it aspired to generalise the incidence of guerrilla war to a range of countries, with the express expectation of 'overextending' the dominant powers. The weakening of the opponent's will to fight was central to guerrilla strategy both within the country directly concerned and internationally: it was *the* central feature of the alternative strategy that revolutionaries proposed. As Andrew Mack has written, these conflicts were *asymmetric*: the insurgents could never win militarily, but provided they could avoid being completely destroyed they could weaken and destroy the external powers' political will:

> For students of strategy the importance of these wars lies in the fact that the simplistic but once prevalent assumption – that the conventional military superiority necessarily prevails in war – has been destroyed. What is also interesting is that although the metropolitan powers did not *win* militarily, neither were they *defeated* militarily. Indeed the military defeat of the metropolis itself was impossible since the insurgents lacked an invasion capability. In every case, success for the insurgents arose not from a military victory on the ground – though military successes may have been a contributory cause – but rather from the progressive attrition of their opponents' *political* capability to wage war. In such asymmetric conflicts, insurgents may gain political victory from a situation of military stalemate *or even defeat*.[31]

In such cases, and as time wore on and casualties mounted, political disagreements within the dominant power grew, leading in the end to a decision to withdraw: such was the case for the French and Americans in Vietnam, for the French in Algeria, for the Portuguese in Africa, for the British in Kenya, Cyprus and South Yemen, and for the Russians in Afghanistan. In each it was not outright military defeat, but the military costs of continuing war, *combined* with the political costs to the country concerned both domestically and in relation to other states, that led to the decision to withdraw.

The guerrillas saw their struggle as involving not just the projection of their conflict into the domestic politics of the opponent, but also as involving the exacerbation of conflict by the spread of revolutionary guerrilla war to a range of societies. Here the long tradition of appeals to revolutionary solidarity of a *political* character were converted into a strategy for convergent *military* action. The appeals of the Sixth Congress of the Comintern in 1928 for an upsurge in struggles of colonial peoples were to find this later, and more specifically military, formulation in the internationalist proclamations of the 1960s. In 1965 Lin Piao was to call for the 'peoples of the world' to unite to encircle the developed world, in an internationalist transposition of the strategy of the Chinese revolution. From Cuba were to come the 'Declarations of Havana', appeals for a continent-wide upsurge of the peoples of Latin America, and Che Guevara's appeals for the creation of 'two, three, many Vietnams', components of the *Defensa Revolucionaria Activa* activated after the April 1961 invasion.

The diffusion of ideas of guerrilla war in the post-1945 period was a striking instance of change in political ideas, given how little attention this form of combat, and indeed its main protagonist, the peasantry, had hitherto received in revolutionary analysis. A new modular form of combat had become available. At the same time, irregular warfare, of various kinds, was to play a major, and in many cases, formative, role in the history of the post-1945 world, accompanying as it did the Chinese revolution, and the wars in Vietnam, Portuguese Africa and elsewhere, as well as the failure of the Soviet intervention in Afghanistan. The central political tenet of guerrilla warfare, the offsetting of military strength by weakening of the enemy's political capacity to continue the war, was vindicated in these instances.

Yet there is, in other respects, a need to set this record of apparent success in some perspective, not least by placing it, even more than is conventional, in an international and comparative light. In the first place, guerrilla war was no prerogative of revolutionary or left-wing movements. Based as it often was on forms of traditional rural resistance and banditry it was an instrument available to any social or political force, as its use by the Reagan administration in the 1980s was to show. It was a curious turn of political phraseology that brought back into political usage the term 'counter-revolutionary', in its Spanish variant *contra*, to denote the Nicaraguan right-wing guerrilla forces. Secondly, despite the myth of invincibility, guerrilla war was no guarantee of success: for every movement that succeeded, there were several that failed, not least because the state against which they were acting was not so weakened, internally or internationally, that it was forced to retreat. Perhaps the most famous of such failures was the guerrilla movement led by Guevara in Bolivia, which was defeated, with his execution in captivity, in 1967. In the Far East, guerrilla movements were defeated in Malaya and the Philippines; in the Middle East, numerous guerrilla forces were crushed, or held at bay; in Latin America, all guerrilla movements, except for those of Cuba and Nicaragua, were contained.[32] Thirdly, even where guerrilla war appeared to be successful some of the favourable outcomes had other, less irregular, explanations. The victories of the Chinese, Yugoslav and Albanian guerrilla movements owed not a little to the fact that the main external enemy they had been fighting against – the Japanese and the Germans – had been defeated in inter-state conflict as part of the outcome of the Second World War. Had this not occurred, then these guerrillas, for all their successes and heroism, would have been contained. Perhaps the most spectacular of all guerrilla actions, that of the Vietnamese communists who in August 1945 took control of their entire country in a matter of weeks in late August and early September, was a result of events far away: the collapse of France in 1940, the surrender of Japan in 1945. Their victory, which it was to take them thirty years to consolidate, was a result of the vacuum produced by global events.

Equally, the line between irregular and regular warfare became blurred in the latter part of the Chinese and Vietnamese wars. It was as much regular military units, with tanks and conventional military command structures, as irregular guerrillas who completed the final stages of these wars; guerrilla theory took account of this, by postulating a final, 'third', stage of people's war when the guerrilla force was transformed into a conventional military one. In many cases, too, the image of the poorly armed guerrilla pitched against the regular opponent was a simplification, if only because the guerrilla forces and their nearest supporters owed much to the indirect participation of other states in the conflict. Without Soviet weapons the Vietnamese and Portuguese African movements would have been much less effective than they were, as would, the Sandinistas in Nicaragua without comparable Cuban help. The conventional international situation, involving both the nuclear stalemate and the competitive provision of weaponry, was therefore a major permissive context for the pursuit of irregular warfare in the Cold War epoch.[33]

In retrospect it is possible to distinguish between a real history of guerrilla warfare in the middle and second half of the twentieth century and a mythical history. Guerrilla warfare served as the vehicle for revolutionary movements in a range of countries and did much to shape the political map of the second half of the twentieth century. It succeeded above all because it combined a strategy for military action and survival within developing countries with an exploitation of the political weaknesses of the more developed, an exploitation made possible by changes within these societies and by the broader pattern of inter-state relations. Divorced from this political and international context, it became a myth, morally inspiring but of limited explanatory value and, in many tragic cases, equally limited practical import. The myth also related to the *political character* of such mobilisations. Presented as a spontaneous upsurge of a people against foreign domination, guerrilla war was in reality underpinned by the most rigorous militarised recruitment and deployment of the peoples involved, that guaranteed their endurance in the face of terrible odds and disproportionate casualties, but also ensured that the post-revolutionary state was itself of a highly militarised kind. China, Vietnam, Korea and Eritrea all bore the marks of such guerrilla pasts. However, the myth was itself significant, in that it served to stimulate guerrilla action in other societies, by providing both moral inspiration and a set of specific guidelines. However, it masked the more conventional forms of military assistance and intervention which accompanied many guerrilla wars.

Three broad periods of mythologisation of guerrilla warfare can be identified: in regard to the resistance to Axis occupation in Europe and the Far East during the Second World War; in respect of Third World revolutionary movements of the 1960s and 1970s; and in regard to the US-backed anti-communist guerrillas of the 1980s. If the Second World War variant marked the beginning of this mythologisation, one that was subsequently used for a variety of political purposes, it was in the 1960s that the full creation of an ideology of guerrilla war, as both invincible strategy and expression of popular will, took place. In its impact on those opposed to guerrilla-based revolutions, this left-wing variant occasioned two contrasted responses: first, in the 1960s, the development of a new doctrine of repression, based on counter-guerrilla action; then, in the 1980s, the adoption by the USA of its own guerrilla strategy, embodied in the Reagan Doctrine.[34]

In each of these three cases – the Second World War, the 1960s, and the 1980s – the mythologisation of guerrilla war was a result not so much of its *success* but of an *impasse*, the impossibility of action in a more conventional vein. What the myth served to do was to distract from the lack of movement on conventional military and political fronts, and to boost the image of what remained a dependent form of conflict. Thus in the Second World War, before the opening of the Second Front in 1944, mythologisation of the anti-Nazi resistance movements served to offset inaction in the West. In the 1960s the incidence of guerrilla war reflected the strategic stalemate between the two blocs, as did, in a different way, the espousal of guerrilla warfare by the Reagan administration in the 1980s. In Aron's phrasing, war was no longer so impossible.

It may be claimed that guerrilla war did, indeed, effect a fundamental shift in the international balance of power during the 1970s and 1980s, in, respectively, the Soviet and US directions. Vietnam represented not just a defeat of the US military intervention in Indochina, but, more generally, enabled a shift in the balance of power throughout the Third World from which other revolutionary movements drew advantage. Afghanistan, by contrast, weakened the USSR and was followed by a more general strategic retreat that contributed to the final collapse of the Soviet system.

These defeats, related as they were to the broader pattern of relations between the competing blocs, did contribute to the shift in the overall relationship, but their impact should not be exaggerated. In the first place, the defeats were themselves only possible because of the ability of the rival bloc to provide significant quantities of conventional weapons *and* to inhibit attacks on base areas (in North Vietnam and Pakistan respectively) through the nuclear balance. Secondly, in the case of Vietnam, the USA, while unable to save South Vietnam, Laos and Cambodia, was able, in alliance with local states, to discourage the spread of revolution elsewhere in

Indochina. The US helped to promote a revitalisation of non-communist regional economies that two decades later was not only greatly to outstrip the communist states but was to provide the incentive for their transformation. On the Soviet side no such recouping was possible, but it must be doubted how far it was Afghanistan, or indeed the other areas where the US challenged Soviet Third World allies, that played the decisive role in the collapse of the Soviet system. The overall historical verdict on guerrilla war in the middle and late twentieth century therefore needs to be one that both recognises its distinctive and formative impact, and sets it in a broader international and historical context.

War as Instrument: (iv) The War of Revolutionary Offensive

As important in the history of revolutionary thought and practice as irregular, or guerrilla war, has been conventional war and in particular the issue of how revolutionary states can use war for the furthering of their overall political strategy. The relationship has been a two-way one: on the one hand, the evolution of conceptions of 'revolutionary' warfare appropriate to the revolutionary state; on the other, the adoption of conceptions of politics derived from the history of conventional warfare, notably Gramsci's contrast, already discussed, between a war of manoeuvre, appropriate to less developed societies, and a war of position, suitable for the more advanced Western states. In conventional, as in guerrilla, war the military and the political have interlocked.

Throughout the history of revolutions, war has been an instrument for the promotion and export of revolution in other states. The ideological formulation of this has been discussed in Chapter 3. Cromwell held that the conflict with Spain would enable England to encourage an anti-Catholic uprising in that country. In 1792 the French revolutionaries were enthusiastic about putting the military resources of the state at the disposal of struggling peoples elsewhere. The Bolsheviks attempted, in the immediate aftermath of 1917, to provide military assistance to the Polish, Iranian and Mongolian revolutions – unsuccessfully in the first two cases, successfully in the third: it was this strategy, and the apparent opportunities, which encouraged Lenin to turn the defensive war against Poland in July 1920 into an offensive one, and occasioned Tukhachevsky's theory of the 'offensive revolutionary war'.[35] Subsequently, and in the context of the Second World War the Soviet army either assisted allied forces to come to power, as in Yugoslavia and Korea, or, as in much of Eastern Europe, imposed communist regimes on conquered countries. In the post-war period China fought a succession of wars, most notably in Korea, while Cuba was to send troops to fight in support of friendly regimes in Angola and Ethiopia, and Iran was to prolong its war with Iraq by six years, from 1982 to 1988, in the hope that military pressure on the regime in Baghdad would precipitate an insurrection in that country, thus bringing a sympathetic Islamic regime to power.

The record of how armed forces have been used as a mechanism for promoting political change abroad is, at best, a mixed one. Where such action has occurred it has been within the context of *an already existing inter-state conflict*: when two states are at war it has become possible to use that war as a context for promoting change in the political system of other states. This was the case of France in the 1790s, and of Russia in the 1940s. Where, in the absence of an inter-state war in which they are involved, revolutionary states have intervened in wars, it has been not to support insurgents but to prevent established allied regimes from being overthrown: thus the interventions of China in Korea in 1950, of Cuba in Angola in 1975 or Ethiopia in 1977 were in support of regimes already established. In no case has a revolutionary state been able to launch a war without prior attack from the other side, and of its own initiative to promote change in another country. In that sense the 'offensive revolutionary war' has been another myth, an impossibility by dint of both the absence of sufficient international legitimacy for such a war and the resistance of the target state society to it. Solidarity and support of a military kind has had to take a more cautious, limited, form. At the same time, where revolutionary states have become embroiled in conflict with other states, the most successful such cases have been ones where they have had clear political goals, relating to the conflict with the other state, beyond which they have not gone.

The revolutionary combination of Clausewitz and Lenin, specifying the need to keep a clear political purpose in mind, was nowhere more evident than in the use made of inter-state war by Mao Tse-tung. During Mao's period as leader (1949–76), China became involved in four military conflicts with its neighbours: Korea (1950–53), India (1962), Russia (1969), and Vietnam (1979). It was also involved in an ongoing confrontation with Taiwan. In each case China fought successful military campaigns, but ones that were guided by a *clear political purpose*. In Korea the goal was to push the American and other 'UN' forces back to the 38th Parallel, the dividing line between the two Koreas, and so ensure both the survival of the North Korean regime and the maintenance of a buffer between themselves and the Americans. The temptation to continue the war, in the hope of unifying all of Korea, the original goal of the adventurist North Koreans, was resisted. In the conflict with India, the goal was not to seize significant areas of territory, or march on the Indian plains, both of which were possible, but to put an end to the border incursions taking place and to reduce New Delhi's ambitions.[36] In regard to Russia, where significant fighting was avoided, China nonetheless mobilised for a general war, using the clashes on the river between the two states to make its point. Its attack on Vietnam in 1979, an initiative both devoid of any legal justification and incompetently carried out, also had a limited goal: it was intended to 'punish' Vietnam for its occupation of Cambodia and the ousting of the Khmer Rouge regime formerly allied to China. As for Taiwan, and despite much rhetoric about reuniting the motherland, Mao never made a concerted effort to attack the island, or even to seize the two small islands, Quemoy and Matsu lying near the mainland: bombardment of these islands and the issuing of hundreds of stern warnings served a *political* purpose that was never allowed to slip into outright war. In each case China, for all its military strength and bellicose rhetoric, fought wars and used force with clear, delimited, political goals.[37]

'Never Invade a Revolution': Mass Mobilisation and Revolutionary Defence

For revolutionary regimes, wars perform not only external but also internal functions. The briefest of historical surveys can show how, faced with an external threat, revolutionary regimes have been able to mobilise sufficient military force to repel an invader and, in so doing, have enhanced their domestic position, through increased administrative control of society, through the socialisation of large numbers of people in the military apparatus, and through the acquisition of enhanced legitimacy. This is a lesson well summarised in the editorial which *The Times* chose to print on 1 October 1980 in the immediate aftermath of the Iraqi invasion of Iran: 'Never Invade a Revolution'. What appear initially to be regimes that are incapable of meeting the test of inter-state conflict, because of the disorganisation of the coercive apparatus and the dispersal of a professional officer corps, turn out to be particularly successful at meeting such challenges. Indeed, in the words of Skocpol, 'the task which revolutionized regimes in the modern world have performed best is the mobilization of citizen support across class lines for protracted international warfare'.[38] The most striking early version of this was the *levée en masse* that followed the counter-revolutionary invasion of France in 1792. The Russian revolution also exemplified this – the poor performance of the Russian army in the First World War contrasting with the stamina and ultimate success of the Soviet army less than thirty years later, and despite the decimation of both the Czarist and Soviet officers corps, in the Second World War.[39]

After 1945, in a range of Third World countries, populations not hitherto noted for military achievement were mobilised into large irregular forces that withheld years of conventional military assault – in China, Vietnam, Algeria, Eritrea, Angola and elsewhere. As remarkable as any was the case of Iran. The 400,000-strong Iranian armed forces almost completely disintegrated during and immediately after the revolution of 1979.[40] When Iraq invaded in September 1980 it might confidently have expected to be able to advance relatively unhindered into the country. Instead, remnants of the old Iranian army, newly recruited regular forces and the separate institutions of the *pasdaran* (guards) and *basij* (mobilisation) were used to halt and then turn back the Iraqi invasion.[41]

The role of such defensive wars in consolidating revolutionary regimes is striking. It illustrates both the potential for political mobilisation present in such situations, and the ingenuity and very administrative capability of civilian revolutionary elites. Yet it would be mistaken to see any simple relationship here between external threat and internal consolidation. In her discussion of the issue, Skocpol indicates how important geopolitical factors are in determining the internal development of revolutionary regimes: those that were not attacked, such as that of Mexico, were less radicalised than those that were, such as Vietnam and Iran. But while the geopolitical context is important, it may be that the causality also works the other way. Those with less radical programmes, internally and internationally, are less likely to be attacked, whereas those that have a commitment to the ongoing promotion of revolution, and which proclaim that commitment, run greater risks. Equally, there is no necessary linkage between external threat and internal response. In some cases external pressure may serve not to strengthen but to weaken the regime, by increasing the costs of revolutionary commitment and promoting economic and social problems. Despite much success in appealing to patriotic sentiment in the initial phases of the *contra* war, it would seem that this more negative outcome was a significant factor in the loss of support for the Sandinistas in Nicaragua, leading to their defeat in the election of 1990.[42]

This contingency is also borne out by the cases where such mobilisations do not occur. Where revolution is carried out 'from above', i.e. by radicalised factions within the military apparatus, the commonsense presumption that they would be especially successful defenders of national security and of patriotic sentiment is belied by the record. Nasser's Egypt and Mengistu's Ethiopia, two leading examples of 'revolution from above', were particularly unable to conduct war or to mobilise their populations for military purposes. Thus Egypt lost two wars, that of 1956 and, even more spectacularly, that of 1967, to surprise Israeli attacks, while the Ethiopian military regime that emerged in 1974 was to prove unable to crush the rebellion in Eritrea and had to call on outside Cuban support to repel an invasion from Somalia.[43] As is discussed in Chapter 10, the external pressures, including the geopolitical context, may in the longer run serve as much to weaken as to consolidate the post-revolutionary regime.

A Contingent Relationship

The relationship between war and revolution is not, therefore, one of cause and effect, so much as of two contrasted and combined forms of mobilisation and conflict, two intertwined expressions of a broader social context. Both are political processes, the organisation and character of which have changed substantially over the past two centuries. Both take on their meaning within a broader context of 'general crisis'. Insofar as any individual revolution, and the international response to it, has to be seen as part of a wider, internationalised pattern of social and political conflict then the revolution can be seen not so much as initiating conflict as exacerbating an already present set of tensions within states. The reason why revolutions lead to war is not therefore that revolutionary states are wilfully belligerent, dissatisfied or revisionist, or that their opponents are militaristic and expansionist. Rather, by dint of the very tensions that led to revolution occurring, other states and societies are affected by them. Thus war is a means by which both groups of states, the revolutionary and the counter-revolutionary, respond to changes in domestic and international politics.

Both groups of states are caught in the difficulty posed by all attempts to link internal political organisation with inter-state relations, namely that of relating but also separating the two dimensions of security. In each case there is an evident relationship between domestic or 'vertical' security, that of the state, and international or 'horizontal' security, peace between states. It is a relationship that allows of no easy resolution. A policy of fully accepting the relationship would mean that any consistent pursuit of international peace would entail regular interference in the internal affairs of other countries. A policy of denying any connection would entail ignoring the international consequences of revolutions and other upheavals. Both revolutionary and counter-revolutionary states are therefore caught in a process that leads to war, but which at the same time is constrained by the political character of states and of relations between them. For both, as discussed in Chapter 5, a set of recurrent dilemmas are evident. Firstly there is that of calculating the benefits of war, in terms of mobilisation and furthering of foreign policy goals, against the costs, in terms of domestic resistance. In both revolutionary and counter-revolutionary states, involvement in external conflict, especially where the ideological rationale seems greater than the national interest, can lead to a loss of support at home. Secondly, both forms of war run the risk of mobilising resistance in the target state on a nationalist basis. The export of revolution, as much as that of counter-revolution, provokes resistance to it. Thirdly, both forms of war violate the principle on which much inter-state relations rest, and which revolutionaries and counter-revolutionaries invoke to legitimise their own cause, namely sovereignty.

The resolution of this problem has, in practice, involved a set of limited commitments, to the export of revolution by revolutionary states, and to the promotion of counter-revolution by status quo powers. If the Soviet Union, China and other revolutionary states of the twentieth century found it difficult to provide support for fellow insurgents in other states, the status quo powers have found comparable difficulties in extending their campaigns. Nowhere was this more striking than in the war in Vietnam, when the USA was

constrained from taking the step that could have decisively weakened the insurgent movement in the south, namely the launch of a
ground offensive against North Vietnam. Yet such violations of the
conventions of sovereignty recur. They are a result of the very
internationalised character of revolutions themselves. While over
time such violations abate on both sides, and while both forms of
external policy have been remarkably ineffective, they recur as long
as revolutionary states themselves remain committed to distinct
paths of domestic development.

10

Systemic Constraints: Revolutionary 'Transformation' and Autarky

Post-Revolutionary Transformation: International Constraints

No study of the international dimensions of revolutions would be complete without analysis of the ways in which international factors shape the development of post-revolutionary states. Analysis of this interaction can do much to identify the ways in which, formal inter-state relations apart, the external shapes the internal evolution of states and societies: such an investigation is relevant for theory, both sociological and international. It highlights the contradictory character of external pressure: radicalising the revolutionary state in the short run, debilitating and pushing it towards conformity with an international norm in the longer run. Such a perspective is equally of historical importance, in helping to explain the outcomes of revolutions. It was Trotsky who in the 1920s perceived the importance of this dimension of competition: 'a Ford tractor is just as dangerous as a Creusot gun, with the sole difference that while the gun can function only from time to time, the tractor brings its pressure to bear upon us constantly'.[1] Revolutions are, above all, attempts to change the societies in which they occurred: beyond the assumption of power itself, they seek to implement domestic transformation – to change political system, economy, social relations. The Jacobins sought to turn French society upside down in pursuit of their rationalist goals; the Bolsheviks and their successors envisaged a socialist transformation, the production indeed of 'new socialist man'; the revolutionaries of Iran pursued Islamisation of politics and society on the model of the Prophet and his immediate successors. It was this post-revolutionary change as much as the actual seizure of power itself that defined the character of revolutions.[2]

The international cannot provide the sole explanation for such policies. The motives behind such post-revolutionary transformation were in considerable part internal: most evidently these were the consolidation of power, and the realisation of the programme in terms of which the revolution itself was made. But as with the ideology and causes of revolution, so with post-revolutionary change, international factors were central to how revolutionaries formulated their aims, and to what they could do: *telos* and outcome were internationally determined. Herein lay one of the paradoxes not only of the revolutionary state, but of the modern state itself: nowhere was the two-sided, the Janus-like character of the state, more evident than in the fate of such authoritarian transformative projects. For while revolutionary states, more than others, sought to intervene in society, to impose change by wielding the coercive or despotic powers that they had, and to do so for reasons of strengthening the state *vis-à-vis* others in the international arena, it was precisely this international dimension that constrained and later undermined what these states could do.[3] The contrast of the two dimensions of state activity was decisive: while the capacities of the revolutionary states were most evident *internally*, it was *internationally* that they were most challenged and these very domestic capacities undermined.

In the first post-revolutionary period, the revolutionary regime proclaimed international goals, but as far as its own society was concerned it sought international rupture: the objective was control, to break contact with the outside world. It aimed to establish national, i.e. state, control over economic resources and to prevent *political* challenges from emerging within. The most consistent example of such a process was that of the Soviet Union. Thus of post-1917 Russia was said:

> In the first phase of the development (from the October revolution to the 'elimination of the exploiting classes'), the functions of the state were: (*a*) 'to suppress the overthrown classes inside the country', (*b*) 'to defend the country from foreign attack', and (*c*) 'economic organization and cultural education'.[4]

Over a longer period, such a breaking served to terminate *social,* *economic* and *cultural* links. Here in the initial post-revolutionary period the external served as an alien opposite, a source of anxiety, corruption, counter-revolution. However, while in the initial period the revolutionaries aimed to insulate their societies as much as possible from external contact, in the longer run they were compelled to interact with it. Therefore revolutions not only began with international causes, to an unacknowledged degree, but their outcomes were also shaped by the external context, to an extent unanticipated by those who had assumed a power that appeared, to friend and foe alike, to be so absolute.

The most abrupt of these pressures was, of course, foreign invasion. Engels, perceiving how war could strengthen the revolutionary regime, was to say of France in the 1790s:

> The whole French Revolution is dominated by the War of the Coalition, all its pulsations depend upon it. If the allied army penetrates into France – predominant activity of the vague nerve, violent heart-beat, revolutionary crisis. If it is driven back – predominance of the sympathetic nerve, the heart-beat becomes slow, the reactionary elements again push themselves into the foreground.[5]

For France, 1815 marked the end of the revolutionary period: Waterloo marked the end of the revolutionary state in France. Invasion ended the Soviet republic in Hungary in 1919, after four months, as surely as it ended the revolutionary experiment in Grenada in 1983, after four years. The Bolsheviks faced external intervention in the civil war of 1918–21, and Nazi invasion in 1941–4. But external pressures also take more subtle forms, as was evident in the early-nineteenth-century United States: the original aspiration to a loose federation of states had to be replaced by a more centralised system because of foreign competition, war with the English in its most direct form, and economic and strategic competition more broadly.[6] It was comparable long-term external pressures which, in the end, eroded the communist system: successfully able to withstand military assault, and the challenge of Cold War, it succumbed to other forms of international competition, not least to what, as we shall see, the Chinese communists termed 'the sugar-coated bullets' of capitalist consumerism and social norms themselves.

This relationship between domestic change and international pressure raises several issues concerning the interaction of revolutions and the international. The first is how far internal transformations are indeed autonomous, independent of international factors. Much is made, by revolutionaries and their opponents alike, of the transnational impact of revolutions; far less of the transnational character of the obverse, domestic transformation. Yet for all the attempts to break with the rest of the world, revolutionary societies remain subject to the external. The appearance of insulation and separation, of rupture with the world system, characteristic of the earlier phase of revolutions, conceals another reality, the costs of such a severing. Even in this period many domestic policies, not least the abrupt shifts of faction and political line, result from calculations about external threats, real and fictitious. Stalin's purges of 1936–8 and Mao's cultural revolution of 1965–9 were both conducted in terms of a struggle against those in league with external powers, 'imperialist' and 'Nazi' agents in the former case, 'capitalist roaders' and sympathisers with the Soviet Union in the latter.

The longer-run picture is one of growing vulnerability to external pressure as insulation breaks down. Such pressure begins to corrode the isolation of states even as they appear most stable. It provides another aspect from which to question the assumption, very much a peculiarity of the middle and late twentieth century, of the power of states.[7] Revolutions at the same time constitute a test of how the constraints of the international system, conventionally assessed with regard to foreign policy, i.e. relations between sovereign states, affect domestic policy – be this through economic sanctions, cultural influence, political propaganda, or, in more extreme cases, support for armed opposition within. Most discussion of such interdependence, or linkage, has been with regard to relations between peaceful, developed, states, within a broadly liberal environment; but such linkage of international and domestic is also present, and with perhaps more explosive results, in the illiberal world of conflict between revolutionary states and their opponents.[8]

Equally challenged is dependency theory. Although this theory developed in Latin America from the 1950s and 1960s in opposition to free trade and, later, neo-liberalism,[9] its underlying premises are those of the Bolshevik experiment itself. One can argue that dependency theory, although formulated in opposition to the

'stagist' theories of orthodox Soviet Marxism-Leninism, is a working out, without explicit reference to the Bolshevik revolution, of
what came to be the assumptions of post-1917 Soviet policy. The
assumption was that the revolutionary state would be capable of
exerting sufficient power both to transform the society and to
sustain the break with the external world. For dependency theory,
the test is central. This theory postulated that it was the very ties,
the links of dependency, between dominant and dominated states
that reinforced dependency, and that a break with this system,
'delinking', was necessary for political and economic development.
Yet the 'independence' that contrasted with 'dependence' was in
some respects a chimera: in the short run the costs were too high, in
the long run the disconnection unattainable.

The issue of external competition went to the heart of the battle
for the consolidation and overthrow of revolutions. For this there
were two main reasons. In the first place, the goal of revolution –
some would argue the very rationale – was not so much the creation
of a new society as the strengthening of a society in the develop-
mental competition with stronger states. Generated by, and in
reaction to, the sharpest points of combined and uneven development, revolutions were above all about 'catching up' with other
more advanced states, a product of a perceived inferiority and the
need for mobilisation of resources the better to compete. Their
cause and goal were a contradictory modernity: as Roman Szporluk
had argued in his *Communism and Nationalism, Karl Marx Versus
Friedrich List* this was reflected in an ideological fusion. The earlier
theoretical contrast of internationalist socialism and nationalist
state-directed economic development, which took form in the
1840s, ended with the Bolshevik revolution; thereafter the two were
conjoined in an authoritarian state-directed industrialisation project.[10] Revolutions were, indeed, attempts by semi-peripheral countries, countries that were incorporated into, but relatively backward
within, the international development competition, to accelerate
and catch up:

> Where socialism became a societal determinant (and did not
> remain just one political force among others within capitalist
> societies), it was the basis and motive force of accelerated,
> delayed development in adverse internal and international con-
> ditions which, as a rule, make successful delayed development
> under the banner of capitalism improbable.[11]

From the 1920s onwards Bolshevism justified itself at home and abroad above all as a successful economic, mainly industrialisation, project, able to rival and outstrip the West. This not only met the requirements of mobilising nationalist sentiment within Russia, but equally served to build a state that could resist, and hopefully prevail over, the capitalist West. After the Second World War, as the threat of war was deemed by the Soviet leadership to have receded, a recognition, formalised in the proclamation in 1956 by Khrushchev of 'peaceful coexistence', the significance of economic competition became even greater: for it was to be in the economic and social sphere that the competition between the two systems would be fought out. Khrushchev proclaimed this as the arena, vowing that the USSR would overtake capitalism within a generation.[12] From a more radical perspective, and without forsaking the possibility of war, China too presented itself as a model for the Third World.

The international mattered, however, not just in the costs of failure to sustain, and win, in an economic competition but also in regard to whether or not the initial revolution spread to other countries. In this, the fate of the revolution depended on events beyond its frontiers. Revolutionaries, for all their postulation of rupture and delinking, had long argued that the fate of any one revolutionary society was dependent on the broader progress of revolution internationally. This was true of Marx's view of the European revolutions, of Lenin's hopes before and after 1917, as of later internationalist aspirations, in Cuba or Iran. One of the most perceptive studies of the dilemmas facing Lenin after the Bolshevik revolution and his incapacitation in 1923, begins with the words:

> In the eyes of its originators the October Revolution had neither meaning nor future independent of its international function as a catalyst and detonator: it was to be the first spark that would lead to the establishment of socialist regimes in countries which, unlike Russia, possessed an adequate economic infrastructure and cultural basis. Unless it fulfilled this function, the Soviet regime should not even have survived.[13]

It was the failure of such revolutions, the unpropitious character of the international system, that for many accounted for the degeneration of the USSR in the 1920s and 1930s. China may have been partially an exception, in that with a quarter of humanity within its territory it could legitimately claim that its revolution was sufficient unto itself. But the Chinese communist regime too had its share of external pressure – the need to cast off the shackles of 'semi-colonial' domination, the aspiration to serve as a beacon to the peoples of the world, the fear of external, US and later Soviet, subversion, the very branding of internal opponents as 'agents' of an externally directed capitalist restoration, the US building in Vietnam after 1965. After close on three decades of defiance of external pressure following the revolution of 1949, the Chinese Communist Party decided in 1978 to embark on a very different path, 'The Four Modernisations', which integrated it into the world market in dramatic form.

The argument that it is external factors which *do* account for the fate of post-revolutionary societies is therefore central to revolutionary thinking itself. The export of revolution, discussed in Chapter 3, has, among other sources, this *internal* rationale. The original Marxist anticipation of a world-wide revolution was reproduced in Lenin's case in the linking of the prospects of the Bolshevik revolution to the broader progress of revolution in more developed European countries. As Trotsky was to say in 1917:

> If the peoples of Europe do not arise and crush imperialism, we shall be crushed – that is beyond doubt. Either the Russian revolution will raise the whirlwind of struggle in the west, or the capitalists of all countries will stifle our struggle.[14]

Stalin later rejected this, by arguing from 1923 onwards that socialism was possible '*in one country*'. His canonical formulations of an official 'Marxism-Leninism' after Lenin's death, *Foundations of Leninism* (1924) and *On the Problems of Leninism* (1926) – thinking reflected in the Fourteenth Congress of the CPSU in December 1925 – argued that while full communism could not be achieved without revolution in other developed countries, socialism could be built in one country.[15] This was explicitly presented as a means of ensuring the survival of the revolution against external intervention.[16]

However, Stalin's critics continued to stress that the revolution had to be internationalised, or it would fail. This connection had been immediately grasped by the leader of the German communist movement, Rosa Luxemburg. While remaining broadly sympathetic to the Bolsheviks, her critique covered both internal policy

– on land, nationalities, the constituent assembly, dictatorship – and external relations. Moreover, she argued that the Bolshevik revolution would, if it remained on its own, become a dictatorship. The solution lay in a revolution elsewhere, above all in Germany:

> Lenin and Trotsky and their friends were the *first* who went ahead as an example to the proletariat of the world . . . But in Russia the problem could only by posed. It could not be solved there. In *this* sense, the future everywhere belongs to Bolshevism.[17]

As her biographer was later to note, Luxemburg 'was far more afraid of a deformed revolution than an unsuccessful one'.[18]

This link between external context and the internal character of the Soviet state was to be one of the central themes of accounts by later revolutionary Marxists of the bureaucratisation of the Soviet state. According to Marcel Liebman, for example, the initial potential for a revolutionary democracy, sustained by an overall sense of Bolshevik optimism, was thwarted by the Brest-Litovsk agreement. For Liebman, Lenin's speeches, in justification of that foreign policy agreement, signalled a broader concession to 'realism', and to the discipline and state control that were to follow. Brest-Litovsk was the first defeat suffered by the Bolsheviks, and it was to be decisive and irreversible.[19] Lenin, as we have seen in Chapter 4, had some sense of what the failure in Poland of 1920 represented. Trotsky, above all, was to link the consolidation of a bureaucracy within the USSR to the failure of the revolution to spread. In *The Third International After Lenin*, and then in exile, having left the Soviet Union in 1929 after his defeat in the inner-party conflict, he claimed that the revolution had been usurped by a bureaucracy that opposed the international spread of revolution. In *The Revolution Betrayed*, his last work, published two decades after Rosa Luxemburg's prophetic analysis, and his supreme analysis of the emergence of Stalinism in Russia, he analyses the forces leading to the ebbing of the revolutionary tide of 1917: Trotsky links the emergence of a bureaucracy both to internal processes – exhaustion in civil war, demobilisation of the Red Army, class formation under the NEP – and to external events:

> The international situation was pushing with mighty forces in the same direction. The Soviet bureaucracy became more self-

confident, the heavier the blows dealt to the world working class. Between these two facts there was not only a chronological, but a causal connection, and one which worked in two directions. The leaders of the bureaucracy promoted the proletarian defeats; the defeats promoted the rise of the bureaucracy. The crushing of the Bulgarian insurrection and in the inglorious retreat of the German workers' party in 1923, the collapse of the Estonian attempt at insurrection in 1924, the treacherous liquidation of the General Strike in England and the unworthy conduct of the Polish workers' party at the installation of Pilsudski in 1926, the terrible massacre of the Chinese revolution in 1927, and, finally, the still more ominous defeats in Germany and Austria – these are the historic catastrophes which killed the faith of the Soviet masses in world revolution, and permitted the bureaucracy to rise higher and higher as the sole light of salvation . . . the continual defeats of the revolution in Europe and Asia, while weakening the international position of the Soviet Union, have vastly strengthened the Soviet bureaucracy.[20]

Surveying the later situation of the 1930s, when the danger of assault on the USSR had once again begun to develop, Trotsky attributes the likelihood of such an attack precisely to the isolation of the USSR, the lack of revolutionary allies in other states:

The danger of a combined attack on the Soviet Union takes palpable form in our eyes only because the country of the Soviets is still isolated, because to a considerable extent this 'one sixth of the earth's surface' is a realm of primitive backwardness, because the productivity of labour in spite of the nationalization of the means of production is still far lower than in capitalist countries, and, finally – what is at present most important – because the chief detachments of the worker proletariat are shattered, distrustful of themselves and deprived of reliable leadership. Thus the October revolution, in which its leaders saw only a prelude to world revolution, but which, in the course of things, has received a temporary independent significance, reveals in this new historic stage its deep dependence upon world development. Again it becomes obvious that the historic question, *who shall prevail?* cannot be decided within national boundaries, that interior successes and failures only prepare more or less favourable conditions for its decision on the world arena.[21]

Mistaken as he was about the prospects for world revolution, Trotsky was to foresee with uncanny intuition two central aspects of the collapse of the Soviet experiment five decades later. On the one hand, he saw that it was the technological superiority of the West in civilian technology, rather than its military preponderance, that would destroy the socialist experiment. On the other, he saw the restoration of capitalism as coming through the conversion of the party and state bureaucracy into a new, private propertied, ruling class, what later became known as a '*nomenklatura* buy-out'.

On the opposite side, for counter-revolutionaries, this vulnerability of revolutions long constituted an opportunity. Economic boycotts and other forms of pressures served to weaken revolutionary regimes, to alienate their populations and to diminish the appeals of such revolutions internationally.[22] Revolution and counter-revolution appeared, in this regard, to make common cause. On its own, such economic pressure may not have served to overthrow the regime: it could, however, as it did in Iran in 1953 or Chile in 1973 and as it was to do over a longer-run period in Eastern Europe up to 1989, intensify popular dissatisfaction and thereby facilitate a political change. When Henry Kissinger said in 1970 that the USA would pressure the Chilean economy 'till it screamed' this was not a casual remark: credit was denied, exports were blocked, striking and disruptive opposition groups were funded, investor confidence was destroyed. Economic pressure on the USSR in the 1980s by the Reagan administration had a similar goal. There is therefore a political economy of counter-revolution, an understanding of how economic pressures, motivated by political and economic goals, could weaken both the domestic and international appeal of revolutionary states, and undermine the hold of the authoritarian state on its population.

Self-Reliance: The Theory

The ideas that underlie the pursuit of autonomy and delinking are by no means specific to the revolutionary, but reflect a confluence, under the pressures of the post-revolutionary process itself, of two trends. One has been present in political economy, and more broadly in philosophy, since classical Greece: 'cosmophobia', as much as cosmopolitanism, has its origins in this time. Fifth-century Athens prohibited the export of grain. Suspicion of contact with the

outside world, and the desire to insulate society, especially in order
to protect programmes of social change, can be found in Plato and
in Rousseau: both argued that their projects for developing an ideal
political community required that contact with the outside world be
kept to a minimum. While not interested in the diffusion of their
message in any revolutionary expansion, they were conscious that
external factors, not least cultural and personal contact, would
undermine their project. This idea of the desirability of insulation
was to recur in the American revolution, where the fact of America's isolation from the rest of the world, and in particular from
Europe, was held to be a virtue of the new republic.[23]

It was in the early nineteenth century, however, that this broad
presumption in favour of insulation, one generally out of keeping
with the liberal temper of the times, was to be formulated in
economic terms, in the writings of the German Friedrich List, in
particular his *Das nationale System der politischen Ökonomie (The
National System of Political Economy)* published in 1840. List was a
political activist; like other German romantics, he opposed liberal
cosmopolitanism, and, in keeping with what came to be 'commu-
nitarian' thinking, he argued that the individual had to be seen in
the context of the broader social unit, in this case the nation.[24] To
this German romanticism he added an economic programme of
strengthening manufacturing and building up German industry, a
theme taken in part from the US vice-president Alexander Hamilton. The essence of List's economic argument was that in order for
states that were lagging behind in the international race for development to compete, they had to reduce the influence of the world
market, and rely on a national path of economic development. Karl
Marx, in an early text, was to criticise List's writings; but List's
argument, for all its nationalist character, was to be the one that
Marxists, once they came to power, were to follow.[25]

Such protectionism as part of a state-directed development
strategy was, over the ensuing century, an argument that was to
appeal to right, as to left. On the right it was evident in the
Germany of Bismarck and Hitler, in the Spain of Franco, the
Ireland of de Valera. But suitably transformed by an analysis that
located such strategies in the context of imperialism, it was also to
be a central theme in the strategies of all communist and revolutionary states: whether individually or in a collective self-reliance,
the seizure of power was to be followed by the breaking of links
with the world market, the construction of a national economy, and

the insulation of society from corrupting or counter-revolutionary external pressures.[26] Such an approach was largely alien to the spirit of Marx, who foresaw a combined and increasingly united capitalist development of the world, leading to an equally combined world revolution. It was central, however, to the thinking of two generations of Marxist thinkers: the Marxists of the early twentieth century, who saw revolution in the context of the struggle against imperialism; and to the dependency school of the 1950s–1970s, for whom the poverty and weakness of Third World states reflected their subordination to global structures.[27]

Mention has already been made of the conflict between the internationalist and anti-statist trend in the classical revolutionary thinking of Marx, and the subsequent record of nationalist and statist economic development in revolutionary states. There are, however, two elements in that classical thinking that were to serve as components of the later strategy. One was the idea of the state itself as the instrument of political power. This concept of the state had been central to what Russian rulers had sought to do from the time of Peter the Great onwards, and was present in much Russian nationalism of the later two centuries. Marx had devoted relatively little space in his work to what would follow the revolution, but in his *Critique of the Gotha Programme* he did provide the elements for such a theory:

> It is by no means the goal of workers who have discarded the narrow mentality of humble subjects to make the state 'free'. In the German Reich the 'state' has almost as much 'freedom' as in Russia. Freedom consists in converting the state from an organ superimposed on society into one thoroughly subordinate to it
> . . .
> Between capitalist and communist society lies a period of revolutionary transformation from one to the other. There is a corresponding period of transition in the political sphere and in this period the state can only take the form of a *revolutionary dictatorship of the proletariat.*[28]

While Marx invokes social needs, what he endorses is a state that acquires authoritarian independence of society, the better to implement that revolutionary dictatorship. The imperatives of economic development, and to the Listian–Leninist pursuit of industrialisation, combine with consolidation of political power to produce the authoritarian revolutionary state. The Soviet state, for all its claims to be democratic, was a centralised body in which the party elite, armed with an ideology of progress and self-fulfilling legitimacy, imposed its will on society.[29]

This strand of calculated insulation from the outside world was compounded from a very different source in the case of late-nine-teenth-century revolutionary thinking – the valorisation of the peasantry and of the pre-industrial past. Revolutionaries were in general believers in progress, a unilinear process urged on by capitalism itself. Yet there was, at the same time, a strand of romanticism, of idealisation of the pre-industrial, that was to influence Marx in his later life, and which was expressed most clearly in the work of the Russian populists. For the latter, the village communities of Russian life could, and should, be preserved, and with them broader patterns of social and cultural life that could provide the basis for a transition to socialism, avoiding the disrup-tions of industrial capitalism itself.[30] This strand in revolutionary thinking was to be strengthened by the link established after the First World War between the revolutionary project and national-ism. The pre-modern and that which was not foreign was thus doubly validated – on *national* grounds as genuine, indigenous and 'authentic', and on *revolutionary* grounds as providing the basis for a rapid, less extended transition to an alternative social order. That revolutions also involved a high degree of cultural isolationism – culturally nationalist in some cases, repressively vigilant in others, viciously petty-minded and suspicious in others – produced an atmosphere of hostility to the outside world that compounded the more rational calculations of economic strategy. The record of revolutionary states throughout the twentieth century is one of the attempts to implement this strategy – state intervention in the economy and society, breaking with the imperialist economic system, mobilisation of domestic resources, pursuit of longer-term investment goals at the expense of shorter-term consumption.[31]

Phase I: The Revolutionary Rupture

The Bolshevik project, the paradigmatic twentieth-century revolu-tion, was implemented in a society where the uneven international impact of development was most acutely felt. On the one hand, Russia had been transformed by its integration into the world capitalist system in the latter part of the nineteenth century; on the other, its backwardness compared to its Western and more industrialised rivals was evident. It was this insertion of a backward Russia into a more developed world that, in the view of Lenin and Trotsky, made possible the Soviet experiment, the leap into a process of accelerated modernity. As Trotsky wrote: 'Savages throw away their bows and arrows for rifles all at once, without travelling the road which lay between these two weapons in the past'.[32] Bolshevism both resulted from, and aimed to redress, this imbalance, producing that fusion of nationalist industrialisation, as expounded by List, and revolutionary statism, as expounded by Lenin.[33] The goal was therefore to defeat capitalism, through socialist construction.

Lenin did not formulate a theory of 'socialism in one country' but the recognition that the revolution would not be simultaneous, even across the more developed countries, led him to articulate ideas which Stalin was to take further.[34] As early as 1915 Lenin had written:

> Uneven economic and political development is an absolute law of capitalism. Hence, the victory of socialism is possible first in several or even in one capitalist country, taken singly. The victorious proletariat of that country, having expropriated the capitalist and organized its own socialist production, would stand up *against* the rest of the world, the capitalist world, attracting to its cause the oppressed classes of other countries, raising revolts in those countries against the capitalist, and in the event of necessity coming out even with armed force against the exploiting classes and their states.[35]

Once in power the Bolsheviks therefore set out to bring foreign and domestic activity under its control. In *The ABC of Communism* published in 1919, Nikolai Bukharin and Evgenii Preobrazhensky begin their section on industry with the words:

> The very first task of the proletariat, and of the Soviet Power as instrument of the proletarian dictatorship, was to wrest the means of production from the bourgeoisie, or, as the phrase runs, to expropriate the bourgeoisie. It is self-evident that we were not concerned with the expropriation of small-scale industry or with the expropriation of artisan production, but with the

seizure of the means of production that were in the hands of the great capitalists, with establishing large-scale industry upon a new foundation, and with organizing it in accordance with new principles . . . Obviously, in the epoch of proletarian dictatorship there is only one way of doing this, namely by *proletarian nationalization*, by which we mean the transfer of all the means of production, distribution, and exchange into the hands of the proletarian State, the greatest and most powerful of working class organizations.[36]

This commitment to nationalisation in part reflected the realities of the post-1917 situation – civil war, conflict with the West, the needs of a war economy. As Bukharin and Preobrazhensky wrote:

Until the world revolution is victorious, Russia must act alone. Now the Russian working class received a disastrous heritage when it conquered power in the year 1917. The whole country was disorganized and impoverished . . . The workers had to clear up the mess which the imperialist lords had made . . . The bourgeoisie continued to do everything in its power to hinder the working class from organizing production, and to prevent the upbuilding of a workers' society.[37]

However, the centralisation of the economy also reflected theoretical orientation: the desire to contrast the planned, directed character of the socialist economy with that of the anarchical capitalist, and the commitment to breaking the hold of foreign capitalist and imperialist interests over the new proletarian economy. By the autumn of 1917, Lenin, who had admitted that when they came to power there was nothing in the Marxist textbooks to tell them how to organise an economy, was expressing the basis of what was to become one of the hallmarks of the Soviet state:

We are for centralism and for a 'plan', but for the centralism and the plan of a *proletarian* state, of proletarian regulation of production and distribution in the interests of the poor, the toilers, and the exploited, *against* the exploiters.[38]

In 1920, in the period of war communism, the Bolshevik leadership as a whole favoured a militarisation of the economic system. At the same time, while some foreign trade was maintained, the goal of 'self-sufficiency' (*samostoyatel'nost*) became a long-term commitment. The Fourteenth Party Congress of December 1925, at which Stalin's theory of 'socialism in one country' was adopted, proclaimed 'economic self-sufficiency' as a goal, one spelt out in a central committee resolution of April 1926:

> The party and the state must take systematic measures to liberate our economy from its dependency on capitalist countries, which has become especially conspicuous in the present year, when the national economy, having utilized all the technique inherited by it from the pre-revolutionary epoch, has come to the end of the restoration period.[39]

This gradual consolidation of state control, linked to separation from the world economy, was to be brought to fruition in the Stalinist planning process that began in 1928.[40]

The subsequent history of the Soviet Union, up to the mid-1980s, was to continue that commitment to state control. Stalin's Five-Year Plans, beginning in 1928, were to aim at a strategy of socialist construction, and of a project fundamentally separate and distinct from that of the capitalist countries. Here the programme spelt out in *Foundations of Leninism* and other renderings of the new official ideology was to be realised.

In both Lenin's and Stalin's vision of the construction of socialism the international perspective was central: for not only was there an imperative to build a separate and distinct model of society, but there was also the opportunity to demonstrate the superiority of a planned society over that of the chaos and cycles of capitalism. Hence the prospect of constructing socialism was interrelated with an expectation of a terminal crisis of capitalism. Therefore, throughout the history of communism the issue of the prospects *for capitalism* was not just of external or long-term importance, but also served as a central legitimating feature of the arguments *for socialism*. In the 1930s, faced with the depression in the West following 1929, Stalin felt confident about the ability of the USSR to outstrip its rivals. Contrasting the situation prior to 1929 when capitalist output and trade were growing, and everyone was 'grovelling to the dollar', he went on:

> And what is the picture today? Today there is an economic crisis in nearly all the industrial countries of capitalism . . . And the

'universal' clamour about the 'inevitable doom' of the USSR is giving way to 'universal' venomous hissing about the necessity of punishing 'that country' that dares to develop its economy when crisis is reigning all around.[41]

The situation after the Second World War appeared to confirm this analysis. In his *Economic Problems of the USSR*, published in 1951, Stalin argued against those, such as the economist Eugen Varga, who believed capitalism could sustain itself without a potentially lethal crisis: the case for 'socialist construction' in the USSR was sustained. Until the 1970s Soviet writers continued, in the face of an unprecedented capitalist boom, to predict the crisis of the free market system; as Kennan had rightly pointed out in 1946, belief in the inevitable failure of capitalism was central and constitutive for the Soviet ideological system.

The model was, with variations, repeated in other revolutions. In post-1949 China, Mao and other communist leaders laid out a strategy of socialist development. For all the vagaries of tempo and emphasis, China sought, from 1949 until the introduction of the 'Four Modernisations' of 1978, to insulate its economy from that of the capitalist world. Mao's was a policy that exalted self-reliance – in revolutionary struggle to achieve power, as in post-revolutionary consolidation:

On what basis should our policy rest? It should rest on our own strength, and that means regeneration through one's own efforts. We are not alone; all the countries and people in the world opposed to imperialism are our friends. Nevertheless, we stress regeneration through our own efforts. Relying on the forces we ourselves organize, we can defeat all Chinese and foreign reactionaries.[42]

The North Korean state propagated its own version, under the name *juche*, to express similar nationalist and statist goals. In Islamic Iran, where the traditional Muslim virtue of *zuhd*, or austerity, was turned to contemporary and autarkic ends, Ayatollah Khomeini articulated a double message: on the one hand he invoked the example of the Prophet, in whose day the faithful ate only two dates per day; on the other he called for an independent industrialisation policy.[43] The first president of the Islamic Republic, Abol-Hasan Bani-Sadr, an Islamist thinker who had studied in the Paris of the 1960s, articulated this integration of self-reliance theory into the Islamic perspective:

> We have had a revolution. If we want to pursue the process of independence we must face certain realistic aspects of this whole thing. We must find out what dependencies our economy has so we may eliminate them through hard work. We must find out about our army's dependencies so we can eliminate them through hard work. We must find out about our cultural dependencies so we can eliminate them. Only then can we have an independent political system.[44]

In the arguments for delinking, considerations of politics, strategy and economics but also of culture are combined. Thus the French revolution sought to transform French culture, and the Bolshevik revolution initiated 'cultural revolution', something taken to higher and instrumental extremes in the Chinese case. The Islamic revolution too had its *inqilab-i farhangi*, a purge of universities and of dissident intellectuals, in 1980–1. In the Portuguese African colony of Guinea-Bissau, Amilcar Cabral, the leader of the guerrilla movement opposed to colonial rule, placed culture at the centre of his revolutionary strategy: he articulated a detailed, four-level campaign for the development of a culture of national liberation:

> The development of a popular culture, comprising all positive values of the indigenous peoples; the development of a national culture, drawn from history and the successes of the liberation struggle itself; the development of a scientific culture, based on the technological needs for progress; and finally, the development of a universal culture, premised on the striving for humanism, solidarity, and respect for people.[45]

The arguments *for* such a delinking strategy, formulated in terms of the demands of revolutionary economic and social strategy, were many. In the first place, such a strategy would break the influence or control which foreign interests had in the national economy. Foreign investment was associated with economic exploitation and broader political and social control: expropriation and the bringing of such enterprises under national control would end that vulnerability. More broadly it would allow for national autonomy in economic matters, reducing the dependence of the domestic market on the fluctuations of the international, and protecting domestic production, agricultural and industrial, from foreign competition. Secondly, state control of the economy would enable a rational planning of economic development, and the planned, socially purposive, distribution of the profits generated by that activity: here the idea of the reappropriation of the 'surplus', of the profit generated by such activity, was a central goal. Thirdly, it would enable the redistribution of wealth, the reallocation of resources from the elite to the mass of the population, be this for economic goals or for such social goals as education, health and housing. Fourthly, it would serve to break the social links between the society in question and the outside world, thereby reducing the distortions which such contacts occasioned: in the terms of an analysis which postulated a binding of the domestic ruling class to a broader international exploitative system, such a sundering of the transnational structures of oppression was essential. Finally, delinking would enable a reformulation of the *cultural* aspirations of society. Revolutionaries, like stoics, puritans and romantics before them, believed in a distinction between real and false needs, essential and luxury items, these latter serving to distort the development of society. Equally, culture, in the sense of art, was also seen as a domain of conflict and competition, one in which the power of the previous ruling group, and foreign exploiters, would, unless checked, reproduce itself. In each case, we may note, revolutionary language and aspiration contain echoes of other, conservative, retrospective and anti-cosmopolitan, themes: behind revolutionary vigilance there lay, too often, the small-minded intrusiveness of the village and the urban neighbourhood.

Through the post-revolutionary periods, the specific economic or other rationale for such delinking overlaps with other *political* goals, that of control of the population and its insulation from potentially counter-revolutionary pressures. The prime goal, to which all other policies are subordinated is that of the consolidation of the post-revolutionary state.[46] This may be most evident in the initial period, when the military and political pressures from outside are most intense. Such pressures are necessarily two-sided, for, while they challenge the very retention of power by the revolutionaries, they also serve to provide justification for consolidation of central control and extreme measures of security and mobilisation.

Phase II: The Impasses of Delinking

For revolutionaries and their opponents alike it may have appeared as if the project of state consolidation and insulation had succeeded. From Robespierre in the 1790s to Khomeini in the 1980s, revolutionaries extolled the ending of foreign dependence, the 'rooting out', extirpation, elimination of ties of dependency and corrupt counter-revolutionary influence. Equally, from the outside, revolutionary states may have appeared to be duly insulated, subject to state control, immune to external pressure. For social scientists too, the record of revolutionary consolidation could be presented as one of an outcome, a stabilisation, once internal and external threats had been contained, of the post-revolutionary regime.[47] At its most extreme, this belief in the strength and immobility of revolutionary regimes was expressed in the theory of totalitarianism, according to which the authoritarian character of the Soviet system gave it potentially decisive advantages over its capitalist rivals, in internal development and external capability alike.

However, such an insulation was, like all such projects, subject to two enduring tensions. The first was that, as with any policy of deliberate challenge to established patterns, it could be achieved *but at a price* – in terms of opportunities forgone and of the costs involved in maintaining it.[48] The second paradox was that while in the shorter run such separation from the external world may have succeeded, the very success of the revolutionary state and the need to sustain that success produced, in the longer run, pressures for opening up to the outside world that undermined this insulation: the emergence of a more educated society on the one hand, the need for access to advanced technology on the other. Thus if revolutionary states sought to defy the international, they did so at a cost, and, over a longer period, at their peril. The working out of these paradoxes, the very mechanisms involved, takes us to the heart of the means by which the international system, via states and other agencies, affects the domestic constitution of societies.

The first problem with the delinking strategy was conceptual and etymological, revolving as it does around the two spellings of the word associated with this project – *autarchy* and *autarky*. Often used interchangeably, these spellings point to different Greek roots – *archo*, to rule, or control, and *arkeo*, to suffice, or be self-sufficient.[49] The former would suggest a policy designed not to end contact with the outside world, but to subordinate all dealings with it to 'national', i.e. state and centralised, control. Thus trade, foreign investment, movements of investment capital and profits, technology transfer, and movements of labour would all be subject to state control, and only authorised if they met given planned targets. The second spelling suggests something much stronger, a self-sufficiency or reduction of contact with the outside world to as near the minimum as possible, the better to rely on national resources and eliminate the uncertainties and corruptions brought on by the international market. The measures designed to achieve the first goal might, in part, have coincided with those propitious to the second; but the goal, and degree of severance with the outside world, were very different. In the history of the communist states, and in those of other experiments in 'delinked' or 'auto-centred' development, the two goals were often confused. This may have reflected uncertainty of purpose in the state concerned. It may also have reflected the difficulties in limiting national economic policy to the goal of control, given that, once such a strategy was embarked on, the international market might, for both economic and political reasons, reduce its contacts with such states.

A second problem associated with such strategies was that of the limits placed on development by the domestic market. This was as true for the availability of raw materials and finished goods as for shortages of skilled personnel. It affected not only supply of all such goods and services, but also demand. This was obviously the case for small countries: a population of under several millions, with a low per capita income, faced special limits on the kind of resources and demand it could muster. Where small capitalist states could develop through trade and specialisation, no such option was open to their socialist counterparts. But even in larger states, including the largest of all, China and the USSR, domestic constraints operated, as a result of shortages of raw materials, because of endemic corruption and low morals, or because of the paralyses and inefficiency that developed when external competition was absent. The political costs of such a policy were also invariably high. Delinking was associated not just with a coercive breaking of links with the outside world, but also, necessarily, with the imposition of state control on society. It therefore denied not only democratic political norms, and freedom of movement of goods and people, but also the mobilisation of 'national' resources around a project that sought to validate such an authoritarian policy. It is not by accident, therefore, that delinking has, throughout its history, been associated with dictatorship, frenzied nationalism, and the cult not just of the nation and its supposedly legitimating past, but often also of the individual leader. Thus in the USSR the cult of Stalin reached its height during the first five year plans (1928–38). In China, both the Great Leap Forward (1958–61) and the Great Proletarian Cultural Revolution (1965–71) were associated with a demented cult of the party chairman, Mao Tse-tung, the 'Great Helmsman'. The experience of the regime in North Korea, in particular its campaign for *juche* or self-reliance, was, to a degree even greater than that seen in the USSR or China, associated with the cult of the leader, in this case Kim Il-sung.

These difficulties of such authoritarian development might, in theory, have been overcome in the event not of individual delinking, a break by one state with the system, but of a shared or collective break by a number of states who could compensate, on a planned and post-revolutionary basis, for the limits of their national economies by forms of cooperation. Such was the idea that lay behind the espousal after the Second World War by the Soviet Union of an inter-socialist trading group, the Council for Mutual Economic Cooperation, or Comecon, and which was reflected more broadly in the aspiration by Third World countries, as part of their campaign for a New International Economic Order, for Economic Cooperation between Developing Countries (ECDC). During its presidency of the Non-Aligned Movement (1979–83), Cuba made a particular point of calling for this ECDC, but to little avail.[50] Logical and practical as these projects appeared to be, they had limited success. On the one hand, cooperation between economies that were themselves planned and state-centred did not overcome the difficulties brought about by lack of competition. On the other hand, these states remained attracted to trading not with their own post-revolutionary or Third World partners, but with the capitalist market, in particular the developed industrialised West; the benefits in hard currency, and in the opportunity provided for the import of needed goods and services, often outweighed the attractions of post-revolutionary solidarity. Neither project constituted a successful collective autarchy, let alone autarky, to offset the costs of delinking.

The most fundamental endogenous problem of all, however, was not associated with the management of ties to the external world, but rather to the very administrative and, since it involved the state, political requirement of delinking itself, and that was authoritarian state domination of the economy. It is here that the issue of international constraint, and of the lack of revolutionary change in other states, can serve not so much as an explanation but as an alibi; even had there been no external pressure – something inconceivable given the aspirations of the revolutionary regimes themselves – or had the Bolshevik model indeed prevailed in the developed world as a whole, the model would still have failed in the goals it set itself. The model was flawed *internally and necessarily*.[51] To introduce and maintain any system of delinking, accompanied as it was with the administrative transformation of social and economic relations, involved a system of coercive intervention and control over society that was in the longer run unable to sustain itself.

Debate will range for many a decade over whether, even in ideal circumstances, the project of planned social development of the Bolshevik or analogous kind could ever have 'worked', in the sense not only of an initial redeployment and mobilisation of economic resources but of a longer-run development that could continue growing and compete successfully with capitalism. A broad but persuasive answer would appear to be *that it could not.* Despite initial successes in the fields of industrialisation and social equity and in the provision of social services, this project was inherently, not just conjuncturally, incapable of sustained development. The particular timing and form of the collapse of Soviet communism and its kindred regimes was contingent, a result of accidents of events, policies, and individuals. The collapse itself was necessary. Post-revolutionary self-reliance therefore contained a fundamental contradiction: projected as a means by which a state could break with, and successfully outstrip, its international rivals, it required a form of economic and political organisation that in the longer run prevented the state from successfully maintaining that competition.[52]

Phase III: The 'Middle Road'

If the more radical or absolute version of delinking could not work, there was, apparently, another option for states wishing to reconcile the pressures of the international system with the demands of post-revolutionary transformation. This was what came to be known as 'the middle road, 'the third way', or 'market socialism'. Some states adopted this in the face of the impasse of their previous planned and state-centred period or because of other irresistible pressures:

Russia in the New Economic Policy of the 1920s and again in the doomed experiment with *perestroika* in the late 1980s, China after 1978, Cuba in the early 1980s, Nicaragua throughout the Sandinista period. The appeal of this was both internal, that it placed less onus on economy and population, and external, that it lessened the pressure from the outside world.

Attractive as it was, however, this 'third way' was an unstable option, a half-way house that, again for internal and external reasons, could not have worked.[53] It contained its own difficulties, ones through which external pressure and internal instability continued to operate. In the first place, any strategy short of large-scale nationalisation of economy – one which allowed an industrial, agrarian and services private sector of significance to survive – enabled part of the economy to remain outside state control: investment would not be made, goods and services would be diverted to private purposes, contacts with the outside world could be maintained. Some of these economies were often referred to as 'mixed'. But the term 'mixed economy' concealed a confusion between two very different kinds: one, such as Sweden in the 1970s, where a strong state sector coexisted with an active private one, and in which the latter predominated; the other, such as Yugoslavia in the same period, where, despite the existence of a private sector it was the state which continued to dominate. Put in other words, there was in the end no sustainable 'third' way, only variations on the two main ways.

Such attempts to promote a middle path also occasioned problems within the revolutionary state itself. Those who worked in the state sector would inevitably have less access to foreign currency and goods, and to travel, and would receive lower wages, than those in the private sector. This would promote resentment. The political crises in Grenada in 1983, which led to a US invasion, and in South Yemen in 1986, which so debilitated the regime that it surrendered to its northern neighbour in 1990, were both provoked in part by a conflict over the disparities, real or imagined, of the middle road.[54] In the Nicaragua of the 1980s the Sandinista regime was never able to overcome the contradictions generated by this middle road – capital strike on the part of the 'national bourgeoisie', constant opposition from the Catholic Church and other social forces tolerated in the name of pluralism, an overvalued currency forced on it to subsidise imports needed by the population.[55] In the Cuba and Vietnam of the 1990s the split between those who had access to dollars or to earnings from tourism, and between the populations as a whole and the tourists with their foreign exchange, sharply accentuated income differentials and social tensions. Most striking of all, of course, was the fate of such economic reform in the USSR and China. In the former, the incoherent and piecemeal dismantling of state economic and political controls after 1985 led, in the space of six years, to the collapse of the communist system and the Soviet state itself.[56] In the Chinese case, the political system remained, for a time, intact; but this was at the price of presiding over a society and economy that retained less and less of its state character and became a managed variant of capitalism, presided over by a one-party state. The middle road, was as unsustainable, for internal reasons alone, as that of authoritarian state socialism.

Exogenous Constraints

These, in summary form, were the endogenous problems with the project of delinking. They were, however, compounded by other, exogenous, factors that made any successful programme of auto-centred development even more difficult. Most obvious was the problem created for the most acute competition of all, that in military terms. For if a revolutionary state was to survive, let alone compete successfully with its rivals on the international plane, it had to be able to match the technological advances of its enemies. This could in part be done through the means associated with delinking: endogenous technological development, or, where this failed, acquisition through purchase, imitation or subterfuge, of the technology of the other side. This was, for example what the USSR did during its long arms race with the USA: it never led in the arms race, except for a period of space exploration in the late 1950s, but sought constantly to keep up with its Western rivals by imitating their development. However, the problem was that this always placed the revolutionary state at a disadvantage, as despite much alarm in the West and reinforcing bombast in the East, the USSR remained behind its rivals. When it came to the more advanced technological developments, mere imitation or other acquisition was not possible. This was what happened in the early 1980s, with the impact of the third industrial revolution on military production. Microelectronics, precision engineering to a thousandth of a millimetre and lasers were not only in advance of what the

USSR was producing but were not replicable within their system on an extensive basis.

The exogenous also affected the very ability of the revolutionary state to continue with its development strategy. For despite the mobilisation and enthusiasm associated with the initial post-revolutionary phase, and the relative success of the revolutionary state in insulating its society from external contact, the external, as an alternative pole of attraction, continued to exert its hold. One obvious dimension where this was so was in the realm of consumer goods. Post-revolutionary transformation increased the availability of social services, but not of consumer goods. In the cast of the post-1945 world the very success of capitalism in providing these, and of generating an accompanying culture of consumerism and popular culture, exerted a growing attraction over the populations of the post-revolutionary states. This was all the more so because the very project, and associated ethos, of the communist states involved the promotion of sacrifices in the present for greater reward in the future. But in the life of a society, as of an individual, such an appeal may have effect for some time, but cannot be sustained indefinitely.

Throughout the history of the revolutionary states, the fear of *political* subversion from abroad was paralleled by that of *cultural* threat: of a demoralisation of the revolutionary mass, an undermining of the spirit of self-sacrifice, a corruption by non-revolutionary cultures, old and new. In the Stalinist period in Russia, and long after, 'imperialist' culture in many of its forms remained suspect. The Chinese in the 1980s complained of the 'sugar-coated bullets' of consumerism, embodied in pop music and fashion clothes. The Iranian revolution, in the mid-1990s, became obsessed with *bombardiman-i tablighati*, 'propaganda bombardment', and *tahajum-i farhangi*, 'cultural aggression'. Equally, the pressures of the external acted to promote a desire in the population of the post-revolutionary states for people to travel either on a temporary basis, as tourists or other forms of visitor, or as permanent emigrants. Post-revolutionary states, of course, allowed no such option. For those who did get out, legally or as refugees, there was no going back; for the great majority, there was no freedom to travel, or migrate. In larger countries, this may for a long time have been of limited import. But as education and living standards increased, and as the consumer attractions of the capitalist world also became more visible, so the pressure to migrate was felt. This was above all the case in a country such as Cuba, where by the 1980s an estimated two million out of thirteen million people had migrated to the USA, and many more were believed to want to. It was equally felt in the German Democratic Republic in the 1980s. It was indeed that pressure, massive but dammed in at first, then diverted through leaks in the Hungarian and Czech frontiers, and finally unleashed on 9 November 1989, that was to signal the end of the post-revolutionary communist experiment in Europe. This collapse, the effective end of the Bolshevik revolutionary experiment that began in 1917, was the outcome of decades of conflict between the communist and Western worlds, the Cold War. It provides an especial vantage point from which to identify the external constraints on revolutionary systems.[57]

The Revenge of Capital

The collapse of Soviet communism in the late 1980s provides a graphic illustration of the ways in which external pressures, of diverse kinds, served to undermine a revolutionary state and, in the end, lead to the reversal of the revolution itself. What began as a project of global ambition, to break with and overtake the capitalist world, ended seven decades later in defeat, as the leading state lost confidence in its aspirations and the mass of the population of the communist states rejected their rulers and sought incorporation with the West. Far from having *caught up with and overtaken* the West, as Khrushchev had predicted in 1961, they had *fallen behind*: hence the pertinence of the phrase, a corrective to Khrushchev, used by Jürgen Habermas – 'the catching up revolution'.[58]

This conflict was one between two heterogeneous blocs, not just military alliances, but rival, distinctly organised, political, economic and social systems: this is why I have elsewhere described it as 'inter-systemic conflict'.[59] Communism set itself the task of breaking with, and rivalling, the capitalist world. Its failure to do so was an international one – in that it competed with capitalism on a world scale, and in that the factors leading to this collapse were in considerable measure international in character. It was precisely through *external* competition that, in the case of communist bloc, the contradictions of the *internal* dimensions of revolution were most unexpectedly and dramatically felt. The law of combined and uneven development which Marxism had deployed to explain the possibility of revolution without its maturing first in the most advanced capitalist countries, here exacted its revenge. It was communism, not capitalism, that was trapped by the combination, and defeated by its own, comparatively deficient, i.e. uneven, performance. Without combination, unevenness would not have mattered so much. In the very domain that had been set as that in which communism would overtake capitalism, that of living standards and political emancipation, it was the capitalist world that in the end prevailed. The end of the Cold War, of the rivalry of capitalism and communism, did not come about in the conventional means by which international conflict is resolved – defeat in war, or the foreign-inspired overthrow of a regime, or in concessions of territory. It came about through the gradual erosion of the insulation of communist societies, of the failure of the post-revolutionary auto-centred project, *and* of a loss of faith by the leaders of these states in their ability to continue with this project.[60] It came about as much as anything through defeat in a battle between two rival systems, each of them representing a distinct set of beliefs, an ideology, about how their political and economic systems, and those of the world as a whole, should be organised. Trotsky's intuition, about the long-run impact of superior Western technology on the Soviet experiment, had been vindicated.

This process of external pressure was matched by evolution within. Far from proceeding towards a triumphant post-capitalist modernity, as revolutionaries believed, or being locked into a stable but effective authoritarian mould, as theorists of totalitarianism supposed, the post-revolutionary societies of the communist world were changing. There are domains in which, in an inversion of the Marxist theory of capitalism creating the conditions for its own supercession, revolutionary regimes produced the conditions for their own demise. Socially, the post-revolutionary projects contained within them the seeds of their own destruction, in that by fostering educational change they produced a new social force, one educated, more pragmatic and materially minded, which had an international perspective markedly at variance with that of the classic revolutionary project.[61] It sought accommodation, where the others had sought confrontation. It was inquiring, where the other had been dogmatic. Ultimately it sought, as Habermas wrote, to 'catch up' with, rather than in a competitive manner, overtake the capitalist world. It was for this reason that many of those who came to realise the failure of the communist experiment were not those who were most excluded: rather it was members of the communist elites, whose greater access to information and travel gave them a critical perspective on the claims of their leaderships.

In sum, while revolutions are caused internationally, and have international aspirations, their very development is shaped, and constrained by these very same factors. International policy, be it the foreign policy of states or transnationalist revolutionary aspiration, is shaped by the international correlation of forces. Over a longer period, the internal development of states is equally subject to external determination. Nothing, therefore, confirms the impact of the international system on revolutions more than the fate of those states that seek to break from the international. The law of combined and uneven development, like that of internationalist solidarity based on class, may tell us more about the workings of capitalism than about those of its supposedly inevitable historical successor.

Part III
Conclusions:
Theoretical and Historical

11

Challenges to Theory

International Relations: Competing Theories

The analysis of revolutions in their international context, both ideological and historical, provides an occasion to assess not only international history itself, but also the ways in which this topic can have implications for theorising international relations. The weight of this historical evidence might suggest that any theory of international relations would have to take the impact of revolutions into account. Yet this has not been so: indeed in much of the international relations literature, be it realist or other, revolutions have a marginal presence. For writers within the transnationalist, or pluralist schools, the reasons are several, and will be examined below. For realists, the reason is clear: it reflects the central orientation of their approach which is the denial of the importance of domestic factors in determining foreign policy. From what appears initially as a commonsense point of view, realism denies that revolutions make much difference to the conduct of foreign policy. It asserts that states continue to pursue national interest and the maximisation of power, whatever their ideological guise. In more theoretical vein, epitomised in the work of Kenneth Waltz, the study of international relations is to be conducted at the 'systemic', i.e. wholly inter-state, level and is to exclude internal processes and factors. Hence in an article written at the height of the Third World upheavals of the late 1960s Waltz was to say: 'The revolutionary guerrilla wins civil wars, not international ones, and no civil war can change the balance of world power unless it takes place in America or Russia.'[1]

Within the literature on revolutions and international relations, there are nonetheless several established approaches to the question of how upheavals affect relations between states. Yet if each of these recognises the importance of revolutions and provides an explanation of their impact, each also raises difficulties which may point to underlying assumptions present in the theory and concepts these explanations deploy. On the one hand, behind every conception of the international impact of revolutions there lies not merely a conception of the international, but also of what constitutes a revolution. On the other hand, each contains within it assumptions about the relation between international and domestic politics, and, not least, an understanding of how the latter is influenced by the former. To disentangle the issue of the international impact of revolutions involves addressing these two, usually obscured, questions. Five main schools of thought can be identified.

(i) 'Dissatisfaction': Henry Kissinger

A pervasive view of revolutionary states is that they are in one way or another 'dissatisfied' with the existing international system. This refusal to accept the existing distribution of power may include such traditional issues of inter-state dispute as territory, strategic balance, and spheres of influence, but is potentially broader in the case of revolutionary states as a result of the 'dissatisfaction' that underlies the revolution itself. This expresses itself in a challenge not only to the legitimacy of the established international balance, but also in the denial of the legitimacy of established regimes, and indeed of the principles on which they rest, be this monarchy or parliamentary democracy. Both 'vertical' and 'horizontal' security are thereby challenged.

A striking example of this approach is contained in the writings of Henry Kissinger.[2] For Kissinger, revolutionary states pose a challenge to the international balance of power: because of the dissatisfaction that underlies the revolution itself, they are states that tend not to accept or recognise limits in the conduct of foreign affairs. From the psychological roots of revolution, Kissinger derives a psychology of international relations, leading to the conclusion that the revolutionary state can only be contained by the establishment and maintenance of a new international equilibrium, based on power. This policy, what Kissinger calls 'a subtle diplomacy of containment and entrapment', can first impose limits on the revolutionary state and thereby induce it to accept the constraints that it is initially prone to deny. In this way, the revolutionary state ceases to be 'dissatisfied' and, hence, to threaten international order.

Kissinger's theoretical maxims on the diplomatic enticement of revolutionary states were to provide guidelines for his own practice, as an official of Republican administrations (1969–76), vis-à-vis both the USSR and China.[3] In addition, Kissinger's analysis contains a number of interesting analytic dimensions. He does have a conception of the relationship between foreign policy and domestic order, expressed in his argument on the threat which revolutionary states pose to both forms of legitimacy. Kissinger, more than most writers on the topic, and following his inspiration the Austrian chancellor Metternich, saw the relation between international peace and domestic stability: to maintain the former, Metternich argued, it was necessary to prevent radical changes within countries – hence his euphemistic title, 'the doctor of revolutions'.

Yet at the centre of his argument there are also several questionable assumptions. In the first place, the underlying premise of what revolutions are is selective. Although never clearly spelt out, it would seem that Kissinger sees revolutions as the product of needlessly dissatisfied individuals and groups, i.e. of forces that should accept the existing system, even if they wish to change it, and whose response is in some sense unnecessary and irrational. Beyond the ethical position contained in this, Kissinger denies any causation of revolutions by the social and economic structures of society. By extension, it suggests a form of transnational impact that is based on irrationality, on the transfer of dissatisfaction from one society to another. From the restricted understanding of the internal causes of revolution the argument therefore proceeds to an equally distorting picture of why revolutions have international effects.

The distortions of this psychologistic approach are also evident in his own experience in the field. Kissinger is wrong to argue that revolutions are necessarily states that cannot accept their limits. While Napoleonic France, the subject of his original study, was indeed such a case, as was the Iran of Ayatollah Khomeini, it was not true of the French Emperor's predecessor, Robespierre. Nor was it true of most twentieth-century revolutionaries, notably Lenin, Stalin, Mao and Castro, all of whom were, whatever their rhetorical flourishes, in practice cautious about international adventures and wary of prejudicing the interests of the revolutionary state. Stalin's caution contrasts with the undoubted recklessness of the man he opposed: Hitler. He indeed told Anthony Eden, the

British foreign secretary, that Hitler's weakness was he did not know when to stop.[4] This prudence was, of course, most evident in the case of the opponents Kissinger faced in his greatest challenge, namely the communists of Vietnam. They neither overreached themselves in their war with the USA, nor became entrapped in the web that Kissinger sought to weave around them. The result was that in 1975, two years after Nixon's administration had been forced to remove its troops from Vietnam, General Giap's tanks crashed through the gates of the presidential palace in Saigon. The Vietnamese communists, denied for three decades the unified state they had briefly seized in 1945, had now triumphed in a signal combination of military and diplomatic achievement. If nothing else, they had shown that they understood when to act.

Perhaps most contentious in Kissinger's analysis is the model of change he proposes. Since revolutions and their impact are viewed as psychological, indeed irrational processes, the impact of revolution internationally is both recognised and confined to this psychologistic level, the acceptance or otherwise of legitimacy. But legitimacy, while part of the domestic constitution of regimes and states, is only one element in a broader pattern of power, ideological and coercive, by which states maintain their control. Moreover, an assessment of the impact of revolutions that is confined to this dimension is inadequate: hence the mistaken title of his book *A World Restored*. The world of the eighteenth century was not and could not have been restored: a fundamentally different world had come into existence as a result of the French revolution.[5] Beyond its ethical position, from which followed his own attempts to 'cure' countries of revolution, Kissinger's is therefore a limited account *both* of why revolutions occur *and* of the means by which revolutions influence events in other countries. His account of the international dimensions of revolution is flawed because of the limits of his conceptions of revolution and of the process of change in international relations, as well as his silence on state–society relations.

(ii) The Challenge to 'International Society': David Armstrong

Kissinger's analysis reflects the perspective of international relations 'realism' as it evolved in the USA in the post-war period, with its preoccupation with order, strategic equilibrium and the containment of hostile powers. An alternative 'realist' perspective can be found in the British school, through its use of the concept 'international society' and the exploration of how revolutions affect this community of states, based on shared 'interests, rules and institutions'.[6] While accepting that in some degree revolutions do challenge the norms of international society, and may even introduce changes in them (e.g. the ending of colonialism), the central conclusion of this approach is that revolutions are in the end tamed, or 'socialised', by the environment in which they operate. David Armstrong's work is the most systematic attempt from within this tradition to meet the challenge posed by revolution. It examines the impact of revolutions on three 'foundations of international order' – international law, diplomacy, and the balance of power. His conclusion is that revolutionary states are compelled to accept the workings of 'international society', by the need to gain benefits from the system, but above all because, once they come to power, revolutionaries find themselves in charge of a state: 'a common sequence, although one that has manifested itself in different ways, is for an initial hostility towards these institutions of international society to give way to a grudging acceptance of their value, albeit sometimes coupled with a desire to reform them'.[7]

The attractions of this approach are several: on the one hand, it recognises that revolutions do promote significant changes in the international system; on the other, it reflects the widespread perception that, in the end, revolutionary states have to 'conform'.[8] There are, however, several points at which it may be questioned. In the first place, the very concept of 'international society' may conceal as much as it reveals, for the concept 'society' that it assumes, namely one of shared norms as between roughly equal units, may be contrasted with an alternative conception of 'society' as a system of structured inequality, in which the appearance of shared norms conceals the imposition by the dominant group on the other members. The character of any challenge to the system changes substantially as between one conception of society and another. Of even greater difficulty is the issue of what the norms of this society pertain to – whether they are wholly about relations between states, as the original conception of 'international society' implied, or whether they also encompass the inner workings of states. If this latter possibility is admitted, as Armstrong in part does, then we are examining not just how states promote change, or respond to challenges from other states, but also at the ways in which societies interact, in a context that encompasses states, but is much broader than that. This is, in terms of the evolution of the concept, a significant break with established notions of 'international society', and suggests a rather different view of how international relations should be conceived.

This theoretical questioning of the 'international society' approach may find support in the historical record itself. For if what is examined is not the state's explicit foreign policy, its relation to the 'institutions' of international society, but its long-run relation to other states and societies, and the response of other states to it, then a much more varied picture emerges. Despite agreements and reductions in tension, and to a considerable extent despite the intentions of their leaders, revolutionary states continue to be in conflict with status quo powers. France did not settle down after the Treaty of Amiens that brought a negotiated peace with Britain in 1802, nor did Russia after it signed commercial agreements with Britain in 1921. Indeed the paradox of the Russian revolution is that it posed its greatest threat to the West not when its most explicitly militant leader, Lenin, was in power, i.e. up to 1924, but when his apparently more cautious successors, Stalin, Khrushchev and Brezhnev, occupied the Kremlin. Some of the 'socialisation' to which Armstrong refers certainly occurred, but this was only part of the picture. On the other hand, the revolutionary state itself continued to feel the pressure of the hostile environment without. In the end no amount of diplomatic reconciliation and strategic agreement could dissolve the underlying conflict derived from the heterogeneity of the two social systems involved in the communist–capitalist conflict. The underlying conflict of social and political systems was resolved not by socialisation at the *international* level, but by the re-socialisation of the communist world into the *domestic* norms of the capitalist, and, it may be added, into an international society marked by an extensive and inescapable hierarchy of power. Capitalist modernity did not just socialise the external norms of the revolutionary state: it crushed that state altogether. The focus on socialisation ignores the underlying dynamics of conflict, and the more long-run incompatibility that arises as much from conflicting norms of *domestic* society as from disputes over international law and diplomacy.[9]

(iii) *Heterogeneity and Misperception: Kim Kyung-won*

An alternative to the emphasis upon the challenge of revolutions to international order is provided in theory which stresses the ways in which revolutions produce misunderstanding and 'misperception' between states and hence lead to a greater likelihood of the outbreak of war. In a perceptive study of the French revolution, Kim Kyung-won argues that conflict between states was less likely when they shared common values, because states more accurately anticipate the reactions of others, and because the room for suspicion and hostility is less.[10] He is particularly interested in the way in which differences in ideology, conceived of as a set of norms about political life, will increase the chances of war. 'What a difference in ideology does is to put an additional strain on a given international system by sharply increasing the chances of international misunderstanding.'[11] Kim takes as a classic example the Pillnitz declaration of 27 August 1791, when the Austrian and Prussian monarchs, in alliance with French exiles, threatened to intervene to free Louis XVI from imprisonment if other powers agreed to collaborate with them. Instead of reducing revolutionary aspirations, this declaration provoked a strong reaction inside France and contributed to the mass mobilisations that led to war in 1792.[12] For Kim there is nothing inevitable or systemic in the foreign policy of revolutionary states, or in the conflicts in which such states subsequently find themselves with status quo powers. Rather, misunderstanding and misperception on both side fuel a process that leads to conflict. The alternative is for conservative powers to avoid provoking revolutionary states and to accept them as part of the international system.

Kim's account of how revolutions come to conflict with other states in the international system goes against theories which stress the inevitability of such confrontations, be they theories of balance of power realism or revolutionary internationalism. It also draws attention to something that is common to both camps in revolutionary situations, namely rhetorical exaggeration of both intention and capability, partly for reasons of political infatuation, partly because statements about external policy are directed more to domestic audiences and reflect internal competition. For these very reasons, it is not surprising to see such analyses recur in discussion of other twentieth-century revolutions: the argument that confrontation could be avoided, that it results from mistakes of perception and the distortions of domestic policy, was to be heard with regard to Russia, China, Cuba, and Nicaragua. One striking application of this approach was Iran. Here the expert on Iran, James Bill, was to write of the 'complex array of mutually reinforcing factors and forces that composed a system built on misperceptions, misunderstandings, and misplaced self-interest' within the US state that led to the failure to predict the revolution and the subsequent clash with the Islamic revolution. His prescriptions for an alternative policy involved greater independence of foreign policy from domestic pressures, the correction of ideological misconceptions, and greater long-run analysis of the society in question. His conclusion, like that of other critics of status quo powers' confrontation with revolution, is that it *was* possible for such states to accept revolutions.[13]

There are, however, several difficulties with this account. In the first place, while the 'perception' school discusses the impact of international politics on the revolutionary state and so recognises the importance of domestic political factors, this is not replicated on the side of the conservative powers. Here the analysis remains based on policies of state, without comparable analysis of how revolutions in another country may affect the domestic political and social situation within states, or in junior allies of such states, and so precipitate a response. Secondly, in common with many such broadly 'liberal' analyses of revolutions it understates the commitment of revolutionary states themselves to confrontation, and the functions of such confrontation, beyond the mere competition of factions at a particular time. As discussed in Chapters 3 and 4, revolutionary states have strong reasons for their own confrontational rhetoric. Thirdly, the 'perception' approach is, in common with too many studies based on political science, ahistorical, in the sense of ignoring the degree to which the past influences present behaviour. In the case of revolutions with a nationalist, 'anti-imperialist' component, the rhetoric of the revolution reflects a long history of resentment at external domination, real and imagined, which no foreign policy adjustments by the state which is the object of that hostility, can remove. Finally, the emphasis on misperception carries with it the implication that such policies are not only avoidable, but are irrational, i.e. do not correspond to a clearly defined need. But in many cases there are identifiable clashes of interest, based not only on pre-revolutionary conceptions of state interest, but also on the particular interests of the revolutionary state in the changed international environment which it has helped to bring about.

The implications and difficulties associated with this approach are evident from the fate of diplomatic contacts between revolutionary and status quo powers both in the time of the French revolution and in the twentieth century: truces, agreements, understandings seemed to break down again and again in the face of resurgent conflict. In the case of the latter part of the twentieth century, there were many who said that the 'West', or the USA in particular, could 'live with' the revolutionary regimes it confronted, in China, Cuba, Iran, Nicaragua and elsewhere. To some extent this was valid: in the end the USA did 'live with' these regimes in the sense that it did not resort to all-out war against them. But this corresponded with long periods of lower-level military and ideological confrontation, born of the incompatibility of interest between the two sides. The belief that such confrontation was unnecessary ignored the realities on both sides, as it underestimated the impact which revolutions had on the international system.

(iv) The Pertinence of Politics: Stephen Walt

Stephen Walt's work *Revolution and War*[14] is, like Kim's, a systematic, in this case comparative, attempt to grasp why revolutions have international effects. As he writes in his conclusion: 'Given the barriers to a revolution spreading beyond a single state's borders, the real mystery is why anybody believes that it will.' He is most ambitious and contentious in regard to the theoretical implications of his work. Walt's is a work of astute historical perceptiveness, cutting through many of the illusions which surround the subject; the questions it leaves open are fruitful products of his analysis. For if Walt is right to show how realism cannot comprehend revolutions, his own resolution is, nonetheless, open to question. Revolutions, Walt argues, matter for theory because the rational assumptions of power politics cannot adequately explain why revolutionary states, and the counter-revolutionary ones opposed to them, act as they do. Balance-of-power analysis therefore needs to be replaced by what Walt terms a balance-of-threat approach, one that accords importance both to the domestic politics of states and to the role of beliefs, ideology, and perception in the conduct of foreign policy. This he terms an 'international-political' perspective, one that simultaneously subsumes power politics and the subjectivity of states in the analysis.

The difficulty here is in part due to circular reasoning: thus the critique of realist theories of socialisation leads him to ascribe the great resistance of the Soviet, Chinese and Iranian revolutions to their having extreme ideologies and orthodox parties. However the invocation of 'extremism' runs a risk of tautology: the Iranian revolution has been characterised by its *not* having any ruling party, while post-revolutionary Mexico and Turkey, two of the ones he sees as moderate and socialised, did. The correlation 'war/extreme revolution', 'no war/less extreme revolution', also sits uneasily with cases Walt does not discuss: Cuba, led by a radical revolutionary elite, did not become embroiled in all-out war; Ethiopia, run by nationalist military officers, did.

More difficult, however, is the 'international-political' framework he proposes. The problem here is that he continues to operate with a limited concept of the international, the state and the system. Revolutions are treated by Walt as 'unit-level' events that then have international results. But revolutions are never unit-level – international, social, economic, ideological and political factors are inscribed in their very causation. Equally, the commitment of revolutionary elites to spreading their message is not a result of misperception, but is part of the very analysis of the international system necessarily present in their ideas. It is not a matter of imperfect information: Lenin knew as much as anyone about Germany, Fidel Castro and the Iranian foreign policy elite of the 1980s were well informed about the USA.

As Walt rightly argues, the international impact of revolutions requires an analysis that combines the role of states with the role of ideologies. The argument advanced here is that it nonetheless requires something further than either of these, a socio-economic concept of the system itself. Symptomatically, and in common with others who are currently uneasy with realism, Walt advocates awareness of the subjective, while distancing himself from 'critical theory'. But critical theory, of course, in its proper sense is not just a discursive adjunct to realism, but involves a view of society, international relations included, as a product of social and economic forces. So understood, and rooted to a re-theorised conception of the international system, it may indeed enable us to understand how revolutions operate. Equally it would focus on something that occupies less space in Walt's account, namely counter-revolution.

This issue is nowhere more evident than in Walt's account of the collapse of Soviet communism. Walt acknowledges the need to provide analysis of this process, but limits it to a discussion of why it did not lead to war. The point, however, is that it demonstrated the ways in which socio-economic factors underpin the more orthodox 'international-political' dimension. The collapse of communism was not so much a result of US *state* policy, but of the pressure of a rival system, in this case Western *capitalism* – a more successful modernity – upon the Soviet bloc. The challenge which revolutions pose to our understanding of the international may therefore be greater than Walt, or cognate realist dissidents, have yet allowed.

(v) The Balance of Power Disturbed: Richard Rosecrance

The work of Richard Rosecrance provides an alternative to that of both the realists and authors such as Kim and Walt.[15] In contrast to the realists, Rosecrance recognises the importance of domestic change within the conduct of foreign policy and develops a theory that links it to international relations. In contrast to Kim, he nonetheless argues that the conflicts produced by revolutions are the product of deep structural changes for which diplomacy alone may provide little remedy. In the eighteenth century prior to the French revolution, Rosecrance argues, a balance of power operated and conflict between states was restricted. States had limited ambitions, and there was a broad sharing of political values between their rulers. The French revolution destroyed this system. The goals of the revolutionary regime, and consequently of its opponents, became much more ambitious, encompassing the restructuring of Europe and the shaping of political systems in other states. The ability of regimes to control their domestic populations declined with the rise of mass movements and nationalism, and the need for states to compensate for domestic insecurity by adopting more belligerent attitudes abroad. The limits on resources, including the numbers available for military mobilisation, no longer constrained states in what they might attempt abroad. And the international system itself no longer had the capacity to contain disruption and to limit the demands of participant states. Of these, in Rosecrance's view, the most important is the inability of the system to contain the demands of a revolutionary actor.

The difficulties with Rosecrance's account begin from his understanding of what constitutes a revolution. This shapes his view both of why and how revolutions occur within specific countries, and how they affect other societies. In the country of origin, revolution is seen as a breakdown of control, as the emergence of a threatening and unstable 'mass society'; it promotes aggression abroad and, through the *levée en masse*, occasions greater mobilisation within. Yet revolutions reflect more than breakdowns of control – they may well reflect long-run structural changes that, among other things, produce new forms of control at least as efficacious as those they replace. Moreover, as a historical generalisation, it is simply not the case that mass societies are more belligerent than more controlled ones; Hitler's Germany, or Saddam's Iraq, which were controlled, contrast with the record of the United States of America, which was not. In regard to international reaction, Rosecrance focuses only on state-to-state relations and does not discuss how revolutions affect other societies, irrespective of what states do. For Rosecrance, the disruption of the international system is the result of the more assertive and ambitious foreign policy of the revolutionary state: the contribution of revolutions to sharpening social and political tensions within other states, and the role of ideas and example, are not encompassed within his theory.[16] Having recognised the importance of bringing in domestic factors at the level of the revolutionary states, these fail to find a place in the analysis of the international, and systemic, reaction. Thus we are left with an account of revolutions as disruptive, and as introducing into the conduct of international politics such factors as ideology that were hitherto absent, but an account which fails to address the structural causes, and consequences, of such upheavals.

(vi) Transnationalism and Violence: James Rosenau

In contrast to the realist approaches, with their emphasis on the role of states, the behaviouralists, notably James Rosenau, have focussed attention on the ways in which societies affect each other – transnationalism – and in particular on the ways in which conflict within one state, taking the form of violence, has affected others. They thus develop analyses for the international sphere that in the sociological work of writers such as Ted Gurr have been applied to the domestic. Within transnationalist approaches, the mechanism by which events in one country influence another is classified as a 'linkage', this allowing of at least three kinds – reactive, emulative and penetrative – as well as of 'fused linkages'. The latter are processes by which events in one country influence another; these latter then influencing the country in which the process originated.[17] This broad category of inter-societal process certainly allows for discussion of many of the ways in which events in one country influence another, whatever the capabilities or intentions of states. For behaviouralists, violence is the most important aspect of this transnational influence. For Rosenau, violence within one state has international effects for at least three reasons: it arouses the interest of others; by creating a situation of amorality it removes constraints on the intervention of others; and by its rapid and unpredictable development it invites responses.[18] The reaction of other societies, be it domestically or by means of intervention in the conflict situation, will be the greater if such conflicts are 'structural', i.e. fought over the basic organisation of society, and if they are of longer duration. Structural conflicts may alter the foreign policy of states and therefore pose particular challenges to other, status quo, powers.

If the great virtue of this work is that it goes beyond the focus on states, it is also limited by some of its theoretical presuppositions. Although arguing for the study of transnational processes, it none-the-less relies to a considerable degree, on the state when it comes to assessing why and how other actors may respond. While it allows for the study of social and ideological processes, it is without any general conception of the central category that would allow this, i.e. society itself, or of revolution as the product of social change that would enable a proper examination of the international conse-quences of revolutions. As with other approaches, such as Peter Calvert in *Revolution and International Politics*, it focuses on 'violence': this is equated not with the structures of dominance within a society, which may or may not resort to overt violence at any particular time, but with discrete 'events' involving violence. A military regime that no one resists openly is as violent as a rebel with a rifle.[19]

Behind the willingness to discuss revolutions, there remains a view of revolutions as aberrant moments, as interruptions, in an otherwise more normal system of international relations. If this transnationalist literature takes discussion beyond the mere discus-sion of states, it does not offer any general picture of what this 'non-state' world would be. We cannot comprehend the ways in which social structure not only generates revolutions, but also acts as the conduit of revolutionary and other influences between societies.

(vii) Antisystemic Movements: Immanuel Wallerstein

A very different approach can be found in the writings of the world-systems theorists, who argue in terms of the development of a broad, world-wide coalition of forces against the dominant system.[20] This approach is distinct, first, in the nature of the system that it identifies as constituting international relations, namely that of capitalism, and, equally, in seeing revolutions as an inevitable and desirable product of the contradictions generated by that system. Broadly influenced by Marxism, but critical of the political and theoretical stance of orthodox communism, the theory of 'anti-systemic' movements argues that we can observe a continued and cumulative development of antisystemic movements. These start with class-based movements, but subsequently encompass both movements of national self-determination and social movements based on status, gender, ethnicity and protest on specific issues. Surveying the changing patterns of domination across the world, and the resistance to them, these authors conclude:

> The central fact of the historical sociology of late-nineteenth- and early-twentieth-century Europe has been the emergence of power-ful social movements which implicitly or explicitly challenged the achievements of triumphant capitalism.[21]

The strengths of this approach are several. On the one hand, it places individual upheavals and movements in a broader compara-tive and international context, and takes the discussion well beyond dissection of the actions of individual states or leaders. On the other hand, it locates these revolts where they should be located, namely in the context of the structures of domination against which they are revolting, rather than as aberrant or inexplicable revolts dis-turbing some pre-existing order. Closely related to these analytic insights is the fact that, alone of the approaches discussed here, it is sympathetic to revolutions.

On the other hand, several difficulties arise with the world-system theory.[22] In the first place, there is an implicit assumption that all movements that are opposed to, and generated in resistance to, capitalism are necessarily part of a broader emancipatory process: while it assumes a global logic, the very existence of such a process is debatable. The attribution of these movements to the workings of capitalism conveys on them a unity, and commonality of direction, that may be spurious: the conditions of their origin, the programmes they articulated, the records in power suggest that there is no single antisystemic movement that can encompass all of these. Moreover, even if some Hegelian unity of historical processes was conceded, it can also be questioned whether some of these movements were in any independent normative or historical sense emancipatory, i.e. tending in the direction identified as desirable by world-systems theorists themselves. Some may be regressive, authoritarian movements that reject modernity *outright*. The period under particular discussion in the work of world-systems theorists, that since the mid-1960s, saw many other social movements whose programme was anything but emancipatory – right-wing populist mobilisations in the USA that heralded the advent of Reagan in 1981, mass racist movements in Western Europe in the 1980s and 1990s, fundamentalist mobilisations of Muslims, Jews and Hindus.

Underlying these particular judgements is the issue that lies at the centre of world-systems theory itself, namely its conception of the system: for in asserting that the whole world is part of the capitalist *system*, the latter defined by the market, it denies the fundamental difference that prevailed between the capitalist and communist world up to the collapse of the Soviet system in the late 1980s. Not only does it mean that within the terms of world-systems theory the collapse of communism was inexplicable – it was, in effect, trivial since these countries were, so the theory claimed, always part of the capitalist world anyway – but it also led to a misunderstanding of the character of the 'antisystemic', i.e. opposition, movements *within* the communist countries themselves. If the 'system' is seen as one, then opposition forces against communist states were part of the same world-wide movement as those opposed to capitalist states; if, however, the system was divided, i.e. there were *two* systems not one, then those opposed to the system on one side were, by dint of this opposition, supportive of the system in the other. The 'antisystemic' movements within the established 'antisystemic' were therefore 'prosystemic': this, indeed, was what the historical function of the opposition movements in the East turned out to be. In a systemically divided world, two negatives make a positive.

Nowhere were the difficulties of asserting a single, world, anti-systemic trend more clear than in the year which supposedly epitomised this global totality, 1968. The protesting student and youth movements of Western Europe and the USA were in a wholly different situation from those in Czechoslovakia whose attempts at emancipation were crushed in August 1968 by Soviet tanks. Distinct from each of these were the participants in the 'Cultural Revolution' in China, an event of horrendous cruelty, mendacity and disaster for the Chinese peoples, too easily indulged, even long after the event, by Western writers, Wallerstein included. Far from constituting part of any emancipatory process, world-wide or other, this phase of Chinese history, in which mass movements were manipulated and traduced by a fractionalised leadership, was one of deepening, arbitrary, repression.[23] This misrepresentation of the global significance of developments in the communist world illustrated the most significant underlying weakness of this approach, namely its continued assertion of a single, global, teleological process leading to some revolutionary future. Neither the critique of philosophy, nor – perhaps even more telling – the failures of the great antisystemic force, two centuries of revolutionary movements, were taken sufficiently into account. Rich in historical insight, world-systems theory when confronted with the future slid rather too easily into mechanistic utopian assertion. More insightful than others, and distinct in ethical stance, world-systems theory proved insufficiently attentive to differences of social context and political system, even as it over-generalised in the positing of a single world-wide emancipatory and antisystemic movement.

Theoretical Assumptions: International Relations, Revolution, Society

Having surveyed the variant approaches within international relations theory to revolutions, it may now be possible to draw together these threads into a more systematic explanation. The starting point of this study has been that revolutions, as historical events, challenge our view both of theory and of history, and that, within theory, this applies both to social science and to historical materialism. The argument that will be developed here, building on earlier suggestions,[24] seeks to see how, by critically combining concepts from international relations with arguments from historical materialism, it may be possible to lay out a more adequate theoretical approach to this issue. The reassessment of international relations involves three arguments: the linking of the analysis of the state with that of socio-economic context and of ideology or culture; the reconceptualisation of the state; the incorporation of social movements and classes. Reassessment of historical materialism involves recognition of the enduring power of states, and a rejection of determinist, or teleological perspectives: it permits the setting of the international relations discussion within a context of the spread of capitalist modernity on the one hand, and its contradictory, combined and uneven, character on the other.

Each of the international relations approaches contains within it not only an argument in explicit terms about how and why revolutions have international effects, but also implicit presuppositions about concepts central to any discussion of revolutions: what revolutions are, their causes, their legitimacy, and, equally, how political and social systems function and hence may be disrupted. No discussion of this issue in purely factual and historical terms, or within the theoretical framework of international relations is sufficient. The very concepts that lie at the core of the international relations literature – state, society, power – require rethinking. A broader examination of the concepts is needed to explain and advance comparative understanding of the international consequences of revolutions. None of these theories, world-systems theory excepted, sees revolutions in the context of a theory of society or of the internationalised mechanism for the maintenance of social order. Equally, none – world-systems theory apart – concedes legitimacy to revolutions. Yet if the other more orthodox theories are indeed flawed by their concepts of revolution and society, as much as by their particular understanding of the international, world-systems theory too has questionable assumptions. This is evident above all in its attempt to produce an account, both global and sympathetic, that allows distortions of those very concepts – international relations, revolution, society – that the others also misrepresent. The historical and specific insights suggested by each of these theories are therefore offset by a range of conceptual misrepresentations.

For all their aspirations to break with conventional inter-state relations, the majority of these explanations remain restricted to the international field, that of relations between states, the latter conceived in conventional terms. What they leave out, or, as with behaviouralism, downplay, are the ways in which revolutions affect the internal constitution of states and how these changes then have their impact on foreign policy. In so doing they miss the role of the transnational in stimulating revolution and in the consequences to it.

In the perspective that I suggest here, revolutions cease to be seen as events that occur within particular national or social contexts alone, but rather, through seeing these national and distinct social contexts as part of a broader transnational formation, they become part of the ongoing interaction of specific states with the international system. To return to the seismological analogy: within the perspective of an international sociology, revolutions occur in particular places, as do volcanoes or earthquakes, but we can only understand these specific explosions by looking at broader contexts and structures within which the revolutions, their causes and their contexts, are located. An earthquake or a volcano tells us to look at underlying structures and faults in the earth's surface as a whole, not just at the site of the explosion itself.

To locate revolutions in such an international context is, however, not to assert their universal character: rather, it emphasises their specificity in place *and* time. On the one hand, revolutions are relatively rare events. The question they pose is why they occurred in the particular place and at the particular time that they did, and, more broadly, why some periods of modern history are more influenced by them than others. To identify the particular periods of revolutionary upheaval – 1760–1815, 1848, 1910–21, 1945–80 – is to pose a question both about individual countries and about the international system as a whole. It is, first of all, to pose a question about what it is in the international system that creates situations – revolutionary conjunctures or general crises – more or less propitious to such upheavals. Such a question cannot be asked only at the level of individual countries – this will miss the ideological, or economic, or power political context in which such internationalised crises occurred. Nor can it be asked solely at the level of inter-state relations: this will not explain why states pursue the policies they do, nor why such policies have the outcomes they have. We have to look at the broader socio-economic and ideological structures of the world at the time when a revolution occurred, at the particular conflicts in modernity that generate revolutions as they do wars. Such an internationalised perspective may, on the other hand, help to explain why revolutions do not occur, why, given the vast range of potential causes, domestic and international, there is not more upheaval in societies than there is.

The transnational dimension is also central to shaping the reasons for the choices revolutionary states make, and the responses, of support and opposition, they occasion in others. It is these considerations – the linkage between international processes and domestic change, and the resulting consequences of domestic change for international relations – that form the context in which revolutions affect the international system.

The Three Dimensions of International Relations

All revolutionaries have sought to defy the reality and necessity for divisions between states. Yet, that states are an essential part of any study of international relations, and of the impact of revolutions on them, would seem to be an inescapable part of any study of revolutions. This is the paradox that all theorists and practitioners of revolution have grappled with. Robespierre, Lenin, Mao, Castro, and Khomeini all defied the system of states, yet sought, in seeking to protect their own revolution, to use it to advantage. Not only do revolutions occur in particular societies, and appropriate particular states, but they consolidate these states and defend their power against challenges internal and external. What the study of revolutions poses is not the displacement of the state, but rather its redefinition: states are to be seen not as undifferentiated legal-territorial entities, nor as units that operate in an abstracted international system, but as the coercive and administrative entities that political and social forces both challenge and appropriate. How they do so, how far they can change them, is a matter for individual analysis – the history of revolution and counter-revolution is one both of success and of failure. What is general is that revolutions are, in both challenge and recomposition, about states, and about stateness. They are equally about those values and communities that are associated contingently but recurrently with states, namely communities, societies and what we have come to term 'nations'. The fallacy of the concept 'nation-state' is not that it denotes something fictional, or recently invented: it is that it *assumes* something that needs to be established. The nation-state has come into existence under particular historical circumstances; the two terms, albeit overlapping, can never be taken as identical. The history of challenges to states, of which revolutions are one form, is precisely about the pressure on that relation: the concept 'nation-state' does not allow these histories to be written, or analysed.

There is therefore a place within any study of the international dimensions of revolutions of what is the conventional concern with states. Those who have proposed revolutions as the supersession of states, be it the anarchist speculation of Lenin in *State and Revolution*, or the recurrent transnationalist enthusiasms that mark every revolution, have been proven wrong. Not only have their policies failed, a failure to be easily explained by claims of 'sellout', 'treason', 'betrayal' and the like, but they do not provide a basis for understanding a central feature of the formation of the modern world, its *parcellised* or *fragmented* nature. Lenin himself was forced to recognise this when, at the Eighth Congress of the Bolshevik Party in March 1919, he declared: 'we are living not merely in a state, but *in a system of states*'.[25] It is in this context, one that presupposes a radically different view of the international system and its history, that revolutions need to be seen. They are not the inevitable end of modern society, nor the gateway to a new one. As with major inter-state war, revolutions express the conflicts and aspirations of political actors in a particular phase of that system's development. Yet the very link between revolutions and the international system shows the enduring character of this world-historical context *and* of the tensions within it. If it is not in revolutions that revolt and protest issue in the globalised context, it is in other forms.

A combination of statist and systemic analysis may go a long way to locating revolutions in the context of international relations, but it still leaves out of the picture the element that is central to the experience and impact of revolutions, namely that of ideas. Such a dimension is, of course, much harder to identify and pin down than the role of states or the vagaries of markets. Both forms of analysis – realism, on the one hand, structuralist or macro-social analysis on the other – present themselves as challenging the role of ideas, of human will, within historical process. In this, as we have seen, the exaggerations of revolutionaries encourage a certain countervailing depreciation. Yet not only are revolutions associated with ideas – the creation of a new world, the transcending of boundaries, the obligation to solidarity – but also they can only be explained by studying how people's attitudes to politics, their own and that of other states, is changed, often in a very rapid time-frame. Revolutions themselves involve two massive ideological shifts – a loss of legitimacy by the rulers, and a belief in an alternative by the dominated. Such a combination alone constitutes an event of enormous proportions. Such events are followed by other ideological shifts: the formulation and imagining of another social order, down to rituals and symbols of dress or language; the articulation of an internationalist vision, within which one's own revolution is but the precursor to a broader global change.

Such an approach, focussing as it does on the cultural and the ideological, has, conventionally, been opposed to that of state-centred or macro-historical analysis. The import of much 'constructivist' writing in international relations seeks to displace analysis from that of institutional or material forces, to that of perceptions, ideas, and belief systems. Yet, as already discussed, it is mistaken to posit *as necessary alternatives* the approach of the ideological and that of the structural. There is, moreover, a need to distinguish between an approach that stresses the importance of ideas and culture, and one that bases its account of change on the role of human will: the former does not entail the latter. Ideas, culture, and language may be part not of the domain of human volition and of meaningful collective action, but rather of that which contextualises and constrains: individuals are born into a world of realities they cannot change, and these include the culture, religion, language, the texture of social meaning that envelops them. These are constraints as important as social or economic structure. When they change, they can, equally, be part of that convulsion of the system that takes individuals and social groups along with it.

Elements of this emphasis on culture, one markedly distinct from constructivism and other forms of cultural reductionism, can be found in both the literature on international relations and that of revolutions. In the former, E. H. Carr famously distinguished, in his *The Twenty Years' Crisis* between three forms of power: political, economic, and power 'over opinion'.[26] It should be noted that, as his phrasing indicates, he did not ascribe to opinion, or ideology, an independent role, but rather sought to show how it constituted one of the ways in which political life was managed and controlled. Later studies of political ideas and their role in international relations have sought to develop analysis of ideas, against a climate generally unfavourable to this theme.[27] In regard to revolutions, the 1980s saw a widespread revision of conventional approaches to the French and other revolutions in which not only outcomes, but also causes and courses, of the revolutions was ascribed to the tensions within political culture. Most famously associated with the work of François Furet and Simon Schama, this approach examined language, symbols and ideology and argued for its centrality in the understanding of revolutionary upheavals.[28]

Examples of this ideological and cultural dimension abound. The impact of the French revolution on the Atlantic region, and over time on the rest of the world, was as much as anything a result of the appeal which its ideas, variously interpreted, had on other countries. In the words of the editors of a volume containing studies of America, Poland, Russia, Africa, the Middle East, Mexico and China:

> the Revolution's power as metaphor and analogue still inspires theorists and political actors throughout the world . . . The dramatic and unexpected events of the late 1980s make it plain that the powerful ideals born two centuries earlier continue to maintain their grip on the modern consciousness.[29]

The appeal of the Russian, and later of the Chinese and Cuban, revolutions was equally one of example, to countries that felt, in some broad sense, a common condition with that of Russia, for which identification with 1917 was a combination of shared political and socio-economic condition, and a common sense of subjugation. When it came to the Iranian revolution the same applied – sympathy for the revolution, the appeal of Khomeini's message, an identification with the particular Islamic revolutionary ideology of the new Iranian state all played their part. Culture and ideology played an equally important part in the collapse of the Soviet model: more than the military pressure of the West, or the erosion of the command economies by market forces, was the force of example and the appeals of Western consumerism and democracy to the populations of the East.[30]

In both the study of established regimes, therefore, and in that of challenges to such regimes, ideas and culture should play a central role. That such ideas and culture are related to power, and are constituted transnationally, has already been argued. This entails that when we look at the workings of any established state and social system we must, whilst looking at the state and at the socio-economic system, also look at the ideology that underpins it, and at the preconditions, internal and external, for that stability. Revolution challenges the stability of ideologies as much as that of states and societies: this explains why revolutions occasion an articulation of an alternative culture within, and without, the promotion of a radical model of society, combined with an alternative view of relations between states and peoples. It is because international relations is comprised of more than relations between states, or economies, that the demonstration effect of revolutions is so strong – for counter-revolutionaries and revolutionaries alike.

Social Movements: Classes as Transnational Actors

Such a tripartite view of international relations opens the way for the study of something central to the analysis of history and of international relations alike, namely social movements. Both orthodox international relations, and more schematic accounts of the emergence of capitalist modernity, tend to downplay these, in favour of structural explanation. Yet it is social movements – political parties, mass movements, uprisings of people, the anger of the dominated – that pose the challenge to states, in both internal and external dimensions: social movements defy the authority of states from within, they overrun or aspire to overrun the frontiers between states. The social movements that make revolutions are, as already seen, ones that are formed in an international context: they respond to change produced within their society by international factors, and at the same time they espouse ideologies that go beyond the frontiers of states.

It is for this reason that many who have written on revolutions and within approaches that are themselves flawed, nonetheless recognise that the forces that make revolutions must be seen in a broader, transnational, context. For Marxists, this means the positing of classes as both internationally constituted and internationally active; for behaviouralists the actions of any group within society are affected by, and in turn affect, the conduct of others, through demonstration effects and a range of transnational linkages. The aspiration of both these approaches is to produce a conception of international relations that displaces the primacy of states and seeks to locate individual revolutions, or political processes in general, within a broader context of transnational action. The illusion of separate states, with discrete politics and upheavals, is replaced by an underlying reality of transnational social forces, distributed differentially into separate segments called states, but ultimately comprehensible only within this wider context.

This challenge of the primacy of states is, of course, compounded by the rhetoric of revolutionaries and counter-revolutionaries themselves. Whether it be in the counter-revolutionary alarm of Edmund Burke, or the revolutionary optimism of a Lenin or a Trotsky, the movements that make revolutions break down the barriers between states, and they drive different societies forward towards a larger solidarity. The implication of such a perspective is that in revolutionary situations the barriers between states and societies are broken down. An otherwise parcellised system of power and domination, i.e. of states, is disrupted. Disruption certainly occurs: 1789 challenged 1648, 1848 challenged 1815, the twentieth-century revolutions repeatedly defied schemes for the maintenance of international order.

However, this focus on revolutions may obscure something of equal importance, and a factor that goes a long way to explaining the international impact of revolutions, which is the permanence of such transnational influence. The constitution and stability of societies is *never* a purely internal matter. In the calmest and apparently most pacific of times, the stability of societies presupposes, *inter alia*, a favourable international economic climate, and the reinforcement, by shared practice, of the political and social practices of the country in question. Homogeneity of internal order is a major precondition of any social order. The cohesion of societies involves the predominance of one set of values, what has been termed the 'dominant ideology'. But for an ideology to be dominant it must not just be instilled into a society by those with power within it, but also reinforced from outside by an appearance of naturalness.[31] Transnationalism of value and political system is not, therefore, an aberration of revolutionary times, but an enduring feature of all social systems. The more the politics and sociology of any particular country are analysed in terms of values and ideology, the more this factor of international reinforcement becomes central. At the same time, the more revolutions are seen in terms of values and political culture, the greater the international impact of any such upheaval. The emphasis on values, ideology and culture, far from serving to distract importance from the study of social and political power may, within this perspective, serve to reinforce it. This was the central argument of Antonio Gramsci's analysis of the functioning of capitalist society, and of the means by which it could be challenged. François Furet's work on the French revolution, counterposed to established Marxist interpretations, can, in such a Gramscian perspective, be related to it: ideologies, values, symbols, are not an alternative to the study of social movements and of state power, but an element in their constitution.

It is also possible to look at the transnational constitution of social groups and classes. The argument on constitution has several dimensions. In the first place, broadly similar conditions in broadly similar societies, a similarity itself produced by transnational forces, create a similarity in social structure, as they do in the form of state, economy and education. Workers, peasants and intellectuals in one society are in large measure constituted by the same transnational context as in others. The same applies to political forms. For all their variations and differences of origin, the political systems of the developed industrialised countries are broadly similar, and are becoming even more alike. This convergence is equally strong in sociological terms: this is the central thesis of sociological writers, from Marx and Weber down to contemporary theorists, on modernity.[32]

That such convergence prevails, however, leaves open the question of in what ways beyond a shared transnational formation it is possible to speak of these social classes as transnational. It is certainly possible to speak of them as transnational in interest, in the sense that their security, prosperity and wealth is to a considerable extent dependent on international conditions. That they have an international *interest* does not, however, entail that classes have a transnational identity or consciousness. Marxism assumed that this was increasingly the case for those without material stake in particular societies, the proletariat. Yet it was probably even more so of the possessing classes, the bourgeoisie. The international constitution of bourgeoisies over the two centuries since the start of the industrial revolution is a revealing chapter of the difficult formation of such a common class interest. Riven by competing economic and strategic interests, most evidently in the epoch up to the end of the Second World War, the possessing classes of the developed world have also globalised their interest. They have sought to an increasing degree to collaborate together, through institutions of shared political, economic and security interest.[33]

That the dominant classes are so constituted internationally does not, however, entail that a similar constitution applies to the dominated. As far as formation is concerned, it can be argued that dominant and dominated are equally shaped by transnational factors. The formation of an industrial proletariat, or of a class of wage-earning plantation workers, or, earlier, of a slave class in the Americas is clearly a product of transnational forces, just as is, in the late twentieth century, the emergence of a vast class of service and part-time workers in the industrialised countries. As for interest, the conflict between different national classes here may, if anything, be greater than for the dominant class between a particular, national or corporatist, interest and the international, for the dominated do not have the investments, the material incentive, to articulate an international interest that the dominant do. As far as organisation is concerned, the balance is even less favourable: international organisation involves both consciousness and material resources, as a contrast between the transnational organisation of enterprises, on the one hand, and of trades unions, on the other, will quickly show. The dominant have more resources – money, air tickets, conference centres, administrative support, time itself – than the dominated.

This conflict between the transnational and the national, or statist, context of social action permeates the history of revolutions, as much as it does non-revolutionary periods. On the one hand, revolutionary movements, propelled by transnational factors and by the anti-state dynamic of their own ideology, do act internationally. In addition, they have an impact far beyond their own frontiers and intentions, an impact made the greater because of the shared, transnational character of the societies in question. The very transnational composition of societies, be it economical, political or ideological, creates a broader interaction, and at times fusion, of revolutionary society and potential imitator. Yet against this, the force of states as political identities and as focuses of specific, non-transnational loyalties endures: counter-revolutionary states mobilise nationalism against revolutionary internationalism; revolutionary states invoke nationalism to mobilise their own support; the revolutionary state is gripped by the logic of competitive and closed state-building.

Neither of the two polar forms of analysis, a militant anarchist or Marxist transnationalism, or an unrepentant restatement of statist logic, can do justice to the transnational impact of revolutions. Social movements act in a context of states and, in the longer run, serve to reinforce states, internally and externally. Yet the changes which are produced in the international system in revolutionary periods cannot be explained by a logic of states, balances of power and *idées reçues*; nor can the international impact of revolutions, the resonances that they create beyond their frontiers, be comprehended in such a logic. Only a dual perspective, incorporating both state and society, can encompass the international dimensions of revolutions.

The Inescapable Context: Combined and Uneven Development

It is against this background that it is possible to address the overall context in which revolutions, and the conflicts of states, classes and ideologies involved in them, are located. The world-historical processes of the past five hundred years associated with the spread of capitalism, and more particularly those since the late eighteenth century, have created a world with common features and global structures. This is the import for the study of international relations of the concept of 'modernity' and for the location of that modernity within capitalism. Something new happened, what Ernest Gellner termed 'The Big Ditch' and Karl Polanyi 'The Great Transformation'. At the same time this change produced a society, globally and within each state, that was marked by the character, ever-changing, of the capitalist whole. These economic, social and cultural changes have taken place through the mechanisms of states and through the division of the world into separate entities, called, variously, states and nations. This parcellisation has created not only separate juridical entities, close on two hundred at the end of the twentieth century, but also separate social structures, cultures, and, again since the eighteenth century, ideological communities. Yet the parts can only be analysed in terms of the larger capitalist whole.

Here, an international sociological perspective, one conscious of historical process and of the global impact of modernity, is essential. Marxism and historical sociology provide one source of such an approach. So too does the work of Karl Polanyi. Polanyi made three arguments central to the comprehension of revolutions and international relations.[34] One was the importance of the changes associated with the industrial revolution, 'The Great Transformation', as he called it: nothing – not states, economies, wars, the family or culture – could be the same after this process. Secondly, Polanyi stressed the inherently conflictual nature of the liberal market society created by this transformation, and hence the enduring role of social revolt, resorts to authoritarian rule, and adjustments in the role of the state. The failure of the Marxist vision of history was thereby compounded by the failure of the liberal economic, market-based, model. Thirdly, Polanyi showed how, despite appearances of difference, each country was subject to similar strains, and thereby to the oscillations and convulsions inherent in this modern system.

The process is, as the Marxists quite aptly termed it, *combined and uneven*.[35] The combination consists in the subjugation of the parts to the workings of the world market, and in the shared economy, stateness, nationalism, and all the attributes of the international community; the unevenness consists in the vast differences of wealth and power. If the distributor of unevenness is the world economy, the mechanisms for both combination and unevenness is the state. International relations, the prerogative of states, manages the combination, while the state separates economies and societies. It was this which led Marxists, conscious that capitalism did not homogenise the world, to argue for the possibility of revolution in less developed states. In Trotsky's formulation:

> The laws of history have nothing in common with a pedantic schematism. Unevenness, the most general law of the historic process, reveals itself most sharply and complexly in the destiny of the backward countries. Under the whip of external necessity their backward culture is compelled to make leaps. From the universal law of unevenness thus derives another law which, for the lack of a better name, we may call the law of *combined development* – by which we mean a drawing together of the different stages of the journey, a combining of separate steps, an amalgam of archaic with more contemporary forms. Without this law, to be taken of course in its whole material content, it is impossible to understand the history of Russia, and indeed of any country of the second, third or tenth cultural class.[36]

The insight of Trotsky was that of locating the history, and revolution, of any one country in a broader, contradictory context, in seeing how ideas, and forms of conflict, like forms of technology or economic activity, could be transposed to contexts very different from that in which they originated. The mistake of the Marxist approach was to conclude that, in the end, the combination would prevail over the unevenness. The unevenness, evident above all in widening income gaps between rich and poor on a world scale, has continued to grow, and is replicated dramatically in an era of capitalist globalisation. But because of the fragmentary character of states, the spatial and political distributor of that unevenness, the combination, *the world revolutionary cataclysm*, did not occur. Trotsky sought to develop his insight into a theory of world revolutionary strategy: but it was the very constrictions of the world system, ones he identified in causing revolution, which spelt the limits of that revolutionary endeavour.

A focus on states, even in a reformulated definition, is, however, insufficient. The two other dimensions of international relations, the socio-economic and the ideological, are equally a product of the world-wide spread of capitalist modernity, and the contradictions – political, social, ideological – it produces.[37] Globalisation in the contemporary period is the latest chapter in a process of internationalisation, *at all three levels*, that has been in train for centuries. States and communities exist in a world increasingly unified by economic and social processes, by both transnational formation and by the pressure on societies to conform with each other with an increasingly unified, and unequal, world. Part of this transformation involves the reproduction of separate political and economic forms, the 'nation-states', but part involves the reproduction within each society of the tensions and conflicts characteristic of the modern world as a whole.

The increasing transformation of the world has therefore produced a global social system, and within this, globalised social conflict. That such conflict is in the first instance located within particular states, and fought out in terms of that state, does not contradict the fact that it is a global phenomenon: nationalism, after all, by definition the most self-regarding of ideologies, is universal – literally no country can be without it. The study of the international dimensions of revolutions is therefore the study of the conflict within this globalised, combined and unequal, social system, of the spread of tensions and conflicts within and between states.

Here is, of course, both the weakness and strength of the Marxist analysis. Marxism recognised the centrality of revolutions in the formation of the modern world. More than other approaches, it located politics and social behaviour within a global context, that of the spread of an uneven but increasingly globalised capitalism. It was mistaken, however, in two central respects: one, in the depreciation of the endurance of states, and the ideologies associated with it; secondly, in ascribing to this globalisation a direction, a teleology, that would necessarily lead to its destruction and supersession by another political and social formation. The global system as we know it today may collapse in the future: no human creation lasts for ever. There is, however, nothing inevitable about this, nor, in the time-frame of the nineteenth and twentieth centuries, was the trend as Marxism had supposed: revolutions were, in the main, associated with the earlier phases of capitalist development; the later phases were ones in which, partly under the impact of the very threat of revolution, capitalist society was able to reform itself, politically and economically, and incorporate its dominated classes into the system.

This said, no analysis of international relations can avoid the formative impact of these world-historical processes, ones too powerful for either status quo rulers or revolutionary challengers to control. The framework of such analysis is not just world history, in the sense of the interaction of states and empires, but that of economic and social history, the formation of modern society, with its inherent tensions, on a global scale.

It is, perhaps, ironic, but all the more suggestive, that what may appear in the context of the domestic or historical explanation of revolutions as two contrasted approaches to revolution – the Marxist and structuralist, on the one hand, and the cultural and ideological, on the other – should have convergent, not rival, significance for the international dimensions of revolutions. If international relations can be seen as a combination of states, economies and ideologies, then the internationalised character of revolutions and their impacts can be comprehended in a combination of all three dominants: as foreign policy, socio-economic context, ideological impact. In the histories of particular revolutions, and the variant phases of each, the relative weight of each will vary. But all are necessary to analysing the ways in which revolutions intersect with the international system, and indeed how the international system has worked over recent centuries, and how it continues to work. The epoch of great social revolutions associated with the early development of the modern world may, or may not, have passed: what is not in question is the insight which the study of such revolutions provides for the history of that system, and for its continued evolution.

12

Revolutions in World Politics

'Der Kommunismus ist nicht radikal. Radikal ist der Kapitalis-
mus.' ('It is not communism that is radical, but capitalism', cited
by Walter Benjamin, review of world premiere of Gorky's *The
Mother*, *Die Literarische Welt*, Berlin, 5 February 1932)

The Great Displacement

If the aim of the preceding chapter was to reflect on the implications
for international relations theory of the interaction of revolutions
with international relations, the aim of this one is to suggest, in
summary form, how this interaction may be viewed in the context of
world history. Such an assessment can begin by recognising a
paradox. Revolution, as idea, and as catalyst of political change,
has been a major force in world history for the past two centuries: in
this sense it has been global. The global spread of that idea was
explored in Chapter 2, that of its international impact as event in
Chapter 7. There is, however, another dimension to this history.
Both idea and impact are distinct from the actual *incidence* of
revolutions. The occurrence of revolutions has not been global, in
the sense of occurring uniformly across the world, let alone
consuming the world in the global cataclysm that Marx and other
revolutionaries envisaged. Discursive universalisation and world-
wide impact have been accompanied by historical fissure.

This tension may be resolved by, in the first place, recognising
that the history of revolutions is really two histories, two developments running on different levels and at different paces. The history

of the idea or myth of revolution is an apparently continuous and increasingly global one, having its origins in the seventeenth and early eighteenth centuries, finding its full formulation in France in 1789, reaching Russia in 1917, sustained by the Second World War through Soviet military power in Europe and social revolution in East Asia, and extending, by the second half of the twentieth century, to Asia, Africa and Latin America. But this history is not purely discursive – ideas spread, and millions of people fight to promote and defend them, because they reflect social and political tensions. Hence the parallel process, the reality of revolution in international revolution. Through this extension revolution has repeatedly come to dominate world politics – be it in the upheavals after 1789 and 1917, or in the four decades of Cold War that began in the late 1940s. This would suggest that the global history of the idea, and its international impact, is one that lasted from 1789 to 1989, the two centuries between the fall of the Bastille and that of the Berlin Wall.

Such a focus may, however, be partial. For what this diffusion obscures is another trend, one associated not with the entropy and collapse of communism in the 1980s, but with the longer-run shift of the incidence of revolutions away from the developed world. Here, more than in the illusion of the permanence of revolutions, the divergence of myth and reality may be the most dramatic. For, in contrast to the other themes unleashed by the French revolution on to the world, most notably democracy and nationalism, that of revolution did not remain associated with the more advanced countries. Rather, what we see in the two centuries since 1789 is a gradual divergence of revolution from the more developed societies, even as it itself continued to dominate world politics, and even as the myth retained its hold within the developed West.

The consolidation of democracy in the developed world was not achieved until the 1960s, and much blood was spilt, in wars civil and international, to get there. But the potential was established much earlier. In this perspective it can be argued that in the more developed states the real turning point was not 1989 at all, nor even 1917, the last incidence of revolution in Europe. Rather it was 1848, the turning point in which, as has often been said, nothing turned. In Britain, the most advanced society, a mass working class and popular protest movement ended in a peaceful demonstration at Kennington Common. In France, a workers' uprising was quelled in June. Elsewhere in Europe national and democratic revolts were crushed.[1] 1848, building on 1789, created the myth of 'Revolution' as an irresistible historical force; but 1848 also signalled the limits of that concept's application. It created the opportunity, indeed, for what was to become, in the Cold War a century later, and after the defeat of authoritarian capitalism, the great division of world politics: this was a conflict between a world in which, revolution having been accomplished, a non-revolutionary democratic politics was possible, and a world of authoritarian, undemocratic, polities in which revolution remained on the agenda.

There were to be no more revolutionary upheavals in Western Europe, and after 1917 no more in Eastern Europe either. The focus of revolution shifted not with the focus of economic and political development, as Marx had hoped, but in a contrary direction, remaining fixed at the point where the conflicts of modernity were sharpest, even as that point moved into the less developed world. The historical verdict was, of course, delayed, first by the Russian revolution and its world-wide impact, then by the Soviet victory in the Second World War, and then by the intersection of popular revolt and East–West conflict in the Cold War. The upheavals of China, Cuba, Vietnam and Iran dominated much of the second half of the twentieth century; they do not presage a new future for the Third World as a whole, let alone for the more developed countries. Delayed as it therefore was, the verdict on revolution as a product of developed modernity was delivered, none the less, in 1989: it was then, one hundred and forty years later, that the import of the failed revolutions of 1848 was decisively established. Modernity contained two potentials, both thwarted and bloody: the revolutionary and the reformist. In the end, with enormous help from the revolutionary, the reformist triumphed.[2]

On a global scale, therefore, the time of the idea, or myth, and of mass upheavals is not the time of revolution as a political end: for the latter, we see less a global process, but rather a constant movement, from Western Europe in the 1790s, through Eastern Europe in the early part of the twentieth century, to the Third World in the post-1945 period. The global spread of the idea masked a regional displacement of the reality. Revolution thus remained a central part of the politics of certain countries, where the tensions of modernity, intensified by global processes of industrialisation, imperialism and nationalism, were most acute. Through this specific incidence, be it in 1917 in Russia, 1949 in China, 1959 in Cuba or 1979 in Iran, revolution continued to exert a predominant influence on world politics. But this migrant earthquake did not, in the sense in which revolutionaries had since 1789, 1848 and 1917 imagined it, presage the future of the developed world as a whole. Global epicentre coincided with a continuous socio-economic and geographical displacement.

Fissures of Modernity

This displacement draws attention to something too easily obscured, both by the proponents of global revolution and by transhistorical, comparative, studies within sociology: the *historicity* of revolutions, their location in particular time, place, and social context. It is not only that revolutions require a set of domestic conditions and an international conjuncture, in themselves a rare combination. Revolutions are also located in a historical time-frame: a product of specific tensions, they are limited by the prevalence of the very contradictions of modernity that produced them, as social events and as ideological myth, in the first place. They are, in other words, bounded by a particular context, itself internationally formed in ideological and social character. Revolutions have occurred in societies that have embarked on, but are at a comparatively early stage of, economic and political development; they express the pressures on traditional societies of international factors, the tensions within societies in transition, the drive for an accelerated development, competitive with other states. Revolutions have not occurred in traditional societies, nor in developed democratic ones. Upheavals with *some* of the elements of the great social revolutions occurred prior to 1789 – in the Netherlands, England, America. It was, however, in absolutist or dictatorial states of the two centuries after 1789 that the great revolutions took place. On the other hand, societies that had gone beyond these stages, while they exhibited some of the tensions associated with states that did have revolutions, did not experience such upheavals, or come near to them: neither Germany in 1918, Britain in 1926, Italy in 1944–5, France in 1968 were in pre-revolutionary situations.

In these countries, as in the USA and Japan, politics was not shaped by violent upheavals within. Rather, while in some states authoritarian regimes plunged their countries into wars that then led to the overthrow of these regimes, in others, strong movements from below, of a social-democratic or reforming character, enhanced by the world wars of the twentieth century, were able radically to alter the social and political composition of these states. As much as there is a history of the international dimensions, formation, ideology and consequences of revolution, so is there a comparable history to be written of reform, including in the sphere of an aspirant internationalism: Bernstein, Kautsky, Bauer, Hilferding, Blum, and Brandt merit a place in the history of commitment to emancipation abroad as much as the revolutionaries. If the latter can, on occasion, be accused of inconsistency, even betrayal, this accusation is no stranger to the supposedly untrammelled revolutionaries.

The revolutionary transformations that affected the countries of Eastern Europe, Asia and elsewhere, and which did so much to shape world politics, were not, therefore, replicated in the core developed countries themselves. The challenge in writing a history of 'Revolution' is to match an account of the globalisation of the idea, and its sustained impact on world politics, with an accurate charting of the shifting specific incidence of revolution itself. The key to that combined history lies, as Marxists have rightly argued, in the contradictory, at once unified and fragmented, character of 'modern society' itself. Herein lies the answer to the paradox of the great displacement: revolution *was* specific to certain societies and times, but the incidence of their occurrence, *and* their global impact, were given by the combined political, economic and ideological character of the global system.

Here, as in so many other ways, there is an analogy to be drawn between the place of revolution in the formation of the modern system and that of two other violent and transformative processes, war and empire.[3] Like revolutions, war has been a feature of modern history, a product of the tensions of development in and between states, and itself a formative influence on states and societies. Little wonder then that many social scientists came to argue that war was an *intrinsic* feature of modern society – a product of the inevitable competition of states and economies, or a result of the drive, fuelled by private business and the momentum of scientific development alike, for technological advance embodied in the arms race. The history of the early part of the twentieth century gave strong support to such an argument, as did the arms race and burgeoning military expenditures of the Cold War period. The alternative view associated with liberal theory, that modern society was intrinsically peaceful because it was democratic or because of the pacific interests of modern business, a theme in much nineteenth-century sociology from Saint-Simon to Comte, appeared to have lost the argument.

The changes in the late 1980s and early 1990s associated with the collapse of communism suggest that this earlier view, of the peaceful potential of the developed areas of modern society, may, *as far as the contemporary period is concerned*, be valid. This means that from a period in which modern society, riven by internal and international tensions, inevitably involved wars on global and local scales, it may now have entered a period when this is not so. Thus the argument as to the inevitability of war, or peace, is mistaken in positing a permanent correlation: both war and revolution are features of modern history, but have contingent relations to the development of that modern world. Modernity has been formed by war and revolution, even as it has generated and shaped them, modernity is not *necessarily* linked to either.

The same conditionality applies to the relation between modernity and empire. The European empires enjoyed two great periods of formation: an earlier phase, lasting from the sixteenth to the end of the eighteenth centuries, and a second phase, lasting from 1870 to after 1945. If, in the early part of the nineteenth century, it was widely believed that formal imperial, i.e. colonial, rule was not essential for the military and economic greatness of the industrialising world, this changed, so that after 1870 advocates and critics alike saw imperialism as a necessary outcome of modernising capitalist states. It was inconceivable, as much to Lord Salisbury and Kaiser Wilhelm as to Lenin, that the modern capitalism of their time could exist without colonies. This imperial system transformed the economies, cultures and societies of the world it dominated. Yet, after two world wars and a globalised revolt against colonialism, the European powers did abandon their formal colonial empires. Imperialism and capitalism were *not* inextricably linked. The relationship was more contingent, necessary for a phase of world history but not permanent.

While revolution did, therefore, reflect a global and contradictory system, it was a phenomenon that was itself limited by time, defined by the specific tensions of industrialisation and ideological and

social change. While revolutionaries proclaimed the universal applicability of revolution, reality and myth diverged dramatically.
The reality was that such tensions would produce the momentous
upheavals they did, and with the international impact they had, but
only on the basis of revolution in certain countries. The myth of the
hypostatisation of 1848 was that such tensions would continue
throughout history, and would, indeed, be accentuated over time,
and that sooner or later, in keeping with a teleological view, the
more developed countries would themselves be consumed. The
continued incidence of revolution *and* the international consequences compounded the illusion of global impact. The more
developed countries were transformed, politically and economically:
but not in the way in which the revolutionaries anticipated.
Bolshevism and later orthodox Soviet Marxism sought to obscure
this issue. The violence and conflicts of capitalist modernity, above
all in the period 1914–45, led millions in Europe and the Third
World to follow the revolutionary path of communism. Yet it was
this tension between radical – in a non-insurrectionary sense,
revolutionary – critique of capitalism and the realities of developed
Western society that preoccupied socialists and Marxists from the
1920s onwards. From Bernstein and Kautsky, through Luxemburg,
Gramsci and the Frankfurt School to the Eurocommunists of the
1970s, this was the reality that the radicals and communists of the
developed world sought to comprehend.[4] Large social movements
contested the authoritarian and bellicose capitalism they endured,
even as that capitalism, at the cost of tens of millions of deaths, was
itself transformed.

The convulsions of capitalist modernity preoccupied the world in
the first half of the twentieth century. In the end, after four further
decades, the revolutionary challenge of communism was to prove
not only unable to overwhelm its capitalist rival, but was to
succumb to the greater strength – economic, social and political,
as well as military – of that rival. The historical tables were turned,
the revolutionary states became those whose conservative order was
challenged. The non-revolutionary states were able, by their enduring competition, to undermine the revolutionary. In 1919 Lenin had
quoted in a letter the Latin verse *volentem ducunt fata, nolentem
trahunt* – 'fate leads the willing, and drags the unwilling'.[5] The
revolutionaries believed themselves to be the willing accomplices of
fate; history was to prove them wrong.

Historical Record

This historical outcome, the clash of statist and social perspectives, and a reaction against revolutionary rhetoric, can easily lead to the conclusion that, in the end, revolutions do not change the nature of the international system. After all, the states system continues, as do the norms of interaction of states, and, as oft noted, revolutionary states can become the most enthusiastic supporters of sovereignty and non-interference. Revolutions do not change the world in the way they proclaim, or intend: this is as true internationally as it is true internally. But to conclude from this that therefore change does not occur internationally as internally is just as mistaken as to claim a wholly new world has arisen.

To ask whether revolutions produce a *complete* change is to ask the wrong question. Whether inside societies or internationally, certain basic features of political and social organisation continue; they are a necessary part of any modernity, be they ministries and the press, or diplomacy and trade.[6] Yet revolutions, whatever their ultimate outcome, do effect permanent change in societies. Witness the paradox of France, scene of a restoration in 1815 and thereafter source of revolutionary upheaval within and inspiration without. The revolutions of 1848, too, although defeated, laid seeds of upheaval and change in many countries, Britain included. Internationally, too, revolutions had an enduring impact. This is true as far as the impact they have on the course of international history is concerned, but it is equally so in the impact they have on the domestic constitution of other states. The very need which status quo powers feel to reform themselves to pre-empt revolutions is an index of how far revolutions change relations between states.

The French revolution was overrun in 1815 yet it transformed European and world politics. The Soviet Union may, in the end, have collapsed, but it left, as we have seen, a legacy in its contribution to the reform of the rest of the world – a powerful impetus to European decolonisation in the Third World, and an equally powerful impetus to the democratisation, and growth of social provision, within the developed industrialised world. It was the fear of Bolshevik 'contagion' and 'pestilence' which in the aftermath of the First World War led the governments of the leading Western nations to introduce wide-ranging reforms: limits on the working week, collective bargaining, graduated incomes taxes, social welfare provision.[7] It was a similar anxiety that propelled the European powers, urged on by the USA, to abandon their colonies after the Second World War. When Bolshevism died in 1991 it succumbed to a competitor that had, in many respects, been transformed from what it had been in 1917; this transformation was itself a result of, among other factors, the very Bolshevik challenge it finally defeated. Perhaps nowhere is the much-misused term 'dialectic' so relevant. For this reason alone revolutions retain a contemporary relevance. Revolutions were not mistakes, or detours, but part of the formation of the modern world.

Revolution in the Age of Globalisation

The alleged irrelevance of revolutions needs questioning in another respect, namely the continued presence in many states of those fissures of modernity that produce such upheavals. No one can say whether there will, in a neutral sense, be any more 'revolutions': if revolutions appear implausible in established democratic societies, this pertains to at most three dozen of the 190-odd states in the world. It assumes moreover that liberal democracy will itself prove 'irreversible', i.e. that once established it will prevail despite the many pressures on it. Since no human institution has, as yet, lasted for ever, it may be premature to suggest that liberal democracy will do so. 'Revolution', the idea of a global *telos* forged from 1789 to 1848, may have been buried: but 'revolutions' as moments of social and political change and as objects of study may well continue.

To say that in the period after 1989 the conditions for revolution do not appear to hold is not, therefore, to make a prediction for ever: it is to reassert the necessary location of revolutions in an international socio-economic context, that of a contradictory and ever-changing modernity, one which, like all contexts, traverses different historical phases. The briefest of overviews of the world after 1989 can show that there are both factors which indicate that revolution is no longer a significant element in world politics, and factors which at the same time favour the continued relevance of this phenomenon.

The argument against the future relevance of revolutions rests on four factors. In the first place, the conditions for revolution, as evident in the authoritarian semi-developed states that did experience it, are not apparently replicated: the spread of democracy on the one hand, and of the prosperity associated with market capitalism on the other, reduce or remove this possibility. The 'end of revolution' reflected a maturing of liberal democracy on a world scale, and the effective end of the conditions that had enabled revolution to occur. Secondly, the strength of states in the contemporary world, a strength born both of indigenous power resources and of international solidarity between states, renders more unattainable the kind of revolutionary challenge seen in earlier times. Revolutions are not mystical events: shifts in economic resources, administrative capability, military technology, and forms of surveillance all affect political outcomes. Thirdly, the international factors favouring revolution are greatly reduced: above all, there are no major states wishing to promote such upheavals. The existence of such states, be they France in the 1790s or Russia in the 1920s, is important not just for material reasons but also for ideological encouragement, as a demonstration that an alternative system is possible. Finally, the ideological climate has fundamentally altered: there are residual groups which believe in a revolutionary social transformation, as there are religious movements that espouse radical programmes. But the period of world history that runs from 1789 to 1989, in which the idea of a revolutionary change, at once possible and desirable, attracted large numbers of people, has effectively ended.

This is, without doubt, the common sense of the post-1989 age – the belief, pervasive throughout the established states and universities of the world, that 1989 marked the end of an epoch. Some of the literature on revolutions has captured this. Thus Theodore Hamerow's *From the Finland Station: The Graying of Revolution in the Twentieth Century* reversed the progressivist teleology implicit in Edmund Wilson's earlier study of socialist thinking, *To the Finland Station*. Hamerow focussed on the gradual loss of revolutionary enthusiasm within states as bureaucratic and elite structures were established, and at the declining appeal which the idea of revolution exerted in the latter part of the twentieth century. Even writers broadly sympathetic to the emancipatory project of socialism had already reflected this waning of the optimistic, progressivist trend – André Gorz's *Farewell to the Working Class* and Eric Hobsbawm's *The Forward March of Labour Halted?*.[8] The 1980s and 1990s saw an extensive literature on this theme: Francis Fukuyama's *The End of History and the Last Man*, François Furet's *Le passé d'une Illusion*, Zbigniew Brzezinski's *The Great Failure*, Walter Laqueur's *The Dream that Failed*.[9] The dialogue in George

Steiner's story *Proofs* is between a communist proof-reader, Tullio, a believer in the perfectability of both text and man, and his moral and historical critic, Father Carlo, an admirer of imperfect, youthful, America.[10] Fukuyama argued that with the collapse of communism history had ended *in the sense that* the world was no longer divided between the partisans and opponents of a grand idea. There was also a sense that a period of rationalised state violence had come to an end: Eric Hobsbawm entitled his history of the twentieth century, *Age of Extremes*; the distinguished British writer Martin Wollacott asked 'Is the era of the breaking and making of peoples at its end?'[11] In raising this question, and giving a cautiously positive answer, the latter was surely right.

There may be, however, a wish within the retrospective dismissal of revolutionary aspiration. Furet, reflecting on a century of admiration for, or indulgence of, communism, concluded that with the collapse of 1989 the idea of revolution had lost its last alibi. His account of the idea of revolution and its relation to communism places this aspiration and myth at the centre of European politics in modern history. Long after the reality of the revolution had receded, the myth lived on. 'The communist idea lived longer in spirit, than in reality.'[12] Yet with the collapse at the end of the 1980s the verdict was, belatedly, final. 'It was as if the largest road offered to the imagination of modern man with regard to social well-being had been closed.'[13] Communism had always appealed to the verdict of history, and that verdict, conveyed in a few final months, was against it. Beyond communism, this collapse forced a rethinking of all ideas of history having a direction and a purpose. Talking of the 'scandal of a closed future', Furet writes: 'Here we are condemned to live in the world in which we live.'[14] It was as if the world had been living through a dream, and had finally, with the collapse of the Berlin wall and the dissolution of the USSR, woken up.

A writer of comparable sensibility and range, the Mexican Jorge Castañeda, was to strike a similar note in his biography of one of the greatest utopian internationalists, Che Guevara. In *Utopia Unarmed* Castañeda had written a fine account of the rise and decline of the Latin American guerrilla movement, focussing on the ideas and personalities of those who promoted this path in the 1960s and 1970s. In a vein comparable in passion and range to the early critical classic of communist internationalism, Borkenau's *World Communism* written in the 1930s, Castañeda had in the 1990s shown how the militant internationalism was both product and victim of a political system it failed in the end to understand, even as it was used and abused by the leading revolutionary state, in this case Cuba. His judgement on Guevara was that he was particular to his time, a man of the 1960s and of the three 'subversions' he represented: the Cuban revolution, the popular uprisings of the decade culminating in 1968, and the critique of communist society. These had become, Castañeda writes in the 1990s, things of the past:

> For the last occasion this century – and doubtless for a long time to come – it seemed reasonable to seek to change the order of things according to a pre-established plan, different from anything already in existence . . . never again would broad sectors from different societies propose to change the world starting not from a status quo or even other existing realities, but from a utopian ideal: to build a world that had simply never existed before, anywhere.[15]

In commentary on this historic outcome there were options: for some, the established opponents of revolution, a note of triumph, not to say complacency; for others, a note of regret, but of equal firmness. While the former danced on the grave of a phenomenon that modernity itself had generated, it is as if the latter had to stifle their own residual affections and illusions the better to kill once and for all the utopian aspirations that had so charged their earlier years.

The Permanence of Unrest

There are, however, reasons for questioning the historical and associated ethical judgement associated with this repudiation of the revolutionary epoch as historically formative and politically relevant. In the first place, as much as any of the other forces discussed above – war and empire – revolution had involved a combination of aspiration and idealism with brutality and coercion, a combination that had gone towards the shaping of the modern world. As this book has sought to argue, revolution was not a madness or an illusion, but a potent combination of ideology and political movement that did much to shape the modern world. On historical grounds alone it continues to merit attention. Secondly, if ethical judgements are to be passed, they must pertain as much to the other formative influences of modern history as to revolution: like war and empire, revolution destroyed the lives of many tens of millions of people, even as it led others to great self-sacrifice, exertion, even exaltation. A retrospective that condemns the one without the other is invalid. Thirdly, there is, in the rejection of revolution, an implicit assumption that the other, non-revolutionary, path was both possible and preferable: whether the former, one can seriously doubt; as to the latter, it needs reiterating, as Barrington Moore above all has, that the human costs of the non-revolutionary road, especially in the case of fascist regimes in Europe, and authoritarian regimes in the Third World, were also high. The radical youth of Latin America turned to armed struggle in the 1960s because of the repeated destruction of parliamentary politics by right-wing forces, aided on occasion by the USA. The critique of myth, the theme of Furet, Laqueur and others, fails the test of explanation, of identifying *against what* revolutionaries and their sympathisers were reacting. Equally, it fails to explain why millions fought and in many cases died for these beliefs. What was lacking from such accounts was a recognition of what it was that had driven millions of people to espouse the revolutionary cause: the revulsion at fascism in Europe in the 1930s and 1940s and at dictatorship in Latin America in the 1960s and 1970s. To espouse such causes involved an act of faith, but so too did a belief that an alternative, liberal outcome was possible. There can be no account of revolution and communism that does not take context and cause into account.

The historical legacy of revolutions is not, however, confined to what was formed in the past but relates equally to the question of the future. For revolutions are pertinent to the future irrespective of whether they continue to occur or not. They are pertinent in the first place because of the *unfinished agenda* that they proclaimed. Revolutionaries stake a claim for the future relevance of revolutions by arguing that there will be more such upheavals: but this is to miss the way in which revolutions affect politics and society. Revolutions are moments of transition which, once passed, may not need replication. Instead, they lay down an agenda for political and social change that through reform, struggles and democracy may take decades, or centuries, to be achieved. This is at once evident from the programmes on rights of the American and French revolutions, the radical egalitarianism and the international programme associated with each;[16] the point is not whether America or France always, or ever, lived up to these ideas, any more than Russia was to do after 1917, but rather how ideas and aspirations that emerged from these revolutions retain their validity in subsequent epochs.

The political system that is so easily counterposed to revolution, democracy, is itself a product, a realisation of the programme, of earlier revolutions – in England, America, France. Here the continued relevance of the American revolution may also become clearer. The debate on the American revolution has been misplaced in its attempt to read back into that revolution subsequent, decidedly unrevolutionary, features of American politics at home and abroad or to validate what America has done in the latter half of the twentieth century by reference to that; but the intellectual and political legacy of 1776 is in some measure independent of that history, as is the chequered history of France after 1789. It is paradoxical, but in no way contradictory, to identify the continued relevance of those eighteenth-century ideals while at the same time questioning the political forms and international hegemonies associated with these states today.

For the world after 1989, such retrospective arguments if coupled to a post-revolutionary triumphalism are also open to question. In the first place, the globalisation of market relations and the collapse of the communist system were associated not with less, but with more, social inequality. This was as true within countries as between them. In the former communist states of Eastern Europe and the USSR the impact of the collapse of communism was catastrophic: income per capita fell across the board, even in the heavily subsidised and exceptional reincorporated *Länder* of east Germany. This was comparable to, or worse than, the impact of war, and with no compensatory burst of reconstruction after the end of hostilities.[17] Elsewhere in the developing world capitalism produced not a diffusion of prosperity, but a brutal and uncontrolled transformation of people's lives. Indices of the distribution of wealth on a world scale showed that the gap between rich and poor had increased in the latter decades of the twentieth century.[18] There was no reason necessarily to expect that this would lead to effective and purposive social upheaval in the absence of an alternative: it did however indicate that there was little room for optimism on humanistic grounds for this new prevalent order, and that anger and resistance were likely to grow. A strong impression given by the

1990s was that in many parts of the world, whether Russia, the Middle East, or Western Europe, the prevailing discontent would be exploited by mass movements of the right, as had occurred in the inter-war period. Secondly, for all the talk of the strength of states, they remained markedly unable to meet the expectations of their people. The democratic and communications revolution of the twentieth century was also one of increased expectations, such that the states, riven with corruption and limited by international pressures, found it difficult to respond. This was one of several lessons of the economic crisis that engulfed East Asia in 1997 and 1998. Thirdly, the expectation of a world-wide spread of democracy was misleading: the majority of the world lived under regimes that were semi-democratic at best, authoritarian at worst, even as they professed adherence to the principles of liberal democracy. In the former USSR, for example, all the former constituent republics, with the exception of the Baltic states, were run by personalised dictatorships, feigning acceptance of international norms even as they consolidated their grip. In Latin America the return to democratic politics, a result of protest movements of the 1970s and 1980s, masked growing social exclusion and popular resentment. Finally, it was too simple to argue that there was no ideological alternative present. There was none with the coherence and universality of communism. But elements of an alternative ideology were certainly there: in hostility to the rich countries of the north and their institutions, supposedly or really responsible for the miseries of the poor; in movements of religious fundamentalism, led and used by competing elites; in admiration for those who, even at high cost in moral terms, defied the West – at the extreme, Saddam Hussein or Ussama bin Ladin.[19] To look for a linear continuation of communism was a mistake. To see in the absence of such a linear continuation the triumph of a global acceptance of the liberal capitalist model, and of the inequality, instability and dislocation associated with it, was equally so.

Here indeed it would be well to remember three of the most easily forgotten lessons of history, ones far more pertinent than any predictions as to the irrelevance, or relevance, of revolutions. If those who established revolutionary states ignored these lessons, at their peril, so did those with power in non-revolutionary contexts. One such lesson is the enduring inability of those with power and wealth to comprehend the depth of hostility to them. The fact that the world is not only more unequal than ever before but is vividly perceived by much of the world's population as so being, may have explosive consequences for states and elites in the next century. Fukuyama has in his *The End of History and the Last Man* reminded us of the importance of Plato's concept of *thymos* or respect. The least we can say is that there is precious little of it in the modern world.

The second lesson is the ability of history, and of social movements in general, to surprise. Few at the beginning of the twentieth century, at a time dominated by the illusions of the *belle époque*, foresaw the wars and social upheavals of the century that were to come. The confidence and complacency characteristic of the end of the twentieth century recalls with unsettling similitude that which prevailed a hundred years before. In more recent times, few events can have been as unexpected as the Iranian revolution of 1978–9 or the collapse of Soviet communism a decade later. What form the crises of the modern state and the tensions of globalisation will take, one cannot foresee. It would be comforting to believe that wise rulers, and honest and efficacious states, embedded in a system of liberal cooperation, will be able to diminish such tensions. This would mean that the world will avoid those convulsions that, in the twentieth century, have indeed been brought about by revolutions, as they have by their contemporary formative forces – wars, empires and aggressive and authoritarian regimes of the right. History does not lend much credence to such an expectation.

Finally, it would be mistaken to minimise or forget the need of people – individually and in mass collective movements – to dream, to believe in alternatives to the world in which they live, as individuals or members of a class, gender, nation or community. For millennia this human aspiration was expressed in, and contained by, religion. For the past two centuries it has taken the form of secular utopias, of which the revolutionary tradition forged in 1789 was the most powerful. That we live in a world that is disenchanted of both forms of collective aspiration does not in any way mean that the human aspiration to find an alternative, to reject the present in the name of something else, attainable or not, has come to an end. Wise souls will say that such dreaming does more harm than good. This may on some occasions be so. It has never prevented humanity, individually and collectively, when faced with inequality and domination, from engaging in one of those activities, the radical rejection of the given, that is central to the human condition.

Notes

1 Introduction: Revolutions and the International

1. Göran Therborn, 'The Rule of Capital and the Rise of Democracy', *New Left Review*, 103, May-June 1977; Barrington Moore, *The Social Origins of Dictatorship and Democracy* (Harmondsworth: Allen Lane, The Penguin Press, 1967).
2. 'The Civil War in France', in Karl Marx, *The First International and After*, edited by David Fernbach (Harmondsworth: Penguin, 1974) pp. 232–3.
3. For an example of a specific national study that is silent on the international, Albert Soboul, *The French Revolution, 1789–1799* (London: NLB, 1974); a comparative study of the sociological literature illustrates the same point: Stan Taylor, *Social Science and Revolutions* (London: Macmillan, 1984).
4. I have gone into this in greater detail in Fred Halliday, *Rethinking International Relations* (London: Macmillan, 1994).
5. Theda Skocpol, *States and Social Revolutions, A Comparative Analysis of France, Russia and China* (Cambridge: CUP, 1979) chapter 1. For an argument challenging the applicability of Skocpol to Latin American cases see Alan Knight, 'Social Revolution: A Latin American Perspective', *Bulletin of Latin American Research*, vol. 9, no. 2, 1990.
6. Engels to Zasulich, 23 April 1885, in Marx and Engels, *Selected Correspondence* (Moscow: Foreign Languages Publishing House, c. 1956) p. 460.
7. E. J. Hobsbawm, 'Revolution' in Roy Porter and Mikulas Teich (eds), *Revolution in History* (Cambridge: Cambridge University Press, 1986) p. 12.
8. Albert Sorel, *L'Europe et la Révolution française* (Paris: Le Plon, 8 vols, 1893–1908).
9. Anthony Giddens, *Sociology* (Cambridge: Polity, 1989) pp. 702–5.
10. On the earthquake analogy see Jack Goldstone, *Revolution and Rebellion in the Early Modern World* (Oxford: University of California Press, 1991) pp. 35, 148–9, 175. In his analysis of the failure of US government policy-making during the Iranian revolution of 1978–9, White House official Gary Sick uses the metaphor of a hurricane, something for which rational calculation and planning are impossible: Gary Sick, *All Fall Down, America's Fateful Encounter with Iran* (London: I.B. Tauris, 1985) pp. 38–3.
11. Karl Marx, 'The Eighteenth Brumaire of Louis Bonaparte', in Karl Marx, *Surveys from Exile* edited by David Fernbach (Harmondsworth: Penguin, 1973) p. 146.

12. I am grateful to Ms. France Henry Labordère, participant in my MSc seminar on revolutions in 1996–7, for emphasising this point.
13. '. . . revolutions do nothing to weaken the institution of the state, but, rather, by stripping away their inefficient *anciens régimes*, actually reinforce the state and make it into a more efficient engine of war, disruption and ultimate creativity, directed inevitably against the *status quo* of the day', Andrew Williams, 'The French Revolution', in Stephen Chan and Andrew Williams (eds), *Renegade States: The Evolution of Revolutionary Foreign Policy* (Manchester: Manchester University Press, 1994) pp. 50–1.
14. Michael Walzer, *Just and Unjust Wars* (Harmondsworth: Penguin, 1977).
15. Karl Radek, *Ein offener Brief an Philipp Scheidemann*, pp. 2–3, quoted in Arno Mayer, *Politics and Diplomacy of Peacemaking: Containment and Counterrevolution at Versailles, 1918–1919* (London: Weidenfeld & Nicolson, 1968) p. 20, note 7.
16. Martin Wight, *International Theory: The Three Traditions* (Leicester: Leicester University Press, 1991).
17. Hence the apt title for Jorge Dominguez's study of Cuba, *To Make a World Safe for Revolution: Cuba's Foreign Policy* (Cambridge, Mass.: Harvard University Press, 1989).
18. For examples of critiques of communism that, though astute in their identification of its mythical character, failed to explain either the broad international appeal of such ideas, or the causes of the mass upheavals that characterised twentieth-century revolutions, see: Bernard Yack, *The Longing for Total Revolution. Philosophical Sources of Social Discontent from Rousseau to Marx and Nietzsche* (Princeton: Princeton University Press, 1986); Theodor Hamerow, *From the Finland Station. The Graying of Revolution in the Twentieth Century* (New York: Basic Books, 1990); Walter Laqueur, *The Dream that Failed, Reflections on the Soviet Union* (London: OUP, 1994); François Furet, *Le passé d'une illusion, Essais sur l'idéé communiste au XXe siècle* (Paris: Laffont, 1995).
19. For example, Richard Pipes in his *The Unknown Lenin* (London: Yale University Press, 1996) sought to document the Bolshevik leaders' commitment to assisting revolution abroad – as if this had ever been in doubt (pp. 135–6, 174–5). Lars Lih makes the same discovery in regard to Stalin's private views on Britain and China, in Lars Lih *et al.* (eds), *Stalin's Letters to Molotov* (London: Yale University Press, 1995) pp. 27–36. In his *We Now Know. Rethinking Cold War History* (Oxford: Clarendon Press, 1997) pp. 195–6, John Lewis Gaddis makes much of the commitment of Stalin to communist ideology, again something on which a reading of his statements from the 1920s would have left little doubt. Similarly, in his messy biography of Lenin, Dmitri Volkogonov documented the jewellery that Lenin had used to help foreign revolutionaries: no doubt this was grist to the theme of Lenin being alien to the interests of the Russian people, an argument with thinly obscured anti-semitic overtones: *Lenin, Life and Legacy* (London: HarperCollins, 1994) p. 69.

20. Fred Halliday, *Revolution and Foreign Policy: The Case of South Yemen 1967–1987* (Cambridge: CUP, 1990).
21. The argument for revolutions as distinctive events had been made by, among others, Karl Marx and Theda Skocpol. The argument against has come from a variety of standpoints. Thus behaviouralists deny the specificity of these events, seeing them as part of a broader continuum of violence, or 'internal war'; Peter Calvert prefers a broad definition of revolution as 'the forcible overthrow of a government or regime' (*Revolution and International Politics*, London: Frances Pinter, 1984, p. 2); the historical sociologist Charles Tilly has sought to establish a broad category of political upheavals, across the range of modern European history; the Marxist Göran Therborn has sought, by developing the etymological and semantic interrelationship of 'reform' and 'revolution', to blunt the political impasse inherited from 1914 and, he argues, to correct an unwarrantedly limited reading of European history ('Revolution and Reform: Reflections on Their Linkages through the Great French Revolution', in J. Böhlin *et al.* (eds), *Samhällsvetenskap, ekonomi, historia,* Göteborg: Daidalos, 1989).

2 An Alternative Modernity: The Rise and Fall of 'Revolution'

1. Amidst a widespread commentary see Martin Kettle reviewing Simon Schama's *Citizens*, 'Debunking the Revolutionary Romance', *The Guardian*, 25 May 1989, and Flora Lewis, 'Revolution Isn't the Way to Change Things', *International Herald Tribune*, 30 January 1989. This literature was to continue through the 1990s.
2. Antonio Gramsci gave the example of the word 'disaster' – originally an astrological term implying an evil start. I have developed this further with regard to misleading etymological investigation in the case of modern Arabic political vocabulary in 'The Delusions of Etymology', *Islam and the Myth of Confrontation* (London: I. B. Tauris, 1996) pp. 205–7.
3. Karl Griewank, *Der Neuzeitliche Revolutionsbegriff, Entstehung und Entwicklung* (Weimar: Hermann Böhlaus Nachfolger, 1955); Raymond Williams, *Keywords, A Vocabulary of Culture and Society* (London: Fontana, 1976); A. T. Hatto, ' "Revolution": An Enquiry into the Usefulness of an Historical Term', *Mind*, vol. LVIII, new series no. 232, October 1949; Hatto, 'The Semantics of 'Revolution" ', in P. J. Vatikiotis, *Revolution in the Middle East and other Case Studies* (London: George Allen & Unwin, 1972); Alain Rey, *'Révolution'*, *Histoire d'un Mot* (Paris: Gallimard, 1989).
4. On the conceptual history see also R. Kosseleck, 'Historical Criteria of the Modern Concept of Revolution', in *Futures Past: On the Semantics of Historical Time* (Cambridge, Mass.: MIT Press, 1985). For the broader history of the idea, see Krishan Kumar (ed.), *Revolution. The Theory and Practice of a European Idea* (London: Weidenfeld & Nicolson, 1971), and David Close and Carl Bridge, *Revolution: A History of the Idea* (London: Croom Helm, 1985).

5. Aristotle, *The Politics* (Hardmondsworth: Penguin, 1968) Book 5, pp. 189–234.
6. David Hume had talked in his *History of England* of the Long Parliament of 1641 as representing a 'revolution in the minds of men', but it was not until 1826 that François Guizot applied the term in its 1789 sense to the English case: Michael G. Finlayson, *Historians, Puritans and the English Revolution* (Toronto: Toronto University Press, 1983), p. 9, n. 16.
7. Griewank, *Der Neuzeitliche Revolutionsbegriff*, chapter 7, pp. 193–205.
8. Discussion of when the modern concept of 'Revolution' can be said to have emerged is similar to that on the modernity, or otherwise, of 'nation' and 'nationalism': elements of the idea can certainly be found in earlier periods, but in both instances I favour a modernist account. For the contrary view, that 'revolution', in its modern political sense had already been formed by the 1750s, see Calvert, *Revolution and Counter-Revolution* (Milton Keynes: Open University Press, 1990), p. 3. There is, mercifully, one difference: revolutionaries are less insistent than nationalists about the perennial and long-established character of their enterprise.
9. Krishan Kumar, *Prophecy and Progress* (Harmondsworth: Penguin, 1978) p. 19.
10. Alain Rey, '*Révolution*' p. 109.
11. Kosseleck, 'Historical Criteria. . .', pp. 46–7.
12. Gellner has written that nationalism 'is primarily a political principle, which holds that the political and the national unit should be congruent' (*Nations and Nationalism*, Oxford: Basil Blackwell, 1983, p. 1). By extension one can argue that 'revolution' is an idea which claims that history and political movement should be congruent. The problems which arise when, in either case, congruence fails to occur, or, to put it another way, history fails to turn up, are comparable: they have been rather serious, especially for those accused of getting in the way, for the past century or two.
13. Therborn, 'Revolution and Reform', p. 8 n.18.
14. Bernard Lewis, 'Islamic Concepts of Revolution', in Vatikiotis (ed.), *The Political Language of Islam* (London: University of Chicago Press, 1988, pp. 92–6). The Arabic aversion for the word *inqilab* may have something to do with the fact that in the Koran one of the meanings of *q-l-b-* is to 'turn away' from the true religion.
15. Davoud Norouzi and Ilse Itscherenska, 'Zur Reflexion der "Islamischen Revolution" in der persischen Sprache', *Asien, Afrika, Lateinamerika* (Berlin) vol. 11 (1983), p. 268. On the vocabulary, often of an inventive kind, of the Iranian revolution see Ervand Abrahamian, *Khomeinism* (London: I.B.Tauris, 1992), and Paul Vieille and Farhad Khosrokhavar, *Le discours populaire de la Révolution iranienne* (Paris: Contemporaneité, 1990).
16. There is a revealing story in the shifts in Turkish usage. The Turkish use of *inqilab*, rendered *inkilâp*, is complicated by the failure of spoken Turkish to distinguish the Arabic letters *q* and *k*: thus there is no difference in pronunciation between Arabic *inqilab*, 'revolution' and

inkilab, literally 'being turned into a dog', from Arabic *klb*, denoting becoming mad, or rabid, or involved in a dogfight, and hence *kalb*, a dog. Since Ataturk had in the official ideology carried out a revolution, this was embarrassing. For this reason the term *devrim* was introduced in the 1930s. However, when in the 1970s the radical left in Turkey began to appropriate the term *devrim*, official Ataturkist usage shifted back to *inkilap*, now, in another shift of meaning, altered to mean 'reform'. I am grateful to Rifaat Kandiyoti and Mete Tuncay for information on this.

17. Maltese has the term *żmien ta'taqlib*, meaning 'time of troubles'. I am grateful to Dennis Sammut for this information.

18. I am grateful to Dr Noah Lucas and Dr Norman Berdichevsky for this information.

19. I am grateful to Isaac Bigio for this information.

20. Alfred Douglas, *The Oracle of Change. How to Consult the I Ching* (Harmondsworth: Penguin, 1971) pp. 185–6.

21. The fate of this word in Chinese is another case of conceptual history shaped by history itself. The term *ge-ming* is, in modern Chinese, ambivalent: it is on the one hand associated with bloody upheaval, and on the other with positive change and is not laden with its premodern meanings. Chinese also has the term *chiyi*, from revolt or rebellion, combining *chi*, to rise, and *yi*, righteous, as well as the term *zao-fan*, for rebellion, as in Mao's slogan 'To rebel is justified'. I am grateful to my colleagues Lin Chun and Michael Yahuda for elucidation of these points.

22. My thanks to Hideaki Shinoda for this information.

23. On progress, see Robert Nisbet, *History of the Idea of Progress, An Enquiry into its Origins and Growth* (New York: Basic Books, 1981); J. M. Bury, *A History of Progress* (London, 1920); Sidney Pollard, *The Idea of Progress, History and Society* (Harmondsworth: Penguin 1971). There is a debate within this discussion of progress as to the novelty of the late-eighteenth-century/nineteenth-century concept thereof: while Bury and most other writers see the idea of progress as linked to historical improvement and hence as specific to the modern age, Nisbet identifies themes in earlier religious thinking, associated with the coming of a Messiah, that predate the enlightenment. Nisbet concentrates on Christianity, but a similar conception is to be found in Shi'ite Islam, where the return of the Twelfth Imam, in hiding since the ninth century, is associated with a golden age: the Iranian revolution was to fuse these two elements, in the myth of the advent of Khomeini, as the Imam's deputy, and the creation of a new age.

24. 'The Eighteenth Brumaire of Louis Bonaparte', in Karl Marx, *Surveys from Exile*, p. 149.

25. Isaac Deutscher, *The Prophet Armed: Trotsky 1879–1921* (London: OUP, 1956) p. 391.

26. David Marr, *Vietnam 1945: The Quest for Power* (London: University of California Press, 1995) pp. 533, 458.

27. See Bernard Yack, *The Longing for Total Revolution*.

28. On anarchist internationalism, see E. H. Carr, *Bakunin* (New York: Octagon Books, 1975) chapters 25 and 26.
29. Quoted in E. H. Carr, *The Romantic Exiles* (Harmondsworth: Peregrine, 1968) p. 134.
30. Erica Benner, *Really Existing Nationalisms* (Oxford: Clarendon Press, 1995).
31. Nisbet, *History of the Idea of Progress*, pp. 258–67.
32. Teodor Shanin, 'The Question of Socialism: A Development Failure or an Ethical Defeat?', unpublished paper, August 1990, p. 11.
33. 'Manifesto of the Communist Party', in *The Revolutions of 1848*, edited and introduced by David Fernbach (London: Penguin, 1973) pp. 70–1.
34. Derek Sayer, *Capitalism and Modernity. An Excursus on Marx and Weber* (London: Routledge, 1991).
35. N. Bukharin and E. Preobrazhensky, *The ABC of Communism*. Part 2, 'The Dictatorship of the Proletariat and the Upbuilding of Communism' (Harmondsworth: Penguin, 1969).
36. Dominique Lecourt, *Proletarian Science? The Case of Lysenko* (London: NLB, 1977).
37. Guozi Shudian, China Publications Centre, 1969 Calendar, July.
38. George Pettee, *The Process of Revolution* (New York: Howard Fertig, 1971) original edition, 1938; Crane Brinton, *The Anatomy of Revolution* (New York: Vintage, 1958)
39. Barrington Moore, *The Social Origins of Dictatorship and Democracy*; Theda Skocpol, *States and Social Revolutions*; Jack Goldstone, *Revolution and Rebellion in the Early Modern World*.
40. German has two words for 'midwife': *Hebamme* and *Geburtshilfer* – literally 'lever-nurse' and 'birth-helper'. Marx uses the former term. I am grateful to Luis Fernandes for this point.
41. Skockpol, *States and Social Revolutions*, p. 4.
42. Samuel Huntington, *Political Order in Changing Societies* (London: Yale University Press, 1968) p. 264.
43. John Keane, *Tom Paine: A Political Life* (London: Bloomsbury, 1995) pp. 230–1.
44. Ellen Trimberger, *Revolution from Above* (New Brunswick, NJ: Transaction Books, 1978). This category had already been identified by Petstee (*The Process*, p. 28).
45. On Egypt and Peru see Trimberger. On the case for Ethiopia as a case for revolution from above, see Fred Halliday and Maxine Molyneux, *The Ethiopian Revolution* (London: Verso, 1981), with the important qualification that, as in Egypt in 1952, mass activity from below is an essential stimulant and accompaniment of the military seizure of power. For the case against, see Christopher Clapham, *Transformation and Continuity in Revolutionary Ethiopia* (Cambridge: Cambridge University Press, 1988) and Andargachew Tiruneh, *The Ethiopian Revolution 1974–1987* (Cambridge: Cambridge University Press, 1993).
46. Contrast: 'The German revolution did happen – in the form of the rise of Hitler to power and his use of that power to carry out far-reaching

changes in German society' (Peter Calvert, *Revolution and Counter-Revolution*, p. 57); 'In no case was an actual revolution against constituted authority launched; fascist tactics were invariably those of a sham rebellion arranged with the tacit approval of the authorities who pretended to have been overwhelmed by force' (Karl Polanyi, *The Great Transformation*, Boston: Little, Brown, 1957, p. 238).

47. Edward Mortimer, 'How History Judges the Revolution', *Financial Times*, 31 January 1989.
48. Norman Cohn, *The Pursuit of the Millennium* (London: Mercury Books, 1962).
49. In late January 1979 I was given a lift by an East End London taxi-driver. 'Ayatollah Khomeini,' he said disparagingly, 'the problem with him is he's not *organised*.' What he meant, of course, was that the Ayatollah was not a member of the Communist Party.
50. Said Arjomand, *The Turban for the Crown: The Islamic Revolution in Iran* (Oxford: OUP, 1988).
51. On the revolution itself, see Shaul Bakhash, *The Reign of the Ayatollahs* (London: I.B. Tauris, 1985). For interpretation of it as a revolution see Ervand Abrahamian, *Khomeinism* (London: I.B. Tauris, 1990); and Fred Halliday, 'The Iranian Revolution in Comparative Perspective' in *Islam and the Myth of Confrontation*.
52. See, for example, the speech by Chief Justice Musavi-Ardebili on the tenth anniversary of the Iranian revolution, where the achievements of the revolution include: guaranteeing national independence ('The only country which can claim to be independent in every aspect, under this blue sky and on earth, is Iran'); improving rural living conditions; safeguarding national wealth; suppressing political parties dependent on foreign powers; developing national, particularly military, industries (*BBC Summary of World Broadcasts Part 4*, ME/0075/A/4-6, 15 February 1988).
53. Fred Halliday, interview with Ehsan Tabari, spokesman of the pro-Soviet *Tudeh* party, *MERIP Middle East Reports* No. 86, March/April 1980.
54. On the modernist content of Khomeini's ideology see Ervand Abrahamian, *Khomeinism*; Sami Zubaida, *Islam, The People and the State* (London: Routledge, 1989); Fred Halliday, 'The Iranian Revolution in Comparative Perspective'. On the modern, Jacobin, concept of the state in Islamist thought, Aziz al-Azmeh, *Islams and Modernities* (London: Verso, 1993).
55. Vieille and Khosrokhavar, *Le discours populaire*, pp. 115–17.
56. Ernst Kux, 'Revolution in Eastern Europe – Revolution in the West?', *Problems of Communism*, vol. XL, no. 3 (May–June 1991).
57. See Krishan Kumar, 'The Revolutions of 1989: Socialism, Capitalism, and Democracy', *Theory and Society*, vol. 21, (1992) pp. 309–56: pp. 320–5 for the 'fronde-like features – a divided and weakened ruling class' of 1989. Reprinted in Kumar, *From Post-Industrial to Post-Modern Society. New Theories of the Contemporary World* (Oxford: Blackwell, 1995).

346   *Notes*

58. 'There is evidently something strange about the revolution of 1989. It seems peculiarly uncreative, unfertile in ideas' (Kumar, 'The Revolutions of 1989', p. 316).

59. Havel himself proposed an 'anti-political politics', Konrad an 'anti-politics' (*Anti-Politics*, London: Quartet Books, 1984): by this they meant limits on the power of the state, and a strong civil society.

60. Jürgen Habermas, 'What Does Socialism Mean Today? The Revolutions of Recuperation and the Need for New Thinking', in Robin Blackburn (ed.), *After the Fall, The Failure of Communism and the Future of Socialism* (London: Verso, 1991) p. 27. The quotation from Fest is from the *Frankfurte Allgemeine Zeitung*, 30 December 1989.

3 Internationalism in Theory: A World-Historical Vision

1. Nisbet, *History of the Idea of Progress*, p. 171.

2. E. H. Carr, *The Romantic Exiles* (Harmondsworth: Peregrine, 1968) pp. 25, 320–1.

3. Amidst the dozens of works on Marx's theories, sympathetic or otherwise, there is hardly ever an extended discussion, or a separate chapter, on his *theoretical* conception of the international system. Some studies do focus on his views on relations between states: Miklos Molnar, *Marx, Engels et la Politique Internationale* (Paris: Gallimard, 1975); Vendulka Kubálková and Andrew Cruickshank, *Marxism and International Relations* (Oxford: OUP, 1986); Michael Doyle, *Ways of War and Peace: Realism, Liberalism and Socialism* (London: W.W. Norton, 1997). Brief summaries on internationalism can be found in Tom Bottomore (ed.), *A Dictionary of Marxist Thought* (Oxford: Blackwell Reference, 1983); George Labica and Gerard Bensussan (eds), *Dictionnaire Critique du Marxisme* (Paris: PUF, second edition, 1985); Miklos Molnar, 'Internationalismns' in *Sowjetsystem und demokratische Gesellschaft* (Freiburg and Vienna: Herder, n.d.). In Lenin's case, there is sometimes a greater attention, a product partly of his theory of imperialism, and partly of what he said about foreign policy after coming to power.

4. Sebastian Balfour, *Castro* (London: Longman, 1990) p. 11.

5. Kosseleck, 'Historical Criteria', p. 49.

6. Arendt, *On Revolution* p. 53.

7. Norman Davies, *Europe*, p. 704.

8. It was one of the curious details of the post-communist regime in Russia that it too involved such legitimation: in 1992 the partly converted Museum of the Revolution in Moscow displayed telegrams from around the world congratulating Yeltsin on defeating the 'anti-constitutional' coup attempt of August 1991.

9. Paolo Spriano, *Stalin and the European Communists* (London: Verso, 1985) p. 7.

10. *Peking Review* no. 10 (3 March 1967); no. 22 (26 May 1967); no. 51 (15 December 1967).

11. Donald Hodges, *Intellectual Foundations of the Nicaraguan Revolution* (Austin: University of Texas Press, 1986) pp. 3–7.

12. On 1947–8, Tad Szulc, *Fidel, A Critical Portrait* (London: Hutchinson, 1986) pp. 100–3, 113–23; on the right to revolt, *History Will Absolve Me* (Havana: Book Institute, 1967) chapter XXIV.

13. Thus in 1996 at an Interamerican Meeting for Humanity and Against Neoliberalism, Subcomandante Marcos, leader of the EZLN, greeted delegates from Canada, the USA, Guatemala, Costa Rica, Venezuela, Puerto Rico, Ecuador, Brazil, Peru, Chile, Uruguay, Argentina, Spain, France and Germany, 'Desafían zapatistas al neoliberalismo', *Reforma* (Mexico) 6 April 1996.

14. *The Shorter Oxford English Dictionary* gives the first use in English of 'internationalist', in 1864 and of 'internationalism', in 1877.

15. Derek Heater, *World Citizenship and Government. Cosmopolitan Ideas in the History of Western Political Thought* (London: Macmillan, 1996); Fred Halliday, 'Three Concepts of Internationalism', *International Affairs*, Spring 1988; C. L. Lange and A. Schou, *Histoire de l'Internationalisme*, vol. 2 (Oslo: Aschehoug, 1954).

16. Barry Coward, *Oliver Cromwell* (London: Longman, 1991) pp. 132–6, 168–74; R. Crabtree, 'The Idea of a Protestant Foreign Policy', in I. Roots (ed.), *Cromwell: A Profile* (London: Macmillan, 1973).

17. Note 16, and Christopher Hill, 'The English Revolution and the Brotherhood of Man', in Heinz Lubasz, *Revolutions in Modern European History* (London: Collier-Macmillan, 1968).

18. Ibid, p. 46.

19. Quoted in ibid, p. 51.

20. Marcel Merle, *Pacifisme et Internationalisme, XVIIe–XXe siècles* (Paris: Armand Colin, 1966); René Pomeau, *L'Europe des Lumières. Cosmopolitisme et Unité Européenne au XVIIIe siècle* (Paris: Stock, 1991). For the continued adherence of enlightenment thinkers to patriotic ideas, see Bayley Stone, *The Origins*, pp. 60–1.

21. Quoted in R. R. Palmer, 'The World Revolution of the West: 1763–1801', *Political Science Quarterly*, vol. 69, no. 1 (March 1954) p. 11.

22. J. M. Thompson, *Robespierre*, vol. 1, *From the Birth of Robespierre to the Death of Louis XVI* (Oxford: Basil Blackwell, 1935) pp. 207–8.

23. On the development of Robespierre's thinking, see Thompson *Robespierre*, vol. 1, chapter VII, 'The Opponent of War (November 1791–April, 1792) and chapter VIII, 'The Defender of the Constitution (April–August 1792); C. Lange and A. Schou, *Histoire de l'Internationalisme*, vol. 2 (Paris, 1954) pp. 373–4; R. R. Palmer, *The Age of the Democratic Revolution*, vol. 2, *The Struggle* (Princeton: Princeton University Press, 1964) pp. 10–16, 50–65; R. R. Palmer, *Twelve Who Ruled* (Princeton: Princeton University Press, 1941) chapter XIV 'The Rush upon Europe'.

24. Heater, *World Citizenship*, p. 70.

25. For a scandalised account of this day – 'a spectacle such as our foolish little Planet has not often had to show' – see Thomas Carlyle,

The French Revolution, A History (Oxford: OUP, 1989) Part I, pp. 352–8.

26.   The sage Anacharsis espoused a vision of unspoiled nature. In 1794 Cloots himself was accused of conspiracy and executed. Lange and Schou, *Histoire*, pp. 375–7. Also A. Soboul, 'Anacharsis Cloots, l'orateur du genre humain', *Annales Historiques de la Révolution Française*, 239 (January–March, 1980).

27.   Antoine-Nicolas de Condorcet, *Sketch for a Historical Picture of the Progress of the Human Mind* (London: Weidenfeld & Nicolson, 1955) p. 141.

28.   Ibid, p. 145.

29.   Ibid, pp. 194–5.

30.   Ibid, pp. 197–9.

31.   The cunning of history was to play a cruel trick on the Corsicans and their supporters. For, as with Cuba in 1898, liberation from one colonial oppressor was to be followed by domination by another, in this case France. The Corsicans were to have their revenge, in the person of the son of an Ajaccio dignitary, Napoleon Bonaparte.

32.   R. R. Palmer, *The Age of the Democratic Revolution* (Princeton: Princeton University Press, 1964) chapter XVI, 'Democracy: Native and Imported'.

33.   R. G. Adams, *Political Ideas of the American Revolution*, pp. 141–52.

34.   Lange and Schou, *Histoire*, chapter 11.

35.   Thomas Paine, *Rights of Man* (Harmondsworth: Penguin Books, 1969) part 2, p. 250. On Paine's international impact, see Keane, *Tom Paine*, and Ian Dyck, *Citizen of the World. Essays on Thomas Paine* (London: Christopher Helm, 1987). Paine's good intentions were, of course, to land him in trouble. He fled from England to France in 1792 after being charged with sedition, was imprisoned in Paris at the end of 1793 after France had declared war on England, and after his release in 1794 wrote a bitter attack on George Washington for neglecting his cause. In 1802 he sailed to America where his attacks on Christianity alienated public opinion and led him to spend the rest of his life in obscurity. The statue in his home town of Thetford, Norfolk, was erected with money from American admirers. 'He did nothing for Thetford' the official of the local tourist office told me.

36.   *Common Sense* (Harmondsworth: Penguin, 1976) p. 120.

37.   *The Rights of Man*, pp. 164–5.

38.   *Rights of Man*, p. 88.

39.   Ibid, pp. 166–8.

40.   *Common Sense*, p. 85.

41.   Ibid, p. 124.

42.   *Rights of Man*, pp. 168–9.

43.   Ibid, p. 178.

44.   Ibid, p. 231.

45.   'On the Reorganization of European Society', in *The Political Thought of Saint-Simon*, edited by Ghita Ionescu (London: Oxford University Press, 1976) pp. 97–8.

46. Nisbet, *History of the Idea of Progress*, pp. 258–67. For commentary, Emile Durkheim, *Socialism and Saint-Simon* (Yellow Springs: The Antioch Press), 'Internationalism and Religion', pp. 170–80.

47. Flora Tristan, *Oeuvres et Vie Mêlées* (Paris: Union Générale d'éditions, 1973) pp. 389–435; Sandra Dijkstra, *Flora Tristan, Pioneer Feminist and Socialist* (London: Pluto Press, 1989). Feminism and internationalism were closely linked at this time, in both Europe and the USA. The first international women's congress was held at Seneca Falls in the USA in 1848.

48. Henry Weisser, *British Working-Class Movements and Europe 1815–48* (Manchester: Manchester University Press, 1975).

49. Nisbet, *History of the Idea of Progress*, p. 261.

50. Lenin, 'Critical Remarks on the National Question', in *Collected Works*, vol. 20, p. 34, quoted in Ephraim Nimni, *Marxism and Nationalism* (London: Pluto Press, 1991) p. 87.

51. 'Ueber Friederich Lists Buch. . .' (1845), in *Sozialistische Politik*, Berlin 1972, no. 19, p. 103, quoted in Michael Löwy, 'Fatherland or Mother Earth? Nationalism and Internationalism from a Socialist Perspective', *The Socialist Register 1989* (London: The Merlin Press, 1989) p. 226, n.8.

52. Karl Marx and Friedrich Engels, *The German Ideology* (London: Lawrence & Wishart, 1965) p. 46.

53. *The German Ideology*, p. 47.

54. Ibid, p. 49.

55. Ibid, p. 76.

56. 'Speeches on Poland', in Karl Marx, *The Revolutions of 1848*, ed. David Fernbach (Harmondsworth: Penguin, 1973) p. 100.

57. Ibid, p. 100.

58. Ibid, p. 101.

59. 'Manifesto of the Communist Party', in Karl Marx, *The Revolutions of 1848*, ed. David Fernbach (Harmondsworth: Penguin, 1973) p. 68.

60. Ibid, p. 71.

61. Ibid, p. 71.

62. Ibid, p. 72.

63. Ibid, p. 78.

64. Ibid, pp. 84–5.

65. Ibid, p. 98.

66. Lenin wanted to alter these lines, to read 'Workers of all countries, and all oppressed peoples, unite!', quoted in Marcel Liebman, *Leninism under Lenin*, p. 372.

67. 'Documents of the First International: 1864–70', *The First International and After* (Harmondworth: Penguin, 1974) pp. 82–3. This cooperative or coordinating interpretation of Marx's internationalism is confirmed by his letter on the subject to Engels of 4 November 1864, in Karl Marx and Frederick Engels, *Selected Correspondence* (Moscow: Foreign Languages Publishing House, c.1956) pp. 179–82.

68. On this, see the excellent discussion by Neil Harding, *Lenin's Political Thought*, vol. 2 (London: Macmillan, 1981) chapter 11, 'The International Dimension of Revolution'.

69. 'On the History of the Communist League', conclusion.
70. Margot Light, *The Soviet Theory of International Relations* (Brighton: Wheatsheaf, 1988) pp. 155–64.
71. Fernando Claudin, *The Communist Movement* (Harmondsworth: Penguin, 1975).
72. Margot Light, *The Soviet Theory of International Relations*, chapter 9.
73. Leon Trotsky, *The Revolution Betrayed* (London: New Park Publications, 1967).
74. G. F. Hudson *et al.* (eds), *The Sino-Soviet Dispute* (London: China Quarterly, 1961) and John Gittings, *Survey of the Sino-Soviet Dispute* (Oxford: OUP, 1968).
75. 'Peaceful Coexistence – Two Diametrically Opposed Policies', *Peking Review*, 51 (20 December 1963). For Soviet writings see V. Zagladin, *Internationalism – The Communists' Guiding Principle* (Moscow: Novosti, 1976); Eduard Bagramov, 'Proletarian Internationalism: Idea and Practice', *New Times*, no. 44 (1978); V. S. Semyonov, *Nations and Internationalism* (Moscow: Progress, 1979).
76. André Fontaine, 'Le declin de l'internationalisme', *Le Monde* 13 May 1976; 'Moscou relance la campagne pour "internationalisme"', *Le Monde*, 21 April 1976.
77. On the East Berlin summit's abandonment of 'proletarian internationalism', *The Guardian*, 1 July 1976, *Le Monde*, 2 July 1976.
78. Gian Carlo Pajetta, *La lunga marcia dell'internazionalismo* (Rome: Riuniti, 1978) pp. 159ff; Sergio Segre, 'L'esigenza di un nuovo internazionalismo', *Rinascità*, 7 April 1978; 'Le P.C.I. prône un "nouvel internationalisme" allant au-delà des frontières du communisme', *Le Monde*, 13–14 April 1980.
79. Heinz Timmermann, *"Proletarischer Internationalismus" aus sowjetischer Sicht. Eine historisch-politische Analyse*, Bundesinstitut fur ostwissenschaftliche und internationale Studien, 1983; Karen Dawisha and Jonathan Valdez, 'Socialist Internationalism in Eastern Europe', *Problems of Communism*, vol. XXXVI, no. 2 (March-April 1987); Light, *The Soviet Theory of International Relkations*, chapter 7.
80. Mikhail Gorbachev, *Perestroika. New Thinking for Our Country and the World* (London: Collins, 1987).
81. 'La "glasnost" à la conquète des PC étrangers', *Le Monde*, 16 April 1988.
82. For a characteristic post-Soviet rejection of internationalism Vladimir Razuvayev, 'Can Moscow afford being the third Rome? or why the Soviet Union has no national interests', *New Times*, no. 32 (1990) p. 16.
83. Carlo Pisacane, *La Rivoluzione* (Turin: Einardi, 1970) pp. 114–32; Giuliano Procacci, *History of the Italian People* (Harmondsworth: Penguin, 1973) pp. 306–9.
84. Sultan Galiev in Stuart Schram and Helène Carrère d'Encausse, *Marxism in Asia* (London: Allen Lane, 1969) pp. 35–7, 178–81, and A. Bennigsen and C. Quelquejay, *Le Sultangalievisme au Tatarestan* (Paris: 1960).

85. Maurice Meisner, *Li Ta-chao and the Origins of Chinese Marxism* (Cambridge: Harvard University Press, 1967) chapter 8, 'Nationalism and Internationalism'.

86. Stuart Schram, *The Political Thought of Mao Tse-tung* (London: Praeger, 1964) section VIII, 'China and the Underdeveloped Countries'.

87. Lin Piao, 'Long Live the Victory of People's War', *Peking Review*, vol. 8, no. 36 (3 September 1965).

88. Teng Hsiao-ping speech to the General Assembly of the United Nations, *Peking Review*, 12 April 1974; Michael Yahuda, *China's Role in World Affairs* (London: Croom Helm, 1978) pp. 238–66; Vendulka Kubálková and Albert Cruickshank, *Marxism and International Relations*, pp. 99–112.

89. Che Guevara, 'Vietnam Must Not Stand Alone', *New Left Review*, no. 43 (May/June 1967). For extensive analysis see Jon Lee Anderson, *Che Guevara: A Revolutionary Life* (London: Bantam Books, 1997).

90. Régis Debray, *Revolution in the Revolution?* (London: Penguin, 1969).

91. Herbert Marcuse, 'Question of Revolution'; *New Left Review*, 45 (September/October 1967). Kurt Steinhaus, *Zur Theorie des internationalen Klassenkampfes* (Frankfurt: Verlag Neue Critik, 1967). Reimut Reiche, *Modele der Kolonialen Revolution* (Frankfurt: Suhrkamp, 1967).

92. 'Khomeini's 20th February Message to the Nation', *BBC Summary of World Broadcasts*, Part 4 The Middle East and North Africa, ME/6352/A/5, 22 February 1980.

93. *Shi'ism and Social Protest*, pp. 100–2.

4 Internationalism in Practice: Export of Revolution

1. Richard Pipes, *The Russian Revolution 1899–1919* (London: Fontana Press, 1992) p. 669.

2. Felix Gilbert, 'The "New Diplomacy" of the Eighteenth Century', *World Politics*, vol. 4, no. 1 (October 1951).

3. Quoted in E. H. Carr, *The Bolshevik Revolution 1917–1923*, vol. 3, p. 86.

4. E. H. Carr, *The Bolshevik Revolution 1917–1923*, vol. 3, p. 103.

5. Leon Trotsky, *My Life* (New York: Grosset & Dunlop, 1960) p. 341. Another source gives his words at the time as: 'I have accepted the post of Commissar of Foreign Affairs just because I wanted to have more leisure for party affairs. My job is a small one: to publish the secret documents and to close the shop', in E. H. Carr, *The Bolshevik Revolution*, vol. 3, p. 28.

6. Jaap van Ginneken, *The Rise and Fall of Lin Piao* (Harmondsworth: Penguin, 1976) pp. 115–17.

7. David Armstrong, *Revolution and World Order* (Oxford: Clarendon, 1993) chapter 7, 'Diplomacy', esp. pp. 263–8.

8. OLAS – *Organisazión Latino-Americana de Solidaridad*; OSPAAAL – *Organisazión de Solidaridad de los Pueblos de Asia, Africa y America Latina*.

9. On China and Vietnam, Bernard Fall, *Le Viet-minh* (Paris: Armand Colin, 1960) pp. 195–6; on Yemen and Dhofar, Fred Halliday, *Revolution and Foreign Policy: The Case of South Yemen 1967–1987* (Cambridge: Cambridge University Press, 1990) pp. 142–57.

10. I have gone into this in greater detail in Fred Halliday, *Revolution and Foreign Policy*. In a speech to the Fourth Congress of the ruling National Liberation Front in March 1968 the secretary-general Abdul Fatah Ismail called for 'the propagation of the revolutionary fire throughout the Arabian Peninsula', through the creation of a popular militia (p. 22).

11. Christel Lane, *The Rites of Rulers. Ritual in Industrial Society – the Soviet Case* (London: Cambridge University Press, 1981) pp. 289–90.

12. Wilfried Buchta, *Die iranische Schia und die islamische Einheit 1979–1996* (Hamburg: Deutsches Orient-Institute, 1997) pp. 102–4.

13. On Brest-Litovsk, Isaac Deutscher, *The Prophet Armed* (Oxford: Oxford University Press, 1954) p. 374; on Castro's criticisms, made after reading Deutscher's biography, K. S. Karol, *The Guerrillas in Power* (New York: Hill & Wang, 1970) p. 383.

14. Quoted in R. K. Ramazani, *Revolutionary Iran: Challenge and Response in the Middle East*, second edition (London: Johns Hopkins University Press, 1988) p. 25.

15. Sorel, *L'Europe et la Révolution française*; Godechot, *La Grande Nation*.

16. Quoted in Kosseleck, 'Historical Criteria of the Modern Concept of Revolution', p. 49.

17. Vol. 2 *La chute de la royauté*, 1889, p. 109.

18. Alexis de Tocqueville, *On the State of Society in France Before the Revolution of 1789*, translated by Henry Reeve (London, 1856) pp. 17–23, quoted in Krishan Kumar, *Revolution – the Theory and Practice of a European Idea* (London: Weidenfeld & Nicholson) p. 113.

19. Text of decree in Jacques Godechot, *La Pensée Révolutionnaire* (Paris: Armand Colin, 1964) pp. 120–1.

20. George Rudé, *Revolutionary Europe 1783–1815* (London: Fontana, 1964) p. 208.

21. Palmer, *The Age of the Democratic Revolution*, vol. 2, pp. 50ff.

22. Marcel Merle, *Pacifisme et Internationalisme XVIIe–XXe siècles* (Paris: Armand Colin, 1966) p. 154.

23. Merle, pp. 154–5.

24. Merle, pp. 155–6.

25. Rudé, p. 222. Godechot, *La Grande Nation*.

26. Leon Trotsky, *History of the Russian Revolution* (London: Sphere Books, 1967) vol. 3, pp. 303–4. See also the account of John Reed in *Ten Days That Shook the World* (Harmondsworth: Penguin, 1977) pp. 129–34.

27. John Reed, *Ten Days That Shook the World*, p. 142.

28. A. Neuberg, *Armed Insurrection* (London: NLB, 1970), esp. chapter 2, 'Bolshevism and Insurrection'.

29. Alexander Orlov, *Handbook of Intelligence and Guerrilla Warfare* (Ann Arbor: University of Michigan Press, 1963), chapter 15, 'Guerrilla Warfare'.

30. Fred Halliday, 'Revolution in Iran: Was It Possible in 1921?', *Khamsin* (London: Ithaca Press) no. 7 (1980); Pezhmann Dailami, 'The Bolshevik Revolution and the Genesis of Communism in Iran, 1917–1920', *Central Asia Survey*, vol. 11, no. 3 (1992).

31. Victor Serge, *Memoirs of a Revolutionary 1901–1941* (London: OUP, 1963) p. 256.

32. 'Political Report of the Central Committee RKP(b) to the Ninth All-Russian Conference of the Communist Party', 20 September 1920, in Richard Pipes (ed.), *The Unknown Lenin*, pp. 97–8.

33. Orlando Figes, *A People's Tragedy* (London: Jonathan Cape, 1996) pp. 698–703; 'Introduction to Tukhachevsky', *New Left Review*, 55 (May-June 1969).

34. *The Prophet Armed*, pp. 471–3.

35. *The Prophet Armed*, p. 471.

36. Mikhail Tukhachevsky, 'Revolution from Without', *New Left Review*, no. 55 (May-June 1969) p. 92.

37. The point about Comintern activism and official Soviet support for it, is most frequently made by critics on the right. During the Cold War this often took the form of selective quotations from Soviet leaders about their global plans, while later they were to draw on released Soviet archives proving their point.

38. For the largest such unacknowledged operation see Jon Halliday, 'Air Operations in Korea: The Soviet Side of the Story', in William J. Williams (ed.), *A Revolutionary War: Korea and the Transformation of the Postwar World* (Chicago: Imprint Publications, 1993).

39. Fred Halliday 'From "Second Mongolia" to "Bleeding Wound"': Soviet Decision-Making and the Afghan War', *Review of International Studies*, forthcoming 1999.

40. 'A Basic Summing-up of Experience Gained in the Victory of the Chinese People's Revolution', *Red Flag*, no. 20–21 (1960), released by New China News Agency, 2 November 1960, quoted in *The Sino-Soviet Dispute* documented and analyses by G. F. Hudson and others (*The China Quarterly*, 1961) p. 167.

41. Chinese government statement of 26 October denouncing the Algerian handling of the summit, *Peking Review*, no. 44 (29 October 1965); on Egyptian policy, author's conversation with Nuri Abd al-Razzaq, general-secretary AAPSO, Cairo, April 1996.

42. Heinrich Bechtoldt speculates on the Chinese plans for a new international organisation, a 'Fifth International', in the period 1963–5: but this came to nothing (*Chinas Revolutionsstrategie mit der dritten welt gegen Russland und Amerika*, Munich: Deutscher Taschenbuch Verlag, 1969, pp. 111–13).

43. Paolo Spriano, *Stalin and the European Communists*, p. 293.

44. How far the Cultural Revolution was a *result* of external setbacks and threats and designed in part to limit their impact on China, and how much it was a *cause*, remains an open question. Some scholars see the Cultural Revolution as having purely internal causes, above all in the factional disputes between Mao and his fellow leaders. Others see it as a response to the break with Moscow and the fear of a pro-Soviet, revisionist or 'capitalist roader' opposition developing in the country. Westad sees the cultural revolution as a response both to the Sino-Soviet dispute *and* to Mao's increased fears of the US threat, following from the escalation in Vietnam (Odd Arne Westad and others, *Conversations between Chinese and foreign leaders on the wars in Indochina, 1964–1977*, Washington, Woodrow Wilson Center 1998).

45. Jaap van Ginneken, p. 115. Chen Yi gave sobering advice, warning against leftist and provocative slogans, to a visiting delegation of revolutionaries from the newly established People's Democratic Republic of Yemen (Hashim Behbehani, *China and the People's Democratic Republic of Yemen. A Report*, London: KPI, 1985). One of those best acquainted with Chinese thinking at the time was the Australian journalist Wilfred Burchett. In 1977 I asked him how many people in China, out of a population of a billion, were informed about the outside world. 'Twenty, perhaps fifteen', he replied.

46. Bechtoldt, p. 180.

47. *Peking Review* no. 7 (14 February 1964) p. 6; Bechtoldt, p. 178. The words attributed to Chou at the time, that Africa was 'ripe for revolution', were later denied by official Chinese sources.

48. Information from Orlando Letelier, Chilean minister of defence at the time of the coup.

49. Gabriel García Marquez, in his *One Hundred Years of Solitude* (Harmondworth: Penguin, 1970) pp. 138–9, tells of Colonel Aurelio Buendía who leaves his own country to fight for the unification of Central America and the elimination of conservative regimes from Alaska to Patagonia.

50. 'The Duty of a Revolutionary is to Make the Revolution: the Second Declaration of Havana', in *Fidel Castro Speaks*, ed. M. Kenner and J. Petras (Harmondsworth: Pelican, 1972) pp. 164–5. For the background, see Andrés Suárez, *Cuba: Castroism and Communism, 1959–1966* (London: MIT Press, 1967) pp. 143–6.

51. Gerassi, *Towards Revolution*, vol. 2, p. 743. The conference set up an Executive Committee with 12 representatives, 4 from each of the three continents. *Primera Conferencia de Solidaridad de los Pueblos de Africa, Asia y America Latina* (Havana: OSPAAAL, 1966).

52. K. S. Karol, *Guerrillas in Power* (New York: Hill & Wang, 1970) p. 364.

53. Suárez, p. 234, citing *Cuba Socialista*, February 1966.

54. 'The Tricontinental: A War to the Finish', in Gerassi, *Towards Revolution*, vol. 2, pp. 755–6.

55. Karol, *Guerrillas in Power*, pp. 364–74.

56. Author's observation, Havana, 1968.

57. In the following I have based myself on the excellent discussion in Jorge Castañeda, *Utopia Unarmed* (New York: Vintage Books, 1994) pp. 51–67. See also the obituary by Richard Gott, 'Manual Piñeiro: Hero of the Revolution', *The Guardian*, 14 March 1998.

58. On the Cuban role in Nicaragua, see Castañeda, *Utopia Unarmed*, pp. 59–60.

59. 'Benigno' (pseudonym of Dariel Alarcón Ramírez), *Vie et Mort de la Révolution Cubaine* (Paris: Fayard, 1996) p. 122.

60. On Operation Carlota, see Gabriel Garcia Márquez, 'Operation Carlota', *New Left Review*, 101/102 (January/April 1977).

61. On the Somali invasion, see Fred Halliday and Maxine Molyneux, *The Ethiopian Revolution*.

62. For general analyses, see Jorge Dominguez, *To Make the World Safe for Revolution*; Susan Eckstein, *Back from the Future: Cuba Under Castro* (Princeton: Princeton University Press, 1996), chapter 7 'Internationalism'; Jorge Castañeda, *Utopia Unarmed*, chapter 3, 'The Cuban Crucible'.

63. Nicaragua, for its part, sustained its own internationalist commitments, to the guerrilla movements in Guatemala and El Salvador. This was, more than in other cases, balanced by an attempt to maintain dialogue with other American and European bodies. For this latter dimension see Hazel Smith, 'The Conservative Approach: Sandinista Nicaragua's Foreign Policy', in Stephen Chan and Andrew Williams (eds), *Renegade States* (Manchester: Manchester University Press, 1994).

64. Castañeda, *Utopia Unarmed*.

65. Kabila's victory owed not a little to the intervention of other forces, themselves revolutionary states that had been undermined by Mobuto in previous years – Uganda and Angola.

66. Ramazani, *Revolutionary Iran*; Buchta, *Die iranische Schia*; Fred Halliday, 'Iranian Foreign Policy Since 1979: Internationalism and Nationalism in the Islamic Revolution', in Cole and Keddie (eds) *Shi'ism and Social Protest*.

67. *BBC Summary of World Broadcasts* Part 4, The Middle East and North Africa, ME/6175/A/7, 24 July 1979.

68. *BBC Summary of World Broadcasts*, ME/6280/A/7, 24 November 1979.

69. *Constitution of the Islamic Republic of Iran*, *The Middle East Journal*, vol. 34, no. 2 (spring 1980) pp. 184–204.

70. *BBC Summary of World Broadcasts*, Part 4, The Middle East and North Africa, ME/6871/A/1, 4 November 1981.

71. *BBC Summary of World Broadcasts*, 2 November 1984, ME/7790/A/4.

72. *BBC Summary of World Broadcasts*, Part 4, The Middle East and North Africa, ME/7930/A/4, 20 April 1985.

73. *BBC Summary of World Broadcasts*, Part 4, 'The Middle East and North Africa', ME/6145/A/7, 19 June 1979.

74. Anoushiravan Ehteshami, *After Khomeini, The Iranian Second Republic* (London: Routledge, 1995) p. 32; Buchta, *Die iranische Schia*,

pp. 118ff. Hashemi was apparently arrested in part for opposition to the secret negotiations with the USA, known as 'Irangate'.

5 The Antinomies of Revolutionary Foreign Policy

1. On Russian accommodation Teddy Uldricks, 'Russia and Europe: Diplomacy, Revolution, and Economic Development in the 1920s', *International History Review*, January 1979.
2. Aléxis de Tocqueville, *L'ancien régime et la Révolution* (Paris: Gallimard, 1967); Albert Sorel, *L'Europe et la Révolution française* (Paris: Le Plon, 1885–1902) 8 vols, and discussion in Pieter Geyl, *Napoleon: For and Against* (Harmondsworth: Peregrine, 1965) part 5.
3. Arthur Schlesinger, 'Four Days with Fidel: A Havana Diary', *New York Review of Books*, 26 March 1992, p. 24.
4. Skocpol, *States and Social Revolutions*.
5. Régis Debray, *Revolution in the Revolution?*
6. Fidel Castro was later to argue that the Alliance had achieved much for the peoples of Latin America.
7. Michel Löwy, *The Politics of Combined and Uneven Development. The Theory of Permanent Revolution* (London: Verso, 1981); Justin Rosenberg, 'Isaac Deutscher and the Lost History of International Relations', *New Left Review*, no. 215 (January-February 1996).
8. David Armstrong, *Revolution and World Order* (Oxford: OUP, 1993). See also Fred Northedge, *The International Political System* (London: Faber & Faber, 1976) pp. 28–30.
9. Andrew Scott, *The Revolution in Statecraft. Informal Penetration* (New York: Random House, 1965).
10. Eckstein, *Back from the Future*, chapter 7, 'Internationalism', pp. 197–200.
11. On Algerian internationalism, Claude Daffarge, 'Alger, capitale des révolutionnaires en exile', *Le monde diplomatique*, August 1972.
12. Ryszard Kapuściński, *The Soccer War* (London: Penguin, 1990) p. 110.
13. Vladimir Razuvayev, 'Can Moscow Afford Being the Third Rome? or Why the Soviet Union Has No National Interests', *New Times*, no. 32 (1990) p. 16.
14. Bailey Stone, *The Genesis of the French Revolution*, pp. 60–1.
15. Jacques Godechot, *La Grande Nation*, second edition (Paris: Aubier Montaigne, 1983) pp. 16–17.
16. Richard Pipes, *Russia Under the Old Regime* (Harmondsworth: Penguin, 1974) p. 223. I am grateful to Dr Monica Herz for this reference.
17. François Furet and Denis Richet, *La Révolution française* (Paris: Hachette, 1973) pp. 429–31.
18. Albert Sorel, *L'Europe et la Révolution française*, part 1, pp. 541–2, quoted in Isaac Deutscher, *Marxism, Wars and Revolutions* (London: Verso, 1984) pp. 40–1. Oswald Spengler believed that the ideas imposed on Europe by France were really *British* ones, but that does not entirely invalidate Sorel's point.

19. Raymond Aron, *Peace and War* (London: Weidenfeld & Nicolson, 1966) pp. 373–81). I have gone into greater detail on this in *Rethinking International Relations*, chapter 5 'International Society as Homogeneity', and chapter 8, 'Inter-Systemic Conflict: The Case of Cold War'.
20. Theodore Hamerow, *From the Finland Station. The Graying of Revolution in the Twentieth Century*, gives one, impressionistic, account of this evolution.
21. On the demise of Soviet communism, see *Rethinking International Relations* chapter 9, 'A Singular Collapse: the Soviet Union and Inter-State Competition'.
22. *The Works and Correspondence of Edmund Burke*, vol. 5, p. 307.
23. Quoted in R. R. Palmer, *The Age of the Democratic Revolution*, vol. 2, p. 62.
24. *The Works and Correspondence of Edmund Burke*, vol. 5, pp. 320–1.
25. 'The Sources of Soviet Conduct', reprinted in George Kennan, *American Diplomacy 1900–1950* (Chicago: University of Chicago Press, 1951) pp. 103–4. The original 'Long Telegram' is in John Lewis Gaddis and Thomas Etzold (eds), *Containment: Documents on American Policy and Strategy* (New York: Columbia University Press, 1978) pp. 49–63.
26. Ibid, p. 105.
27. On Kennan, see Michael Cox, 'Requiem for a Cold War Critic: the Rise and Fall of George F. Kennan, 1946–1950', *Irish Slavonic Studies*, 11 (1991), and my interview with Kennan in *From Yalta to Potsdam: Conversations with Cold Warriors* (London: BBC Publications, 1995).

6 The International as Cause

1. On the historical character of interaction between states, see *Rethinking International Relations*, chapter 1. The term 'transnational' came into common currency in the 1970s to denote those activities – such as trade, movement of peoples, intellectual and cultural exchange – that took place across frontiers but were not 'international' in the sense of controlled by states.
2. Michael Mann, *States, War and Capitalism* (Oxford: Basil Blackwell, 1988); Felix Gilbert (ed.), *The Historical Essays of Otto Hintze* (New York: Oxford University Press, 1975).
3. Skocpol, *States and Social Revolutions*; Goldfrank, 'Theories of Revolution and Revolutions without Theory'.
4. Jack Goldstone, 'Theories of Revolution: the Third Generation', *World Politics*, April 1980; Anthony Giddens, *Sociology*, chapter 19, 'Revolutions and Social Movements'.
5. George Pettee, *The Process of Revolution* (New York: Harper & Brothers, 1938); Crane Brinton, *The Anatomy of Revolution*, second edition (New York: Anchor Books, 1965).
6. Brinton, *Anatomy*, p. 92.

7. Jack Davis, 'Political Violence in Latin America', International Institute for Strategic Studies, *Adelphi Papers* no. 85 (February 1972) p. 18, talks of how states seek to 'artificially inseminate' revolution in other states.

8. James Davies, 'Towards a Theory of Revolution', *American Sociological Review*, vol. 27, no. 1 (February 1962).

9. Herein lies the weakness of orthodox functionalist and systemic analysis, be it in the work of sociologists like Talcott Parsons or political scientists like David Easton and Harold Lasswell. The very stability of such societies and polities is both maintained by forms of coercion and reliant upon forms of international reinforcement.

10. Chalmers Johnson, *Revolutionary Change*, second edition (Harlow, Essex: Longman, 1982) p. 72.

11. S. N. Eisenstadt, *Revolution and the Transformation of Societies* (London: Collier-Macmillan, 1978).

12. For further discussion of this sociological approach, see Michael Kimmel *Revolution: A Sociological Interpretation* (Cambridge: Polity Press, 1990).

13. Jeffrey M. Paige, *Agrarian Revolution: Social Movements and Export Agriculture in the Underdeveloped World* (New York: Free Press, 1975).

14. Eric Wolf, *Peasant Wars of the Twentieth Century* (London: Faber & Faber, 1971); Eric Hobsbawm, *Primitive Rebels* (Manchester: Manchester University Press, 1963). While the emphasis of Paige's work is on social movements arising from newly created economic situations, Wolf emphasises the revolt of those relatively excluded by modernisation and then subjected to state interventions. Hobsbawm writes (p. 3): 'The men and women with whom this book is concerned differ from Englishmen in that they have not been born into the world of capitalism as a Tyneside engineer, with four generations of trade unionism at his back, has been born into it. They come into it as first-generation immigrants, or what is even more catastrophic, it comes to them from outside, insidiously by the operation of economic forces which they do not understand and over which they have no control, or brazenly by conquest, revolutions and fundamental changes of law whose consequences they may not understand, even when they have helped to bring them about.'

15. Jack Goldstone, *Revolution and Rebellion in the Early Modern World*. The question of how far demographic change can, or cannot, be considered an international or transnational factor is itself an interesting one: in some ways – changes in climate, agricultural technique, medical knowledge – these are transnational factors, and it would be hard to see a set of contemporaneous and parallel changes as reflecting separate endogenous processes. But the degree and mechanisms of such a transnationalism remain to be specified – see John Foran, 'Revolutionizing Theory/Theorizing Revolutions', in Nikki Keddie (ed.), *Debating Revolutions* (London: New York University Press, 1995) p. 120.

16. Ellen Trimberger, *Revolution from Above*. For critical discussion, see Ralph Miliband, 'State Power and Class Interests', *New Left Review*,

138 (March/April 1983); Jack Goldstone, 'Theories of Revolution'; Fred Halliday and Maxine Molyneux, *The Ethiopian Revolution*, chapter 1; Simon Bromley, *Rethinking Middle East Politics* (Cambridge: Polity, 1994) pp. 161–2.

17. On these revolutions from above, and the particular ideology associated with them, see Halliday and Molyneux, *The Ethiopian Revolution*. The case of Afghanistan, often represented as just a result of an external, Soviet, intervention, also contains a vivid and cruel case of a small, impatient, modernising elite forcing abstractly conceived of 'reforms' on the society: see Raja Anwar, *The Tragedy of Afghanistan* (London: Verso, 1988); Fred Halliday and Zahir Tanin, 'The Communist Regime in Afghanistan, 1978–1992: Institutions and Conflicts', *Europe-Asia Studies*, vol. 50, no. 8 (1998); Barnett Rubin, *The Fragmentation of Afghanistan: State Formation and Collapse in the International System* (London: Yale University Press, 1995).

18. Thus in the Parsonian theory societies are *self-regulating* systems, within which external factors act as something outside, and disruptive of, the society's equilibrium. The conception being advanced here is that in addition to the contentious equilibrium assumptions contained within it, this theory is mistaken in seeing the regulation as being constituted from within the society alone.

19. I was told by the former country analyst in the CIA for Iran, Jesse Leaf, that he *had* in 1977–8 predicted major upheaval in Iran: he had never been there and had never met an Iranian, but he had read de Tocqueville. His report was rejected, his promotion blocked, and he resigned.

20. I am grateful to Philip Windsor for this information.

21. *Recollections*, p. 68, quoted in Kumar, *Revolution*, p. 174.

22. *States and Social Revolutions*, pp. 14–18.

23. '"Left-Wing" Communism – An Infantile Disorder', in V. I. Lenin, *Selected Works*, vol. 3 (Moscow: Progress Publishers, 1971) p. 401.

24. Skocpol *States and Social Revolutions*, pp. 51–67.

25. Bailey Stone, *The Genesis of the French Revolution*, p. 2.

26. David MacLaren McDonald, *United Government and Foreign Policy in Russia, 1900–1914* (London: Harvard University Press, 1992) p. 10.

27. On the case for the importance of nationalist factors in the communist success, see Chalmers Johnson, *Peasant Nationalism and Communist Power, The Emergence of Revolutionary China 1937–1945* (London: Oxford University Press, 1962); for the argument on the social programme see Elinor Lerner, 'The Chinese Peasantry and Imperialism: A Critique of Chalmers Johnson's Peasant Nationalism and Communist Power', *Bulletin of Concerned Asian Scholars*, vol. VI, no. 2 (April–August 1974). This argument does not, however, address the issue of how far the communists, behind nationalist rhetoric, sought to use the Japanese in order to weaken the KMT.

28. In the same year, the regime of the colonels in Greece fell, in the wake of their disastrous handling of the situation in Cyprus: after provoking a coup by right-wing Greek Cypriot soldiers, the junta in Athens were unable to act when, some days later, Turkey invaded and

occupied part of the island. In 1982, a similar fate was to befall the military regime in Argentina: after invading the Malvinas islands, the regime was defeated in a British counter-attack and was forced to hand over to a civilian government.

29. This withdrawal of US support is seen in one cogent comparative study as one of the *five necessary conditions* for the success of guerrillas in Cuba and Nicaragua, as compared with other states: Timothy Wickham-Crowley, *Guerrillas and Revolution in Latin America* (Princeton: Princeton University Press, 1992), especially table 11-3, p. 300 and chapter 12, 'Winners, Losers, and Also-Rans: Toward an Integration of Revolutionary Theories'. Wickham-Crowley (pp. 315–6), for both liberal and structuralist reasons, is drawn towards downplaying the role of Cuban military support in the success of the Nicaraguan revolution.

30. Mohammad Reza Pahlavi, *The Shah's Story* (London: Michael Joseph, 1980) chapter 29.

31. R. B. Merriman, *Six Contemporaneous Revolutions* (Hamden, CT: Archon Books); Eric Hobsbawm, 'The Crisis of the Seventeenth Century', *Past and Present*, 5 and 6 (1954); Geoffrey Parker and Lesley Smith, (eds), *The General Crisis of the Seventeenth Century* (London: Routledge & Kegan Paul, 1978).

32. Parker and Smith, *The General Crisis*, p. 6. They are, however, sceptical, pp. 19–21, of accounts that seek to unify disparate events or postulate unwarranted solidarities.

33. Although not in the main the result of revolutions, the ending of European colonialism after the Second World War was another case of such a conjunctural crises – a system hitherto maintained by a set of competing but reinforcing states proved unsustainable and disappeared within the space of two or three decades.

34. Fred Halliday, *The Making of the Second Cold War* (London: Verso, 1983), chapter 4, 'A New Period of Third World Revolutions'.

35. George Rudé, *Revolutionary Europe*, p. 74.

36. Quoted in Herbert Aptheker, 'Power in America', in Hoyt Bollard and William Domhoff (eds), *C. Wright Mills and the 'Power Elite'* (Boston, MA: Beacon Press, 1968) p. 157.

37. Mao in Edgar Snow, *The Long Revolution* (1972) p. 217, quoted in Chalmers Johnson, *Autopsy on People's War* (Berkeley: University of California Press, 1973) p. 33.

38. *On the State of Society in France before the Revolution of 1789* (1856), quoted in Kumar, *Revolution*, p. 207.

39. Arendt, *On Revolution*, pp. 24–5.

40. Parker and Smith, *The General Crisis*, p. 20.

41. Edward Thompson, *The Making of the English Working Class* (Harmondsworth: Penguin, 1974) p. 911.

42. Nelson Mandela, *Long Road to Freedom* (London: Little, Brown, 1994) chapters 4, 6–8.

43. Palmer, 'The World Revolution of the West', p. 10.

44. A third candidate for such discussion of insulated revolutions would be Mexico in 1910. Alan Knight has argued that interstate competi-

tion of the kind analysed by Skocpol was not present and indeed that any general theory is suspect in regard to Latin American revolutions ('Social Revolution: a Latin American Perspective'). Yet, it can be argued, the determining external factors were two: the pattern of incorporation of Mexico into the global economy as a semi-peripheral state; and the influence on the Mexican social system of ideas of liberalism and reform. See Walter Goldfrank, 'Theories of Revolution and Revolution Without Theory: The Case of Mexico'.

45. Lawrence Stone, *The Causes of the English Revolution 1529–1642* (London: Routledge, Ark Paperbacks, 1986) pp. 76–9.
46. Robin Clifton, 'Fear of Popery', in Conrad Russell (ed.), *The Origins of the English Civil War* (London: Macmillan, 1973).
47. Conrad Russell, *The Causes of the English Civil War* (Oxford: Clarendon Press, 1990), chapter 2, 'The Problem of Multiple Kingdoms c. 1580–1630'; Norman Davies, *Europe: A History*, pp. 545–53.
48. J. H. Elliott, 'England and Europe: A Common Malady?', in Russell (ed.), *The Origins of the English Civil War*.
49. For one exceptionally lucid exposition of this, see Christopher Hill, 'The English Revolution and the Brotherhood of Man'.
50. Stone, *Causes*, pp. 88–90.
51. Ibid, p. 106.
52. During a visit to Baghdad in April 1980, i.e. a few months prior to the outbreak of war between Iraq and Iran, I asked some people in the bazaar what they thought of the Iranian revolution. 'What are they shouting about?', one man said. 'We were Shi'ites before they were Shi'ites. We had a revolution before they did.'
53. Theda Skocpol, 'Rentier Stone and Shia Islam in the Iranian Revolution', in Theda Skocpol, *Social Revolutions in the Modern World* (Cambridge: Cambridge University Press, 1994) chapter 10.
54. Fred Halliday, *Iran: Dictatorship and Development* (Harmondsworth: Penguin, 1978) and *Islam and the Myth of Confrontation*, chapter 3,'The Iranian Revolution in Comparative Perspective'.
55. Ervand Abrahamian, *Khomeinism* (London: I. B. Tauris, 1993).
56. The Shah himself subscribed to this view: Mohammad Reza Pahlavi, *The Shah's Story*, chapter 29. He even quotes, with apparent agreement, the remark by General Rabii, the former commander of the air force, to the effect that the American envoy General Huyser threw the Shah out 'like a dead mouse'.

7 Revolutions and International History

1. Hedley Bull, *The Anarchical Society: A Study of Order in World Politics* (London: Macmillan, 1977).
2. Martin Wright, *Power Politics* (London: Penguin, 1966) p. 92.
3. Voltaire *Essai sur les Moeurs*, quoted in Parker and Smith, *The General Crisis of the Seventeenth Century*, p. 3.
4. Jack Goldstone, *Revolution and Rebellion in the Early Modern World*.

5. R. Palmer, 'The World Revolution of the West, 1763–1801', *Political Science Quarterly*, March 1954; R. Palmer, *The Age of the Democratic Revolution*, 2 vols (Princeton: Princeton University Press, 1959 and 1964); *New Cambridge Modern History*, vol. viii, *The American and French Revolutions 1763–93* (Cambridge: CUP, 1986), chapter 1, 'Introductory Survey', chapter 24, 'Reform and Revolution in France: October 1789–February 1793'; Jacques Godechot, *La Grande Nation*, second edition, chapter 1, 'La révolution de l'Occident, Révolution "française", ou Révolution occidentale' (Paris: Aubier Montaigne, 1983). Palmer ends his period in 1801, with the triumph of Napoleon: I extend it to 1815, since despite the imperial political character of Napoleonic rule, the impact of the French revolution, in ideas and the form of direct military confrontation, was to continue until the final defeat at Waterloo.
6. Norman Davies, *Europe*, pp. 690–3.
7. I am grateful to Ekkehardt Krippendorff for this observation.
8. Eric Hobsbawm, *Echoes of the Marseillaise*, p. 4, pp. 111–12; Geoffrey Best (ed.), *The Permanent Revolution: The French Revolution and its Legacy 1789–1988* (London: Fontana, 1988). Contrast the observation of my colleague Dr David Starkey at lunch one day, after I had told him, in response to his enquiry, that I was about to give a lecture on the French revolution: 'My dear boy, don't you know there wasn't one?'
9. Norman Davies, *Europe*, p. 805.
10. Eric Hobsbawm, *The Age of Empire 1875–1914* (London: Weidenfeld & Nicolson, 1987), chapter 12, 'Towards Revolution'.
11. Arno Mayer, *Politics and Diplomacy of Peace-making*.
12. This was to be used for apologetic purposes by later German nationalist writers: the misuse of the argument does not, however, obliterate the historical connection.
13. But not entirely. Revolutions since the end of the Cold War have shown just how far Soviet forces were involved in Third World conflicts.
14. Halliday, *The Making of the Second Cold War*, chapter 3, 'The Decline of US Military Superiority'.
15. Gabriel Kolko, *Anatomy of a War* (New York: Pantheon Books, 1985); Andrew Mack, 'Why Big Nations Lose Small Wars: The Politics of Asymmetric Conflict', *World Politics*, vol. 27, no. 2 (January 1975); Henry Kissinger, *Diplomacy* (London: Simon & Schuster, 1994) pp. 694–704.
16. Raymond Garthoff, *Reflections on the Cuban Missile Crisis* (Washington: Brookings Institution, 1987); Philip Brenner, 'Cuba and the Missile Crisis', *Journal of Latin American Studies*, vol. 22 (February 1990); James Nathan (ed.), *The Cuban Missile Crisis Revisited* (New York: St Martin's Press, 1992); Arthur Schlesinger, 'Four Days with Fidel: A Havana Diary', *New York Review of Books*, 26 March 1992; John Lewis Gaddis, *We Now Know: Rethinking Cold War History* (Oxford: Clarendon Press, 1997) chapter 9, 'The Cuban Missile

Crisis'. Earlier accounts by European observers include Karol, *Guerrillas in Power*, chapter 3; and Saverio Tutino, *L'ottobre cubano, lineamenti di una storia della rivoluzione castriasta* (Turin: Einaudi, 1968) chapter 7.

17. Anatoli Gribkov and William Smith, *Operation ANADYR. U.S. and Soviet Generals Recount the Cuban Missile Crisis* (Chicago: edition q, 1994) pp. 166–8, text of draft Soviet–Cuban treaty 'On military cooperation for the defense of the national territory of Cuba in case of aggression', pp. 185–8.
18. Kennedy to Secretary of State Rusk, quoted in Hershberg, p. 243.
19. Max Holland, 'Cuba, Kennedy and the Cold War', *The Nation*, 29 November 1993; William Breuer, *Vendetta! Fidel Castro and the Kennedy Brothers* (New York: Wiley & Sons, 1998).
20. Many US officials involved in the decision-making at that time, including former Secretary of Defense Robert McNamara, have denied that there was any plan to invade *before* October 1962. As ever, intention and contingency planning have to be separated. The evidence of what would have appeared to the Cubans not only as an invasion plan but of a real preparation, short of decision, is strong. On this, see in particular James Hershberg, 'Before "The Missiles of October"': Did Kennedy Plan a Military Strike Against Cuba?', in James Nathan (ed.), *The Cuban Missile Crisis Revisited*; Brenner, 'Cuba and the Missile Crisis'; Pierre Salinger, 'Kennedy and Cuba: The Pressure to Invade Was Fierce', *International Herald Tribune*, 6 February 1989. Part of Salinger's argument covers the period of the crisis itself, when there certainly was such an intention to invade, if the USSR had not withdrawn its missiles.
21. I am grateful to Domingo Amuchastegui, formerly a Cuban intelligence officer, for his insights into the divergence between the Cuban leadership and the intelligence services on this issue.
22. Information from Domingo Amuchastegui.
23. There was a third consideration which, while subordinate to the other two, also affected the formation of policy by the Soviet and Cuban leaderships. This was the concern of both Khrushchev and Castro to quell challenges from within their own ranks, in the former's case from a Soviet military anxious about Khrushchev's reduction in military expenditure, in the latter's from a pro-Soviet faction he had clashed with in March 1962. The stationing of missiles enabled the Soviet leader to appear as the patron of a major military initiative, and Castro to present himself as the closest ally of the USSR.
24. On the no invasion pledge, Garthoff, *Reflections*, pp. 52–5, 80–3.
25. See Chapter 4, pp. 116–124 above.
26. Gaddis, *We Now Know*, pp. 278–9. For Cuban criticisms of the Soviet withdrawal, Brenner, pp. 134–5; Castro interview, *Le Monde*, 22 December 1993; and Hugh Thomas, *Cuba or the Pursuit of Freedom* (London: Eyre & Spottiswoode, 1971) pp. 1414–15, quoting a disparaging Cuban song about Khrushchev, 'Nikita, Nikita! Lo que se da, No se quita', ('Nikita, Nikita!, What you give away, You shouldn't take

back'). A hitherto unpublished 12–hour denunciation by Castro of the Russians was published in 1997 (*The Guardian*, 15 August 1997).

27. This was true even in the state where conventional argument held that the confrontation with the USSR had inhibited domestic liberalisation, namely the USA. While the McCarthyism of the early 1950s did indeed reduce political freedom, the 1960s saw a massive increase in rights for millions of previously disenfranchised blacks.

28. W. W. Rostow, *The Stages of Economic Growth: A Non-Communist Manifesto* (Cambridge: Cambridge University Press, 1962).

29. One hegemonic state that may appear to have escaped such a costly involvement was Britain, which never faced a test such as those of Algeria to France or Vietnam to the USA. There are, however, analogies, albeit on a smaller scale, in the relation of Britain to Ireland, the latter constituting the topic which, from the 1880s until the First World War was to dominate and significantly divide British politics.

30. Justin Rosenberg, *The Empire of Civil Society* (London: Verso, 1994).

8 Counter-Revolution

1.   Quoted in A. J. P. Taylor, *Revolutions and Revolutionaries* (London: Hamish Hamilton, 1980) p. 141.

2.   There is little general literature on this subject: one exception is Arno Mayer, *Dynamics of Counterrevolution in Europe, 1870–1956: An Analytic Framework* (London: Harper Torchbooks, 1971). The subject has to be constructed largely on the basis of historical cases studies, and international relations literature on intervention.

3.   William Doyle, *The Oxford History of the French Revolution* (Oxford: Oxford University Press, 1989) chapter 13, 'Counter-Revolution 1789–1795'; Jacques Godechot, *La Contre-Révolution: Doctrine et Action 1789–1804* (Paris: PUF, 1961).

4.   Henry Kissinger *A World Restored: Europe After Napoleon* (Gloucester, Mass.: Peter Smith, 1973).

5.   Trotsky, who at first resisted the application of this analogy to the Russian case, came round to doing so in 1935 and, later, in *The Revolution Betrayed*. Yet, for all its appeal, it raised more problems than it resolved. Isaac Deutscher, *The Prophet Outcast*, pp. 53–5, 313–18.

6.   Al McCoy, 'Land Reform as Counter-Revolution', *Bulletin of Concerned Asian Scholars*, vol. 3, no. 1 (Winter–Spring, 1971).

7.   Hedley Bull (ed.), *Intervention in International Politics* (Oxford: Clarendon Press, 1984).

8.   William Doyle, *The Oxford History of the French Revolution*, pp. 308–13.

9.   Kissinger, *A World Restored*, pp. 185–6.

10. F. H. Hinsley, *Power and the Pursuit of Peace* (Cambridge: Cambridge University Press, 1963).

11. Clemens von Metternich, 'A Confession of Faith', in Peter Viereck (ed.), *Conservatism* (London: Van Nostrand, 1956) pp. 135–6.

12. Trotsky, *The Revolution Betrayed* (London: New Park, 1967) p. 189.

13. For analyses of Nazi ideology see Arno Mayer, *Why did the Heavens Not Darken?*. *The 'Final Solution', in History* (London: Verso, 1990) chapter 4 'The Syncretism of *Mein Kampf*'; Enzo Collotti, *La Germania Nazista. Dalla repubblica de Weimar al crollo del Reich hitleriano* (Turun: Einaudi, 1962) chapter 1, 'Premesse storico ideologiche'.

14. Ian Kershaw, *The Hitler Myth. Image and Reality in the Third Reich* (Oxford: OUP, 1987) p. 230.

15. Kershaw, *The Hitler Myth*, pp. 81, 174.

16. On the counter-revolutionary crisis of Germany in the 1920s see Arno Mayer, 'Internal Crisis and War Since 1870', in Charles Bertrand (ed.), *Revolutionary Situations in Europe, 1917–1922* (Montreal: ICES, 1977); Gabriel Kolko, *Century of War, Politics, Conflicts, and Society since 1914* (New York: New Press, 1994).

17. Robert Gates, *From the Shadows* (New York: Simon & Schuster, 1996); James Scott, *Deciding to Intervenue: The Reagan Doctrine and American Foreign Policy* (London: Duke University Press, 1996).

18. The main thrust was one of incorporation into Western Europe, a process assisted by abandonment of the outdated commitment to the African colonies.

19. On Afghanistan, it has been argued that the Soviet commitment there did bring down the Soviet system, but the arguments for this are overstated. Had there not been a shift in Moscow for other reasons the Afghan policy could, and would, have been maintained. See Fred Halliday, 'From "Second Mongolia" to "Bleeding Wound": Soviet Decision-Making on Afghanistan'.

20. Fred Northedge, *Britain and Soviet Communism. The Impact of a Revolution* (London: Macmillan, 1982) p. 29.

21. Michael Brown, 'Vietnam, Learning from the Debate', *Military Review*, February 1987.

22. Robert Gates, *From the Shadows*, chapter 16, 'Central America, 1983–1984: Our Own Worst Enemy'. For an account at the time, Hedrick Smith, 'U.S. Policy on Nicaragua: A Tale of Confusion', *International Herald Tribune*, 12 April 1984.

23. Fred Halliday, 'From "Second Mongolia" to "Bleeding Wound"'.

24. Andrew Mack, 'Why Big Nations Lose Small Wars: The Politics of Asymmetric Conflict'.

25. Mayer, 'Internal Crisis and War Since 1870'.

26. George Kennan in Fred Halliday, *From Potsdam to Perestroika: Conversations with Cold Warriors*; Hans Morgenthau, *Politics in the Twentieth Century* (London: University of Chicago Press, 1962).

27. Burke ascribed a third principle to the French revolution, 'cannibalism': but this was stretching it a bit.

28. Eisenhower speech at a press conference, 7 April 1954, in *Public Papers of Presidents 1954* (1960) p. 383, quoted in *The Oxford Dictionary of Quotations*, fourth edition (Oxford: OUP, 1992) p. 268.

9 War and Revolution

1. 'A War for Eternal Peace', in Stuart Schram, *The Political Thought of Mao Tse-tung* (London: Praeger, 1964) pp. 267–9.
2. Tad Szulc *Fidel. A Critical Portrait* (London: Hutchinson, 1986) pp. 7–8.
3. According to *The Oxford English Dictionary* the term entered English in 1809 as a result of the Peninsular War (1808–14). It referred first to a combatant engaged in such a war, then to the war itself. For general histories, see Gerard Chaliard (ed.), *Stratégie de la Guerrilla* (Paris: Mazarine, 1979); Walter Laqueur, *Guerrilla: A Historical and Critical Study* (London: Weidenfeld & Nicholson, 1977).
4. von Clausewitz, *On War*; Raymond Aron, *Clausewitz* (London: Routledge & Kegan Paul, 1985), chapter 5, 'The Moral and the Physical'.
5. It is worth noting that those within the social sciences who wish to dissolve the distinction tend to be those who deny the importance of revolutions, while those who do so within political rhetoric tend to downplay the costs of war.
6. Arno Mayer, 'Internal Crisis and War Since 1870'.
7. Ernest Mandel, *The Meaning of the Second World War* (London: Verso, 1986) p. 45, distinguishes *five* different conflicts within the overall process of the Second World War.
8. Kissinger, *Diplomacy*, p. 790.
9. Paul Kennedy, *The Rise and Fall of the Great Powers* (London: Unwin Hyman, 1988). For later, supportive, use of this argument, see Henry Kissinger, *Diplomacy*.
10. On Trotsky *The Prophet Armed*, pp. 214–15; on Lenin, George Lukacs, *Lenin, The Unity of His Theory* (London: Verso, 1970) chapter 4, 'Imperialism: World War and Civil War'.
11. On the role of anti-Bolshevism in Hitler's ideology and foreign policy, see Chapter 8 above.
12. Friedrich Katz, *The Secret War in Mexico: Europe, the United States and the Mexican Revolution* (Chicago: Chicago University Press, 1981).
13. Mayer, 'Internal Crisis and War Since 1870', pp. 230–1.
14. Ibid, p. 201.
15. For analysis and edited texts, see Bernard Semmel, *Marxism and the Science of War* (Oxford: Oxford University Press, 1981). A perspective discussion of Marx, Engels and Lenin is in W. B. Gachie, *Philosophers of Peace and War* (Cambridge: CUP, 1978).
16. Raymond Aron, *Clausewitz*, chapter 11, 'The Meeting of Two Revolutions', pp. 267–77.
17. V. I. Lenin, *Selected Works* (London: Lawrence & Wishart, 1969) 'Marxism and Insurrection', p. 361.
18. Neuberg, *Armed Insurrection*, p. 25.
19. Neuberg, *Armed Insurrection*, p. 29 (italics in original).
20. For a study of one later attempt, see my 'The Ceylonese Insurrection', *New Left Review*, 69 (September-October 1971).

21. Perry Anderson, 'The Antinomies of Antonio Gramsci', *New Left Review*, 100 (November 1976–January 1977) pp. 8–10.
22. Bernard Semmel (ed.), *Marxism and the Science of War*, section V, 'Soviet Marxism and A Nuclear Strategy'.
23. 'Reactionaries and Atom Bombs Are Paper Tigers', in Schram, *Political Thought*, pp. 279–80; John Gittings, *The World and China 1922–1972*, pp. 230–2, 249–50; Michael Yahuda, *China's Role in World Affairs*, pp. 134–8.
24. ' "Castro had no control of Cuban missiles crisis" paper reveals', *The Guardian*, 15 August 1997.
25. Castro was later to say that Khrushchev had misunderstood his message, reading it as an encouragement to launch a pre-emptive nuclear strike on the USA in response to *air* attacks on Cuba. But Castro confirms that he had called for such a strike in the event of a *land* invasion ('Castro, Khrouchtchev et l'apolcalypse', *Le Monde*, 2 November 1990, and Arthur Schlesinger, 'Four Days with Fidel', p. 24). In the speech released in 1997 (see previous note) he is reported as having called for a 'massive and total' attack on the USA.
26. Quoted in Hugh Thomas, *Cuba or the Pursuit of Freedom* (London: Eyre & Spottiswood, 1971) p. 1417. A few weeks after the crisis Guevara was to tell a British journalist, as he fumed against the Soviet betrayal, that if the missiles had been under Cuban control they could have fired them (Jon Lee Anderson, *Che Guevara*, p.545).
27. Mao Tse-tung, *Strategic Problems of China's Revolutionary War* (Peking: Foreign Languages Press, 1954). For Vietnam, Vo Nguyen Giap, *People's War, People's Army* (Hanoi: Foreign Languages Publishing House, 1961).
28. Che Guevara, *Guerrilla War* (New York: Monthly Review Press, 1961).
29. Régis Debray, *Revolution in the Revolution?*. See also *Regis Debray and the Latin American Revolution* (New York: Monthly Review Press, 1968); Hartmut Ramm, *The Marxism of Regis Debray: Between Lenin and Guevara* (Lawrence, Kansas: The Regents Press of Kansas, 1978).
30. For a perceptive and critical account of the post-war evolution, and one that lays proper stress on the role of ideology and strategic vision in revolutionary movements, see Chalmers Johnson, *Autopsy on People's War* (London: University of California Press, 1973). In the short term, Chalmers Johnson was proved spectacularly wrong: within two years of the publication of his autopsy, revolutionary guerrillas had taken power in Vietnam, Cambodia and Laos, and in the former Portuguese colonies of Africa; in 1979 the FSLN were to triumph in Nicaragua. Yet the ideological history he wrote, and the analysis of flaws within the theory, have been vindicated in the longer run.
31. Mack, 'Why big nations lose small wars', p. 177.
32. For retrospective reflection on the mixed experience, see the political critiques of Régis Debray *Che's Guerrilla War* (Harmondsworth: Penguin, 1975) and *La Critique des Armes*, 2 vols (Paris: Seuil, 1979); João Quartim, *Armed Struggle in Brazil* (London: NLB,

1971) and Jorge Castañeda, *Utopia Unarmed*. For an academic assessment of the successes and failures see Timothy Wickham-Crowley, *Guerrillas and Revolution in Latin America*.

33. Much was made during the 1970s in particular of the 'proxy' character of Third World conflicts, be this on behalf of US or Soviet allies, the implication being that these states acted *solely* at the behest of their patrons. This was always a dubious argument, confusing assistance with instigation, and denying the indigenous reasons that impelled these states to act – in Israel, Iran and South Korea on the US side, or Cuba and South Yemen on the Soviet.

34. James Scott, *Deciding to Intervene*.

35. Pipes (ed.), *The Unknown Lenin*, pp. 95–100.

36. On the lessons of the 1962 Indian campaign see 'Introduction to Tukhachevsky', *New Left Review*, no. 55 (May-June 1969) pp. 85–6. Also Neville Maxwell, *India's China War* (London: Cape, 1970).

37. Most discussion of Mao as a theorist of war has focussed on his theory of guerrilla war, and the relation of politics to military strategy and tactics. On this aspect of Mao as Clausewitzian, see Raymond Aron, *Clausewitz* (London: Routledge and Kegan Paul, 1983).

38. Theda Skocpol, 'Social Revolutions and Mass Military Mobilization', in *Social Revolution in the Modern World* (Cambridge: Cambridge University Press, 1994) p. 281.

39. A comparable case, without concomitant revolutionary changes, was that of the Turkish army. Defeated in the First World War it was remobilised by Mustafa Kemal in the patriotic resistance to external intervention after 1918 and succeeded by 1923 in reasserting control of the whole of Turkey.

40. Author's interview with Admiral Madani, the first Minister of Defence of the Islamic Republic of Iran, 1980.

41. On the Iranian army in war, Shahram Chubin and Charles Tripp, *Iran and Iraq at War* (London: I.B. Tauris, 1989).

42. For a feminist perspective on the erosion of support for the FSLN as a result of the war, see Margaret Randall, *Sandino's Daughters Revisited* (New Brunswick, N.J.: Rutgers University Press, 1994).

43. Fred Halliday and Maxine Molyneux, *The Ethiopian Revolution*.

10 Systemic Constraints: Revolutionary 'Transformation' and Autarky

1. Leon Trotsky, *The Third International After Lenin* (New York: Pathfinder, 1975) p. 48.

2. Skocpol, *States and Social Revolutions*, part II, 'Outcomes of Social Revolutions in France, Russia and China'. For a critique of Skocpol that ascribes causation more to the internal and civil war aspects of state consolidation than to the external challenges, see Rosemary O'Kane, 'The National Causes of State Construction in France, Russia and China', *Keele Research Paper* no. 8 (1994), and her *Terror, Force, and States: The Path from Modernity* (Cheltenham: Edward Elgar, 1996). O'Kane is right to point to the internal dimensions of

state consolidation, but rather underplays the importance of external factors, typically seen by revolutionary states as *mediated through* domestic counter-revolutionaries. In the third of her cases, China, it is inappropriate to begin with the establishment of the People's Republic in 1949: the consolidation of state and party organisation took place in the twenty years of guerrilla and then conventional war prior to that, a decisive part of it against the Japanese in the period 1937–45.

3. Michael Mann, 'The Autonomous Power of the State', in his *States, War and Capitalism* (Oxford: Basil Blackwell, 1988) p. 5, terms despotic power 'the range of actions which the elite is empowered to undertake without routine, institutionalized negotiation with civil society groups'. This he contrasts to 'infrastructural' power, the ability to penetrate society and effect its will. Communist states were powerful in both senses, though less so in the latter regard than appeared when they were initially established.
4. Herbert Marcuse, *Soviet Marxism, A Critical Analysis* (Harmondsworth: Penguin, 1971), chapter 5, 'The Dialectic of the Soviet State', p. 86.
5. Engels To Adler, 4 December 1889, in Marx and Engels, *Selected Correspondence*, p. 489.
6. Anne Tickner, *Self-Reliance versus Power Politics* (New York: Columbia University Press, 1987).
7. For discussion of 'stateness' and 'state capacity', J. P. Nettl, 'The State as a Conceptual Variable', *World Politics*, vol. xx, no. 11 (July 1968); Joel Migdal, *Strong Societies and Weak States* (London: Princeton University Press, 1988); Nazih Ayubi, *Overstating the Arab State* (London: I. B. Tauris, 1995).
8. James Rosenau, *Linkage Politics* (New York: The Free Press, 1969); Robert Keohane and Joseph Nye (eds), *Transnational Relations and World Politics* (London: Harvard University Press, 1972); *Power and Interdependence* (Boston: Little, Brown 1977).
9. Amidst a large literature see Dudley Seers (ed.), *Dependency Theory: A Critical Reassessment* (London: Pinter, 1981).
10. Roman Szporluk, *Communism and Nationalism, Karl Marx Versus Friedrich List* (Oxford: Oxford University Press, 1988), especially chapter 13, 'List and Marx in Russia'.
11. Dieter Senghaas, *The European Experience: A Historical Critique of Development Theory* p. 180.
12. Isaac Deutscher, *The Great Contest, Russia and the West* (London: OUP, 1960).
13. Moshe Lewin, *Lenin's Last Struggle* (London: Wildwood House, 1973) p. 3.
14. Quoted in E. H. Carr, *The Bolshevik Revolution*, vol. 3, p. 29.
15. J. Stalin, *The Foundations of Leninism, On the Problems of Leninism* (Moscow: Foreign Languages Publishing House, 1950).
16. Ibid, pp. 232–3.
17. J. P. Nettl, *Rosa Luxemburg*, abridged edition (London: OUP, 1969) p. 435.
18. Ibid, p. 434.

19. Marcel Liebman, *Leninism under Lenin* (London: Jonathan Cape, 1975) pp. 226–7.
20. Leon Trotsky, *The Revolution Betrayed* (London: New Park Publications, 1967) pp. 90–1.
21. *The Revolution Betrayed*, pp. 190–1.
22. The most striking instance of this policy by the USA was the blockade imposed on Cuba in 1961 and sustained throughout the ensuing four decades. For one account Morris Morley, *Imperial State and Revolution. The United States and Cuba, 1952–1986* (Cambridge: CUP, 1987) chapter 5.
23. Stephen Neff, *Friends But No Allies: Economic Liberalism and the Law of Nations* (New York: Columbia University Press, 1990) chapter 1, 'From *Polis* to *Kosmos*: Expanding Horizons of International Political Economy'.
24. Eric Roll, *A History of Economic Thought* revised edition (London: Faber & Faber, 1973) pp. 227–31.
25. Szporluk, *Communism and Nationalism*.
26. Gabriel Palma, 'Dependency and Development: A Critical Overview', in Dudley Seers (ed.), *Dependency Theory: A Critical Assessment* (London: Pinter, 1981).
27. Among a large literature Paul Baran, *The Political Economy of Growth* (New York: Monthly Review Press, 1957); Johan Galtung, 'The Politics of Self-Reliance', in Heraldo Muñoz (ed.), *From Dependency to Development* (Boulder: Westview, 1981); Thoma Weisskopf, 'Self-Reliance and Development Strategy', in Ngo Manh-Lam, *Unreal Growth* (Delhi, 1984) vol. 2.
28. Karl Marx, 'Critique of the Gotha Programme', in Karl Marx, *The First International and After*, ed. David Fernbach (Harmondsworth: Penguin, 1974) pp. 354–5.
29. George Lichtheim, *Marxism Historical and Critical Study* (London: Routledge & Kegan Paul, 1961), part four, chapter 2, 'State and Society'; Herbert Marcuse, *Soviet Marxism*.
30. Teodor Shanin (ed.), *Late Marx and the Russian Road. Marx and 'the Peripheries of Capitalism'* (London: Routledge & Kegan Paul, 1984).
31. For contemporary analysis of Third World socialist states, see *World Development*, vol. 9, no. 9/10 (September–October 1981), special issue 'Socialist Models of Development'; Christopher Chase-Dunn (ed.), *Socialist States in the World-System* (London: Sage, 1982); Cal Clark and Donna Bahry, 'Dependent Development: A Socialist Variant', *International Studies Quarterly*, vol. 27 (1983); Ann Helwege, 'Three Socialist Experiences in Latin America: Surviving US Economic Pressure', *Bulletin of Latin American Research*, vol. 8, no. 2 (1989). For discussion of how the Soviet model was adjusted for 'state capitalist' development, see Stephen Clarkson, *The Soviet Theory of Development. India and the Third World in Marxist-Leninist Scholarship* (London: Macmillan, 1979).
32. Leon Trotsky, *History of the Russian Revolution*, vol. 1, pp. 24–5.
33. The fusion of Marxism and nationalism in the Bolshevik authoritarian model was reflected in the meaning of the Russian word *gosudarst-*

vennost', literally 'statehood' or 'state system', but also synonymous with the English term 'nation-building'. The suggestion is that state and nation were, in the Russian case, even more closely fused than was the case in other, more Western, cases where an element of distinction between state and civil society had been evident for some centuries.

34. Roy Medvedev, *Leninism and Western Socialism* (London: Verso, 1981), chapter 5, 'Socialism in One Country'.
35. 'On the Slogan for a United States of Europe', in V. I. Lenin, *Selected Works* (Moscow: Progress Publishers, 1970) vol. 1, pp. 664–5.
36. Bukharin and Preobrazhensky, *The ABC of Communism*, p. 311.
37. *ABC of Communism*, pp. 210–11.
38. Quoted in E. H. Carr, *The Bolshevik Revolution 1917–1923*, vol. 2, p. 361.
39. Quoted in E. H. Carr, *Foundations of a Planned Economy 1926–1929* (Harmondworth: Pelican, 1974) p. 429.
40. Neil Harding, 'Socialism, Society and the Organic Labour State', in Neil Harding (ed.), *The State in Socialist Society* (London: Macmillan, 1984).
41. Stalin, *Works* (Moscow: Foreign Languages Printing Press, 1953–1955) XII, pp. 242–3, quoted in Richard Day, *The 'Crisis' and the 'Crash'. Soviet Studies of the West (1917–1939)* (London: NLB, 1981) p. 202.
42. 'The Situation and Our Policy After the Victory in the War of Resistance Against Japan'(August 13, 1945), *Selected Works*, vol. IV, p. 20.
43. This was the answer which Ayatollah Khomeini gave to his adviser Abol-Hasan Bani-Sadr, when the latter warned him that a prolonged confrontation with the USA over the detention of US diplomats as hostages would provoke an economic blockade (author's interview with Bani-Sadr, Auvers-sur-Oise, France, August 1981).
44. 'Bani-Sadr's Speech at 6th April Gas Seminar', BBC *Summary of World Broadcasts*, ME/6392/A/9, 11 April 1980.
45. Amílcar Cabral, *Return to the Source: Selected Speeches of Amílcar Cabral* (New York: Monthly Review Press, 1973) p. 55, quoted in Ronald Chilcote, *Amilcar Cabral's Revolutionary Theory and Practice: A Critical Guide* (London: Lynne Rienner, 1991) p. 38.
46. Theda Skocpol, *States and Revolutions*, chapter 4, 'What Changed and How: A Focus on State Building', pp. 161–73.
47. Skocpol, part II, is phrased very much in terms of 'outcomes', suggesting a final achievement.
48. For an early prescient analysis of these costs, see George von Vollmar, 'Der isolirte sozialistische Staat', *Jahrbuch für Sozialwissenschaft und Sozialpolitik*, ed. I. Richter, Zurich, 1879. I am grateful to the late Adam Westoby for drawing this to my attention.
49. I am grateful to my brother Jon Halliday for this point.
50. Fidel Castro, *The World Economic and Social Crisis: its impact on the underdeveloped countries, its somber prospects and the need to struggle if we are to survive*, Report to the Seventh Summit Conference

of Non-Aligned Countries (Havana: Publishing Office of the Council of State, 1983).

51. It was argued by one Soviet-bloc economist that however successful the socialist economies, they would always need to preserve one capitalist economy in existence, in order to determine real prices.

52. For one cogent argument as to the necessary impasse of the state social model, see Wlodzimierz Brus and Kazimierz Laski, *From Marx to the Market* (Oxford: Clarendon Press, 1989). See also Senghaas, *The European Experience*, chapter 6; Ivan Szelenyi and Balazs Szelenyi, 'Why Socialism Failed: Towards a Theory of System Breakdown – Causes of Disintegration of East European Socialism', *Theory and Society*, vol. 23, no. 2 (1994); Stanislaw Gomulka, 'Soviet Equilibrium Technological Gap and the Post-1975 Productivity Slowdown', *Economics of Planning*, vol. 22, nos. 1–2 (1988).

53. Richard Fagen, Carmen Diana Deere and Jose Luis Coraggio (eds), *Transition and Development, Problems of Third World Socialism* (New York: Monthly Review Press, 1986); E. V. K. Fitzgerald and L. M. Wyts (eds), *Markets Without Planning: Socialist Economic Management in the Third World* (London: Cass, 1988).

54. Courtney A. Smith, *Socialist Transformation in Peripheral Economies* (Aldershot: Avebury, 1995) documents the accumulating economic problems of the Grenada regime, not least an investment code that deterred both foreign and domestic investment, and a set of state policies that the regime lacked the resources to implement. At the same time Smith makes clear that the political crisis of the New Jewel movement, i.e. its imposition of a Leninist model on the island, predated the economic crisis that matured in 1983. On the People's Democratic Republic of Yemen, see Fred Halliday, *Revolution and Foreign Policy*, pp. 41–53.

55. Forrest Colburn, *Post-Revolutionary Nicaragua* (Berkeley: University of California Press, 1986).

56. David Lane, *The Rise and Fall of State Socialism* (Cambridge: Polity, 1996), chapter 5, 'Movements for Market and Political Reform'.

57. I have discussed the history and nature of the Cold War in a number of earlier writings, notably *The Making of the Second Cold War* (London: Verso, 1983); 'The Ends of Cold War', in Robin Blackburn (ed.), *After the Fall: Rethinking International Relations* (London: Macmillan, 1994), chapters 8, 'Inter-Systemic Conflict: The Case of Cold War', and 9, 'A Singular Collapse: The Soviet Union and Inter-State Competition'; *From Potsdam to Perestroika: Conversations with Cold Warriors* .

58. As note 54, Chapter 2.

59. *Rethinking International Relations*, chapter 8.

60. Jerry Hough, *Democratization and Revolution in the USSR 1985–1991* (Washington: Brookings Institution, 1997); David Lane, *The Rise and Fall of State Socialism*.

61. Moshe Lewin, *The Gorbachev Phenomenon* (London: Radius/Hutchinson, 1988); Jerry Hough, *Democratization and Revolution*; David Lane, *The Rise and Fall of State Socialism*. The East German

opposition writer Rudolf Bahro, writing then in a Marxist framework, developed the idea of the production, under 'actually existing socialism', of a form of 'surplus consciousness', an excess of intellectual and potentially critical power that would challenge the bureaucratic dictatorship of the ruling party: Rudolf Bahro, *The Alternative in Eastern Europe* (London: Verso, 1978) pp. 256–7. This would be the gravedigger of the system, just as in the classic Marxist analysis of capitalism the proletariat, a product of the system's development, would perform this role. To a considerable degree Bahro was right: the intelligentsia in particular, and more generally the mass of the population educated to be receptive to Western consumerist and political ideas, did, during the 1980s come to reject the system and when in 1989 it had the opportunity to act, spontaneously and in mass, it did so. In the former communist countries it was, of course, the intelligentsia who were to lose most in the transition to capitalism.

11 Challenges to Theory

1. Kenneth Waltz, 'The Politics of Peace', *International Studies Quarterly*, 11, no. 3 (September 1967) p. 205, quoted in Chalmers Johnson, *Autopsy on People's War*, p. 105.
2. Henry Kissinger, *A World Restored*.
3. For his own resumé of this combination, see Henry Kissinger, *Diplomacy*.
4. Gordon Craig, 'Above the Abyss', review of Alan Bulloch, *Hitler and Stalin: Parallel Lines, New York Review of Books*, 9 April 1992, p. 5.
5. Tony Judt, 'Counsels on Foreign Relations', *New York Review of Books*, 13 August 1998, p. 59 n.15.
6. David Armstrong, *Revolution and World Order, The Revolutionary State in International Society* (Oxford: Clarendon Press, 1993) pp. 8–9.
7. *Revolution and World Order*, p. 302.
8. Northedge, *The International Political System* (London: Faber & Faber, 1976) pp. 28–30; James Der Derian, *On Diplomacy* (Oxford: Basil Blackwell, 1987) p. 198; Kenneth Waltz, *Theory of International Politics* (New York: Random House, 1979) pp. 127–8.
9. A less elaborated variant of this approach is to be found in the discussion of revolutions as proponents of a 'new diplomacy', in the sense of one based on rejection of conventional norms of diplomatic interaction, sponsoring of opposition groups, and the use of terrorism. For example: Andrew M. Scott, *The Revolution in Statecraft, Informal Penetration*. This approach is doubly flawed: on the one hand it suffers from a degree of historical and moral amnesia about the flagrant violations of sovereignty by status quo powers over the past two centuries of colonial conquest and domination; on the other, it confines the international impact of revolutions to one of *method*, ignoring the broader social and ideological context in which such policies are pursued.

10. Kim, *Revolution and the International System.*
11. Ibid, p. 123.
12. William Doyle, *The Oxford History of the French Revolution* (Oxford: OUP, 1989) pp. 156–7.
13. James Bill *The Eagle and the Lion* (London: Yale University Press, 1988) pp. 440–8.
14. Stephen Walt, *Revolution and War* (Ithaca and London: Cornell University Press, 1996).
15. Richard Rosecrance, *Action and Reaction in World Politics* (Boston: Little, Brown and Company, 1963).
16. While discussing the role of ideology in motivating state behaviour, Rosecrance seems (p. 299) to treat as similar ideologies of social revolution and nationalism. The latter may be disruptive of an existing international system, but not in the manner in which the former is so. Again, neglect of the internal, social and political content of states leads to a misrepresentation of international processes.
17. James Rosenau, *Linkage Politics*, chapter 3, 'Internal War as an International Event'.
18. James Rosenau, *International Aspects of Civil Strife* (Princeton: Princeton University Press, 1961).
19. The critique of the behaviouralist theory of violence rests on the argument that an apparent *absence* of conflict or violence may reflect oppression by established *structural* violence.
20. Giovanni Arrighi, Terence K. Hopkins and Immanuel Wallerstein, *Antisystemic Movements* (London: Verso, 1989) and '1989, The Continuation of 1968', Fernand Braudel Center for the Study of Economies, Historical Systems and Civilizations, State University of New York at Binghampton 1991. See also Wallerstein, *Historical Capitalism* (London: Verso, 1984).
21. *Antisystemic Movements*, p. 77.
22. For other critiques see, on revolution, Kimmel, *Revolution: A Sociological Interpretation*, pp. 98–115, and, on world systems theory in general, Charles Ragin and Daniel Chirot, 'The World System of Immanuel Wallerstein', in Theda Skocpol (ed.), *Vision and Method in Historical Sociology* (Cambridge: CUP, 1984), and Peter Worsley, 'One World or Three: A Critique of the World System of Immanuel Wallerstein', *Socialist Register*, 1980.
23. For a cogent indictment, see Jung Chang, *Wild Swans* (London: HarperCollins, 1991).
24. See in particular chapters 3 and 4 of my *Rethinking International Relations* in which I assess the encounters of, respectively, historical materialism and historical sociology with theories of international relations.
25. Quoted in Liebman, *Leninism under Lenin*, p. 369.
26. E. H. Carr, *The Twenty Years' Crisis 1919–1939* (London: Macmillan, 1983) chapter 8.
27. Ralph Pettman, *International Politics: Balance of Power, Balance of Production, Balance of Ideologies* (London: Lynne Rienner, 1991). Such an approach is, of course, quite different from those which seek

to replace analysis of political and other processes by arguing for the primacy of the semiotic or cultural.

28. François Furet, *Interpreting the French Revolution* (Cambridge: Cambridge University Press, 1981) and Simon Schama, *Citizens: A Chronicle of the French Revolution* (London: Viking, 1989). For discussion see Edward Berenson, 'The Social Interpretation of the French Revolution', in Nikki Keddie (ed.), *Debating Revolutions* (London: New York University Press, 1995); Jack Censer, 'The French Revolution after Two Hundred Years', in Joseph Klaits and Michael Haltzel (eds), *The Global Ramifications of the French Revolution* (Cambridge: Cambridge University Press, 1994); Eric Hobsbawm, *Echoes of the Marseillaise: Two Centuries Look Back on the French Revolution* (London: Verso, 1990).

29. Klaits and Haltzel (eds), p. 6.

30. Fred Halliday, *Rethinking International Relations*, chapter 9, 'A Singular Collapse: The Soviet Union and Inter-State Competition'.

31. Nicholas Abercrombie, Stephen Hill and Bryan Turner, *The Dominant Ideology Thesis* (London: Unwin Hyman, 1980).

32. Derek Sayer, *Capitalism and Modernity. An Excursus on Marx and Weber* (London: Routledge, 1991).

33. For contrasting theorisations of the international formation of classes, see Kees van der Pijl, *The Making of an Atlantic Ruling Class* (London: Verso, 1984) and Carolyn Vogler, *The Nation State, The Neglected Dimension of Class* (Aldershot: Gower, 1984).

34. Karl Polanyi, *The Great Transformation: The Political and Economic Origins of Our Time* (Boston: Beacon Press, 1957). The arguments on the specificity of the modern international system are taken further in Justin Rosenberg, *The Empire of Civil Society*.

35. The classic formulation of this argument is in Leon Trotsky, *The History of the Russian Revolution*, vol. 1, pp. 23–31. This was a development, after 1917, of the overarching view of revolutionary strategy first sketched in his *Results and Prospects* of 1906: here Trotsky had argued that it was the very apparent 'backwardness' of Russia that made it possible for a socialist revolution to be made, provided this then led to revolution elsewhere. For analysis, see Isaac Deutscher, *The Prophet Armed, Trotsky: 1879–1921* (London: OUP, 1954) pp. 149–63. For later discussion, Justin Rosenberg, 'Isaac Deutscher and the Lost History of International Relations', *New Left Review*, 215 (January–February 1996).

36. Trotsky, *History of the Russian Revolution*, vol. 1, pp. 25–6.

37. For discussion of these three dimensions in the context of the end of the Cold War, see *Rethinking International Relations*, chapter 9.

12 Revolutions in World Politics

1. A. J. P. Taylor, *Revolutions and Revolutionaries*; Eugene Kamenka and F. B. Smith (eds), *Intellectuals and Revolution: Socialism and the*

Experience of 1848 (London: Edward Arnold, 1979); J. A. S. Grenville, *Europe Reshaped 1848–1878* (London: Fontana, 1976).

2. This argument entails a rethinking of the *social character* of revolutions: the conventional distinction into 'bourgeois', and other variants, 'proletarian', 'peasant', 'petty-bourgeois', combines a claim about *agency* – who were the *primary actors* in that revolution – with one about *direction* – who benefited, or, more broadly, *to what socially defined stage of history* did the revolution tend. The implication of what is said here is that claims about direction need to be discounted. Hence the linking of agency to historical process, the latter usually tied to a historical materialist schema, is not sustainable. If it is clear that the term 'bourgeois' refers only to agency, then it might have more utility, provided the evidence sustains the claim.

3. Fred Halliday, 'War and the Making of Modern Europe', in Jarroe Wiener and Stephen Chan (eds), *International Currents in the Twentieth Century* (London: Macmillan, 1999).

4. For commanding surveys Herbert Marcuse, *Soviet Marxism*, and Perry Anderson, *Considerations on Western Marxism* (London: Verso, 1978).

5. In Pipes (ed.), *The Unknown Lenin*, pp. 62–3.

6. David Armstrong, *Revolution and World Order*, Conclusion.

7. Arno Mayer, *Politics and Diplomacy*, p. 14.

8. André Gorz, *Farewell to the Working Class* (London: Pluto Press, 1982). Eric Hobsbawm in *The Forward March of Labour Halted?*, edited by Martin Jacques and Francis Mulhern (London: Verso, 1981).

9. Walter Laqueur, *The Dream that Failed. Reflections on the Soviet Union*.

10. George Steiner, *Proofs and Three Parables* (London: Faber & Faber, 1992).

11. *The Guardian*, 22 February 1997.

12. *Le passé*, p. 13.

13. Ibid, p. 807.

14. Ibid, p. 809.

15. Quoted in Patrick Markee, 'Semper Fidel', review of Jorge Castañeda, *Compañero: The Life and Death of Che Guevara* (New York: Knopf, 1997) *The Nation*, 5 January 1998, p. 29.

16. On the ideals of the American revolution, R. R. Palmer, *The Age of the Democratic Revolution* chapter XVI, 'America: Democracy Native and Imported'; Joyce Appleby, *Capitalism and a New Social Order. The Republican Vision of the 1790s* (London: New York University Press, 1984); David Brion Davis, *Revolutions. Reflections on American Equality and Foreign Liberations* (London: Harvard University Press, 1900). All three discuss how the original radicalism of 1776 was taken further in the agitation of the 1790s that culminated in Jefferson's election as president in 1800 and the defeat of the elitist Federalist party. For a later chapter see James Farr, 'Discordant Chorus: The United States and the European Revolutions of 1848', in Joachim

Remak (ed.), *War, Revolution and Peace* (London: University Press of America, 1987).
17. According to the European Bank for Reconstruction and Development, GDP in every former communist country, except Poland, was lower in 1997 than in 1989, the non-Soviet countries' GDP falling by an average 50%, that of the former USSR republics by 44% (*The Economist*, 15 November 1997).
18. Between 1965 and 1990 the share of world income owned by the richest 20% rose from 69% to 83% of world GDP, representing an average of 60 times per capita income in the poorest quintile (*The Economist*, 20 September 1997). The UNDP *Human Development Report* for 1998, based on figures from 1995, showed that the top 20% of the world's population accounted for 86% of expenditures for personal consumption, the bottom 20% for 1.3% (*Financial Times*, 10 September 1998).
19. Graham Fuller, 'The Next Ideology', *Foreign Policy*, no. 98 (Spring 1995).

Select Bibliography

1. Revolution: General Works

Arendt, Hannah, *On Revolution*, Harmondsworth, Penguin, 1963.
Aya, Rod, 'Theories of Revolution Reconsidered', *Theory and Society*, vol. 8, no. 1, 1979.
Aya, Rod, *Rethinking Revolutions and Collective Violence: Studies on Concept, Theory and Method*, Het Spinhuis Amsterdam, 1990.
Bertrand, Charles (ed.), *Revolutionary Situations in Europe, 1917–1922*, Montreal, Interuniversity Centre for European Studies, 1977.
Blackey, Robert, *Revolutions and Revolutionaries: A Guide to the Literature*, Santa Barbara, CA, ABC-Clio, 1982.
Brinton, Crane, *The Anatomy of Revolution*, New York, Anchor Books, 1965.
Calvert, Peter, *Revolution and Counter-revolution*, Milton Keynes, Open University Press, 1990.
Chaliand, Gerard, *Revolution in the Third World*, Hassocks, Harvester, 1977.
Close, David and Bridge, Carl, *Revolution: A History of the Idea*, London, Croom Helm, 1985.
Cohan, A. S., *Theories of Revolution: An Introduction*, London, Nelson, 1975.
Comparative Politics, Special Issue, vol. 5, no. 2, April 1973.
Davies, James, 'Towards a Theory of Revolution', *American Sociological Review*, vol. 27, no. 1, February 1962.
Davies, Norman, *Europe: A History*, Oxford, Oxford University Press, 1996.
Decouflé, André, *Sociologie des Révolutions*, Paris, PUF, 1968.
Deutscher, Isaac, *Marxism, Wars and Revolution*, London, Verso, 1984.
Dunn, John, *Modern Revolution: An Introduction to the Analysis of a Political Phenomenon*, Cambridge, Cambridge University Press, 1972.
Eisenstadt, S. N., *Revolution and the Transformation of Societies*, New York, The Free Press, 1978.
Foran, John (ed.), *Theorizing Revolutions*, London, Routledge, 1997.
Freeman, Michael, 'Theories of Revolution', *British Journal of Political Science*, no. 2, 1972.
Gerassi, John, *Towards Revolution: vol. 1 China, India, Asia, the Middle East; vol. 2 The Americas*, London, Weidenfeld & Nicolson, 1971.
Goldfrank, Walter, 'Theories of Revolution and Revolution without Theory: The Case of Mexico', *Theory and Society*, vol. 7, 1979, pp. 135–65.
Goldstone, Jack, 'Theories of Revolution: The Third Generation', *World Politics*, vol. 32, no. 3, April 1980.

Goldstone, Jack (ed.), *Revolutions: Theoretical, Comparative and Historical Studies*, London, Harcourt Brace Jovanovich, 1986.

Goldstone, Jack, *Revolution and Rebellion in the Early Modern World*, Oxford, University of California Press, 1991.

Goldstone, Jack, Gurr, Ted and Moshiri, Farrokh (eds), *Revolutions of the Late Twentieth Century*, Oxford, Westview, 1991.

Griewank, Karl, *Der Neuzeitliche Revolutionsbegriff*, Weimar, Hermann Böhlaus, 1955.

Gurr, Ted, *Why Men Rebel*, Princeton, Princeton University Press, 1970.

Halliday, Fred, *The Making of the Second Cold War*, London, Verso, 1983, chapter 4.

Halliday, Fred, *Revolution and Foreign Policy, The Case of South Yemen 1967–1987*, Cambridge, Cambridge University Press, 1990.

Halliday, Fred, and Molyneux, Maxine, *The Ethiopian Revolution*, London, Verso, 1982.

Hamerow, Theodor, *From the Finland Station: The Graying of Revolution in the Twentieth Century*, New York, Basic Books, 1990.

Hatto, A. T., '"Revolution": An Enquiry into the Usefulness of an Historical Term', *Mind*, vol. LVIII, October 1949.

Heater, Derek, *World Citizenship and Government: Cosmopolitan Ideas in the History of Western Political Thought*, London, Macmillan, 1996.

Hobsbawm, Eric, *Primitive Rebels*, Manchester, Manchester University Press, 1959.

Hobsbawm, Eric, *Revolutionaries*, London, Weidenfeld & Nicolson, 1973.

Hobsbawm, Eric, *The Age of Empire 1875–1914*, London, Weidenfeld & Nicolson, 1987.

Hobsbawm, Eric, *Age of Extremes: The Short Twentieth Century, 1914–1991*, London, Michael Joseph, 1994.

Huntington, Samuel, *Political Order in Changing Societies*, London, Yale University Press, 1968.

Johnson, Chalmers, *Revolutionary Change*, second edition, London, Longman, 1983.

Kamrava, Mehran, *Revolutionary Politics*, New York, Praeger, 1993.

Keane, John, *Tom Paine: A Political Life*, London, Bloomsberg, 1995.

Keddie, Nikki (ed.), *Debating Revolutions*, London, New York University Press, 1995.

Kimmel, Michael, *Revolution: A Sociological Interpretation*, Cambridge, Polity, 1990.

Knight, Alan, 'Social Revolution: A Latin American Perspective', *Bulletin of Latin American Research*, vol. 9, no. 2, 1990.

Kosseleck, Reinhard, 'Historical Criteria of the Modern Concept of Revolution', in *Futures Past: On the Semantics of Historical Time*, Cambridge, Mass., MIT Press, 1985.

Kumar, Krishan (ed.), *Revolution – the Theory and Practice of a European Idea*, London, Weidenfeld & Nicolson, 1971.

Leiden, Carl and Schmitt, Karl, *The Politics of Violence: Revolution in the Modern World*, Englewood Cliffs, NJ, Prentice-Hall, 1968.

Lubacz, Heinz, *Revolutions in Modern European History*, London, Collier-Macmillan, 1968.

McDaniel, Tim, *Autocracy, Modernization and Revolution in Russia and Iran*, Princeton, Princeton University Press, 1991.

Miliband, Ralph, 'State Power and Class Interests', *New Left Review*, no. 138, March–April 1983.

Moore, Barrington, *The Social Origins of Dictatorship and Democracy*, Harmondsworth, Allen Lane, 1967.

Nisbet, Robert, *History of the Idea of Progress*, New York, Basic Books, 1980.

O'Kane, Rosemary, 'The National Causes of State Construction in France, Russia and China', *Keele Research Papers*, no. 8, 1994.

O'Kane, Rosemary, *Terror, Force and States: The Path from Modernity*, Cheltenham, Edward Elgar, 1996.

Paige, Jeffrey, *Agrarian Revolution and Export Agriculture in the Underdeveloped World*, New York, The Free Press, 1975.

Paine, Thomas, *The Rights of Man*, Harmondsworth, Pelican, 1969.

Parker, Geoffrey and Smith, Lesley (eds), *The General Crisis of the Seventeenth Century*, London, Routledge & Kegan Paul, 1978.

Pettee, George, *The Process of Revolution*, New York, Harper, 1938.

Petras, James, 'Socialist Revolutions and their Class Components', *New Left Review*, no. III, Sept.–Oct. 1978.

Polanyi, Karl, *The Great Transformation: The Political and Economic Origins of Our Time*, Boston, Little Brown, 1957.

Porter, Roy and Teich, Miklos, *Revolution in History*, Cambridge, CUP, 1986.

Reid, Anne, *Revolution*, unpublished manuscript, 1985.

Rey, Alain, *'Révolution': Histoire d'un Mot*, Paris, Gallimard, 1989.

Rice, Ellen (ed.), *Revolution and Counter-revolution*, Oxford, Basil Blackwell, 1991.

Schutz, Barry and Robert Slater (eds), *Revolution and Political Change in the Third World*, Boulder, CO, and London, Rienner, 1990.

Skocpol, Theda, *States and Social Revolutions*, Cambridge, CUP, 1979.

Skocpol, Theda, *Social Revolutions in the Modern World*, Cambridge, CUP, 1994.

Sohrabi, Nader, 'Historicizing Revolutions: Constitutional Revolutions in the Ottoman Empire, Iran and Russia, 1905–1908', *American Journal of Sociology*, vol. 100, no. 6, May 1995.

Stone, Lawrence, 'Theories of Revolutions', *World Politics*, January 1966, vol. 18, no. 2.

Stone, Lawrence, *The Causes of the English Revolution 1529–1642*, London, Routledge, 1986.

Stone, Norman, *Europe Transformed 1878–1919*, London, Fontana, 1983.

Taylor, A. J. P., *Revolutions and Revolutionaries*, London, Hamish Hamilton, 1980.

Taylor, Stan, *Social Science and Revolutions*, London, Macmillan, 1984.

Therborn, Göran, 'Revolution and Reform: Reflections on their Linkages through the Great French Revolution', in J. Böhlin *et al.*, *Samhällsvetenskap, ekonomi, historia*, Götebord, Daidalus, 1989.

Tilly, Charles, *From Mobilization to Revolution*, New York, McGraw-Hill, 1978.
Tilly, Charles, *European Revolutions, 1492–1992*, Oxford, Blackwell, 1993.
Trimberger, Ellen, *Revolution from Above: Military Bureaucrats and Development in Japan, Turkey, Egypt and Peru*, New Brunswick, Transaction, 1978.
Vatikiotis, P. J., *Revolution in the Middle East and Other Case Studies*, London, George Allen & Unwin, 1972.
Yack, Bernard, *The Longing for Total Revolution: Philosophical Sources of Social Discontent from Rousseau to Marx and Nietzsche*, Princeton, Princeton University Press, 1968.

2. Revolutions and International Relations

Akhavan Kazemi, Masood, *Dimensions Internationales des Révolutions*, doctoral thesis, Université de Rennes, Faculté de Droit et de Science Politique, 1995.
Armstrong, David, *Revolution and World Order: The Revolutionary State in International Society*, Oxford, Basil Blackwell, 1993.
Arrighi, Giovanni, Hopkins, Terence and Wallerstein, Immanuel, *Antisystemic Movements*, London, Verso, 1989.
Boswell, Terry, *Revolution in the World System*, London, Greenwood, 1989.
Calvert, Peter, *Revolution and International Politics*, London, Frances Pinter, 1984.
Cassels, Alan, *Ideology and International Relations in the Modern World*, London, Routledge, 1996.
Chan, Stephen and Williams, Andrew (eds), *Renegade States: The Revolution of Revolutionary Foreign Policy*, Manchester, Manchester University Press, 1995.
Holsti, Kal (ed.), *Why Nations Realign*, London, Allen & Unwin, 1982.
Horowitz, Irving, *Beyond Empire and Revolution*, New York, OUP, 1982.
Ikenberry, John and Kupchan, Charles, 'Socialisation and Hegemonic Power', *International Organisation*, vol. 44, no. 3, summer 1990.
International Institute for Strategic Studies, *Civil Violence and the International System*, 1971.
International Institute for Strategic Studies, *Third World Conflict and International Security*, 1981.
Katz, Mark, *Revolutions and Revolutionary Waves*, London, Macmillan, 1997.
Kim Kyung-won, *Revolution and International System*, New York, New York University Press, 1970.
Klare, Michael, *Rogue States and Nuclear Outlaws: America's Search for a New Foreign Policy*, New York, Hill & Wang, 1995.
Mack, Andrew *et al.*, *Imperialism, Intervention and Development*, London, Croom Helm, 1979.
Neumann, Sigmund, *Permanent Revolution: Totalitarianism in the Age of International Civil War*, second edition, 1965.

Rosecrance, Richard, *Action and Reaction in World Politics*, Boston, Little, Brown, 1963.

Rosenau, James (ed.), *International Aspects of Civil Strife*, Princeton, Princeton University Press, 1964.

Scott, Andrew, *The Revolution in Statecraft*, New York, Random House, 1965.

Spanier, John, *World Politics in an Age of Revolution*, New York, Praeger, 1967.

Wight, Martin, *Power Politics*, Harmondsworth, Penguin, 1966.

3.   Counter-Revolution and Intervention

Barnett, Richard, *Intervention and Revolution: The United States in the Third World*, London, Paladin, 1972.

Bull, Hedley (ed.), *Intervention in World Politics*, Oxford, Clarendon Press, 1984.

Burke, Edmund, in *The Works and Correspondence of Edmund Burke*, London, Francis Rivington, 1852, vol. 5.

Chomsky, Noam, *Deterring Democracy*, London, Vintage, 1992.

Collotti, Enzo, *La Germania Nazista*, Turin, Einardi, 1964.

Duner, Bertil, *Military Intervention in Civil Wars: The 1970s*, Aldershot, Gower, 1985.

Gates, Robert, *From the Shadows*, New York, Simon & Schuster, 1996.

Godechot, Jacques, *La Countre-Révolution Doctrine et Action, 1789–1804*, Paris, PUF, 1961.

Halliday, Fred, *From Potsdam to Perestroika: Conversations with Cold Warriors*, London, BBC Publications, 1995.

Horowitz, David (ed.), *Containment and Revolution: Western Policy Towards Social Revolution, 1917 to Vietnam*, London, Anthony Blond, 1967.

Katz, Friedrich, *The Secret War in Mexico: Europe, America and the Mexican Revolution*, Chicago, Chicago University Press, 1981.

Kennan, George, 'The Sources of Soviet Conduct', in *American Diplomacy 1900–1950*, London, Secker & Warburg, 1964.

Kissinger, Henry, *A World Restored: Europe After Napoleon*, Gloucester, Mass., Peter Smith, 1973.

Little, Richard, *Intervention: External Involvement in Civil Wars*, London, Robertson, 1975.

MacFarlane, Neil, *Intervention and Regional Security*, London, International Institute for Strategic Studies, 1985.

Mayer, Arno, *Politics and Diplomacy of Peace-making: Containment and Counter-Revolution at Versailles, 1918–1919*, London, Weidenfeld & Nicolson, 1968.

Mayer, Arno, *Dynamics of Counterrevolution in Europe, 1870–1956: An Analytic Framework*, London, Harper Torchbooks, 1971.

Mayer, Arno, *Why Did the Heavens Not Darken? The 'Final Solution' in History*, London, Verso, 1990.

Polanyi, Karl, *The Great Transformation*, Boston, Beacon Press, 1957.
Scott, James, *Deciding to Intervene: The Reagan Doctrine and American Foreign Policy*, London, Duke University Press, 1996.
Thomas, Caroline, *New States, Sovereignty and Intervention*, Aldershot, Gower, 1985.
Vincent, John, *Non-Intervention and International Order*, Princeton, Princeton University Press, 1974.
Welsh, Jennifer M., *Edmund Burke and International Relations: the Commonwealth of Europe and the Crusade Against the French Revolution*, London, Macmillan, 1995.

4. Historical Materialism: The Concept of World Revolution

Barker, Colin (ed.), *Revolutionary Rehearsals*, London, Bookmarks, 1987.
Blackburn, Robin (ed.), *Revolution and Class Struggle*, London, Fontana, 1978.
Colburn, Forrest, *The Vogue of Revolution in Poor Countries*, Chichester, Princeton University Press, 1994.
D'Encausse, Hélène Carrère and Schram, Stuart, *Marxism and Asia*, London, Allen Lane, 1969.
Deutscher, Isaac, *Marxism in Our Time*, Berkeley, CA, Ramparts Press, 1971.
Doyle, Michael, *Ways of War and Peace: Realism, Liberalism and Socialism*, London, W.W. Norton, 1997.
Harding, Neil, *Lenin's Political Thought*, vol. 2, London, Macmillan, 1981, chapters 2, 3, 11.
Horowitz, David, *Imperialism and Revolution*, Harmondsworth, Allen Lane, The Penguin Press, 1969.
Kubálková, Vendulka and Cruikshank, Albert, *Marxism and International Relations*, Oxford, Oxford University Press, 1985.
Lenin, V. I., *Selected Works*, 3 vols, Moscow, Progress Publishers, 1970–71.
Lichtheim, George, *Imperialism*, Harmondsworth, Penguin, 1971.
Light, Margot, *The Soviet Theory of International Relations*, Brighton, Harvester, 1989.
Löwy, Michael, *The Politics of Combined and Uneven Development: The Theory of Permanent Revolution*, London, Verso, 1981.
Löwy, Michael, 'Fatherland or Mother Earth? Nationalism and Internationalism from a Socialist Perspective', *The Socialist Register*, London, The Merlin Press, 1989.
Lukacs, G., *Lenin*, chapter 4, 'Imperialism: World War and Civil War', London, NLB, 1970.
Mandel, Ernest, *Revolutionary Marxism Today*, London, Verso, 1975.
Marx, Karl, *The Revolutions of 1848*, ed. David Fernbach, Harmondsworth, Penguin, 1973.
Marx, Karl, *The First International and After*, ed. David Fernbach, Harmondsworth, Penguin 1974.
Miliband, Ralph and others (eds), *Revolution Today: Aspirations and Realities Socialist Register 1989*, London, The Merlin Press, 1989.

Molnar, Miklós, *Marx, Engels et la Politique Internationale*, Paris, Gallimard, 1975.

Narkiewicz, Olga, *Marxism and the Reality of Power, 1919–1980*, London, Croom Helm, 1981.

Parkinson, Fred, *The Philosophy of International Relations*, London, Sage, 1977.

Pieterse, Jan, *Empire and Emancipation, Power and Liberation on a World Scale*, London, Pluto, 1990.

Rosenberg, Justin, 'Isaac Deutscher and the Lost History of International Relations', *New Left Review*, no. 215, January–February 1996.

Steinhaus, Kurt, *Zur Theorie des Internationalen Klassenkampfs*, Frankfurt, Verlag Neue Kritik, 1967.

Therborn, Göran, 'From Petrograd to Saigon', *New Left Review*, no. 48, 1967.

Thorndike, Tony, 'The Revolutionary Approach: The Marxist Perspective' in Trevor Taylor (ed.), *Approaches and Theory in International Relations*, London, Longman, 1978.

Timmermann, *"Proletarischer Internationalismus" aus sowjetischer Sicht. Eine historisch-politische analyse*, Bundesinstitut für ostwissenschaftliche und internationale Studien, 1983.

Trofimenko, Henry, 'The Third World and US–Soviet Competition: A Soviet View', *Foreign Affairs*, Summer 1981.

Trotsky, Leon, *The Revolution Betrayed*, London, New Park, 1967.

Wickham-Cowley, Timothy, *Guerrillas and Revolution in Latin America: A Comparative Study of Insurgents and Regimes Since 1956*, Princeton, Princeton University Press, 1992.

5. Revolutions and War

Adelman, Jonathan, *Revolution, Armies and War*, Boulder, CO, Rienner, 1986.

Aron, Raymond, *Clausewitz*, London, Routledge & Kegan Paul, 1983, chapters 11 and 12.

Asprey, Robert, *War in the Shadows: The Guerrilla in History*, New York, Doubleday, 1994.

Best, Geoffrey, *War and Society in Revolutionary Europe 1770–1870*, London, Fontana, 1982.

Chaliand, Gérard (ed.), *Stratégie de la guerrilla*, Paris, Mazarine, 1979.

Debray, Régis, *Revolution in the Revolution?*, Harmondsworth, Penguin, 1969.

Debray, Régis, *Che's Guerrilla War*, Harmondsworth, Penguin, 1975.

Debray, Régis, *La Critique des Armes*, 2 vols, Paris, Seuil, 1979.

Ellis, John, *A Short History of Guerrilla Warfare*, London, Ian Allan, 1975.

Gallie, W. D., *Philosophers of Peace and War*, Cambridge, Cambridge University Press, 1978.

Gearty, Conor, *Terror*, London, Faber & Faber, 1991.

Giap, Vo Nguyen, *People's War, People's Army*, Hanoi, Foreign Languages Publishing House, 1961.

Guevara, Ernesto, *Guerrilla Warfare*, New York, Monthly Review Press, 1961.

Johnson, Chalmers, *Autopsy on People's War*, London, University of California Press, 1973.

Kolko, Gabriel, *Century of War: Politics, Conflicts and Society Since 1914*, New York, New Press, 1994.

Laqueur, Walter, *Guerrilla: A Historical and Critical Study*, London, Weidenfeld & Nicolson, 1977.

Lin Piao, 'Long Live the Victory of People's War', *Beijing Review*, vol. 8, no. 36, 3 September 1965.

Mack, Andrew, 'Why Big Nations Lose Small Wars: The Politics of Asymmetric Conflict', *World Politics*, vol. 27, no.2, 1975.

Mandel, Ernest, *The Meaning of the Second World War*, London, Verso, 1986.

Mao Tse-tung, *Selected Works*, 4 vols, London, Lawrence & Wishart, 1954–6.

Neuberg, A., *Armed Insurrection*, London, NLB, 1970.

Pomeroy, William, *Guerrilla and Counter-Guerrilla Warfare*, New York, International Publishers, 1964.

Pomeroy, William (ed.), *Guerrilla Warfare and Marxism*, London, Lawrence & Wishart, 1969.

Quartim, João, *Armed Struggle in Brazil*, London, NLB, 1971.

Sarkesian, Sam (ed.), *Revolutionary Guerrilla Warfare*, Chicago, Precedent Publishing, 1975.

Semmel, Bernard (ed.), *Marxism and the Science of War*, Oxford, OUP, 1981.

Walt, Stephen, *Revolution and War*, London, Cornell University Press, 1996.

Wolf, Eric, *Peasant Wars of the Twentieth Century*, London, Faber & Faber, 1971.

6. Self-Reliance and Post-Revolutionary 'Transformation'

Amin, Samir, *Delinking*, London, Zed, 1990.

Bassand, Michel and others, *Self-Reliant Development in Europe Theory, Problems, Actions*, Aldershot, Gower, 1986.

Bukharin, Nikolai and Preobrazhensky, E., *The ABC of Communism*, Harmondsworth, Penguin, 1969.

Chase-Dunn, Christopher (ed.), *Socialist States in the World-System*, London, Sage, 1982.

Clark, Cal and Bahry, Donna, 'Dependent Development: A Socialist Variant', *International Studies Quarterly*, vol. 27, 1983.

Colburn, Forrest, *Post-Revolutionary Nicaragua: State, Class and the Dilemmas of Agrarian Policy*, Berkeley, University of California, 1986.

Fagen, Richard, Deere, Carmen Diana, and Coraggio, Jose Luis (eds), *Transition and Development: Problems of Third World Socialism*, New York, Monthly Review Press, 1986.

Galtung, Johan, O'Brien, Peter and Preiswerk, Roy (eds), *Self-Reliance: A Strategy for Development*, London, Bogle-L'Ouverture for Institute for Development Studies, 1980.

Halliday, Fred, 'Self-Reliance in the 1980s', *Monthly Review*, February 1988.

Helwege, Ann, 'Three Socialist Experiences in Latin America: Surviving US Economic Pressure', *Bulletin of Latin American Research*, vol. 8, no. 2, 1989.

Marcuse, Herbert, *Soviet Marxism: A Critical Analysis*, Harmondsworth, Penguin, 1971.

Senghaas, Dieter, *The European Experience: A Historical Critique of Development Theory*, Leamington Spa, Berg Publishers, 1985.

Smith, Courtney A., *Socialist Transformation in Peripheral Economies: Lessons from Grenada*, Aldershot, Avebury Publishing, 1995.

Szporluk, Roman, *Communism and Nationalism: Karl Marx versus Fiedrich List*, Oxford, Oxford University Press, 1988.

Tickner, J. Ann, *Self-Reliance Versus Power Politics: The American and Indian Experience in Building Nation States*, New York, Columbia University Press, 1987.

Utting, Peter, *Economic Reform and Third-World Socialism: A Political Economy of Food Policy in Post-Revolutionary Societies*, London, Macmillan, 1992.

Weisskopf, Thomas, 'Self-Reliance and Development Strategy', in Ngo, Manh-Lam, *Unreal Growth*, Delhi, 1984, vol. 2. OC.

White, Gordon, Murray, Robin and White, Christine (eds), *Revolutionary Socialist Development in the Third World*, Brighton, Wheatsheaf, 1983.

Wiles, Peter (ed.), *The New Communist Third World*, London, Croom Helm, 1982.

World Development, special issue on 'Socialism and Development', vol. 9, nos 9/10, 1981.

7. Case Studies

(a) France

Best, Geoffrey (ed.), *The Permanent Revolution: The French Revolution and its Legacy*, London, Fontana, 1989.

Blackburn, Robin, *The Overthrow of Colonial Slavery, 1776–1848*, London, Verso, 1988.

Blanning, T. C. W., *The Origins of the French Revolutionary Wars*, London, Longman, 1986.

Brinton, Crane, *A Decade of Revolution, 1789–1799*, London, Harper & Brothers, 1934.

Cobban, Alfred, *The Debate on the French Revolution*, 2nd ed., London, Black, 1960.

Cobban, Alfred, *A History of Modern France*, vol. 1, Harmondsworth, Penguin, 1957, vol. 2, Harmondsworth, Penguin, 1961.

Crawley, C. W. (ed.), 'War and Peace in an Age of Upheaval, 1793–1830', vol. IX of *The New Cambridge Modern History*, 1965.

Doyle, William, *The Oxford History of the French Revolution*, Oxford, OUP, 1989.

Elliott, Marianne, *Partners in Revolution: The United Irishmen and France*, New Haven, Yale University Press, 1982.

Furet, François, *Interpreting the French Revolution*, Cambridge, Cambridge University Press, 1981.

Furet, Francois, *Revolutionary France 1770–1880*, Oxford, Blackwell, 1992.

Geyl, Pieter, *Napoleon: For and Against*, Harmondsworth, Penguin, 1965.

Godechot, Jacques, *La Grande Nation*, 2nd ed., Paris, Aubier Montaigue, 1983.

Hampson, Norman, *The First European Revolution, 1776–1815*, London, Thames & Hudson, 1969.

Hobsbawm, Eric, *The Age of Revolution: Europe 1789–1848*, London, Weidenfeld & Nicolson, 1962.

Hobsbawm, Eric, *Echoes of the Marseillaise: Two Centuries Look Back on the French Revolution*, London, Verso, 1990.

Klaits, Joseph and Haltzel, Michael, *The Global Ramifications of the French Revolution*, Cambridge, CUP, 1994.

Meikle, A. W., *Scotland and the French Revolution*, Glasgow, 1912.

Merle, Marcel, *Pacifisme et Internationalisme, XVIIIe–XXe siècles*, Paris, Armand Colin, 1966.

Palmer, R. R., 'The World Revolution of the West: 1763–1801', *Political Science Quarterly*, March 1954.

Palmer, R. R., *The Age of the Democratic Revolution, 1760–1800*, 2 vols, Princeton, Princeton University Press, 1959, 1964.

Pomeau, René, *L'Europe Lumières. Cosmopolitisme et unité européenne au xxiiie siècle*, Paris, Stock, 1991.

Rudé, George, *Revolutionary Europe 1783–1815*, London, Fontana, 1964.

Rudé, George, *The French Revolution*, London, Weidenfeld & Nicolson, 1988.

Schama, Simon, *Citizens: A Chronicle of the French Revolution*, London, Viking, 1989.

Soboul, Albert, *The French Revolution 1787–1799*, London, NLB, 1975.

Sorel, Albert, *L'Europe et la Révolution française*, 8 vols, Paris, Le Plon, 1893–1908.

Stone, Bayley, *The Genesis of the French Revolution*, Cambridge, CUP, 1994.

(b) Russia

Borkenau, Franz, *World Communism*, Ann Arbor, University of Michigan, 1963.

Carr, E. H., *Socialism in One Country*, Penguin, 1964, vol. 3.

Carr, E. H., *The Romantic Exiles: A Nineteenth Century Portrait Gallery*, Harmondsworth, Penguin, 1968.

Carr, E. H., *The Bolshevik Revolution*, Harmondsworth, Penguin, 1973, vol. 3.

Claudin, Fernando, *The Communist Movement: From Comintern to Cominform*, Harmondsworth, Penguin, 1976.

Deutscher, Isaac, *The Prophet Armed: Trotsky 1879–1921*, Oxford, Oxford University Press, 1954.

Deutscher, Isaac, *The Great Contest*, Oxford, OUP, 1960.

Deutscher, Isaac, *Russia, China and the West, 1953–1967*, Oxford, OUP, 1968.

Deutscher, Isaac, *Stalin*, Harmondsworth, Penguin, 1968.

Edmonds, Robin, *Soviet Foreign Policy in the Brezhnev Years*, OUP, 1984.

Eudin, Xenia and North, Robert, *Soviet Russia and the East 1920–1927*, Stanford, Stanford University Press, 1957.

Figes, Orlando, *A People's Tragedy*, London, Jonathan Cape, 1997.

Gourfinkel, Nina, *Lenin*, London, Evergreen, 1961.

Laqueur, Walter, *The Dream that Failed: Reflections on the Soviet Union*, Oxford, OUP, 1994.

Lenin, V. I., *On Proletarian Internationalism*, Moscow, Progress Publishers, 1967.

Lenin, V. I., *On the Foreign Policy of the Soviet State*, Moscow, Progress Publishers, 1970.

Lewin, Moshe, *Lenin's Last Struggle*, London, Wildwood House, 1973.

Liebman, Marcel, *Leninism under Lenin*, London, Merlin Press, 1975.

Light, Margot, *The Soviet Theory of International Relations*, Brighton, Wheatsheaf, 1988.

Northedge, F. S. and Wells, Audrey, *Britain and Soviet Communism: The Impact of a Revolution*, London, Macmillan, 1982.

Pajetta, Giancarlo, *La lunga marcia dell'internazionalismo*, Rome Riuniti, 1978.

Pipes, Richard, *The Russian Revolution, 1890–1919*, London, Fontana, 1992.

Pipes, Richard, *The Unknown Lenin: From the Secret Archive*, London, Yale University Press, 1996.

Reed, John, *Ten Days that Shook the World*, Harmondsworth, Penguin, 1966.

Schapiro, Leonard, *1917: The Russian Revolutions and the Origins of Present-Day Communism*, Harmondsworth, Penguin, 1985.

Spriano, Paolo, *Stalin and the European Communists*, London, Verso, 1985.

Steele, Jonathan, *The Limits of Soviet Power: The Kremlin's Foreign Policy – Brezhnev to Chernenko*, revised and updated edition, Harmondsworth, Penguin, 1985.

Toynbee, Arnold, introductory essay in Degras, Jane (ed.), *The Impact of the Russian Revolution, 1917–1967: The Influence of Bolshevism on the World Outside Russia*, Oxford, Oxford University Press for RIIA, 1967.

Trotsky, Leon, *The History of The Russian Revolution*, 3 vols, London, Victor Gollancz, 1932.

Trotsky, Leon, *The Revolution Betrayed*, London, New Park, 1967.

Tukhachevsky, Mikhail, 'Revolution from Without', *New Left Review*, no. 55, May–June 1969.

Ulam, Adam, *Expansion and Coexistence: The History of Soviet Foreign Relations Policy, 1917–1967*, second edition, London, Holt, Rinehart & Winston, 1974.

Ulam, Adam, *Dangerous Relations: The Soviet Union in World Politics 1970–1982*, New York and Oxford, Oxford University Press, 1984.

Uldricks, Teddy, 'Russia and Europe: Diplomacy, Revolution and Economic Development in the 1920s', *International History Review*, January 1979.

Ullman, Richard, *Anglo-Soviet Relations, 1917–1921: Intervention and the War*, Oxford, Oxford University Press, 1961.

Volkogonov, Dmitri, *Lenin, Life and Legacy*, London, HarperCollins, 1994.

Weber, Herman, *Die Wandlung des deutschen Kommunismus*, Frankfurt, Europäische Verlag Sanstalt, 1969.

Westoby, Adam, *The Evolution of Communism*, Cambridge, Polity, 1989.

White, Stephen, *Britain and the Bolshevik Revolution*, London, Macmillan, 1979.

Wilson, Edmund, *To the Finland Station: A Study in the Writing and Acting of History*, London, Fontana, 1974.

(c) China

Armstrong, J. D., *Revolutionary Diplomacy: Chinese Foreign Policy and the United Front Doctrine*, Oxford, Clarendon Press, 1978.

Bechtoldt, *China's Revolutionsstrategie. Mit der dritten welt gegen Russland und Amerika*, Munich, dtv, 1969.

Benton, Gregor, 'Bolshevizing China: From Lenin to Stalin to Mao, 1921–44', *Journal of Communist Studies and Transition Politics*, vol. 12, no. 1, March 1996.

Brandt, Conrad, Schwartz, Benjamin and Fairbank, John, *A Documentary History of Chinese Communism*, 2nd ed., London, George Allen & Unwin, 1959.

Gittings, John, *Survey of the Sino-Soviet Dispute*, Oxford, OUP, 1968.

Gittings, John, *The World and China 1922–1972*, London, Eyre Methuen, 1974.

Goncharov, S. Lewis, J. and Xue, Litai, *Stalin, Mao and the Korean War*, Stanford University Press, 1994.

Johnson, Chalmers, *Peasant Nationalism and Communist Power: The Emergence of Revolutionary China, 1937–1945*, London, OUP, 1962.

Kim, S. K. (ed.), *China and the World: Chinese Foreign Policy Faces the New Millenium*, 4th edition, Boulder, CO, Westview Press, 1998 (previous editions, 1984, 1989, 1994).

Lerner, Elinor, 'The Chinese Peasantry and Imperialism: A Critique of Chalmers Johnson's Peasant Nationalism and Community Power', *Bulletin of Concerned Asian Scholars*, vol. VI, no. 2, April-August, 1974.

Maitan, Livio, *Party, Army and Masses in China*, London, NLB, 1976.

Maxwell, Neville, *India's China War*, London, Cape, 1970.

Meisner, M., *Li Ta-chao and the Origins of Chinese Marxism*, Cambridge, Mass. Harvard University Press, 1967.

Schram, Stuart, *The Political Thought of Mao Tse-tung*, London, Praeger, 1963.

Schram, Stuart, *Mao Tse-tung*, Harmondsworth, Penguin, 1966.

Van Ginneken, Jaap, *The Rise and Fall of Lin Piao*, Harmondsworth, Penguin, 1976.

Van Ness, Peter, *Revolution and Chinese Foreign Policy: Peking's Support for Wars of National Liberation*, Berkeley, CA, University of California Press, 1970.

Yahuda, Michael, *China's Role in World Affairs*, London, Croom Helm, 1978.

Yahuda, Michael, *Towards the End of Isolationism: China's Foreign Policy After Mao*, London, Croom Helm, 1983.

(d) Cuba

Anderson, Jon Lee, *Che Guevara: A Revolutionary Life*, London, Bantam Books, 1997.

Balfour, Sebastian, *Castro*, London, Longman, 1990.

'Benigno', *Vie et mort de la révolution cubaine*, Paris, Fayard, 1996.

Blasier, Cole and Mesa-Lago, Carmelo, *Cuba in the World*, Pittsburgh University Press, 1979.

Brenner, Philip *et al.*, *The Cuba Reader: The Making of a Revolutionary Society*, part I (the setting), part IV (foreign policy), Grove Press, 1989.

Casteñeda, Jorge, *Utopia Unarmed: The Latin American Left after the Cold War*, New York, Knopf, 1993.

Dominquez, Jorge, *Cuba: Internal and International Affairs*, London, Sage, 1982.

Dominguez, Jorge, *To Make a World Safe for Revolution: Cuba's Foreign Policy*, Cambridge, Mass., Harvard University Press, 1989.

Dumont, Rene, *Is Cuba Socialist?*, London, Deutsch, 1974.

Erisman, Michael, *Cuba's International Relations: The Anatomy of a Nationalistic Foreign Policy*, Boulder, CO, Westview, 1985.

Erisman, H. Michael and Kirk John (eds), *Cuban Foreign Policy Confronts a New International Order*, Boulder, CO, Lynne Rienner, 1991.

Garthoff, Raymond, *Reflections on the Cuban Missile Crisis*, Washington, Brookings Institution, 1987.

Guevara, Che, 'Vietnam Must not Stand Alone', *New Left Review*, no. 43, May/June 1967.

Huberman, Leo and Sweezy, Paul, *Régis Debray and the Latin American Revolution*, London, Monthly Review, 1968.

Karol, K. S., *The Guerrillas in Power*, London, Jonathan Cape, 1971.

LeoGrande, William, *Cuba's Policy in Africa, 1959–1980*, Institute of International Studies, Berkeley, 1980.

Levine, Harry (ed.), *The New Cuban Presence in the Caribbean*, Boulder, CO, Westview, 1983.

Mesa-Lago, Carmelo, *The Economy of Socialist Cuba*, Albuquerque, University of New Mexico Press, 1981.

Morley, Morris, *Imperial State, The United States, and Revolution and Cuba*, London, Cambridge University Press, 1987.

Nathan, James (ed.), *The Cuban Missile Crisis Revisited*, New York, St Martin's Press, 1992.

Ritter, Archibald and Kirk, John, *Cuba in the International System: Normalisation and Integration*, London, Macmillan, 1995.

Suárez, Andrés, *Cuba: Castroism and Communism, 1959-1966*, London, MIT Press, 1969.

Szulc, Tad, *Fidel: A Critical Portrait*, London, Hutchinson, 1986.

Thomas, Hugh, *Cuba or the Pursuit of Freedom*, Eyre & Spottiswoode, 1971.

Tutino, Saverio, *L'ottobre cubano: lineamenti di una storia della rivoluzione castrista*, Einandi, Turin, 1968.

Weinstein, Martin (ed.), *Revolutionary Cuba in the World Arena*, Philadelphia, Institute for the Study of Human Issues, 1979.

White, Mark, *The Cuban Missile Crisis*, London, Macmillan, 1996.

(e) Indochina

Charlton, Michael and Moncrieff, Anthony, *Many Reasons Why: the American Involvement in Vietnam*, London, Scolar Press, 1978.

Duiker, William, *The Communist Road to Power in Vietnam*, Boulder, CO, Westview, 1981.

Evans, Grant and Rowley, Kelvin, *Red Brotherhood at War: Indo-China Since the Fall of Saigon*, London, Verso, 1984.

Fall, Bernard, *Le Viet-minh: La République Démocratique du Viet-Nam 1945–1960*, Paris, Armand Colin, 1960.

Fall, Bernard, *The Two Vietnams*, 2nd ed., London, Pall Mall, 1963.

Herring, George, *America's Longest War: The United States and Vietnam, 1950–1975*, Chichester, Wiley, 1979.

Karnow, Stanley, *Vietnam: A History*, Harmondsworth, Penguin, 1985.

Kiernan, Ben, *How Pol Pot Came to Power*, London, Verso, 1985.

Kolko, Gabriel, *Anatomy of a War: Vietnam, the United States and the Modern Historical Experience*, New York, Pantheon Books, 1985.

Leifer, Michael, *Cambodia: The Search for Security*, London, Praeger, 1975.

Marr, David, *Vietnam 1945: The Quest for Power*, Berkeley, University of California Press, 1995.

Porter, Gareth, *A Peace Denied: The United States, Vietnam and the Paris Agreement*, Bloomington, IN, Indiana University Press, 1975.

Post, Ken, *Revolution, Socialism and Nationalism in Vietnam*, 5 vols, Brookfield, VT, Dartmouth, 1989–1994.

Shawcross, William, *Sideshow: Kissinger, Nixon and the Destruction in Vietnam*, London, Fontana, 1980.

Smith, Ralph, *An International History of the Vietnam War*, vol. 1, *1955–61*, 1983, vol. 2, *1961–65*, 1985; vol. 3, *1965–66*, 1990.

Turley, William, *The Second Indochina War: A Short Political and Military History, 1954–75*, Boulder, CO, Westview, 1986.

(f) Iran

Abrahamian, Ervand, *Khomeinism*, London, I. B. Tauris, 1990.
Arjomand, Said Amir, 'Iran's Islamic Revolution in Comparative Perspective', *World Politics*, April 1986.
Arjomand, Said, *The Turban for the Crown; the Islamic Revolution in Iran*, Oxford, OUP, 1988.
Bakhash, Shaul, *The Reign of the Ayatollahs*, London, I. B. Tauris, 1985.
Bill, James, *The Eagle and the Lion*, London, Yale University Press, 1988.
Buchta, Wilfried, *Die iranische schia und die islamische einheit 1979–1996*, Hamburg, Orient-Institut, 1997.
Chubin, Shahram, *Iran's National Security Policy*, Washington, Carnegie Endowment, 1994.
Cole, Juan and Keddie, Nikki (eds), *Shi'ism and Social Protest*, London, Yale University Press, 1986.
Ehteshami, Anoushiravan, *After Khomeini, The Iranian Second Republic*, London, Routledge, 1995.
El-Azhary, M. S., *The Iran–Iraq War*, London, Croom Helm, 1984.
Esposito, John (ed.), *The Iranian Revolution, Its Global Impact*, Miami, Florida International University Press, 1990.
Farhi, Farideh, *States and Urban-based Revolutions: Iran and Nicaragua*, Illinois University Press, 1990.
Foran, John, *Fragile Resistance: Social Transformation in Iran from 1500 to the Revolution*, Boulder, Westview Press 1993.
Halliday, Fred, 'The Iranian Revolution in International Affairs: Programme and Practice', *Millennium*, Spring 1981.
Halliday, Fred, 'The Iranian Revolution in Comparative Perspective', in *Islam and the Myth of Confrontation*, London, I.B. Tauris, 1996.
Ismael, Tareq (ed.), *Iran and Iraq: Roots of Conflict*, Syracuse University Press, 1982.
Kazemi, Farhad, 'Models of Iranian Politics, the Road to the Islamic Revolution and the Challenge to Civil Society', *World Politics*, vol.27, no.4, July 1995.
Keddie, Nikki, *Iran and the Muslim World, Resistance and Revolution*, London, Macmillan, 1995.
Kemp, Geoffrey, *Forever Enemies? American Policy and the Islamic Republic of Iran*, Washington, Carnegie Endowment, 1994.
Milani, Mohsen, *The Making of Iran's Islamic Revolution*, Boulder, Westview, 1988.
Pahlavi, Mohammad Reza, *The Shah's Story*, London, Michael Joseph, 1980.
Parsa, Misagh, *Social Origins of the Iranian Revolution*, Rutgers University Press, 1989.
Piscatori, James (ed.), *Islam in the Political Process*, London, Royal Institute of International Affairs, 1982.
Ramazani, R. K., *Revolutionary Iran: Challenge and Response in the Middle East*, London, Johns Hopkins University Press, 2nd ed., 1988.
Rubin, Barry, *Paved with Good Intentions: Iran and the American Experience*, Oxford, OUP, 1980.

Sick, Gary, *All Fall Down: America's Tragic Encounter with Iran*, London, I. B. Tauris, 1985.

Vieille, Paul and Khosrokhavari, Farhad, *Le discours populaire de la Révolution irannienne*, Paris, Contemporaneité, 1990.

Yodfat, Aryeh, *The Soviet Union and Revolutionary Iran*, London, Croom Helm, 1984.

Zubaida, Sami, *Islam: The People and the State*, London, Routledge, 1989.

(g) Central America

Blakemore, Harold, 'Central America Crisis: Challenge to US Diplomacy', *Conflict Studies*, 1984.

Blasier, Cole, *Hovering Giant: US Responses to Revolutionary Change in Latin America*, Pittsburg, University of Pittsburg, 1976.

Booth, John, *The End of the Beginning: The Nicaraguan Revolution*, 2nd ed., Boulder, CO, Westview, 1985.

Dunkerley, James, *Power in the Isthmus: A Political History of Modern Central America*, London, Verso, 1988.

Feinberg, Richard (ed.), *Central America: International Dimensions of the Crisis*, New York, Holmes & Meier, 1982.

Hodges, Donald, *Intellectual Foundations of the Nicaraguan Revolution*, Austin, University of Texas Press, 1986.

Journal of Latin American Studies, special issue, vol. 15, part 2, November 1983.

LaFeber, Walter, *Inevitable Revolutions: The United States in Central America*, expanded edition, London, Norton, 1985.

Leiken, Robert (ed.), *Central America: Anatomy of Conflict*, Oxford, Pergamon, 1984.

Millennium, special issue, 'The Central American Crisis', vol. 13, no. 2, Summer 1984.

Smith, Hazel, 'Revolutionary Diplomacy Sandinista Style: Lessons and Limits', *Race & Class*, vol. 33, no. 1, 1991.

Spalding, Rose (ed.), *The Political Economy of Revolutionary Nicaragua*, London, Allen & Unwin, 1987.

Walker, Thomas (ed.), *Nicaragua: The First Five Years*, New York, Praeger, 1985.

Walker, Thomas (ed.), *Reagan Versus the Sandinistas*, Boulder, CO, Westview, 1987.

Wiarda, Howard, *Rift and Revolution: The Central American Imbroglio*, Washington, DC, American Enterprise Institute, 1984.

Vilas, Carlos, *The Sandinista Revolution*, New York, Monthly Review, 1986.

(h) Collapse of Communism: Eastern Europe/USSR

Allan, Pierre and Goldmann, Kjell, *The End of the Cold War: Evaluating Theories of International Relations*, Dordrecht, Boston, M. Nijhoff, 1992.

Ash, Timothy Garton, *The Uses of Adversity*, Harmondsworth, Penguin, 1989.

Bahro, Rudolf, *The Alternative in Eastern Europe*, London, Verso, 1978.

Bauman, Zygmunt, 'Living Without an Alternative', *Political Quarterly*, January–March 1992.

Blackburn, Robin (ed.), *After the Fall: The Failure of Communism and the Future of Socialism*, London, Verso, 1991.

Brus, Wlodzimierz and Laski, Kazimierz, *From Marx to the Market*, Oxford, Clarendon Press, 1989.

Calvocoressi, Peter, *The Cold War as Episode*, London, David Davies Memorial Institute, occasional paper, 1993.

Cox, Michael, 'From the Truman Doctrine to the Second Superpower Detente: The Rise and Fall of the Cold War', *Journal of Peace Research*, vol. 27, no. 1, 1990.

Cox, Michael, 'Rethinking the End of the Cold War', *Review of International Studies*, vol. 20, no. 2, April 1994.

Crockatt, Richard, *The Fifty Years War: The United States and the Soviet Union in World Politics, 1941–1991*, London, Routledge, 1995.

Dawisha, Karen, *Eastern Europe, Gorbachev and Reform: the Great Challenge*, 2nd ed., Cambridge, Cambridge University Press, 1990.

Deudney, Daniel and Ikenberry, John, 'Soviet Reform and the End of the Cold War: Explaining Large-Scale Historical Change', *Review of International Studies*, vol. 17, no. 3, July 1991.

Fowkes, Ben, *The Rise and Fall of Communism in Eastern Europe*, London, Macmillan, 1993.

Furet, François, *Le passé d'une illusion. Essai sur l'idée communiste an XXe siècle*, Paris, Laffont, 1995.

Gaddis, John Lewis, *We Now Know: Rethinking Cold War History*, Oxford, Clarendon Press, 1987.

Gaddis, J. L., 'International Relations Theory and the End of the Cold War', *International Security*, vol. 17, no. 3, 1992–3.

Garthoff, Raymond, *Détente and Confrontation: American–Soviet Relations from Nixon to Reagan*, revised edition, Washington, Brookings Institution, 1994.

Halliday, Fred, 'The Ends of Cold War', *New Left Review*, no. 180, March–April 1990.

Hamerow, Theodore, *From the Finland Station: The Graying of Revolution in the Twentieth Century*, New York, Basic Books, 1990.

Hechter, Michael, Szelenyi, Ivan and Szelenyi, Balacs in 'Theoretical Implications of the Demise of State Socialism', special issue of *Theory & Society*, vol. 23, no. 2, April 1994.

Hogan, Michael (ed.), *The End of the Cold War: Its Meaning and Implications*, Cambridge, Cambridge University Pres, 1992.

Hough, Jerry, *Democratization and Revolution in the USSR 1985–1991*, Washington, Brookings Institution, 1997.

International Organization, Special Issue, vol.48, no.2, Spring 1994, symposium on the end of the Cold War and theories of international relations.

Konrad, George, *Anti-Politics*, London, Quartet, 1984.

Kumar, Krishan,'The Revolutions of 1989: Socialism, Capitalism, Democracy', *Theory and Society*, vol. 21, 1992.

Lane, David, *The Rise and Fall of State Socialism*, Cambridge, Polity Press, 1996.

Laqueur, Walter, *The Dream that Failed: Reflections on the Soviet Union*, London, OUP, 1994.

Lebow, Richard Ned, and Risse-Kappen, Thomas, *International Relations Theory and the End of the Cold War*, New York, Columbia University Press, 1995.

Lewin, Moshe, *The Gorbachev Phenomenon*, London, Radius, 1988.

Lohman, Susanne, 'The Dynamics of Informational Cascades: The Monday Demonstrations in East Leipzig, 1989–91', *World Politics*, vol. 47, no. 1, 1994.

Nevers, R. de, *The Soviet Union and Eastern Europe: The End of an Era*, London, International Institute for Strategic Studies, 1990, Adelphi Paper.

Partos, Gabriel, *The World That Came In From the Cold*, London, Royal Institute of International Affairs, 1993.

Prins, Gwyn (ed.), *Spring in Winter: The 1989 Revolutions*, Manchester, Manchester University Press, 1990.

Pryce-Jones, David, *The War That Never Was: The Fall of the Soviet Empire, 1985–1991*, London, Weidenfeld & Nicolson, 1995.

Rothschild, Joseph, *Return to Diversity: A Political History of East Central Europe since World War II*, New York, OUP, 1989.

Schopflin, George, 'Why Communism Collapsed', *International Affairs*, January 1990.

Steele, Jonathan, *Eternal Russia: Yeltsin, Gorbachev, and the Mirage of Democracy*, London, Faber & Faber, 1994.

Steiner, *Proofs and Three Parables*, London, Faber & Faber, 1992.

Stern, Geoffrey, *The Rise and Decline of International Communism*, Aldershot, Edward Elgar, 1990, part III.

Stokes, Gale, 'The Lessons of 1989', *Problems of Communism*, September–October 1991, vol. XL, no. 5.

Wallerstein, Immanuel, *After Liberalism*, New York, The New Press, 1995.

Index